RULES OF LAW AND LAWS OF RULING

Rules of Law and Laws of Ruling

On the Governance of Law

Edited by

FRANZ VON BENDA-BECKMANN,
KEEBET VON BENDA-BECKMANN AND JULIA ECKERT
Max Planck Institute for Social Anthropology, Germany

ASHGATE

Published by
Ashgate Publishing Limited
Wey Court East
Union Road
Farnham
Surrey, GU9 7PT
England

Ashgate Publishing Company
Suite 420
101 Cherry Street
Burlington
VT 05401-4405
USA

www.ashgate.com

British Library Cataloguing in Publication Data
Rules of law and laws of ruling : on the governance of law.
- (Law, justice and power series)
1. Ethnological jurisprudence 2. Legal polycentricity
3. Rule of law
I. Benda-Beckmann, Franz von II. Benda-Beckmann, Keebet von
III. Eckert, Julia M.
340.1'15

Library of Congress Cataloging-in-Publication Data
Benda-Beckmann, Franz von.
Rules of law and laws of ruling : on the governance of law / by Franz von Benda-Beckmann, Keebet von Benda-Beckmann and Julia Eckert.
p. cm. -- (Series: law, justice, and power)
Includes bibliographical references and index.
ISBN 978-0-7546-7239-5 -- ISBN 978-0-7546-9132-7 (ebook) 1. Rule of law. 2. Sociological jurisprudence. 3. Administrative law. I. Benda-Beckmann, Keebet von. II. Eckert, Julia. III. Title.

K3171.B45 2009
340'.115--dc22

2008049052

ISBN 978 0 7546 7239 5
eISBN 978 07546 9132 7

Mixed Sources
Product group from well-managed forests and other controlled sources
www.fsc.org Cert no. SA-COC-1565
© 1996 Forest Stewardship Council
FSC

Printed and bound in Great Britain by
MPG Books Ltd, Bodmin, Cornwall.

Contents

List of Figures

Notes on Contributors

Franz von Benda-Beckmann is head of the Project Group 'Legal Pluralism' at the Max Planck Institute for Social Anthropology in Halle/Saale, Germany, since 2002 Honorary Professor for Legal Anthropology at the University of Leipzig, and since 2004 Honorary Professor for Legal Pluralism at the University of Halle/Saale. He holds a PhD in Law (1970), and obtained his *Habilitation* in Anthropology at the University of Zurich (1979). Before 2000 he was Professor for Law in Developing Countries at the Agricultural University Wageningen. He has done fieldwork and supervised research in Malawi, West Sumatra, the Moluccas and Nepal. He has written and co-edited several books and published widely on issues of property rights, social (in)security and legal pluralism in developing countries, and on legal anthropological theory. He co-edited, together with Keebet von Benda-Beckmann and Anne Griffiths, *Mobile People, Mobile Law: Expanding Legal Relations in a Contracting World* (Ashgate 2005), and with Keebet von Benda-Beckmann and Melanie G. Wiber, *Changing Properties of Property* (Berghahn 2006). He published *Social Security between Past and Future: Ambonese Networks of Care and Support* (LIT Verlag 2007) jointly with Keebet von Benda-Beckmann.

Keebet von Benda-Beckmann is head of the Project Group 'Legal Pluralism' at the Max Planck Institute for Social Anthropology in Halle/Saale, Germany, since 2003 Honorary Professor for Legal Anthropology at the University of Leipzig, and since 2004 Honorary Professor for Legal Pluralism at the University of Halle/Saale. She has carried out research in West Sumatra and on the Moluccan island of Ambon, Indonesia, and among Moluccan women in the Netherlands. She has published extensively on dispute resolution, social security in developing countries, property and water rights, decentralization and on theoretical issues in the anthropology of law. She co-edited, together with Franz von Benda-Beckmann and Anne Griffiths, *Mobile People, Mobile Law: Expanding Legal Relations in a Contracting World* (Ashgate 2005), and with Franz von Benda-Beckmann and Melanie G. Wiber, *Changing Properties of Property* (Berghahn 2006). She published *Social Security between Past and Future: Ambonese Networks of Care and Support* (LIT Verlag 2007) jointly with Franz von Benda-Beckmann.

Arthur Bull lives in Digby Neck in the Bay of Fundy region of Nova Scotia, where he is an Associate Staff Member of the Bay of Fundy Marine Resource Centre. Over the past fifteen years he has worked with inshore fishermen in the capacity of Executive Director of the Fundy Fixed Gear Council, and President of the Bay of Fundy Inshore Fishermen's Association.

Jean Comaroff is a Distinguished Professor of Anthropology at the University of Chicago, Director of the Chicago Center for Contemporary Theory, and an Honorary Professor at the University of Cape Town. Her current research is on crime, policing, post-colonial politics and state sovereignty, religious revitalization, and the commodification of identity. Her books, co-authored and co-edited with John Comaroff, include *Of Revelation and Revolution*, Volumes I (University of Chicago Press 1991) and II (University of Chicago Press 1997), *Ethnography and the Historical Imagination* (Westview Press 1992), *Modernity and its Malcontents: Ritual and Power in Africa* (University of Chicago Press 1993), *Civil Society and the Political Imagination in Africa* (University of Chicago Press 1999), *Millennial Capitalism and the Culture of Neoliberalism* (*Public Culture* 2000), *Law and Disorder in the Postcolony* (University of Chicago Press 2006) and *Ethnicity, Inc.* (University of Chicago Press 2009).

John L. Comaroff is a Distinguished Professor of Anthropology at the University of Chicago, a Research Professor at the American Bar Foundation, and an Honorary Professor at the University of Cape Town. His current research is on crime, policing and the workings of the state, on democracy and difference, on postcolonial politics, and on the commodification of identity. His books, co-authored and co-edited with Jean Comaroff, include *Of Revelation and Revolution*, Volumes I (University of Chicago Press 1991) and II (University of Chicago Press 1997), *Ethnography and the Historical Imagination* (Westview Press 1992), *Modernity and its Malcontents: Ritual and Power in Africa* (University of Chicago Press 1993), *Civil Society and the Political Imagination in Africa* (University of Chicago Press 1999), *Millennial Capitalism and the Culture of Neoliberalism* (*Public Culture* 2000), *Law and Disorder in the Postcolony* (University of Chicago Press 2006) and *Ethnicity, Inc.* (University of Chicago Press 2009).

Bill Derman is a Professor of Anthropology at Michigan State University, and a Visiting Professor at the Department of International Environment and Development Studies at the Norwegian University of the Life Sciences. His current interests are in land and water reform in southern Africa. Some recent publications include: *Citizenship and Identity: Conflicts over Land and Water in Contemporary Africa*, edited with Rie Odgaard and Espen Sjaastad (James Currey 2007), and 'Whose Water? The Political Ecology of Water Reform in Zimbabwe', co-authored by Anne Ferguson, in *Political Ecology Across Spaces, Scales and Social Groups*, edited by Lisa Gezon and Susan Paulson (Rutgers University Press 2005).

Julia Eckert is Associate Professor at the Max Planck Institute for Social Anthropology, Halle/Saale, Germany, where she heads the research group 'Law against the State', which examines the juridification of protest and the globalization of transnational legal norms. Her research interests are in legal anthropology, conflict theory, the anthropology of the state, social movements and the anthropology of security. She is currently writing a book on the police in Bombay, focusing on everyday conflicts over norms of justice, citizenship and authority. Among her publications on this research are 'The Trimurti of the State' (*Sociologus* 2005) and 'From Subject to Citizen: Legalism from below and the Homogenization of the Legal Sphere' (*Journal of Legal Pluralism* 2006). Her work on a Hindu nationalist movement in India resulted in her book *The Charisma of Direct Action* (Oxford University Press 2003). Other than India, she has conducted research in Uzbekistan and Afghanistan. She was a researcher at the German Institute for International Pedagogical Research, Frankfurt am Main, and lecturer at the Humboldt University, Berlin and the Free University of Berlin, from where she holds a PhD.

Marie-Claire Foblets, Lic. Iur., Lic. Phil., PhD Anthrop. (Leuven, Belgium) is Professor Ordinarius of Law and Anthropology at the Universities of Leuven, Brussels and Antwerp, Member of the Flemish Royal Academy of Sciences (Vlaamse Koninklijke Academie voor Wetenschappen) and Honorary Member of the Brussels bar. She won the Francqui Prize 2004 (Human Sciences). She has done extensive research and published widely on issues of immigration, integration and nationality law in Belgium. In the field of anthropology of law, her research focuses on the application of Islamic family laws in Europe. Her publications include authoring *Les familles maghrébines et la justice en Belgique. Anthropologie juridique et immigration* (Karthala 1994), editing *Familles – Islam – Europe. Le droit confronté au changement* (L'Harmattan 1996), editing *Femmes marocaines et conflits familiaux en immigration. Quelles solutions juridiques appropriées?* (Maklu 1998), editing, with J.Y. Carlier, *Le nouveau Code marocain de la famille. Son application en Europe* (Bruylant 2005) and authoring *Culturen voor de rechter* (Maklu forthcoming).

Anne Griffiths holds a Personal Chair in the Anthropology of Law at the School of Law at Edinburgh University. Her research focuses on anthropology of law, comparative and family law, African law, gender, culture and rights. Her most recent project involves a UN Study on Informal Justice. Over the years she has held visiting appointments at various institutions, including Distinguished Visiting Professor, Faculty of Law, University of Toronto, the Max Planck Institute for Social Anthropology, Halle/Saale, Germany, the International Institute for the Sociology of Law Oñati – Gipuzkoa, Spain, the University of Texas at Austin, School of Law, and the Southern and Eastern African Regional Centre for Women's Law at the University of Zimbabwe. She is currently President of the Commission on Folk Law and Legal Pluralism, a branch of the International Union of Anthropological and Ethnological Sciences.

Anne Hellum is Doctor Juris and Professor at the Department of Public and International Law at the University of Oslo. She is Director of the Institute of Women's Law and Visiting Professor at the Southern and Eastern African Centre of Women's Law at the University of Zimbabwe (SEARCWL). Her research interests lie in exploring women's human rights and legal pluralism in struggles over claims to equality and non-discrimination in relation to family, land and water reform. Her most recent book, *Human Rights, Plural Legalities and Gendered Realities: Paths are Made by Walking* (Weaver Press 2007), was co-edited with Julie Stewart, Shaheen Sardar Ali and Amy Tsanga.

Randy Frances Kandel is an Adjunct Associate Professor at John Jay College of Criminal Justice, City University of New York, and an Administrative Law Judge. She has written many recent chapters and articles on children and the law with her co-researcher/writer, Anne Griffiths. They include 'Half-told Truths and Partial Silence: Managing Communication in the Scottish Children's Hearings' in *The Power of Law in a Transnational World: Anthropological Enquiries* (Berghahn forthcoming) and 'Reconstructing Space and Legal Interventions in Scottish Children's Hearings: The Myth of the Transparent Table' in *Spatializing Law: An Anthropological Geography of Law in Society* (Ashgate 2009), both edited by F. and K. von Benda-Beckmann and A. Griffiths, and 'Custody and Coming of Age: Three American Cases' in *Reframing Parenthood and Childhood: Global Trends, Institutional Transformations, and Local Responses*, edited by T. Thelen and H. Haukanes (Berghahn forthcoming).

Tobias Kelly is a Senior Lecturer in Social Anthropology at the University of Edinburgh. His research interests include legal anthropology, the Israeli–Palestinian conflict and the politics of rights. He has carried out long-term fieldwork amongst West Bank Palestinians, concentrating on issues of citizenship, violence and human rights. More recent work explores the role of ethics, medicine and law in the recognition of cruelty, drawing on fieldwork in Israel/Palestine, the UK and at the UN. He received a PhD in Anthropology from the London School of Economics in 2003, and has worked at Birzeit University, the LSE and Oxford University. His publications include the monograph *Law, Violence and Sovereignty among West Bank Palestinians* (Cambridge University Press 2006) and the co-edited volume *Paths to International Justice: Social and Legal Perspectives* (Cambridge University Press 2007).

Tania Murray Li is Professor in the Department of Anthropology at the University of Toronto, where she holds the Canada Research Chair in the Political Economy and Culture of Asia-Pacific. Her books include *The Will to Improve: Governmentality, Development, and the Practice of Politics* (Duke University Press 2007) and *Transforming the Indonesian Uplands: Marginality, Power and Production* (Routledge 1999). She has published many articles on development, resource struggles, community and indigeneity in Indonesia, among them 'Practices of Assemblage and Community Forest Management' (*Economy and Society* 36(2)). Through the collaborative research programme 'Challenges of Agrarian Transition in Southeast Asia', she is currently co-authoring *Powers of Exclusion: Land the New Enclosures in Rural Southeast Asia*.

Bill Maurer is Professor and Chair of the Department of Anthropology at the University of California, Irvine. He has written widely on the anthropology of money, finance and property for *Cultural Anthropology*, *American Ethnologist*, *American Anthropologist*, *Annual Reviews in Anthropology*, *Environment and Planning D: Society and Space*, *Comparative Studies in Society and History* and other publications. He is the editor of several collections, as well as the author of *Recharting the Caribbean: Land, Law and Citizenship in the British Virgin Islands* (University of Michigan Press 1997), *Pious Property: Islamic Mortgages in the United States* (Russell Sage Foundation Publications 2006) and *Mutual Life, Limited: Islamic Banking, Alternative Currencies, Lateral Reason* (Princeton University Press 2005). The latter received the Victor Turner Prize in 2005. He is currently conducting research on the shifting regulatory landscape in the offshore Caribbean, innovations in Native American banking (with Justin B. Richland), and the cultural and legal implications of new forms of electronic money and payment systems.

David Nelken is Distinguished Professor of Sociology at the University of Macerata, Italy, and also Distinguished Research Professor of Law at the University of Cardiff, Wales, and Honorary Professor of Law at the LSE, UK. In 2007–2008 he was Wiarda Chair at the Willem Pompe Institute of Criminal Law at the University of Utrecht, and in 2008–2009 he will be the S.T. Lee Visiting Professor at London University's Institute of Advanced Studies. Specializing in comparative sociology of law, recent books include *Adapting Legal Cultures*, edited with J. Feest (Hart 2001), *Law's New Boundaries: The Consequences of Autopoiesis*, edited with J. Pribán (Dartmouth, UK 2001), *L'integrazione subita: (im)migrazioni, flussi, trasformazione*, edited by Franco Angeli (Rome 2005), *European Ways of Law*, edited with V. Gessner (Hart 2007), *Comparative Law: A Handbook*, edited with E. Orucu (Hart 2007), *Exploring Legal Cultures*, edited with Freek Bruinsma (special issue of *Recht der Werkelijkheid*, Elsevier 2007), and *Beyond the Law in Context: Collected Essays in Legal Philosophy* (Ashgate 2008).

Monique Nuijten is Associate Professor at the Rural Sociology Group of Wageningen University, the Netherlands. In Mexico and Peru she has conducted extensive research on state–peasant relations, agrarian reform and communal land tenure institutions. At present she directs a research project about social organization and the construction of space in urban slums in Recife, Brazil. She is author of the book *Power, Community and the State: The Political Anthropology of Organization in Mexico* (Pluto Press 2003), editor, together with G. Anders, of the book *Corruption and the Secret of Law: A Legal Anthropological Perspective* (Ashgate 2007), and has written numerous articles, including 'Between Fear and Fantasy: Governmentality and the Working of Power in Mexico' (*Critique of Anthropology* 2004) and 'External Interventions and Rituals of Resistance: The Implementation of Participatory Approaches in Rural Mexico' (*Journal of Peasant Studies* 2004).

David Lorenzo is a PhD candidate at the Department of Society and Globalization of Roskilde University, Denmark. After having conducted research in a Mexican *ejido* for his MSc in Social Forestry at Wageningen University, the Netherlands, he started his PhD research in Andean communities in the Central Highlands of Peru. A special focus of his research is the role of law, violence and state–peasant relations.

Diana Sidakis received her Master's degree in Law, Society and Anthropology from LSE, and her BA in English from New York University. She is currently a student at Columbia Law School, where she is focusing on international law.

Melanie G. Wiber is Professor of Anthropology at the University of New Brunswick, Canada. Her primary focus is natural resource management, with research on irrigation, dairy and fishery quota, and community-based management. Her publications include *Politics, Property and Law in the Philippine Uplands* (Wilfrid Laurier Press 1993), *The Role of Law in Resource Management*, co-edited with Joep Spiertz (Vuga 1996) and *The Changing Properties of Property*, co-edited with F. and K. von Benda-Beckmann (Berghahn 2006). With Chris Milley, she recently co-edited a special issue of the *Journal of Legal Pluralism*, *After Recognition: Implementing Special Rights in Natural Resource Management* (2007).

Acknowledgements

This volume resulted from an international conference on 'Law and Governance' at the Max Planck Institute for Social Anthropology in Halle, Germany, 9–11 November 2006. The theme had emerged from the work of the Project Group 'Legal Pluralism' during the first phase at the Max Planck Institute. The conference was organized to mark the end of the first exploratory phase. We are indebted to Gesine Koch, Philipp Humpert and Titus Rebhann for preparing the manuscript and index.

Chapter 1

Rules of Law and Laws of Ruling: Law and Governance between Past and Future[1]

Franz von Benda-Beckmann, Keebet von Benda-Beckmann and Julia Eckert

Introduction

The past twenty years have witnessed important changes in the ways in which government is exercised. A plurality of non-state actors has become involved in what until recently was considered the sole domain of state agencies. At the same time, the academic and political perception of these changes has changed as well. To capture these processes, the term 'governance' was coined, and it has generated a substantial body of literature. Two major strands can be discerned in the literature on governance (Engel and Olsen 2005). The first, particularly prominent in the literature on international law and political science, is strongly policy-oriented. It takes state sovereignty as a crucial point of departure, discussing the loss of internal or external sovereignty and looking for new legitimate and effective ways of governing under conditions of globalization.[2] The second, less prominent, strand of literature takes a descriptive and analytical stance and tries to understand the dynamic changes in governance activities and the intended and unintended consequences of such transformations. It does not focus on a state-centred approach with the associated methodological nationalism predominant in conventional analyses of rule (cf. Glick Schiller and Wimmer 2002; Beck 2007; Zürcher 2007), but rather on a notion of governance in the sense of administration of access to and provision of rights, services and goods, which also implies the definition of categories of inclusion and entitlements either explicitly or implicitly in governmental practices. The concept of 'governance' thus points to a turn from a normative substantive conception of government exclusively tied to the national state based on constitutional and international law towards a functional characterization of governing activities. It embraces the possibility of a multiplicity

1 We thank Sally Merry and Brian Donahoe for their insightful and critical comments, and Anja Sing for correcting our English.

2 See Held (1995) for the quest for legitimate global governance. The World Bank (1989, 135–47; 1991; 1992) and Shihata (1990) have been active in this strand of thought and its emphasis on good governance and related issues. See Healy and Robinson (1992, 163f.); F. von Benda-Beckmann (1994); Santos (2002, 31); Engel and Olsen (2005).

of governance agents, who engage in new modes of exercising power, often guided and legitimized by 'alternative' legalities.

This volume is situated within this second strand of literature. The chapters contribute to an understanding of modes of governance that are emerging from and embodied in practices and social relationships where neither the law of a national state nor state agents are dominant *per se*. They examine the emergence, persistence and growth of relatively independent, parallel networks and centres of governance authority and the legal forms they bring about. The chapters thus document the broadening variety of actors involved in governance practices and the widening ranges of regulation and legal structures. They also investigate the relationship between changing modes of governance and the rules that organize and legitimize governance. They analyse how plural legal orders structure governance processes and examine the effect this has on matters of legal responsibility, liability and accountability for acts of governance. The volume discusses the paradox that the binding power of law for governmental authority is simultaneously increasing and decreasing. Central in all chapters is the question of how these changing modes of governance affect social inequality.

New Constellations of Governance

One might easily consider the attention to the multiple sites of governing authority simply as a late awakening to the fact that state authorities have rarely been the exclusive locus of governance. History is full of multiple or polycentric (Petersen and Zahle 1995) constellations of governance and rule-making by non-state actors. Colonial regimes often relied on indirect rule through what would now be called plural centres of governance.[3] Power and authority structures based on traditional, neo-traditional or religious legitimizations have long been agents of governance in many states; self-regulatory orders in professional, social and economic corporations and networks are not new either.[4] Transnational flows of ideas, legal forms, resources and people occurred long before anyone talked about 'transnationalization' or 'globalization'. Tsing (2000, 333) has therefore rightly cautioned us that 'one of the worst faults of the assumption of global newness is that it erects stereotypes of the past that get in the way of appreciating both the past and the present'.

However, for several reasons it would be inaccurate to say 'it has all been seen before'. For once, the paradigm shift among policy makers and academics from a state-centrist approach to that of governance beyond government was born out of an assessment that the state was in crisis, both by its adversaries advocating the market as a substitute and by its defenders, who saw it reduced to a night

3 In the earlier political and legal anthropology, these were often referred to as 'primitive government' (Mair 1962).

4 On earlier historical manifestations, see Held et al. (1999); Schuppert (2007).

watchman. The politics from which the attention to governance arose have thus affected the ways in which governance is thought about, and have affected policies towards plural constellations of governance. These range from decentralization, to structural reform, all the way to interventionist politics when constellations of governance appear to be far removed from what is considered 'good governance'. Dismissing the current interest in governance by pointing to the historical fact that governance has never been the sole prerogative of states would mean missing out on understanding the impacts of these new governance policy discourses and practices. It would also mean missing out on understanding what is new.

So what is new? While competitive or co-operative constellations of governance have always affected governing processes, the talk of governance beyond government is not simply due to epistemological state-centrism giving way to a more realistic assessment of how governance is conducted. There has been a change in the plurality of governance actors and the conditions under which they compete or co-operate. Current constellations are shaped by novel relations between different agents of government (Castells 1997). The number and range of international and transnational actors involved in governance is higher than ever. Non-state actors, such as transnational companies, have also taken on governance tasks, playing a role in regulating marketing structures, in access to resources, in surveillance, acting as security and military entrepreneurs, and in providing public infrastructure that extends far beyond their primary company goals. The vastly expanding group of NGOs, ranging from transnational to very local organizations, has acquired a firm place in the line-up of governance players. In some states they have become more resourceful and sometimes more powerful than the state bureaucracy.[5] So the sheer number of actors involved, their character, as well as the global networks they are each involved in, are of a different scale than previous constellations of plural governance. Moreover, the normativity that shapes their relations has been transformed through international law, transnational legal norms and international conventions. These are all contested in their interpretation and application. The emerging constellations of governance, shaped as they are by global economic relations, power structures and legal pluralism, confront us with questions regarding their effect on inequality, on legal responsibility for acts of governance, and the role of law in these processes.

Governance and Legal Pluralism

Law is a crucial aspect of governance, for '[g]overnance encapsulates complex dynamics of shaping binding rules, procedures and behaviours in different social

5 See, among others, Rösel and von Trotha (1999). But see Anders (2005) for a critique of the assumption that the state bureaucracies of poor countries depending on development co-operation have virtually no power at all. See also Randeria (2003) on 'cunning states'. On decentralization in Indonesia, see von Benda-Beckmann and von Benda-Beckmann (2007).

spaces' (Engel and Olsen 2005, 10). It constitutes, organizes, and legitimizes positions of authority of governance agents and governance activities. Like governance, the concept of law is not by definition exclusively connected to the state, but allows for the possibility of a plurality of co-existing legal orders, generated and used by different sets of actors, with different sources of legitimacy. The concept 'legal' thus covers a wide range of constellations of law that are highly variable in form and scope.[6] There has been enormous diversification and proliferation of legal forms generated and sanctioned by non-state actors. Besides the official law of the state, international law, and neo-traditional and religious legal orders, there is a wide variety of rules, principles and procedures made or generated by non-state actors under the labels of 'soft law', 'project law', 'standard-setting' or the *lex mercatoria*.[7] Often these are 'recognized' as valid and legitimate in official legal orders; in other cases, such rules are not recognized. State law may even criminalize other governance rules and agents. On their part, the actors generating and using such rules and procedures may also not necessarily seek official 'legal' legitimacy and keep their rules secret. Bureaucratic organizations develop sets of rules for their internal operation and relations with outside agents that differ markedly from the official rules. Such an 'undocumented order' (Wassenberg 1987) may in the worst case be illegal itself, as in cases of corruption; see, for instance, the internal rules governing the appointments of Italian university professors described by Nelken in this volume.[8] There is also an increasing proliferation of 'soft law', 'a variety of processes ... which have normative content [but] are not formally binding' (Trubek, Cottrell and Nance 2006, 65). The sources of soft law are varied. They include multilateral international organizations like the OECD as well as non-governmental organizations and private actors. Besides soft law, another type of rule set, which does not have official legal status, is the 'project law' generated and enforced by powerful agents of development co-operation.[9] Project law is generated in two connected social fields, which shape the relations and interactions between development agencies, their partners and so-called target groups. Li in Chapter 11 of this volume illustrates how the World Bank governs through such project law in many parts of Indonesia.

---

6 For further elaborations of the concept, see Vanderlinden (1971); J. Griffiths (1986); Merry (1988); K. von Benda-Beckmann (2001); F. von Benda-Beckmann (2002); A. Griffiths (2002).

7 See Teubner (1997); von Benda-Beckmann and von Benda-Beckmann (2007). See Wiber (2005) on law-making by epistemic communities.

8 Already in 1965, Lev (1965, 304) spoke of a 'folk law of corruption'. For earlier discussions of corruption and normative pluralism as two sets of rules that are not independent, see Mooij (1992, 229). See also Wade (1984; 1985) and Nuijten and Anders (2007).

9 On project law, see Thomson (1987); F. von Benda-Beckmann (1989; 1991); K. von Benda-Beckmann (1991); Günther and Randeria (2001); Weilenmann (2004; 2005).

As a result, many people and governance agencies operate under conditions of legal pluralism and have to find their way in diverse modes of constituting governance authority, rules of governance and ways in which the legal basis for governance activities is defined. As the chapters in this volume show, this may lead actors to engage in selectively mobilizing certain legal orders in one context but switching to another in a different context, as the example described by Maurer in Chapter 10 of the states engaged in soft law governance shows. It may also involve situations in which the same actors have to balance out two sets of norms for the same activities, as in the appointment procedures in Italian universities described by Nelken in Chapter 12. Or it may lead to a situation where private companies backed by a powerful state manage to evade compliance to national and international law, as Sidakis describes for Iraq in Chapter 3.

The Changing Role of the State

Within these constellations, the role of the state has changed: The centralizing drive by state agencies has been redirected to incorporate new (and old) alternatives or additional agencies of governance. More precisely, states, rather than governing directly, now attempt to determine the shape of the constellations of governance. As Santos stressed: 'The centrality of the state lies to a significant extent in the way the state organises its own decentring …' (Santos 1995, 118). The processes of the formal or informal, and of actively initiated or passively enforced devolution of governance competences from the state to alternative organizations can take at least five principal forms:

- devolution of state productive and distributive tasks to private organizations like charitable organizations or commercial companies, which possibly also informally devolve regulation as much as it is inherent in distribution and production;
- formal decentralization and devolution of regulatory tasks in specific legal fields, be they of the kind of personal status regulations or the devolution of regulation for and jurisdiction over the internal affairs of corporations, but also of development projects and international NGOs; these also affect other legal fields than those specified, as well as persons not immediately part of the entity thus empowered;
- the independent constitution of parallel centres of governance authority that wield control over specific territories, specific groups of people, or specific economic spheres and that do not stand in a subsidiary, complementary relation to the state but in a parallel and autonomous one; the establishment of such autonomy has often been treated as a sign of state crisis, or the infringement of state sovereignty, as an instance of 'fragmented sovereignties' (Randeria 2003);
- a nearly world-wide resurgence and revitalization of political authorities

and legal frameworks based on neo-traditional religious, ethnic or local legitimizations which show resurgence of claims and modes of governance based on religious and neo-traditional law; with the greater emphasis on political freedom and equality and an increasing social and economic interdependence between the formerly more detached spheres of governance, the former legal and political asymmetries have become contested again;[10]
- scaling up of tasks and the assuming of competences by international agencies.

These trajectories of organizing the pluralization of governance have been the subject of intense political activity – also on the part of the state. The policies directed towards them diverge enormously, including public–private partnerships, conditionalities connected to development co-operation, and military interventions. Which of these measures are employed depends on the actors involved in these constellations and their integration into the international system and international economy.

The Paradox of Deregulation and Juridification

These dynamics are full of contradictions which are particularly obvious in the discourses and processes of simultaneous deregulation and juridification. When in the 1980s and 1990s it was asserted that the state ceased to be the central site of governance, this was lauded in certain circles (for example, Friedman 1999) and bemoaned by others (for example, Strange 1996). Since then, the state has made a comeback, aided not least by such agencies of governance as the World Bank (1997). 'Good governance' has given the state a new lease of life even among its strongest adversaries. At the same time, it has made the legitimizing role of law ever more prominent: The 'rule of law' has become the linchpin of legitimate governance.

The debate about the centrality of the state, however, continues. It has diversified from a pro and contra position to one that distinguishes various and sometimes contradictory processes. On the one hand, we have the changing scope of sovereignty in the international system. In the legal dimension, the classical notions of sovereignty and the authority to govern which it encompasses are increasingly restricted by international law, transnational law and international conventions. International agencies take on governing roles that enter deeply into the internal affairs of national states and affect the lives of their citizens. These developments do not necessarily mirror a parallel loss of political power

10 For Africa, see Comaroff and Comaroff (1999); Hellum and Derman (Chapter 6 in this volume); Rouveroy van Nieuwaal and Zips (1998); Oomen (2002; 2005); Hinz and Pateman (2006); Ubink (2008). For Indonesia, see Davidson and Henley (2007); F. von Benda-Beckmann et al. (2003).

and autonomy for all countries, and they often mask power differences between different states, as between the US and the EU and many states in the Third World. They form a constraining factor for many governments (McGrew 1998).

Internally, the contours of state sovereignty have undergone change as well, in particular due to deregulation and the rising security paradigm. Deregulation usually concerns specific fields of governmental activity. By now, it has become clear that deregulation has been paralleled by and partly only achieved through an unprecedented wave of *re*-regulation and new law. The emphasis on de-juridification and the presumed weakening of state power masked processes whereby state bureaucracies capture governance powers that previously have not been within their ambit. So while state sovereignty is increasingly challenged by the international legal system, at the same time state governments assume controlling and surveillance powers, imposing restrictions on the rights of citizens or peoples that are unprecedented in recent legal history (Castells 1997, 301; Eckert 2008; Kelly 2008; Schiffauer 2008; Peter 2008; von Benda-Beckmann and von Benda-Beckmann 1998; 1999). This is especially the case since the rise of an international security paradigm in the 1990s, and culminated in the efforts of co-ordinating 'the war on terror' internationally (Eckert 2008).

Together, the rise of international law and conventions and the international security paradigm signify a shift in the delineations of external sovereignty. International law and conventions limit the exercise of internal sovereignty with regard to the rights of citizens. At the same time, the rise and international co-ordination of the security paradigm has introduced new standards for legitimate and illegitimate violence, as for example in the debate on torture. It has introduced new categories of participants such as enemy combatants, rendering them ineligible for protection under international law. And it has transformed the legitimacy of surveillance as well as the scope of prevention. It has thereby created new forms of legitimate and legal violence, while at the same time international law and various international conventions have de-legitimized other forms of state violence by declaring them illegal. On first sight, these complementary legal trajectories seem entirely born from geopolitical power relations.

The Comaroffs (Chapter 2 in this volume) call attention to the relation between the assumed dissolution of centres of governmental authority, the pluralization of governance, and the fear of disorder. This fear of disorder was 'encouraged', so to speak, by the dissolution of central authority, and as we will discuss below, the concomitant dissolution of state liability legitimizes the proliferation of intrusive and far-reaching forms of governance. Bubandt (2005) showed that this very fear of chaos and the 'onto-politics' of security have generated more fear rather than security, setting off a never-ending spiral of ever more intrusive measures.

Paradoxically, this process is accompanied by what the Comaroffs call the 'fetishization' of law, that is, the belief in law's capacity to generate order. Evidence of this is an explosion of 'rights talk' and an increasing juridification of politics and conflicts. The latest waves of transnational legal engineering in law and development are a case in point (see Dezalay and Garth 2002; F. von Benda-

Beckmann 2006; World Bank 2006). So is the ever-increasing reliance on legal claim-making by oppositional movements. And the more the rule of law becomes a battle cry in intra- and international politics, the greater the need to turn to law for legitimization. However, the law of the state no longer has the privileged position it was assumed to have. Rights talk and the fetishization of law are therefore not restricted to state law, but increasingly include reference to legalities based on different legitimacies by a variety of actors such as NGOs and ethnic and faith-based groups. Since governance is one important way of exercising power, the question of who is entitled to engage in governance, and under whose terms governance may legitimately be carried out, is a hotly contested issue in most societies, each authority claiming superior rights or freedom to self-regulation in the name of the state's sovereignty, the *sharia*, ethnic customary law, or international law (such as the ILO Convention on the Rights of Indigenous Peoples no. 169). Thus, those opposing this specific law-based power increasingly counter it with law themselves, be it the same law of the state interpreted differently, or alternative legal systems such as the law of indigenous peoples, religious communities or ethnic groups, or a higher-level international law.

The fetishization of law often appears as a spectacle, which deflects from concomitant processes of dissolving legal responsibility for acts of governance, or from the fact that social processes might be shaped by quite different social and normative forces other than law, in which ostensibly all hope is vested. The extent to which governance practices are actually structured by law, and by which law, is not self-evident, particularly not where people operate under a plurality of governance rules. It cannot be deduced from the law itself or from the ways actors normatively arrange plural rule sets in terms of recognition and subordination. The way state law defines its relationship towards other types of law is not necessarily followed. In cases where the state is so weak that it cannot impose its recognition of rules on other actors, the question of how much scope non-state legal orders leave for the recognition of other legal orders (including that of the state) and governance authorities becomes more important. And there are examples of governance by non-state actors against the prerogatives of state governments and the effective takeover of governance from the state (see, for example, Humphrey 1999; Schlichte and Wilke 2000; Volkov 2000). The co-existence of different rules for the conduct of governance may lead to peaceful, relatively unstructured and complementary forms of governance co-existing side by side. It may lead to co-operation between state representatives and private persons and organizations in ways that may be considered either legal or illegal.[11] However, co-existing governance regulations may also lead to intense, and at times violent, conflicts in which reference to different legal orders rationalizes and justifies opposing economic or political objectives.

11 On such 'illegal' collaborations of state and non-state organizations, see Eckert (2003; 2004).

Public and Private

Many of these changes affect the normative and empirical boundaries between private and public authority and responsibility that were previously taken for granted, at least according to the social-democratic European canon of state tasks of the twentieth century. But they equally affect the distribution of governance authority and power in Third World states, in which the state organization never came anywhere near assuming and fulfilling state tasks as they had developed in Europe. All over the world, under the recent conditions of globalization, we seem to face a proliferation of fully privatized and hybrid governance practices, *ad hoc* or institutionalized, such as so-called 'public–private partnerships', in which a variety of agents co-operate and which give rise to the emergence of new constellations of rules authorizing and organizing governance, which we have discussed earlier.[12] These new governance institutions not only provide services; they are often also endowed with secondary rule-making authority. Increasingly, such hybrid modes of governance are emerging and being popularized as means to guarantee 'good governance', leaving the question open whether this is meant in the ideal social-democratic sense or in the sense of a liberal economy.[13]

Numerous scholars from a range of disciplines have drawn attention to the increasing role of soft law in solving problems of international governance and regulation that cannot be addressed through the hard laws of individual sovereign states or by enforceable international treaties.[14] Maurer (Chapter 10 in this volume) suggests we use the term 'soft law' in a broad analytical sense to refer to governance through peer review, consultation, peer pressure, shaming and the creation of non-binding guidelines and recommendations. As de Búrca and Scott (2006, 2–3) state, soft law is a key component of the so-called 'new governance', based on participation, networked decision-making, diversity, consultation rather than the formal mechanisms or the centralized 'command and control' regime

12 There is a burgeoning body of literature on privatized governance, concerted actions between private and public actors. See Streeck and Schmitter (1985); Brunsson and Jacobsen (2000); Benz (2004); Pattberg (2005); Schepel (2005); Budäus (2006). On 'horizontal' or 'negotiating' governance in the Netherlands, see K. von Benda-Beckmann and Hoekema (1987).

13 Schuppert (2007) distinguished three major types of what he called 'hybrid' governance modes, which also express law and governance intersections:

legal hybridization, cases in which legal orders themselves provide legal constructions that make the co-operation between governmental and private action modes possible;

organizational–institutional hybridization, where governmental and private actors are joined in the administration of domains or sectors;

functional hybridization, in which the actual provision of statehood functions is complementary or mutually substitutive (see Eckert, Dafinger and Behrends 2003; Eckert 2004).

14 Mörth (2006, 121) provides a convenient ideal-typical sketch, contrasting hard law 'government' with soft law 'governance'.

of association with law and constitutionalism. In Europe, soft law has become the hallmark of the Open Method of Co-ordination (OMC) in the creation and maintenance of European integration (Trubek and Trubek 2005). Especially in development co-operation, the 'project law', generated and enforced by powerful agents of development co-operation, becomes a more important means of governance than the law of the state (and often also the customary law) in the area in which the development project is carried out (see Li's Chapter 11 in this volume). Nelken provides us with a particularly interesting example of the kinds of linkages that are being created. Analysing practices of appointments in Italian universities, Nelken suggests that the law of the state that officially regulates such appointments, and the law of patronage that in practice determines who gets appointed and why, are linked in an inextricable embrace, feeding upon each other while seemingly mutually exclusive in effect.

The reasons why governance passes on to, or is acquired by, hybrid or private institutions vary. In the cases of resource management as described by Hellum and Derman (Chapter 6) and Wiber and Bull (Chapter 7), it is done by the government to enhance participation of all stakeholders. Griffiths and Kandel show that it may also be more of an unintended consequence of an ideological change in dealing with unruly youths. In the case of Iraq, it is ostensibly for reasons of efficiency, and powerful private organizations have managed to convince the government that they are better positioned to keep violence in check, though this may generate problematic violence on the side of these very organizations, for which neither the state nor the organization seems to take responsibility. The pattern seems to be that in situations where reliance on plural constellations of governance is high, large areas of law-making are 'outsourced' together with the various governance tasks for which private companies are given licences. The specific issues of governance, for which the hybrid or privatized institution has been established, are effectively separated from the wider public interests and the social and political implications that might have receded to the background. The mechanisms built into state governments that force them to consider broader public interests when making policies for more specific purposes do not work for privatized governance.[15]

This raises important issues about what is and belongs to the role of the public realm of the state as such, as well as about how the interests of the socially and economically disadvantaged are to be protected. Old ideas that the state is responsible for the public good no longer hold, if they ever did. And the old ways in which protection was granted do not seem to work any more. Many of the chapters in this volume testify to the problematic consequences, especially for marginalized, poorly organized and poor sections of the population. The organization of these new governance structures is often highly unequal and dominated by powerful actors, while others are excluded. As Maurer warns us in Chapter 10, the rise of 'social' forms of governance through participation and consultation often masks

15 See Sikor (2008) on new modes of public–private mixes in natural resource management.

the fact that powerful actors are much more resourceful and powerful than many states. The powers of governance are not always conferred upon private institutions by the state; often powerful private institutions capture this power against the will of the state. As Sidakis shows in Chapter 3, some of these institutions assume so much power and operate so independently that they in effect are private institutions performing public tasks and assuming public authority while dodging any public responsibility. Kapferer (2005) even argues that these modes can better be understood as new forms of state-formation – formations that are, however, exclusive rather than inclusive. These developments also raise serious questions concerning the notions and practices of 'participation' and partnership. The notion of participation suggests a high degree of equality of the partners or 'stakeholders' and is therefore often no more than a thin veneer, as Chapter 6 by Hellum and Derman, Chapter 7 by Wiber and Bull and Chapter 8 by Griffiths and Kandel all demonstrate. Some of these stakeholders, the less well organized and least endowed, are virtually excluded from the decision-making processes and are governed over, rather than being participants to governance.

The driving force behind privatization and the technical mode of such governance also conceal the fact that serious issues of legal responsibility are involved. These will be discussed in more detail below. It also conceals that we are witnessing an ideological turn in the role of the government. This leads to a paradox that the raised insistence that the state should adhere to international and constitutional law is undermined by privatization of hitherto vital governmental tasks to institutions that do not feel bound by international law constitution. The new constellations of governance thus confront us with questions regarding their effect on inequality, on legal responsibility for acts of governance, and the role of law in these processes.

Law, Pluralization and Inequality

The proliferation of actors involved in governance activities, as well as the frequent dividing up of tasks among governing actors, have an effect on structures of inequality. Typically, plural legal configurations are part of and affect the social and political environment, in which governance activities take place, whether state governments recognize the existence of other governance agents and rules or not, whether they join forces with them or fight against them. Firstly, changing plural legal structures might change the structures of inequality in that they create new constraints for some and new opportunities for others. Secondly, structures of inequality affect the chances to act within plural legal situations in contradictory ways.

On the one hand, plural legal constellations and a plurality of governing actors open up a certain room for manoeuvring in which parties can choose a forum of decision-making or a legal order, which they expect to be beneficial for their purposes.[16] On the other hand, this room for manoeuvring is usually structured unequally. What shapes the interaction between different governance actors and what legal order they refer to, or which decision-making forum they employ in their strategies, depends on a wide range of factors.[17] Among the important factors are the extent to which a specific rule set or procedure fits the economic or political objectives of actors, and the extent to which their power and social networks enables them to mobilize a given legal order or decision-making authority successfully. It also depends on the relationships of power and dependence between the parties and the respective institutions of decision-making. Frequently, it tends to be the stronger parties, that are those which can bring to bear their accumulated social, political and financial capital, who determine which forum and which set of rules are to govern a particular situation. Therefore, plurality may actually reinforce structures of inequality as the plurality of forums available decreases the binding power of any law.

Structures of inequality might also be reinforced when those engaged in deciding on which rules should govern governance agree on the necessity to co-operate in order to 'de-pluralize' legal diversity. This happens in efforts to close regulatory gaps and contradictions and to 'harmonize' or centralize regulatory systems. As the case of EU legislation on Third Country Nationals discussed by Foblets in Chapter 9 in this volume shows, the attempt to co-ordinate the differing national laws governing migration leads to what she calls a downward harmonization, resulting in a bare minimum standard for the protection of rights of migrants being agreed upon. The driving forces of such efforts to homogenization, harmonization or centralization are often state agents or other powerful governance actors. However, sometimes such de-pluralization is also pursued by citizens precisely because they lose out in the plurality of forums (see Eckert 2006).

As the contributions to this volume demonstrate, there are many situations in which the seeming openness and flexibility inherent in the plurality of rules and governing bodies work against the weaker parties involved in an interaction. But sometimes weaker parties can use the contradictions in the rules established by a plurality of governing bodies and this may open up possibilities for circumvention. Often gaps emerge in decentralized and compartmentalized governance constellations, which provide at least some space for creative strategies of those adversely affected by certain legal regimes. Whether they can indeed use these possibilities depends on the extent to which they can mobilize their social and political capital effectively. For example, wherever numbers count and a powerful party depends on a poor electorate, the scales in decision-making are weighted differently than in situations were only purely economic capital determines the course of events.

---

16 On practices of 'forum shopping', see K. von Benda-Beckmann (1981).

17 These have been widely discussed in the literature: see, for instance, Nader and Todd (1978); K. von Benda-Beckmann (1981); J. Griffiths (1983); Galanter (1974).

Several chapters in this volume suggest that there are limits to such 'weapons of the weak' (Scott 1985) as circumvention and avoidance, and that these stand in complex relation to more overt means of strengthening one's position. This volume also suggests that the role such strategies have in the stabilization of power relations or in their transformation might deserve further study. One instance of the contradictory effects which new modes of governance have on the possibilities of differentially situated parties is 'soft law' governance. This concerns negotiated rule-making for controlling taxation among states, as discussed by Maurer. It also concerns rule-making by international organizations, as discussed by Li, or by a set of state and non-state actors as in the cases of Hellum and Derman, Wiber and Bull and Griffiths and Kandel. Soft law seems to leave more room for compromise and the taking into account of situational needs and necessities; on the other hand, it lacks the binding power over stronger parties. Power relations are therefore negotiated differently, under so-called 'soft' regulations rather than under 'hard' ones – and soft regulations with their reliance on social relations privilege those who can bring the necessary capitals into the fray of negotiation. However, Maurer demonstrates that there are circumstances, under which a weaker party manages to resist compliance with the rules forced upon them by stronger actors, invoking these very principles and rules against the stronger party, who does not comply with them themselves. Maurer's examples suggest that this is only possible because of the status actors have under international law. With respect to the choice for disputing forums, Nader (1996) suggested that the preference for 'soft' non-judicial mechanisms over allegedly more rigid ones as implied in court proceedings was related to the increasing success with which 'harder' rules and forums were used by the weaker parties to a negotiation. In practice, the less powerful participants to a negotiation then often have no recourse to sanctioning mechanisms, and lose out in negotiations, in which they are forced to participate.

Li's illustration of the World Bank's project law (Chapter 11 in this volume) shows how 'hard' such 'soft' unofficial law may be if one partner controls the allocation of resources in a legal and governance context, in which the weaker partners in the relationship have little choice of action. As Li argues, the assumptions underlying neoliberal policies, which are premised on a rational choice model, are deeply flawed. This model emphasizes the agency of all participants, but fails to address the question of what the choices are that the unequal partners in fact have. While the weak states of Maurer's example can derive considerable strength from their position as sovereign states in the international legal order, the weak Indonesian partners of the World Bank that Li discusses have no recourse to such legal support, and this is reflected in their bargaining position. However, Li's chapter also shows the limitations of the power of such powerful actors. They can shape the context for resource allocation and control the conditions for allocation, but in the end they often cannot really control the process of distribution of such resources afterwards.

Chapter 6 by Hellum and Derman and Chapter 7 by Wiber and Bull describe the intricate new intermeshing of state regulation, non-state associations and newly formed market oriented 'private partners'. While notions of equity, transparency and participation figure high in the constitutional setup of the modes of governance, the practice is quite different. For issues that are being negotiated at a sub-national level, it is far less easy for poorly organized population groups to mobilize effective support than for the well-organized and powerful companies and state agents. Likewise, the children described by Griffiths and Kandel have little scope for negotiating the rules that govern unruly juveniles, but depend on a diverse, and for them incomprehensible, set of actors who approach the rules from very diverse perspectives.

The issue of inequality is thus central to the questions that are raised in relation to the plurality of legal orders and governance actors. The chapters in this volume testify to the importance of subjecting to scrutiny complex negotiation procedures and informality, in which unequal participants are forced to compete for their interests. The contradictory effects which the pluralization of rule-making and the proliferation of governing bodies have on structures of inequality, or the new role which different forms of inequality gain within the configurations of power, have to be explored further.

Legal Responsibility for Acts of Governance

The pluralization of governance actors and the dividing up of tasks among different governing actors also have an effect on the organization and practice of legal responsibility. Outsourcing, sub-contracting, devolving, delegating, co-operation, competition and usurpation – the chains of command, the alliances, and linkages of governance extend in capillary quality; responsibility is dispersed and compartmentalized, if not diffused altogether. Most importantly, responsibility may no longer be directly tied to authority. The contradictions, overlaps and gaps inherent in most plural governance constellations not only produce opportunities for weaker parties mentioned above; they also make it possible for governance bodies to shift responsibility from one to the other, hide behind each other, or claim non-liability.[18] In the course, claimants run from pillar to post, often facing a complete dissolution of legal responsibility. This is the case where governing tasks are allotted according to areas of specialization or the principle of subsidiarity, but also when the involvement of several governing bodies is less formally organized. As Sidakis shows in her contribution to this volume on Iraq in Chapter 3, it can be a direct result of the specific forms of public–private partnership, which make all conventional legal forms of liability non-applicable, circumventing both private and public law. Moreover, it is the separation of specific governance tasks from the wider political and legal process which leads to the dispersion, if not dissolution, of legal responsibility. Analysing the World Bank approach to introducing a development project with far-reaching political implications,

18 For an excellent analysis of such strategies by 'cunning states', see Randeria (2003).

Li uses Ferguson's (1994) notion of the 'anti-politics machine' to characterize the project's depoliticization. Interestingly, such dissolution of legal liability and 'technicization' of what clearly are political rules and principles frequently go hand in hand with a demonstrative celebration of the importance of law and good governance. Spectacles of international law and constitutional law mask both the privatization of law-making and the erosion of legal responsibility in many fields of governance. The fetishization of law thus deflects from concomitant processes of dissolving legal responsibility. Such public 'spectacles' of the rule of law often provide the legitimacy for the laws of ruling to operate. However, they can easily backfire when most participants regard it as a cynical enactment of the 'emperor's new clothes', as often is the case in political show trials, faked elections or unconvincing justifications for military interventions.

Dissolution of responsibility is not exclusively related to privatization and devolution of state authority. Both Kelly (Chapter 4) and Nuijten and Lorenzo (Chapter 5) point at ways in which state agencies enter into illegal acts of governance, confronting the public and the population with *faits accomplis* to proceed in legalizing the situation that was created by illegal means. Kelly analyses the ways in which the state tries to respond to feelings of fear among a deeply divided population, whose groups are nevertheless intimately dependent upon each other. The government creates spaces and boundaries separating the Israeli and Palestinian population by erecting walls and border posts the population has to pass. These are often entirely illegal according to Israeli law. The normative effect of these physical constructions renders them legal at a later point in time. However, these very modes of governance create and exacerbate the very fears they intend to take away.

The issue of legal responsibility and liability is particularly pressing with regard to issues of violence perpetrated by governing bodies. Plural constellations of governance, old and new, challenge not only state claims to external and internal sovereignty, but particularly state aspirations to the monopoly on legitimate coercive force. These aspirations have always been relative and unstable in actual practice, and the periods in which state violence was actually subservient to law have been short and reserved for a relatively limited number of states. In most instances of colonial history, largely uncontrolled and legally unjustified violence established an order which was then 'legalized' in ways that affirmed very specific interests. These were concealed by the very employment of the term 'governance' and its implication of a largely apolitical effective conduct of administration. The legal order established thereby continued the violence by other means; or rather, it established long-term economic and political structures which precluded the sovereign and democratic decision-making about the latter promised by the simultaneous spectacles of constitutional law.

We have now entered into a new era in which the current developments in the pluralization of governance effectively imply a retreat of the state from its liability to prevent undue violence and reveal the Janus-like nature of governance. The aspiration to sovereignty, which had as its correlate the presumption of responsibility, seems to be abandoned. Feeding on a 'culture of fear', governmental agencies establish far-reaching and intrusive measures of control. The laws of ruling are often fraught with opaqueness, violence, and inequality, which the rules of law seem to be subjected to. The diffusion and privatization of governmental controlling and surveillance practices in the exercise of their internal sovereignty, however, diffuse and compartmentalize liabilities, which in effect threaten to dissolve responsibility. This connection is demonstrated clearly by Sidakis in her discussion of private military companies (Chapter 3). Similarly, Kelly in Chapter 4 examines the different governmental propositions on how violence against Israel and Israeli citizens could most effectively be prevented which have underlain the security policies of Israel since the 1960s. While all security policies were inspired by the aim to prevent violence, they related differently to the employment of force, or to different types of force, in the efforts to produce security. Their legacies of structures of inclusion and exclusion produce insurmountable contradictions which give rise to ever more insecurity. Kelly's discussion of Israel's policies of spatial control is an extreme example of how a culture of fear came to dominate a legal system, creating its own insecurities and invitations to violence.

Moreover, the scope of governance structures, and the pace at which they are changing, tend to make the procedures opaque for ordinary citizens. This lack of transparency provides powerful actors with the space to pursue their interests and to force less powerful actors into compliance with the wishes of the former. They may do so by referring to state law, if it suits their goals, or to self-regulation and negotiation, if that is more amenable to their interests. But the lack of transparency also allows powerful actors to exert violence, whether legitimate, illegitimate or balancing on the borderline between illegal and legal violence. Due to the equally opaque diffusion or dissolution of legal responsibility mentioned above, the victims have hardly any recourse to institutions that might curb this unabashed force and violence.

In Chapter 5, Nuijten and Lorenzo therefore argue that violence as a mode of governance needs to be examined more closely again. They emphasize the importance of taking into account how different segments of the population are targeted by different forms of power and governmentality, making some subject to the seemingly 'softer' forms discussed above, and others to brute force. This is also due to the fact that the overwhelming preoccupation with fears of disorder and the resurgence of a security paradigm allows for a degree of force and violence that is ostensibly quite unintended (Eckert 2008). The forms of legal pluralism generated by neoliberal policies, such as public–private partnerships, decentralization, privatization and so on, have created systems of differential citizenship in which segments of the population have citizenship rights that are seriously curtailed, while others enjoy unprecedented freedoms and privileges. Citizenship has never been equal and homogeneous; however, the emerging forms of differentiation correlate to the emerging forms of governmental pluralism. Far from adhering to the new institutionalized claims for universalism, such as in the human rights regime and in international law, these new differentiations most often pertain to the particular positions within the global economy or within the emerging security regimes.[19]

Thus, although governance beyond the state has historically been the norm rather than the exception, an exploration of its current forms poses a series of new questions. The field of governance has broadened and relations between the various authorities have changed, both in terms of the actors included and the conditions for co-operation or competition. The normative and institutional complexity under which they operate is of a different kind than previous ones. In various ways, old hierarchies between agents and levels of governance are being reshuffled, while new linkages are being forged between local, regional, national and transnational bodies of governance. The level of experimenting with new modes of governance and the strategic, and at times haphazard, alliances being created in the process are quite remarkable. In view of the political and economic goals that different actors pursue, these new modes of governance require critical scrutiny.

The Chapters

John L. and Jean Comaroff, in Chapter 2, 'Reflections on the Anthropology of Law, Governance and Sovereignty', argue that it is time again to put law at a central position in social theory. They explore three major sets of issues that need to be addressed by a critical legal anthropology. These are, in the first place, the 'hyper-extended, often counter-intuitive, deployment of legalities in the social, geographical, political, moral, and material reconstruction of the universe' engendered by neoliberalism. This has led to a 'fetishism of law', 'a process whereby … the law … is objectified, ascribed a life-force of its own, and attributed the capacity to configure a world of relations in its own image'. The over-determination of law also finds expression in a culture of legality, which affects everyday life in an obsession with order, rights and legality. Resistance is as much clothed in terms of law as is governance from the powerful. These processes go hand in hand with a dramatic outsourcing of government, including policing and warfare. With reference to Benjamin (1978 [1921]) and Foucault, the Comaroffs draw attention to the dark sides of the law: '*law*fare', the legitimate use of penal powers, administrative procedures, states of emergency, mandates and warrants to discipline its subjects by means of violence. One of the consequences is a shift of politics towards the courts, of democracy to law, and political issues being turned into technical–legal problems.

This leads to a fragmented field of partially overlapping horizontal and vertical sovereignties. The kind of sovereignty that emerges is no longer based on an assumed homogeneity, but on cultural or religious diversity. The authors

19 On variegated citizenship, see also Ong (2006); Holston (2007). On the specific impact of the security regime on citizenship, see Eckert (2008); Schiffauer (2006; 2008); Cole (2002); Mamdani (2004).

discuss the political consequences this has for groups claiming self-government in a vernacular of 'living customary law' that refers to tradition and the ethics of social connections, but at the same time is deeply modern in their focus on rights, freedom of choice and on courts. The Comaroffs point at a third major set of related issues arising from the pervasive focus on fear for criminality that is used to legitimize a proliferation of governance, control, policing and law enforcement that has, however, to a great extent been privatized.

Sidakis, in 'Private Military Companies and State Sovereignty: Regulating Transnational Flows of Violence and Capital', provides us with a normative and reflexive analysis of the growing military industry of private military companies and the effects these have on state sovereignty. The author discusses the developments in the US Department of Defense and today's mercenaries in the first privatized war – that in Iraq. Arguing that the monopoly of legitimate violence has only briefly been at the core of state sovereignty and the implied strict separation between the public and the private sphere, we are now in a period in which this strict opposition is dissolved. And this occurs not in marginal sectors, but in what was considered the centre of state tasks – the realm of military action. Violence has become a market commodity that is supposed to be controlled by sovereign power, but in practice cannot be controlled. The power of the sovereign, the author argues, is contracted away from the government, redefined and reallocated to the market, allowing the government to keep a distance from actions they would not be allowed to take themselves. While private military companies are subject to national, international and contract law, they produce governance when exerting violence and design codes of conduct which should serve to regulate this industry. The chapter discusses why these companies have such a striking ability to evade legal responsibility, and why the usual legal tools designed to keep them under control do not work. Not only is the government not interested in monitoring them too closely; the contractual relationships are exceedingly complex, making control virtually impossible. Moreover, the chapter argues that the actual activities of these companies, the regulations and contractual relationships pertaining to these activities, as well as the discourses legitimizing their involvement, are constantly in flux, undergoing the same extreme rapid change as transnational capital flows. This makes the companies and their actions powerful institutions of governance that are immune to effective control by the state, crucial parts of which have neither an interest in public control nor in assuming responsibility.

Kelly, in his chapter on 'Laws of Suspicion: Legal Status, Space and the Impossibility of Separation in the Israeli-occupied West Bank', discusses how the Israeli government created a spatial regime of governance based on two contradicting premises that have to do with security, given that Palestinians are considered a political threat to the Israeli state and a physical threat to the Israeli population. One response that was particularly important up to the 1990s was to create maximum economic and social dependency by the Palestinian population on the Israeli economy. This would deeply link the two population groups and would provide the Palestinians with a sound economic basis which would buy enough political support so that they would no longer actively oppose the Israeli state and government. Settlement movements into the West Bank and East Jerusalem reinforced this physical integration. The other way of dealing with this was by creating maximum separation between the Israeli and the Palestinian populations. This was done by means of the partial inclusion of the West Bank in the state of Israel and the installation of a complex system of parallel legal systems for the Israeli and Palestinian populations in the West Bank. This was further strengthened by zoning and the installation of an ever-increasing number of checkpoints and a wall, together with a differential system of identity cards. The civilized Israeli population needed zones of safety where civilian life was possible, apart from and excluding the Palestinian population, who were regarded as being so fundamentally different that they had to be excluded. In line with the American obsession with security and anti-terrorism, the Israeli government has imposed a military governance structure that follows a criminological model and is based on 'punitive segregation'. Kelly also explores the tensions inherent in this legal regime of spatial control and their violent outcome. He argues that the tensions due to the contradicting security policies of the Israeli state in the West Bank create their own insecurities.

Nuijten and Lorenzo, in 'Ritual and Rule in the Periphery: State Violence and Local Governance in a Peruvian *Comunidad*', show how, throughout Peruvian history, a culture of fear on the side of the state seems to have guided policies towards marginal segments of the population. Violence related differently, though, to both the rule of law and the laws of ruling in the logics of state governmentality in different periods, indicating a to and fro between governance through violence, and violence as a rescue of governance. However, for those subjected to these various state efforts at control and exclusion, the changing relations between law and violence appear to have made little difference. Nuijten and Lorenzo argue for an analysis of the co-existence and complementarity of different modes of power, and the resultant emergence of variegated citizenship.

Populations in the periphery, like the ones of highland Peru which they discuss, experience domination in terms of sovereign power, expressed through laws governing territory and brutal physical violence. 'Softer' techniques of governance are not applied to them. Being kept in a relation of exclusion and the absence of state care, highland communities have developed a high degree of autonomy in governance and jurisdiction and turned into small peasant republics with elaborate mechanisms of discipline and punishment. These local regimes of order include a mimicry of state rule, rituals and symbols. Rather than a form of resistance or struggle for independence, Nuijten and Lorenzo analyse this mimicry of the state as a desperate desire and claim to be incorporated in the national project as 'worthy citizens'.

Hellum and Derman, in 'Government, Business and Chiefs: Ambiguities of Social Justice through Land Restitution in South Africa', explore a new governance model set up by the government of South Africa for the process of restitution of communal land. Faced with the enormous scale of developmental responsibilities involved in the demand for a just and sustainable post-restitution process, the government has altered the land restitution process, at least in the case of relatively high-value farms. Through the mandatory formation of new non-state institutions, the government seeks to democratize land use by popular participation and the inclusion of women and the poor. As a condition for the return of their land, claimant communities are required to form strategic partnerships with agribusiness corporations for a minimum period of ten years. This strategic partnership model represents the reliance of the government upon a market approach to land restitution. Hellum and Derman explore how this new governance model for land restitutions changes both the role of law and the roles of the state, the market and the community. The new structure relies to a greater degree chiefly on power than the earlier state-orchestrated development model. While chiefs neither figure in the CPA Act nor in the agreements, they play a significant role in negotiating workers' rights, hiring practices and the use of potential profits. The re-institutionalization of chiefs is likely to have South Africa divided again by two primary systems of land tenure: communal land and freehold land. The authors address the question of how co-existing general law and official customary law can be reconciled with the constitutional equality imperative through a 'living customary law' as interpreted and made in the state court system. In the claimant communities, local law and practice are not in concordance with the state-court version of living customary law. In their interpretation of their respective CPA constitutions, older and strongly male-biased interpretations of patrilineal customs trump the equality principle in the South African Constitution. Paradoxically, the new business model thus reproduces a dual property system, strengthening the positions of chiefs and older versions of customary law.

Wiber and Bull, in 'Re-scaling Governance for Better Resource Management?', analyse policies of a community-based management system for the marine resources in the Nova Scotia area of Eastern Canada. They show how access to clams, which formed a significant source of food and income for many native and non-native families, has shifted from the local population towards one industrial monopolist causing severe hardship among the local population. The authors analyse the reasons why local communities have effectively become excluded from access and from participating in any relevant decision about allocation or improvement of resources. They document the use of property rights to force a marginalized population of indigenous and non-indigenous fishing families into compliance with the monopolist's interests with harassment, unfair labour practices and prohibition of unionization, with government agencies standing by. Moreover, large-scale privatization, licensing, zoning, a deficient quality control and an overall lack of transparency, all combined with the refusal to provide the relevant information to the local population, have effectively concentrated the benefits in the hands of one large company at the expense of local fisher families. This company, riding the rough edges of legality by chasing the local population from leased beaches, banning union membership and harassment, forces the local population to refrain from organizing resistance. The only possible further resistance might be to claim constitutional rights in courts, but the outcome is uncertain with such powerful commercial and administrative opponents. The other open path is to base claims on the alternative legality of first nations, but it would be open for native fishermen and their families only. It would drive a wedge between members of an already marginalized population, laying the seeds for violence within the coastal communities. Thus, the law that was seen as the tool to facilitate devolving powers, roles and responsibilities to the grassroots level has had quite different effects.

Griffiths and Kandel, in 'The Governance of Children: From Welfare Justice to Proactive Regulation in the Scottish Children's Hearings System', explore the consequences of shifting legal approaches to compulsory measures of supervision and care for children under the age of 16. They argue that a system designed to protect children who have suffered from child abuse and neglect, as well as children who are dropping out of school or who have committed criminal offences, underwent two shifts: first towards a rights-based approach and then to a proactive regulatory regime. Underlying this turn, the authors argue, was a change in the conception of children as primarily subjects to and the product of an environment, towards a conception in which children are rational and responsible agents, responsible for their deeds, but who also have rights in legal processes. Focusing on the responses of the various participants in such models reveals a number of paradoxes. The first paradox is that a focus on rights leads to more and more bureaucratic compulsory measures lacking transparency, which in turn lead to contracting rights of the children and parents. Secondly, more emphasis on due process creates more formalization, and therefore makes the process less comprehensible to the children due to the technical language involved. Thus, the focus on rights, intended to strengthen the position of the children for whom the intervention was designed, has actually seriously weakened their position within the network of involved actors and in the hearings' settings, and has increased the number of compulsory measures. The move to a preventive model meant that a wide array of governance measures can be forced upon the juveniles, even if they have not committed any criminal act. These measures are forced upon them by non-governmental agencies, installed to create an informal procedure that would guarantee that these juveniles stay out of a judicial process. Along this path, principles of transparency are dropped, and the youths and their families are forced to undergo a degree of governance they do not understand, and which they feel intrudes on their rights.

The main contention of Foblets in 'Migration and Integration of Third-country Nationals in Europe: The Need for the Development of an Efficient, Effective and Legitimate System of Governance' is to show that in issues relating to immigration and integration, European Union member states have so far given preference to a mode of governance that leaves them a wide margin of discretion in the process of transposing EU rules into their own domestic legal systems. This explains why a coherent regulatory framework at EU level relating to the issues of family reunification and long-term residents cannot (yet) be constituted.

As Foblets shows in her discussion of the efforts to harmonize EU migration law, gaps and contradictions between the different national legislations have been creatively used by migrants to different EU countries. However, they affect the groups towards which they are targeted in a variety of ways, enabling some migrants to benefit from the contradictions between differing national legal regimes in their migratory strategies, and subjecting others to further dependence on costly, if not exploitative and frequently physically dangerous, opportunities provided by entrepreneurs of illegal migration. Foblets concentrates on the arduous process of harmonization – the attempts by participating national governments to create a unitary legal regime spanning the different governing bodies. This results in a process of downward harmonization, born both from the pressures which individual actors (countries) put on the common legislative process, as well as from the response of countries with higher standards to the strategic actions by migrants, who seek out the most liberal regimes.

Maurer, in 'From the Revenue Rule to Soft Law and Back Again: The Consequences for "Society" of the Social Governance of International Tax Competition', discusses the OECD's attempt at governance through soft law in its struggle to curb tax competition and gain greater control over financial crime and money laundering. In its attempt to achieve governance based on persuasion rather than force, the OECD had to invite 'society' to the table, including the International Trade and Investment Organization (ITIO), a multilateral body of tax haven countries that was explicitly modelled on the OECD itself as a consultative body made up of representatives from its own member states. In the newly established Global Forum on Taxation, including the ITIO, the OECD was opposed by a collection of unlikely partners who used the OECD's own practice of partnership to demand a level playing field, not to reduce, but to protect tax competition. Once they became part of the consultative process, the tax havens and their advocates made the call for universal rules of the tax game the centrepiece of their counter-campaign, so that large states would be subject to exactly the same forms and level of scrutiny as small states. Meanwhile, many of these same small countries struck individual deals in the form of Double Taxation Treaties with the big players, such as the United States. This, in effect, killed the multilateral effort for global tax regulation. In the end, these relatively weak small states, like the British Virgin Islands and the Cayman Islands, were able to 'trump' the concerted efforts of the powerful OECD countries by using the very tools of organizations like the OECD: peer pressure, and the deployment of rhetoric about reputation and fairness in the context of new social networks that were created through the consultative process. The international effort against 'harmful tax competition' at the turn of the century, Maurer argues, can thus be seen as a story of the limits of social governance or multilateral regulation of the financial sphere.

Li, in 'The Law of the Project: Government and "Good Governance" at the World Bank in Indonesia', shows how the World Bank attempts to restructure community empowerment programmes in Indonesia via project funds and 'project law'. Drawing on Foucault's notion of government, she describes how the World

Bank uses such project law as a tactic to educate the desires and reform the practices of the target population. The Kecamatan ('Sub-district') Development Programme (KDP) is hugely ambitious, aiming at implementation in tens of thousands of villages and absorbing $1 billion of loan funds. In what Li considers a striking example of government in a neo- or advanced-liberal form, rules, incentives and other tactics are used to set the conditions under which project funds can be acquired, 'artificially arranging things so that people, following only their self interest, will do as they ought'. The project largely bypassed the state apparatus. The consultants on private-sector contracts, almost all of them Indonesian, operated as a loyal, parallel bureaucracy, answerable to the World Bank and KDP's official sponsor, the Central Planning Agency.

As Li points out, the team operated in the manner of an 'antipolitics machine', reducing political and economic problems such as poverty and powerlessness to 'technical problems'. This 'technicization' and depolitization also showed in the 2004 World Bank publication *Village Justice in Indonesia*. The World Bank would only supply the 'mediating institutions' and the 'meta-rules', or at least the 'minimum standards' for meta-rules, that villagers would craft 'from below' within the space the World Bank's programme would provide. The reason for these omissions lies in the fact that the effectiveness of the 'law of the project' as a means of social transformation is limited to arenas that can plausibly be turned into projects of a technical kind. Li's chapter also shows, however, the limitations of such policies. By the time the project funds are no longer controlled by the World Bank, it seems that the further 'implementation' again becomes subject to local power relationships and political objectives.

The final chapter by Nelken on 'Corruption as Governance? Law, Transparency and Appointment Procedures in Italian Universities' draws attention to a relation between law and governance 'that is usually outside the ambit of legal or political science models'. This is where governance practices involve two sets of rules, principles and sanctioning mechanisms that relate to the same activities of the same actors. In contrast to the better-known instances of normative or legal plurality, in which actors often mobilize different legal forms with differing legitimacies against each other, Nelken discusses 'corruption as governance' using the example of the *concorso*, the appointment system to university positions at Italian universities. As a professor at an Italian university who participated in such procedures and had to find a way to understand what was going on, he presents one of the rare examples of true observant participation. He shows how decisions are taken on the basis of patronage relations within academia that trump a relatively impartial weighing of the candidates' academic qualifications as required by the law. All participants are involved in such patronage links. Thus, approaching corruption from a legal pluralist perspective, and emphasizing that one does not deal with acts of individual deviance from law, the paper shows that these practices are well structured – rules exist also in the illicit. And he shows that the appointment process is largely governed by a set of rules that has emerged from and within these patronage relationships. The networks profit from the trust and the positions of authority delegated to them by the state. The main function of the state law in this process is to conceal the range of extra-legal criteria that have in fact been taken into account. Nelken argues that both rule sets are inextricably involved in the process. Rather than offering an alternative to official law, the unofficial rules of the concourse live in parasitic symbiosis with it. The need to provide a patina of legality itself produced a 'dirty togetherness' that makes the system so robust.

References

Anders, G. (2005), *Civil Servants in Malawi: Cultural Dualism, Moonlighting and Corruption in the Shadow of Good Governance*, PhD Dissertation, Erasmus University, Rotterdam.

Beck, U. (2007), 'The Cosmopolitan Condition: Why Methodological Nationalism Fails', *Theory, Culture and Society* 24(7–8): 286–90.

Benda-Beckmann, F. von (1989), 'Scapegoat or Magic Charm: Law in Development Theory and Practice', *Journal of Legal Pluralism* 28: 129–48.

—— (1991), 'Pak Dusa's Law: Thoughts on Legal Knowledge and Power', in E. Berg, J. Lauth and A. Wimmer (eds), *Ethnologie im Widerstreit: Kontroversen über Macht, Geschäft, Geschlecht in fremden Kulturen. Festschrift für Lorenz G. Löffler*, Munich: Trickster Verlag, pp. 215–27.

—— (1994), 'Good Governance, Law, and Social Reality: Problematic Relationships', *Knowledge and Policy* 7: 55–67.

—— (2002), 'Who's Afraid of Legal Pluralism?', *Journal of Legal Pluralism* 47: 37–82.

—— (2006), 'The Multiple Edges of Law: Dealing with Legal Pluralism in Development Practice', in C.M. Sage and M. Woolcock (eds), *The World Bank Legal Review, Volume 2: Law, Equity and Development*, The Hague: The World Bank and Martinus Nijhoff, pp. 51–86.

—— (1999), 'Community-based Tenurial Rights: Emancipation or Indirect Rule?', in K. von Benda-Beckmann and H.F. Finkler (eds), *Papers of the XIth International Congress 'Folk Law and Legal Pluralism: Societies in Transformation' of the Commission on Folk Law and Legal Pluralism, Moscow 18–22 August 1997*, Ottawa: Department of Circumpolar Affairs, pp. 169–87.

—— (2007), 'Between Global Forces and Local Politics: Decentralization and Reorganization of Village Government in Indonesia', in C. Antons and V. Gessner (eds), *Globalization and Resistance: Law Reform in Asia since the Crisis*, Oxford and Portland, OR: Hart Publishing, pp. 211–52.

—— and Benda-Beckmann, K. von (1998), 'Das Recht der Dinge: Verrechtlichung und Entrechtlichung im Verhältnis zwischen Erster und Dritter Welt', in J. Brand and D. Strempel (eds), *Soziologie des Rechts*, Baden-Baden: Nomos, pp. 343–54.

——, Benda-Beckmann, K. von, Eckert, J., Pirie, F. and Turner, B. (2003), 'Vitality and Revitalization of Tradition in Law: Going Back to the Past or Future-oriented Development?', in Max Planck Institute for Social Anthropology (ed.), *Report 2002–2003*, Halle/Saale: Druck-Medienverlag, pp. 296–306.

Benda-Beckmann, K. von (1981), 'Forum Shopping and Shopping Forums: Dispute Processing in a Minangkabau Village', *Journal of Legal Pluralism* 19: 117–59.

—— (1991), 'Development, Law and Gender-skewing: An Examination of the Impact of Development on the Socio-legal Position of Indonesian Women, with Special Reference to Minangkabau', *Journal of Legal Pluralism* 30/31: 87–120.

—— (2001), 'Legal Pluralism', *Tai Culture* VI: 11–17.

—— and Hoekema, A.J. (1987), 'Hoe Horizontaal Bestuurt de Overheid', *Recht der Werkelijkheid* 8: 3–12.

Benjamin, W. (1978 [1921]), 'Critique of Violence', in P. Demetz (ed.), *Reflections: Essays, Aphorisms, Autobiographical Writings*, trans. E. Jephcott, New York: Schocken Books, pp. 237–52.

Benz, A. (2004), 'Einleitung: Governance – Modebegriff oder nützliches sozialwissenschaftliches Konzept?', in A. Benz (ed.), *Governance – Regieren in komplexen Regelsystemen*, Wiesbaden: Verlag für Sozialwissenschaften, pp. 11–28.

Brunsson, N. and Jacobsson, B. (eds) (2000), *World of Standards*, Oxford: Oxford University Press.

Bubandt, N. (2005), 'Vernacular Security: The Politics of Feeling Safe in Global, National and Local Worlds', *Security Dialogue* 36: 275–96.

Budäus, D. (ed.) (2006), *Kooperationsformen zwischen Staat und Markt: Theoretische Grundlagen und praktische Ausprägungen von Public Private Partnership*, Baden-Baden: Nomos.

Búrca, G. de and Scott, J. (2006), 'Introduction: New Governance, Law and Constitutionalism', in G. de Búrca and J. Scott (eds), *Law and the New Governance in the EU and US*, Oxford: Hart Publishing, pp. 1–12.

Castells, M. (1997), *The Power of Identity*, Oxford: Blackwell.

Cole, D. (2002), 'Enemy Aliens', *Stanford Law Review*, 54: 953–1,004.

Comaroff, J.L. and Comaroff, J. (1999), *Civil Society and the Political Imagination in Africa: Critical Perspectives*, Chicago, IL and London: University of Chicago Press.

Davidson, J.S. and Henley, D. (eds) (2007), *The Revival of Tradition in Indonesian Politics: The Deployment of Adat from Colonialism to Indigenism*, London and New York: Routledge.

Dezalay, Y. and Garth, B.G. (2002), *Global Prescriptions: The Production, Exportation, and Importation of a New Legal Orthodoxy*, Ann Arbor, MI: University of Michigan Press.

Eckert, J. (2003), *The Charisma of Direct Action: Power, Politics, and the Shiv Sena*, Oxford: University Press.

—— (2004), 'Urban Governance and Emergent Forms of Legal Pluralism in Mumbai', *Journal of Legal Pluralism* 50: 29–60.

—— (2006), 'From Subjects to Citizens: Legalism from Below and the Homogenization of the Legal Sphere', in F. von Benda-Beckmann and K. von Benda-Beckmann (eds), *Dynamics of Plural Legal Orders: Special Double Issue of the Journal of Legal Pluralism and Unofficial Law* nos 53–4, Berlin: Lit Verlag, pp. 45–75.

—— (2008), 'Laws for Enemies', in J. Eckert (ed.), *The Social Life of Anti-terrorism Laws*, Bielefeld: Transcript, pp. 7–31.

——, Dafinger, A. and Behrends, A. (2003), 'Towards an Anthropology of Governance', in Max Planck Institute for Social Anthropology (ed.), *Report 2002–2003*, Halle/Saale: Druck-Medienverlag, pp. 19–30.

Engel, U. and Olsen, G.R. (2005), 'The African Exception: Conceptual Notes on Governance in the New Millennium', in U. Engel and G.R. Olsen (eds), *The African Exception*, Aldershot: Ashgate, pp. 1–13.

Ferguson, J. (1994); *The Anti-politics Machine: 'Development', Depolitization, and Bureaucratic Power in Lesotho*, Minneapolis, MN: University of Minnesota Press.

Friedman, T.L. (1999), *The Lexus and the Olive Tree: Understanding Globalization*, New York: Anchor.

Galanter, M. (1974), 'Why the "Haves" Come out Ahead: Speculations on the Limits of Legal Change', *Law and Society Review* 9: 95–160.

Glick Schiller, N. and Wimmer, A. (2002), 'Methodological Nationalism and Beyond: Nation-state Building, Migration and the Social Sciences', *Global Networks* 2: 301–34.

Griffiths, A. (2002), 'Legal Pluralism', in R. Banakar and M. Travers (eds), *An Introduction to Law and Social Theory*, Portland, OR: Hart Publishing, pp. 289–310.

Griffiths, J. (1983), 'The General Theory of Litigation: A First Step', *Zeitschrift für Rechtssoziologie* 2: 145–201.

—— (1986), 'What is Legal Pluralism?', *Journal of Legal Pluralism* 24: 1–5.

Günther, K. and Randeria, S. (2001), *Recht, Kultur und Gesellschaft im Prozeß der Globalisierung*, Bad Homburg: Werner Reimers Stiftung.

Healy, J. and Robinson, M. (1992), *Democracy, Governance and Economic Policy: Sub-Saharan Africa in Comparative Perspective*, London: ODI.

Held, D. (1995), *Democracy and the Global Order: From the Modern State to Cosmopolitan Governance*, Cambridge: Polity Press.

——, McGrew, A., Goldblatt, D. and Perraton, J. (1999), *Global Transformations: Politics, Economics and Culture*, Cambridge: Polity Press.

Hinz, M. (ed.) in collaboration with Pateman, H. (2006), *The Shade of New Leaves: Governance in Traditional Authority. A Southern African Perspective*, Münster: LIT Verlag.

Holston, J. (2007), *Insurgent Citizenship: Disjunctions of Democracy and Modernity in Brazil*, Princeton, NJ: Princeton University Press.

Humphrey, C. (1999), 'Russian Protection Rackets and the Appropriation of Law and Order', in J. Heyman (ed.), *States and Illegal Practices*, Oxford: Berg, pp. 199–232.

Kapferer, B. (2005), 'Oligarchic Corporations and New State Formations', in B. Kapferer (ed.), *Oligarchs and Oligopolies: New Formations of Global Power*, New York and Oxford: Berghahn, pp. 1–23.

Kelly, T. (2008), 'Documents, Security and Suspicion: The Social Production of Ignorance', in J. Eckert (ed.), *The Social Life of Anti-terrorism Laws*, Bielefeld: Transcript, pp. 109–29.

Lev, D. (1965), 'The Lady and the Banyan Tree: Civil Law Changes in Indonesia', *American Journal of Comparative Law* 14: 282–307.

Mair, L. (1962), *Primitive Government*, Harmondsworth: Pelican Books.

Mamdani, M. (2004), *Good Muslim, Bad Muslim*, New York: Pantheon Books.

McGrew, A.G. (1998), 'Global Legal Interaction and Present-day Patterns of Globalization', in V. Gessner and A.C. Budak (eds), *Emerging Global Certainty: Empirical Studies on the Globalization of Law*, Aldershot: Ashgate, pp. 325–45.

Merry, S.E. (1988), 'Legal Pluralism', *Law and Society Review* 22: 869–96.

Mörth, U. (2006), 'Soft Regulation and Global Democracy', in M.-L. Djelic and K. Sahlin-Andersson (eds), *Transnational Governance: Institutional Dynamics of Regulation*, Cambridge: Cambridge University Press, pp. 119–35.

Mooij, J. (1992), 'Private Pockets and Public Policies: Rethinking the Concept of Corruption', in F. von Benda-Beckmann and M. van der Velde (eds), *Law as a Resource in Agrarian Struggles*, Wageningen: Pudoc, pp. 219–40.

Nader, L. (1996), 'Civilization and its Negotiations', in P. Caplan (ed.), *Understanding Disputes: The Politics of Argument*, Oxford and New York: Berg, pp. 39–63.

—— and Todd, H.F. (eds) (1978), *The Disputing Process: Law in Ten Societies*, New York: Columbia University Press.

Nuijten, M. and Anders, G. (eds) (2007), 'Corruption and the Secret of Law: An Introduction', in M. Nuijten and G. Anders (eds), *Corruption and the Secret of Law: A Legal Anthropological Perspective*, Aldershot: Ashgate, pp. 1–24.

Ong, A. (2006), *Neoliberalism as Exception: Mutations in Citizenship and Sovereignty*, Durham, NC: Duke University Press.

Oomen, B. (2002), *Chiefs! Law, Power and Culture on Contemporary South Africa*, PhD Dissertation, University of Leiden.

—— (2005), 'McTradition in the New South Africa: Commodified Custom and Rights Talk with the Bafokeng and the Bapedi', in F. von Benda-Beckmann, K. von Benda-Beckmann and A. Griffiths (eds), *Mobile People, Mobile Law: Expanding Legal Relations in a Contracting World*, Aldershot: Ashgate, pp. 91–109.

Pattberg, P. (2005), 'The Institutionalization of Private Governance: How Business and Nonprofit Organizations Agree on Transnational Rules', *Governance* 18: 589–610.

Peter, F. (2008), 'Political Rationalities, Counter-terrorism and Policies on Islam in the United Kingdom and France', in J. Eckert (ed.), *The Social Life of Anti-terrorism Laws*, Bielefeld: Transcript, pp. 79–108.

Petersen, H. and Zahle, H. (eds) (1995), *Legal Polycentricity: Consequences of Pluralism in Law*, Aldershot: Dartmouth.

Randeria, S. (2003), 'Globalization of Law: Environmental Justice, World Bank, NGOs and the Cunning State in India', *Current Sociology* (Special Issue) 51: 305–28.

Rösel, J. and Trotha, T. von. (eds) (1999), *Dezentralisierung, Demokratisierung und die lokale Repräsentation des Staates: Theoretische Kontroversen und empirische Forschungen*, Cologne: Köppe Verlag.

Rouveroy van Nieuwaal, E.A.B. van and Zips, W. (eds) (1998), *Sovereignty, Legitimacy, and Power in West African Societies: Perspectives from Legal Anthropology*, Hamburg: Lit Verlag.

Santos, B. de Sousa (1995), *Toward a New Common Sense: Law, Science and Politics in the Paradigmatic Transition*, London, New York: Routledge.

—— (2002), *Toward a New Legal Common Sense: Law, Globalization, and Emancipation*, 2nd edn, London: Butterworths.

Schepel, H. (2005), *The Constitution of Private Governance: Product Standards in the Regulation of Integrating Markets*, Oxford and Portland, OR: Hart Publishing.

Schiffauer, W. (2006), 'Enemies within the Gates: The Debate about Citizenship of Muslims in Germany', in T. Modood, A. Triandafyllidou and R. Zapata-Barrero (eds), *Multiculturalism, Muslims and Citizenship: A European Approach*, London: Routledge, pp. 94–116.

—— (2008), 'Suspect Subjects: Muslim Migrants and the Security Agencies in Germany', in J. Eckert (ed.), *The Social Life of Anti-terrorism Laws*, Bielefeld: Transcript, pp. 55–77.

Schlichte, K. and Wilke, B. (2000), 'Der Staat und einige seiner Zeitgenossen', *Zeitschrift für Internationale Beziehungen* 2: 359–84.

Schuppert. G.F. (2007), 'Governance – auf der Suche nach den Konturen eines "anerkannten uneindeutigen Begriffs"', in G.F. Schuppert and M. Zürn (eds), *Governance in einer sich wandelnden Welt*, Politische Vierteljahresschrift Sonderhefte 38, Wiesbaden: VS-Verlag.

Scott, J.C. (1985), *Weapons of the Weak: Everyday Forms of Peasant Resistance*, New Haven, CT and London: Yale University Press.

Shihata, I. (1990), *Issues of 'Governance' in Borrowing Members: The Extent of their Relevance under the Bank's Articles of Agreement*, Memorandum of the Vice President and General Counsel, 21 December, Washington, DC.

Sikor, T. (ed.) (2008), *Public and Private in Natural Resource Governance: A False Dichotomy?*, London and Sterling, VA: Earthscan.

Strange, S. (1996), *The Retreat of the State: The Diffusion of Power in the World Economy*, Cambridge: Cambridge University Press.

Streeck, W. and Schmitter, P.C. (eds) (1985), *Private Interest Government: Beyond Market and State*, Beverly Hills, CA and London: Sage Publications.

Teubner, G. (ed.) (1997), *Global Law without a State*, Aldershot: Dartmouth.

Thomson, J.T. (1987), 'Land and Tree Issues in Three Francophone Sahelian Countries: Niger, Mali and Burkina Faso', in J.B. Raintree (ed.), *Land, Trees and Tenure*, Nairobi and Madison, WI: International Council for Research in Agroforestry (ICRAF) and Land Tenure Center, pp. 211–16.

Trubek, D. and Trubek, L. (2005), 'Hard and Soft Law in the Construction of Social Europe: The Role of the Open Method of Co-ordination', *European Law Journal* 11(3): 343–64.

——, Cottrell, P. and Nance, M. (2006), '"Soft Law", "Hard Law", and EU Integration', in G. de Búrca and J. Scott (eds), *Law and the New Governance in the EU and the US*, Oxford: Hart Publishing, pp. 65–94.

Tsing, A.L. (2000), 'The Global Situation', *Cultural Anthropology* 15: 327–60.

Ubink, J.M. (2008), *In the Land of the Chiefs: Customary Law, Land Conflicts, and the Role of the State in Peri-urban Ghana*, Law, Governance, and Development Dissertations series, Leiden: Leiden University Press.

Vanderlinden, J. (1971), 'Le Pluralisme Juridique: Essai de Synthèse', in J. Gillissen (ed.), *Le Pluralisme Juridique*, Brussels: Université Libre de Bruxelles, pp. 19–56.

Volkov, V. (2000), 'Gewaltunternehmer im postkommunistischen Russland', *Leviathan* (2000/2): 173–91.

Wade, R. (1984), 'The System of Administrative and Political Corruption: Canal Irrigation in South India', *Journal of Development Studies* 18: 287–328.

—— (1985), 'The Market in Public Office: Why the Indian State is Not Better at Development', *World Development* 13: 467–97.

Wassenberg, A.F.P. (1987), 'Kunnen Organisaties Elkaar Vertrouwen? Oefeningen in Horizontaal Bestuur', *Recht der Werkelijkheid* 8: 106–32.

Weilenmann, M. (2004), 'Die Wirklichkeit: "Good Governance" und sozio-kulturelle Entwicklung', in Deutsche Gesellschaft für Technische Zusammenarbeit (ed.), *Good Governance und Demokratieförderung zwischen Anspruch und Wirklichkeit – Ein Diskussionspapier*, Eschborn: GTZ, pp. 16–25.

—— (2005), 'Project Law – Normative Orders of Bilateral Development Cooperation and Social Change: A Case Study from the German Agency for Technical Cooperation', in F. von Benda-Beckmann, K. von Benda-Beckmann and A. Griffiths (eds), *Mobile People, Mobile Law: Expanding Legal Relations in a Contracting World*, Aldershot: Ashgate, pp. 233–55.

Wiber, M.G. (2005), 'Mobile Law and Globalism: Epistemic Communities versus Community-based Innovation in the Fisheries Sector', in F. von Benda-Beckmann, K. von Benda-Beckmann and A. Griffiths (eds), *Mobile People, Mobile Law: Expanding Legal Relations in a Contracting World*, Aldershot: Ashgate, pp. 131–51.

World Bank (1989), *Sub-Saharan Africa: From Crisis to Sustainable Growth*, Washington, DC: The World Bank.

—— (1991), *The Challenges of Poverty: World Development Report 1991*, Washington, DC: The World Bank.
—— (1992), *Governance and Development*, Washington, DC: The World Bank.
—— (1997), *The State in a Changing World: World Development Report 1997*, Washington, DC: The World Bank.
—— (ed.) (2006), *The World Bank Legal Review, Volume 2: Law, Equity and Development*, The Hague: Brill.
Zürcher, C. (2007), 'When Governance Meets Troubled States', in M. Beisheim and G.F. Schuppert (eds), *Staatsverfall und Governance*, Baden-Baden: Nomos, pp. 11–27.

Chapter 2
Reflections on the Anthropology of Law, Governance and Sovereignty

John L. Comaroff and Jean Comaroff

Prolegomenon

Just over a quarter century ago, John Comaroff and Simon Roberts opened *Rules and Processes*, their study of African jurisprudence, with a statement that did not win them many friends among their colleagues at the time. 'It is doubtful', they wrote, 'whether [legal anthropology] should exist at all' (Comaroff and Roberts 1981, 3). Their point was not that the comparative study of law was too insignificant or too marginal to claim a discursive domain of its own. Quite the contrary. It was because its subject matter – and especially its theory-work – was too important to be confined to an island unto itself. Nor were they alone in thinking this. Max Gluckman was wont to assert that legal anthropology was the root of *all* anthropology: not only did much of modernist Western thought owe its understanding of the social to one or another version of contract theory, but it rested on the implicit truth that *Homo sapiens* was, everywhere, *Homo juralis*. Gluckman also liked to say that, were apprentice anthropologists to read just one text, there was no question what it should be: Henry Maine's *Ancient Law* (1919). Anthropology in the Maine-stream, some of his younger Manchester colleagues used to joke (J.L. Comaroff 2002).

Now, an epoch later, this seems more than a little overdrawn. Comparative law is *not* everything. Nor, patently, ought it to be the primary source of social theory. But there *is* reason to believe that legal anthropology warrants a more prominent place at the core of the social sciences than ever before: that it is fundamental to making sense of our Brave Neo World, a world whose lineaments are only beginning to make themselves visible, a world for which we do not yet have adequate analytic equipment. If the idea of anthropology in the Maine-stream appeared first as farce, it returns to history a second time in deadly earnest. So much so that, in thinking out loud here about the present and future, we shall concern ourselves with two things, in counterpoint: one is to consider *why* it is impossible to approach the contemporary global order without close attention to law; to law especially in its polyvalent relation to governance. We shall argue, in this regard, that the latest chapter in the *longue durée* of capital, the chapter often titled 'neoliberalism', has led to a hyper-extended, often counter-intuitive deployment of legalities in the social, geographical, political, moral and material reconstruction of the universe, a process most usefully estranged, and grasped, by a critical legal anthropology. Our second objective is part programmatic, part problematic: it is to sketch three potential directions for that anthropology, three directions – among many, we stress – in which it may do both forensic and theory-work at the vanguard of the social sciences.

Before we begin, let us digress for just a moment. Much of what we shall say would have been impossible without the development of a discursive field now known as 'legal pluralism', a field productively cultivated at the Max Planck Institute in Halle, under whose aegis this chapter began its life.[1] Notwithstanding the critiques it has attracted (for example, Moore 1978; Merry 1988; Roberts 1998), legal pluralism – as an orienting sensibility, as a call to re-conceptualize the scope of the law, as provocation (F. von Benda-Beckmann 2002, 37) – sent a wave of creative energy through our discipline. Intersecting with other scholarly initiatives, it has compelled us all to look anew both at the colonial past and at the neo-modern present – in particular, at the legal institutions, practices and processes to which they have given rise. The question for us now, though, is not what has been accomplished. That has been answered cogently by von Benda-Beckmann and von Benda-Beckmann (2006) and others. For us, the question is the future. Where do we go from here? As we shall see, the move from legal pluralism, as orienting gaze, to law and governance, as *problematique*, turns out to be a highly productive one.

Cardinal Pointers: Mapping the Anthropology of Law and Governance

We begin with the most general of our three cardinal directions. For want of a better signpost, since it will take us down several intertwined pathways, let us refer to it as …

The Fetishism of the Law

The modernist nation-state, we hardly need say here, has always been erected on a foundation of legalities.[2] Not only the modernist nation-state – among the pre-modern Nuer of the Sudan, who had no government *sensu stricto*, the line between a tribe and its exteriors, that Schmittian frontier between friend and enemy, was, according to Evans-Pritchard (1940, 278–9), precisely the point at which the law gave way to war, the legal to the lethal. It was similar in classical Greece, where, Arendt (1998 [1958], 194–5) observes, 'the laws [were] like the wall around the city'. Since the destruction of The Wall that marked the end of the Cold War, law

1 It was written originally as a Keynote Lecture to a conference on 'Law and Governance' at the Max Planck Institute for Social Anthropology, Halle, in November 2006.

2 This section, in abbreviated and amended form, is extracted from the introduction to our recent *Law and Disorder in the Postcolony* (Comaroff and Comaroff 2006b).

– specifically, that species of law held to underpin public order – has been yet further fetishized; even as, across the world, ever more forbidding walls are put up to protect the propertied from the unruly. Note that, in speaking of fetishism, we refer to the process of displacement whereby an abstraction – in this case, 'the law' – is objectified, ascribed a life-force of its own, and attributed the mythic capacity to configure a world of relations in its own image.

Striking, in this regard, is the number of new national constitutions written since 1989: 105, and rising.[3] Even more striking is the millennial faith in their capacity to conjure up equitable, ethically-founded polities (cf. Ackerman 1997, 2, 5) – and social order. It is a faith owed largely to the fact that the promulgation of a new Legal Order, in the upper case, signals a break with the past, with its embarrassments, its nightmares, its torments, its traumas. Throughout the global South, moreover, these national constitutions have become the paradigm for a wide range of lower-order analogues. In South Africa, everyone is acquiring them: chiefdoms, churches, NGOs, taxi drivers, even street gangs. As salient as the sheer *quantum* of new national constitutions, though, is a change in their *content*. This, Schneiderman (2000) argues, is owed to a global shift in 'constitutional design' from a state capitalist to a neoliberal model – itself the product of an epochal transformation in the relationship between the economics and politics of capitalism; also of a re-visioning of the relationship between law and governance. Thus, whereas post-Second World War constitutions stressed parliamentary sovereignty, executive discretion, bureaucratic authority and cultural homogeneity, recent ones focus, if unevenly, on the primacy of civil and political rights, the freedoms of the citizen, the limitations of state power, the tolerance of difference, and the rule of law.

This is the case even when both the spirit and the letter of that law are despoiled, distended, desecrated; even as more regimes suspend it in the name of emergency, expediency, exception; even as they expropriate its sovereignty unto themselves; even as they franchise it out.

The enchanted faith in constitutionalism speaks to something yet deeper: a '*culture* of legality' seems to be infusing everyday life almost everywhere, becoming part and parcel of the obsession with order that haunts many nation-states nowadays. The term itself – 'culture of legality' – underwrites a new citizenship education programme in Mexico, for example.[4] It also describes the object of a game invented in Sicily, mythic home of northern banditry; the game is called *Legalopoli*.[5] Even the Vatican is using it. In 1998, *Jubilaeum* carried an essay entitled 'A Strong Moral Conscience for a Culture of Legality' (Dalla

3 See *World Fact Book*, 14 July 2005, <www.odci.gov/cia/publications/factbook/fields/2063.html>, accessed 27 July 2005. The number includes only countries that had either enacted entirely new constitutions (92) or had heavily revised existing ones (13).

4 See <http://bibliotecadigital.conevyt.org.mx/transparencia/Formacion_ciudadana_Gto071103.pdf>, accessed 30 January 2009.

5 *Legalopoli: The Game of Legality* has its own website, <www.legalopoli.it>. We came across it at <www.cmecent.org/Legalopoli.htm>, accessed 1 August 2005.

Torre 1998). It said, among other things, that we have entered an age in which humanity knows itself by virtue of its rights – spelled r-i-g-h-t-s. A new chapter in the 'judicial experience has been opened', the essay added, a chapter we might 'call the "rights of [individual] desires" …'. In fact, this age appears to be one in which rites and rights conjoin in parallel significance as rarely before: faith and the law, arguably, are the twin fixations of *this*-worldly being at the new millennium. Ours is the epoch not of theodicy or theocracy, but of theo-legality. *Pace* Karl Schmitt, it is not just about *political* theology that we ought to be vexing ourselves. It is also *legal* theology. Nor is this true only of the Judaeo-Christian world. As we shall see, it applies as much to Islam.

That humanity knows itself more than ever before by virtue of its rights – or, at least, that more of humanity knows itself in these terms – seems evident from the planetary explosion of human rights advocacy, and also from the spread of law-oriented NGOs, especially in the global South. The civilizing missions of the new century, these NGOs, which ply the intersection between the public and the private, encourage citizens to deal with their problems by legal means. In the upshot, even those who break the law appear ever more litigious. In South Africa – which introduced a 'law train' in 1998 to traverse the country giving free counsel[6] – a plumber recently convicted of drunk driving sued the state for imprisoning him when, by rights, it should have had him in rehabilitation.[7] And alumni of the liberation struggle, members of the Umkhonto we Sizwe Veterans Association, squared up for a struggle in the courts in 2005 over the assets of the organization.[8] In times past, this intra-ANC conflict would have been fought by political means. But then, in times past, Umkhonto Veterans Association would have been a commons for ex-guerillas, not an investment company.

The global effect of all this is such that it is not unusual any more to hear the Euro-language of jurisprudence in the Amazon or Aboriginal Australia. Or among the poor of Mumbai, Madagascar, Cape Town and Trench Town. Even in places

6 The train was operated by *Legal i*, a non-profit enterprise with a board of directors representative of the law societies, the Black Lawyers Association, the National Association of Democratic Lawyers and various consumer agencies. It was supported by the European Union.

7 See, for example, Fatima Schroeder, 'Drunk Driver Sues over Being Kept in Jail Instead of Rehab', *Cape Times*, 8 August 2005, p. 7. The plaintiff, Andre Schlebusch, was given a three-year sentence, suspended on condition he had treatment, by a magistrate who ordered that he be jailed until he could be placed in rehabilitation; Schlebusch argued that the court had been obliged to require that the Director-General of Health designate an appropriate institution and ensure immediate treatment, and had failed to do so.

8 See Wiseman Khuzwayo, 'MK Veterans' Row Heads for Court', *The Sunday Independent*, 14 August 2005, Business Report, p. 1. Under a banner headline, the story made it clear that MKMVA has a complex corporate existence: the two people against whom the interdict was sought were referred to as the 'directors' of MKMVA Investment Holdings (which, allegedly, represents 60,000 members and their dependents), and of its financial arm, the Mabutho Investment Company.

where trafficking outside the law is as common as trafficking within it – Nigeria, Russia, Zimbabwe – the self-imaginings of citizenship, and actions taken in its name, tend to be infused with that language. Nor is it just rights, interests, identities and injuries that have become saturated with legality. Politics *itself* is migrating to the courts. Conflicts once joined in parliaments, by means of street protests, media campaigns, strikes, boycotts, blockades, tend more and more to find their way to the judiciary; note Julia Eckert's observation that, in India, the 'use of the law' now 'complements or replaces' other species of counter-politics (Eckert 2006, 46 *et passim*). As we have noted before (Comaroff and Comaroff 2006b, 27), class struggles are giving way to class actions in which people drawn together by material predicament, culture, race, sexual preference, residence, faith and habits of consumption become legal persons as their common plaints turn them into plaintiffs with common identities. Citizens, subjects, governments, congregations, chiefdoms, communities and corporations litigate against one another in an ever-mutating kaleidoscope – changing 'constellations', legal pluralism might call it – often at the intersections of tort law, human rights law, constitutional law and the criminal law. Even democracy has been judicialized: few national elections these days go by without some resort to the courts. No need to mention the American presidential election of 2002, which was decided by an ideologically stacked judiciary, thereby aborting the democratic process – this in the imperium that imposes its political theology of 'freedom' upon much of the rest of the planet.

For their part, states are having to defend themselves in courts against unprecedented sorts of things in unprecedented ways and against unprecedented sorts of plaintiff. The legal struggle between the ANC and AIDS sufferers in South Africa is legend. But there are many others: like that of the Brazilian government, which in 2000 was ordered to pay damages, by its *own* high court, for the death and suffering of Panará Indians; or Nicaragua, held to account a year earlier by the Inter-American Court for violating the territory of Tingni Indians by granting a timber concession to a Korean company.[9] Suits of this species – which exemplify Eckert's 'legalism from below' (Eckert 2006, 50–54) – are often abetted by advocacy groups. In them, the law connects political means to political ends. At times, too, legalities are directed against unexpected sites of authority – in a manner that reverses the Foucaldian notion of capillary biopower. Thus, 16,000 graduates of Indian schools recently filed suits in Canada against the Anglican, Presbyterian and Catholic Churches, alleging physical, sexual and cultural abuse.[10]

9 See *Amazon Update*, no. 63, November 2000, published by the Amazon Alliance for Indigenous and Traditional Peoples of the Amazon Basin, <www.amazonalliance.org/upd_nov00_en.html>, accessed 15 July 2005.

10 Perhaps the best popular account of these remarkable lawsuits, which ended in the payment of major sums of money to the plaintiffs – most of whom had been forced into the schools – is to be found in James Booke, 'Indian Lawsuits Threaten Canadian Churches', *Incite Newsletter*, May 2001, <www.incite-national.org/news/lawsuits.html>, accessed 9 August 2005.

They won. But many such initiatives fail. Thus, the Ogoni lost a claim against Shell for its complicity in killing those opposed to its presence in Nigeria. Patently, the law often comes down on the side of the powerful, and of big business, which also flexes its legal muscles as far as possible to create deregulated environments conducive to its workings.

In sum, while the law has always been a battle-ground, it appears ever more so; ever more, people seek and find, legal justifications and jurisdictions on the basis of which to attack rogue capital, the state and their enemies, real or imagined – extending, in the process, what has long been known as 'forum shopping'. Note here the increasing appeal to the Alien Torts Claims Act in the USA, which allows those who have suffered wrongs at the hands of American parties abroad to take their suits to federal courts. Their efforts have enjoyed some success. Unsurprisingly, mega-corporations have responded by trying to have the Act repealed, and by offering as an alternative 'corporate social responsibility' and 'soft law' – that is, self-regulation and mediation. A *luta continua*. But what this means is that the political geography of the planet is no longer sufficed by the kind of thing taught in school, the kind of geography that began with Kant and von Humboldt. The cartography of our times transects the order of nation-states with another, equally significant set of co-ordinates: the jurisdictional axes of effective collective action. Indeed, an urgent task of legal anthropology, which will have to await another occasion, is to establish the epistemic basis for this new geography.

Let us return, though, to the judicialization of politics.

It is not only the politics of the present that are being judicialized. The past, too, is being fought out in court. As Anja Peleikis (2006) and Judith Beyer (2006) have shown for Lithuania and Kyrgyzstan, history enters the law in diverse ways, often insinuating itself into the cultural underpinnings of everyday jurisprudence, into its ways and means, its materialities and motivations. But we mean here something yet more specific: the struggle actually to repossess and reposition the past. Just as Brazil has had to recognize its part in the ethnocide of the Panará Indians and to make material amends for it, so Britain is having to answer for atrocities in East Africa (cf. Anderson 2005; Elkins 2005): for having killed local leaders at whim, for having alienated land from one people to another, and for other such illegalities. By these means is colonialism itself rendered criminal. Hauled before a judge, history is made to break its silences, to submit to the scales of justice at the behest of those who suffered it – and to be reduced to a cash equivalent, payable as the tender of damage, dispossession, loss, trauma. What imperialism is being indicted for, above all, is *lawfare*: the use of penal powers, administrative procedures, states of emergency, mandates and warrants to discipline its subjects by means of violence made actual by its own sovereign word.

As a species of displacement, lawfare – the resort to legal instruments, to the violence inherent in the law, for political ends – becomes most visible when those who 'serve' the state conjure with legalities to act against its citizens. Outside the USA, the most infamous instance right now, perhaps, is Zimbabwe, where the Mugabe regime consistently passes statutes to justify the silencing of its critics.

Operation Murambatsvina, which forced dissidents out of urban areas under the banner of 'slum clearance', took this to unprecedented depths. Murambatsvina, said the authorities, was merely an application of existing statutes to raze dangerous 'illegal structures'.[11] Lawfare may be limited, or it may reduce people to 'bare life'. And it may mutate into necropolitics. Typically, it seeks to launder power in a wash of legitimacy as it is deployed to strengthen the sinews of state or enlarge the capillaries of capital, all under the sign of governance. Hence Benjamin's (1978 [1921]) thesis that the law originates in violence and lives by violent means; that the legal and the lethal animate one another. Of course, in 1921, when he wrote his critique, Benjamin could not have envisaged the possibility that lawfare might also become a weapon of the weak, turning authority back on itself by commissioning courts to make claims for resources, recognition, voice, integrity, sovereignty.

But this still does not lay to rest the key questions: *Why* the fetishism of legalities? What are its wider implications?

Modernist nationhood seems to be undergoing a tectonic shift: the *ideal* of cultural homogeneity on which it was founded, always more aspiration than achievement, is giving way to a *recognition* of greater heterogeneity. It is a move marked almost everywhere by nervous xenophobia, a move closely linked to the rise of neoliberalism, to its impact on population flows, on the dispersion of images, objects, desires, identities, on new geographies of production and accumulation. And heterogeneity begets more law. Why? For one thing, because legal instruments appear – we stress, *appear* – to offer a means of commensuration: a repertoire of standardized signs and practices that, like money in the realm of economics, permit the negotiation of values and interests across otherwise intransitive lines of difference. Hence the planetary flight into a constitutionalism that explicitly embraces heterodoxy in highly individualistic, universalistic Bills of Rights, even where states are paying less of those bills. Hence the effort to make human rights into an ever more global, ever more authoritative discourse. Hence the extension of the model of the market to ever more domains of everyday existence – and, to close an epistemic circle, to legal theory itself. Hence the displacement of so much politics into jurisprudence.

But there is something else at work, too. Another well-recognized feature of the neoliberal turn has been the outsourcing by government of many of its conventional operations, including those integral to the management of 'bare life'. The Weberian bureaucratic state has mutated into a rather different beast: a state that is not just a corporate management enterprise – although, as Rancière (1999,

11 For a persuasive explanation of the Zimbabwean government initiative, see Allister Sparks, 'Now It's a Crime against Humanity: A Million Zimbabweans Left Homeless', *Cape Times*, 29 June 2005, <www.capetimes.co.za/index.php?fSectionId=332&fArticleId=2604095>, accessed 30 January 2009. The official line of the Mugabe regime, including its talk of 'slum clearance' and 'illegal structures', is spelled out in a letter from its embassy in Indonesia in response to a critical report published by *The Jakarta Post*; see <www.zimbabwesituation.com/jun29a_2005.html>, accessed 30 January 2009.

113) says, it *is* ever more overtly just that – but one whose principal *regulatory* work lies in franchising and licensing, not least in the realm of policing and warfare. Where the modernist state undertook the redistribution of private wealth for public ends, the neoliberal state redistributes public wealth into private hands. Bureaucracies *do* retain some of their old functions, of course. But most regimes have reduced their administrative reach, entrusting ever more to the market and devolving ever more responsibility to citizens as individuals, communities or classes of consumer. This has a number of corollaries, variably felt across the world. One is that, with states no longer the sole guarantor of the security of citizens – with many shrinking their policing operations and relinquishing their monopoly over the means of violence to the private sector – populations tend to become more fearful about the prospect of disorder, more anxious about criminal violence, real or imagined (of which, more later). A second corollary is that, with the outsourcing of government, counter-politics tends to be criminalized; this because it is treated not as the expression of democratic dissent, but as illicit action against the property, persons and prerogatives of those who act, contractually, in the name of authority. Which in turn quickens the resort to lawfare on all sides. A third corollary is that, with the sacrifice of the originary ideal of *Leviathan* to the deities of self-regulation, self-protection and self-interest, the court – one institution still securely under the purview of the state, the one ostensibly capable of commensuration – becomes a utopic site to which human agency believes it may turn in order to pursue a widening horizon of ends.

Put all this together, and the fetishism of the law seems over-determined. Not only is public life becoming more legalistic, but so, in regulating their own affairs and in dealing with others, are sub- and transnational 'communities': cultural communities, corporate communities, residential communities, communities of faith or interest. Sometimes, as in India, these communities appropriate the law of the state unto themselves, which, Eckert (2006, 47–8) notes, dissolves legal pluralism into judicial pluralism; sometimes they assert autonomy in specific domains, but leave others to government. And sometimes, as we shall see, they seek juridical independence. Nor is it only the communities of *civil* society that are saturated with legality. So are its criminal undersides. In the USA, South Africa, Brazil, Russia and elsewhere, 'gangs' of various scale – that is, organized crime – mimic both the state and the market. Many provide their 'tax-paying' clients with the policing and protection that government has stopped supplying; some have shadow judiciaries to try offenders against the persons, property and social orders over which they exert sovereignty. In South Africa, recall, a number have constitutions. Several are structured as franchises. A few even offer 'alternative citizenship' to their members. Tilly (1985, 170–71) once noted that the modern state operates much like organized crime. These days, organized crime is operating ever more like the modernist state – concretely, we mean, not just, as Derrida (1994) once suggested, in the manner of a spectre.

In the process of becoming ever more legalistic, communities of all kinds, including outlaw communities, appear increasingly to evince a will to sovereignty;

by 'sovereignty', we mean the exercise of control over the lives, deaths and conditions of existence of those who fall within its purview – and the extension over them of the jurisdiction of some kind of law (cf. Hansen and Stepputat 2005). 'Lawmaking', said Benjamin, 'is power making' (Benjamin 1978 [1921], 295). But 'power [is] the principal of all … lawmaking'. In sum, to transform itself into sovereign authority, power demands an architecture of legalities or their simulacra. Perhaps because of changes in the relationship between law and governance in the age of neoliberalism, perhaps because so many of the operations of the bureaucratic state now live within the realm of the market, perhaps because the outsourcing of its authority has stretched so deep into the management of 'bare life' – in short, because we live in a world at once post-Weberian and post-Foucauldian – more and more non-state institutions, from corporations through cultural communities and churches to criminal organizations, are asserting sovereignty of greater or lesser scale. Modernist political theory, of course, allows only one sovereignty to any nation, a vertically integrated one vested in the state. Increasingly, however, polities consist in a horizontal tapestry of partial sovereignties: sovereignties over terrains and their inhabitants, over people conjoined in faith or culture, over transactional spheres, networks of relations, regimes of property; sovereignties at war or peace with each other; sovereignties longer or shorter lived, protected by more or less violence. Under such conditions, the social world tends to be imagined as an archipelago of zones of civility, of Arendt's 'walled' spaces of legality, under one or another sovereign jurisdiction; civil zones joined by corridors of tenuous safety in environments otherwise presumed to be, literally, out of control – inhabited by criminals, warlords, druglords, immigrants and other alien non-persons – with the mediating reach of government over the whole being distinctly uneven.

If vertical and horizontal sovereignties are archetypical ends of an imaginary continuum, the states of the global North tend to be associated more with the former, those of the South with the latter. But the global North seems to be edging southward. Russia has found as much with Chechnya and Tatarstan, two notable, if very different, instances of centrifugal sovereignty. So has the UK with the devolution of its Celtic fringe; also the USA, where Native Americans are claiming ever more autonomy under the sign of exception, where mega-churches are asserting ever more regulatory control over the lives of their congregants, and where inner cities, increasingly seen as a problem of human waste-management by the state, are the exclusionary domain of underworld syndicates. And these are only the most dramatic instances of a thoroughgoing, often dispersed, process. The more general point? That sovereignty – as Agamben, Arendt, Bataille and Benjamin understood – is the root construct, the encompassing algorithm, on which the unfolding, labile relationship between law and governance is wrought. How it is exercised, by whom, in what name and with what effect; how it interpellates itself in the state, the market, civil society, faith, identity, even criminality; how it constructs a geography of jurisdictions and a cartography of violence; in these things lie the present and future of the Brave Neo World, of its social character, of its political life, of its architecture, of its ethics, even of its aesthetics. It is towards a confrontation with this clutch of problems, towards interrogating the nature of sovereignty, we believe, that legal anthropology is being inexorably drawn. A great deal hangs on it.

This first cardinal direction leads directly to our other two. But, before we move on, we should like to stress that several things quickly passed by here demand more attention from legal anthropology. We have only scratched the surface of the problems of sovereignty, of constitutionalism and of the fetishism of law. The triangulation of these three *axes mundi* – and, concomitantly, the move from a world in which politics reigned over law and economy to one in which law seems to reign supreme – may turn out to be as consequential to our understanding of the neoliberal age as, say, the process of rationalization was to Weber's analysis of modernity, or the commodity to Marx's reading of capitalism; both, interestingly, were also concerned with enchantment and commensuration. Indeed, what we have called legal theology – or theo-legality, the twenty-first-century mutation of Carl Schmitt's political theology – is, we would suggest, a critical grail to be followed, to whatever theoretical end-point it leads. So, we believe, is the mapping of a new jurisdictional geography through which to make sense of the unfolding logic of collective action in the world. All of these questions are profoundly the subject of a legal anthropology that, as we said at the outset, ought to play a key part in theorizing the twenty-first century.

But let us move off in our second direction. We signpost it as …

Difference, ID-ology and the Limits of Liberalism

The turn towards legal self-imaginings on the part of communities of diverse kinds, like the changing cartography of sovereignty, is, we reiterate, not just uneven. It is visibly polymorphous. So, too, is the relationship between sovereignties and the sorts of legality on which they base themselves. Some operate with shadow juridical orders that replicate or replace those of the state, some stress their alterity, some resort to modes of regulation that are only tenuously law-like, some strive for very limited autonomy. For their part, states tend to regard such sovereignties with deep ambivalence: Those that contend in the economy of violence, or spill over into polite, propertied society, are likely to be criminalized – or recommissioned – by government, if it has the capacity to do so. Others may be tolerated, particularly if they limit themselves to the 'private' sphere, which, according to the liberal theory at the core of modernist governance, is the domain in which difference *ought* to express itself.

One species of sovereignty poses particular problems for states on this front: sovereignty based on cultural or religious difference of the kind that refuses altogether the antinomy between the private and the public; the kind that invokes intransitive, and often intransigent, ontologies of being-in-the-world; the kind whose alterity extends, as well, to governance. These sovereignties may be wilfully self-limiting. Fernanda Pirie's Tibetan pastoralists, for example (Pirie 2006, 78–9, 93), are fiercely protective of the autonomy of their cultural patch when it comes to managing internal affairs and conflicts – and defer voluntarily to the Chinese authorities in matters of criminal violence. But the appeal to the sovereignty of culture or faith against government seldom stops at this felicitous border, the border of disorder. With neoliberal nationhood having to admit ever-increasing heterodoxy, with its explicit recognition in post-1989 constitutional design, ontological otherness is widely invoked these days to make substantial claims to autarkic self-regulation – claims that exceed the polite politics of recognition proffered by liberal philosophers as a panacea for the demands of difference in multicultural times. We have written of this in respect of South Africa (Comaroff and Comaroff 2003), which may exemplify a phenomenon spreading with exponential gravity.

South Africa, being a postcolony, was erected from the first on difference. Like most other places, it has seen a significant shift in the dialectic of law and governance. Here as elsewhere, neoliberalism has emerged triumphant, its language spoken as a national vernacular, albeit not without challenge. Here, too, it has hidden its ideological scaffolding, reducing government to, and representing it as, technical management. Here, too, partisan politics has become a tournament in the promise of competing profitabilities and efficiencies. Here, too, there has been a displacement from the struggle between political visions to struggles in the name of interest and affect. And interest and affect, in their collective voice, congeal in identity – itself naturalized, as though it were a generic and genetic condition of human being. For more and more people, the site of politics has shifted from ideology, theology of the idea, to ID-ology, the '-ology' of identity.[12] Notwithstanding all the noisy debate about the future of the country that swirls around the African National Congress, its leadership and its policies, the 'vast majority' of South Africans think of themselves first and foremost as members of 'an ethnic, cultural, language, religious or some other group' to which they attach their personal fate (Gibson 2004, 2).

The most comprehensive assertions of ID-ology, as we have already implied, are those made in the name of culture and faith; most comprehensive because they are *existential* in their foundations – based, in the instance of faith, on transcendent truths and sacrally sanctioned ways and means, and in the instance of culture, on shared essence and bio-genealogical alterity. Let us take each in turn.

ID-ology under the sign of culture and shared essence, when it is translated into a will to sovereignty, yields *poli*culturalism. The prefix 'poli-' denotes *both* plurality and a political claim to the exercise of governance over, well, everything; this through the instrumentation of a law accountable to no temporal authority. In South Africa, it asserts itself most articulately, perhaps, in the argot of cultural jurisprudence, of the right of Zulu, Xhosa, Tswana and others to rule and be ruled

12 See Rapule Tabane and Ferial Haffajee, 'Ideology is Dead, Long Live ID-ology', *Mail and Guardian*, 27 June–3 July 2003, p. 6. To our knowledge, this is the first time that the term 'ID-ology' appeared in public discourse. Tabane and Haffajee use it in a manner slightly different from the way we do here and elsewhere.

according to their own customary ways. Note that this is taken to be quite different from the custom of colonialism, although it *may* unwittingly reproduce some of its effects. It is, quite expressly, a living, Afro-modern law (Comaroff and Comaroff 2004a), one that – now unencumbered by the *ancien régime* – is said, from within, to be vital and growing, but in vernacular ways that apply long-standing principles of Africanity to the life and times of the postcolony.

The cause of policulturalism here has been most fervently fought – no surprise, given what we have said about the fetishism of law – on the terrain of the South African constitution. Its primary protagonist is the Congress of Traditional Leaders (Contralesa). For the past decade, Contralesa has put pressure on government to change the Bill of Rights, which subjects all forms of difference to the universal rights of citizens;[13] it argues that 'chiefs and kings' ought to enjoy sovereign authority over their realms. By statute, their formal powers, although amended several times, are confined to the administration of 'customary law', the co-ordination of cultural activities, any 'function ... delegated by a competent authority', and such odds and ends as 'the gathering of firewood'.[14] Matters came to a head at a national conference held in August 2000[15] to discuss '[indigenous] leadership and institutions' with a view to producing a parliamentary White Paper.[16] Contralesa refused to take part, although many of its members were physically present. Even more, it declined to talk to anyone other than the president – and only about constitutional change. There have been times when the organization was sure that the state had been persuaded to do its bidding and times when it has declared that the ANC, acting in bad faith, has never intended 'to accommodate [chiefly authority in] the making of the new South Africa'.[17] Such assertions have typically drawn denials from government, leaving behind them a trail of ambiguity, to the extent that there remains 'considerable confusion as to what exactly the constitutional recognition [of chiefs] implies'[18] – all the more so since the state has enacted laws, like the Recognition of Customary Marriages Act (no. 120 of

---

13 Section 36 of the Constitution allows that some constraints on those rights are 'reasonable and justifiable in an open and democratic society', but stresses that any such constraint is to remain bound by the Bill of Rights. As we shall see, protagonists of the sovereignty of tradition have invoked this 'justifiable' and 'democratic' limitation in their struggles with the state.

14 This is a virtual paraphrase of the Local Government: Municipal Structures Amendment Bill, 2000.

15 'A National Conference on Traditional Leadership', Midrand, 17–18 August 2000, Department of Provincial and Local Government.

16 The document that was finally produced, *Traditional Leadership and Governance Draft White Paper* (Gazette 23984, Notice 2103), 29 October 2002, can be read at <www.info.gov.za/view/DownloadFileAction?id=68780>, accessed 30 January 2009.

17 These were the words of Mangosuthu Buthelezi; see M. Jubasi and T. Mkhize, 'Unite against ANC Treachery – Buthelezi', *Sunday Times*, 4 August 2002, p. 4.

18 L. Ntsebeza and F. Hendricks, 'The Chieftancy System is Rooted in Apartheid', *Mail and Guardian*, 18–24 February 2000, p. 33.

1998), that authorize some vernacular practices, including ones once deemed 'repugnant',[19] and, by implication, delegate to indigenous rulers the sovereign authority to administer them.

The upper echelons of the judiciary, which occasionally embrace Africanity in their jurisprudence,[20] have added to the confusion by acting incoherently on the sovereignty of culture and, by extension, of those institutions in which it is vested. On one hand, for example, in May 2000, in *Mthembu* v. *Letsela*, the Supreme Court of Appeal decided that women married under African customary law were subject to the rule of male primogeniture, and thereby excluded from inheriting conjugal property. The 'interests of the community' as expressed in its 'mores and fundamental assumptions', said the bench, were of paramount importance in cases of this sort.[21] In short, it declared that there *are* situations in which culture ought to take precedence over the Bill of Rights, in this instance over its gender equality clause. The decision drew criticism from some quarters, notably feminist, but that is another story. On the other hand, in a vividly contrasting, controversial judgment four years later, *Bhe and Others* v. *Magistrate, Khayelitsha and Others*, the Constitutional Court concluded that 'the rule of male primogeniture … is … inconsistent with the Constitution and invalid …'.[22] This outcome, too, evoked outrage, now from those who rule over the polities of indigenous South Africa, many of whom retain a high level of legitimacy among their subjects (see, for example, Oomen 2005); they complained that the court had violated the constitution by criminalizing their cultures.

Nor did *Bhe* bring an end to the confusion or to the struggle over policulturalism. As we write, a female ANC member of parliament, Tinyiko Nwamitwa-Shilubana, is embroiled in a dispute that replays, in a new key, the uneasy dialectic of sovereignty against the state. Ms Shilubana claims that the chiefship she inherited

19 The Customary Marriages Act allows polygamy, this notwithstanding the fact that it had long been treated by South African law, and by 'native administration', as 'repugnant' to civilization. The Act also raises questions of gender equality, to which the Constitution and statutory law give a great deal of anxious attention.

20 This is most notable in respect of the 'principle' of *ubuntu*, a notion of humanity founded on a sense of social and ethical connectedness. It was famously cited by the Constitutional Court in *The State* v. *T. Makwanyane and M. Mchunu*, 6 June 1995 (CCT3/94), which outlawed the death penalty. At note no. 244, a long list of other cases is given in which this vernacular concept has figured. In his judgment, Justice Madala (no. 237) argued that, while *ubuntu* appears only in the postamble, it 'permeates the Constitution'. Added Justice Yvonne Mokgoro (no. 307): 'It is a] value and ideal that runs like a golden thread across cultural lines … in this country.'

21 *Mildred Hleziphi Mthembu* v. *Henry K. Letsela*, 30 May 2000 (SCA, 71/98), pp. 31–2.

22 *Bhe and Others* v. *Magistrate, Khayelitsha and Others*, 15 October 2004 (CCT49/03). The quoted passage is from *The Order* (para. 4, p. 80). One justice, Ngcobo, wrote a cogent dissent, arguing that African vernacular practice could and should be brought into line with the Law of the Land.

from her father, Fofoza – who ruled the Valoyi of Limpopo Province until his death in 1962 – has been 'stolen' by her cousin, Sidwell Nwamitwa. The intricacies of the conflict need not detain us, save to say that Fofoza died without male heirs at a time when daughters could not succeed to office, and was therefore followed by his brother, Richard, also now deceased, and then by Sidwell, Richard's son. Most significant about the story is the fact that, in 1996, when Ms Shilubana approached the Valoyi people with her desire to become their ruler, they agreed, citing the gender equality clause of the Constitution and recognizing her genealogical status. But Sidwell went to law, asserting the principle of patriliny. He won a decision from the Pretoria High Court and then from the Supreme Court of Appeal; why either entertained a quarrel that, by 'tradition', fell within the purview of the sovereign *politics* of an African chiefdom was never broached (cf. Tebbe 2008). Both benches ignored the publicly sanctioned change in Valoyi succession rules; they paid no heed when Ms Shilubana insisted, correctly, that 'customary law' is constantly evolving. And both, acting like colonial tribunals, held that male primogeniture ought to prevail since, 'pursuant to tribal custom and tradition, a Hosi [chief] is born not elected'.[23] This simply ignored *Bhe*. The case, not surprisingly, has been taken on by the Constitutional Court. What *is* surprising, however, is that Ms Shilubana is opposed by many of her ANC parliamentary comrades, who think that a victory for her would lead to 'instability' throughout Southern Africa's traditional communities.[24] To tamper with vernacular sovereignty, they believe, is to enter a policultural minefield, with explosive consequences. Not to do so, of course, is to affirm that sovereignty, at least by omission – and to limit the jurisdictional reach of the Constitution.

The struggle for sovereign indigeneity – and against Euromodern liberal democracy, conventionally conceived – seems to be spreading across the legal terrain of the country. A few instances, true social dramas in the old anthropological sense of the term, have come to stand as paradigmatic of this struggle. While often arising out of conflicts of value *within* African polities, their intended audience, and ultimate respondent, is the state itself. And, not infrequently, they play on the incoherence of the judiciary in dealing with Afromodern 'custom'. One, a *cause célèbre* in the late 1990s,[25] pitted a staunch Jehovah's Witness, Mrs Kedibone Tumane, against Chief Nyalala Pilane of the Bakgatla, under whose jurisdiction in

23 For the Supreme Court of Appeal case, see *Nwamitwa Shilubana* v. *Nwamitwa*, [2006] SCA 174 (RSA); for the latest documentation on the Constitutional Court case, see *Shilubana and Others* v. *Nwamitwa*, 27 November 2007 (CCT03/07). It is from the media summary in the Constitutional Court record that the quotations in the previous sentences are taken.

24 The South African press has covered the case extensively. This particular quotation is from 'Woman Fights for Right to Lead Clan in Case that Weighs Constitution and Custom', *Cape Times*, 17 May 2007.

25 See 'Clash of Custom, Constitution', *The Mail* (Mafikeng), 31 July 1998, p. 17; we have also analysed the case *in extenso* (Comaroff and Comaroff 2003).

the North West Province she was then resident. For reasons of faith, Mrs Tumane had violated a burial taboo which enjoins bereaved women to remain confined for a specified period and, when going abroad, to sprinkle a herb (*mogaga*) on their paths; not to do so is to risk spreading death pollution (*sefifi*), with potentially lethal consequences for the 'nation' (*morafe*). When Mrs Tumane tried to leave her home and refused to broadcast *mogaga*, she was stopped from doing so by the Tribal Authority. Some of her neighbours, reacting with a mixture of fear and fury, called for her banishment. In contemporary South Africa, riddled with AIDS and other perennial threats to life, dicing with death evokes deep existential anxieties – and mass anger.

To cut a tortuous story short, Mrs Tumane, abetted by the South African Human Rights Commission (SAHRC), took Chief Pilane to court late in 1998.[26] Her constitutionally protected rights had been deliberately traduced, she said. Having been put under 'house arrest' – note her use here of an apartheid-saturated term – she had been forced to 'live … [as] an outcast'.[27] In an affidavit sworn prior to the case, Mrs Tumane claimed that, in June 1998, the ruler had agreed to call a mass gathering and had promised to announce the end of her confinement, but had failed to do so. Pilane replied that he could not 'release' her at the meeting in question, since 'the tribe' had taken a 'democratic' decision there to the contrary. He added that Mrs Tumane was 'confined' not by the tribal authority, but by 'her own custom', which could not be changed save by the 'consent of the Kgatla nation', of which she herself was a member. Her rights had been respected, he said, except where they were in tension with the Section 36 of the Constitution, which acknowledges that some limitations on individual freedoms are 'reasonable and justifiable in an open … society'.[28] For Kgatla, a received practice whose transgression presented a clear and present danger to their community and was recognized as such in a democratically constituted public forum, was just such a justification.[29] To this, the complainant answered that, while an indigenous people *is* entitled to promote its culture and religion, it has to do so within the compass of the Bill of Rights, which places individual freedoms above all things. This argument won, at least in the short run: in July 1998, the court agreed that the compulsory performance of *mogaga* violated the Constitution. An interim order instructed the chief to lift Mrs Tumane's confinement immediately.

Nothing happened. Political pressure from the state mounted. Counter-pressure came from the House of Traditional Leaders, which put three questions to the state. In paraphrase: Why did the Constitution place individual rights above those of 'tribes'? Why were cultural practices not similarly protected? And why was the Tumane case being handled by the High Court and not by their own House,

26 High Court of South Africa (Bophuthatswana Provincial Division), Case no. 618/98.

27 Ibid., Founding Affidavit, p. 3.

28 See note 13 above.

29 Ibid., Answering Affidavit, 13 November 1998, pp. 7–10.

where it belonged? For its own part, Pilane's defence fused British functionalist anthropology with Agamben on sovereignty: 'Tradition is the glue that holds the tribe together, gives it purpose, sustains its identity …'. Virtually all Kgatla, irrespective of religion or education, observe *mogaga*, it went on. The transgression of death rituals endangers social life. Only Jehovah's Witnesses refuse to comply. This explained why his people, following due democratic procedures, had decided to sacrifice Mrs Tumane's 'rights' and – deploying the exception authorized by Section 36 of the Constitution – to condemn her to social death. This was their right as a sovereign nation; his sovereign obligation was to do their will. What is more, the SAHRC, clearly seen here as a cipher of government, had exploited the circumstances to criminalize an unobjectionable rite in the hope of bringing a cultural practice under the penumbra of the Bill of Rights. Pilane added, in a subtle legal stratagem that seemed to reverse his earlier statement, that *mogaga* was a ritual *voluntarily* followed by Kgatla, and that Mrs Tumane had therefore not suffered compulsion. *Per contra*, being 'eccentric', she had shown contempt for a constitutionally protected practice.[30] Stressing that *mogaga* had been 'declared voluntary' – that it belonged to the 'private' domain of individual choice and did not compel anyone to violate their religious beliefs – the court dismissed the case. It clearly did not want to enter deep constitutional waters by being seen to outlaw an indigenous rite. As it happened, Mrs Tumane's period of mourning was by then long over.[31]

Here, then, is a paradigmatic instance in which policulturalism expressed itself. Here, the sovereignty of a vernacular jurisprudence, and the political order in which it is embedded, was asserted against the state.[32] Here, the fundamental lines drawn by the Constitution – between the private and the public, the religious and the secular, the prerogatives of the individual and the imperatives of the communal – were directly challenged. Here, an existential struggle over sovereignty itself was conducted by means of lawfare, displacing the political into the legal. Note that this was also a confrontation between Euromodernity and Afromodernity: Pilane did not simply invoke 'custom'. He sought to re-write it into the thoroughly contemporary language of democratic decision-making, jural exception, freedom of choice, rights-talk. Thus do constitutional jurisprudence and culture recast each

30 Ibid. All the quoted phrases in this paragraph are from the same passage in the Answering Affidavit.

31 The SAHRC regretted Pilane's strategic decision to 'declare' *mogaga* voluntary, an ambiguity that left unclear whether this was meant as a statement of existing practice or a change of rules. It sought to contest chiefly authority, *not* by criminalizing tradition, but, more subtly, by preventing indigenous rulers from 'interfering' with the freedom of movement and other fundamental rights of their subjects (Comaroff and Comaroff 2003).

32 Other chiefs have challenged the state over the practice of initiation, corporal punishment and the like. Some have chosen to be less confrontational, opting to assert sovereignty through a politics of avoidance; yet others have sought to amend cultural practices just enough to render them inoffensive to the Constitution.

other – and the political geography of a nation-state now built on the irreducibility of difference. Thus does policulturalism, its imbrications and its effects, become the urgent object of legal anthropology.

But it is not merely on the rarified scape of constitutionality that policulturalism is making itself felt. The confrontation between the Euromodern and the Afromodern, the displacement of the politics of sovereignty into the juridical, and the reworking of legal subjectivities are occurring in more mundane contexts as well. For example, so-called customary courts across the country are constantly having to deal with practices that are outlawed or unrecognized, yet are part of everyday life for much of the population. Most notable in this respect are conflicts arising out of the African occult – whose practice, real or alleged, remains illicit – which call into doubt the capacity of the state to impose both its rule of law and its monopoly over the means of violence (cf. Geschiere 2006). Precisely because they do, they provide a theologico-legal space for indigenous rulers to assert sovereign control over their realms. On occasion, these kinds of conflicts also filter into the lower reaches of the judiciary, where they compel the authorities to deal with the ineluctable pragmatics of difference. Which, at times, has called forth a strikingly novel, and an analytically unexpected, species of jurisprudence (Comaroff and Comaroff 2004a).

Because we know it best, we have taken South Africa as the ground on which to open up the matter of policulturalism, of the processes it sets in motion, of its capacity to transform the interiors of both the national and the native, of its challenge to liberal notions of legality, of the analytic and theoretical issues that it raises. We could equally have looked elsewhere; for example, to France and its treatment of Muslim head scarves, or to the banning of female circumcision, most lately in Eritrea, or to the outlawing of *sati* in India. Also, as in our discussion of the fetishism of the law, we have barely scratched at its surfaces. For now, though, let us turn to the other domain of ID-ology that poses important questions of sovereign difference, and its implications, for legal anthropology: faith.

We said earlier that faith and the law are the twin obsessions of the twenty-first century, that we are living in an age of legal theology, of theo-legality: faith, it seems, is taking more and more to the law to re-make the world in its own image, to extend is sovereignty, to police populations. Not everywhere, patently, nor always in the same way, but palpably. Many religions, of course, not least those that bear the capitalized adjectives 'Great' or 'World', have long had a juridical scaffolding. What appears different nowadays is the degree to which they are resorting to lawfare to extend their imperium and to displace liberal reason, albeit often by liberal means.

Take orthodox Islam. Where there have been efforts to recast the foundations of nation-states in its name, they have been deeply invested in the rule of Sharia law. The same applies to regions within states, as in Northern Nigeria, and Aceh, Indonesia; also to Muslim initiatives that would extend the dominion of both the faith and the faithful, like the Salafiyya movement in Morocco, which propagates a 'return' to *legal* Islam (Turner 2006, 101). Indeed, the force of Sharia law in the lives of Muslim populations was dramatically affirmed in early 2008 when, of all people, the Archbishop of Canterbury, Dr Rowan Williams, suggested that some measure of official recognition be given to it by the British state for purposes of everyday governance in predominantly Islamic communities – perhaps the first time, this, that a religious leader of his stature has called for the policultural acceptance of (even partial) sovereignty for another faith. 'As a matter of fact,' he noted, 'certain provisions of Sharia are already recognised in our society and under our law' – as they are in India and Egypt – to the extent that their adoption was 'unavoidable'.[33] Predictably, his statement sparked a bitter controversy. Said his predecessor, Lord Carey, 'there can be no exceptions to the laws of our land'.[34] What is significant, however, is that the argument has been joined at all. Clearly, we have reached a historical juncture in the convergence of faith and the law at which it has become thinkable.

But it is not only for the governance of everyday life that Muslim theo-legality has been evoked in policultural assertions of sovereignty. The religion *itself* is being reframed in these terms. A dramatic instance is to be found in Pakistan. It began in the 1970s, when the *ulema,* orthodox religious authorities, sought and won an injunction against the Ahmadis, a movement they declared heretical, to prevent them from using any of the *Sha'ir* ('signs') of Islam; these, they said, belonged solely to 'proper' Muslims (Ahmed 2006, 19–24, 40–45). When, in 1978, the Ahmadis appealed to the Lahore High Court,[35] counsel for the *ulema* again argued 'that Muslim-ness [is] the exclusive property of Muslims alone, that certain Muslim terminology [is] analogous to copyright and trademarks', and that their improper use is therefore 'an infringement of the rights' of the faithful (Ahmed 2006, p. 21). On this occasion, the judge found against the religious authorities on the technical ground that they could not show that a material loss had been incurred (Ahmed 2006, p. 41). But fifteen years later, in 1993, in a Pakistan Supreme Court case[36] that addressed the constitutional bases of Muslim identity, the same argument was accepted by a majority of the justices: 'They argued that certain signs were not just distinctive characteristics and practices but the exclusive property of Islam' (Ahmed 2006, pp. 41–2). Thus was Islam transformed 'into property, something that could be owned, possessed and bounded off from others' (Ahmed 2006, ibid.),

33 See 'Archbishop Defends Sharia Remarks', *BBC News*, 9 February 2008, <http://news.bbc.co.uk/2/hi/uk_news/7236174.stm>, accessed 30 January 2009; 'Sharia Law in the UK is "Unavoidable"', *BBC News*, 7 February 2008, <http://news.bbc.co.uk/2/hi/uk_news/7232661.stm>, accessed 30 January 2009.

34 See 'Carey Weighs into Sharia Law Row', *BBC News*, 10 February 2008, < http://news.bbc.co.uk/1/hi/uk/7236849.stm>, accessed 30 January 2009.

35 *Abdur Rehman Mubashir* v. *Syed Amir Ali Shah*, PLD 1978 Lahore 113. We were made aware of this case, and derive our summary of it, from the doctoral dissertation research of Asad Ahmed (2006, ch. 3); all the page references in this paragraph are to Ahmed's study.

36 *Zaheeruddin* v. *The State* (1993, *Supreme Court Monthly Review*: 1,718); again, see Ahmed (2006, 40–41).

something whose true nature vested in the law. In some religions, as we have observed elsewhere (Comaroff and Comaroff 2009), divinities may themselves have a jural identity. In 1986, when the Indian government sued for the return of a twelfth-century bronze Shiva that had been looted from a village in Pathur, '*it did so on behalf of the offended god himself*', who was the 'named … plaintiff in the case' (Keefe 2007, 60–61; emphasis added). Thus does a Deity, and the faith for which it stands, become a legal person.

Contemporary Christianity is also interpellating itself into the law – and, through it, into governance – in the effort to extend the reach of faith-based sovereignty. This, too, has precedents: Protestant and Catholic missions have, throughout their history, sought to create more or less closed, sovereign communities, thereby to exercise an authority over their citizens at once institutional and capillary. And the Church, in its various denominational guises, has always taken pains to exert influence on political society and the state. But we appear to be seeing an acceleration, and an accretion, of this tendency, evident both in small Christian movements and in large evangelical awakenings across the world. Henning Mankell, the noted crime novelist and organic anthropologist of Sweden, writes of these movements in *One Step Behind* (2003): 'No longer [are they] simply charismatic,' he observes, 'They are corporate franchises run by lawyers and accountants' (Mankell 2003, p. 351), legal persons that strive to change the world by means of legal ploys. The extent to which this is true has been brought to light in the US, on unprecedented scale, since the turn of the new century: reminiscent of the rise of Christian Political Economy (CPE) at the dawn of the modern Age of Capital (Waterman 1991), conservative Protestantism would render social, moral and material life according to the dictates of faith – although, in its second coming, CPE seems much more anxious to insinuate itself directly into the workings of state.

Witness, in this respect, the spread of so-called dominionism, whose 'global "kingdom" agenda' is founded on the belief that Jesus will not return 'until the Church has taken … control of the earth's governmental and social institutions (Leslie 2008, 2, 3), including the market and the courts; its 'three-legged stool' subsumes the state, business and civil society (Leslie 2008, 6). Even among Christians who do not explicitly see themselves as part of this movement, many support the effort to entrench 'godly dominion over our neighborhoods, our schools, our government, our literature and arts, our sports arenas, our … media, our scientific endeavors – in short, over every aspect and institution of human society'.[37] For some, the longer-term objective is to make the country over into a theocracy, thereby to reverse the course of history, and to put an end to the hegemony of secular reason. The ideology of the religious right is too familiar to bear repeating: its assaying of 'family values' and *laissez-faire*, its antipathy to

37 This quotation, from the late Pastor D. James Kennedy of Coral Ridge Ministries, is taken from 'The Rise of the Religious Right in the Republican Party', *Theocracy Watch*, <www.theocracywatch.org>, accessed 30 January 2009. The remaining words in quotes are taken from the same (unsigned) article.

abortion, homosexuality, welfare and stem cell research, its hard-nosed positions on poverty, the environment, theological and cultural relativism, immigration, 'just' wars and the like. In pursuing its imperial ends, conservative Christianity has been quick to resort to the means of lawfare.[38] Recall the disturbing *Jesus Camp* (2006, directed by Rachel Grady and Heidi Ewing), a documentary about the indoctrination of very young people, who spend their summers learning to 'seize back' the USA for Christ. The film may seem extreme in its choice of subject matter and in the matter of its subjects' choices. But it captures a rising tide in modern America. Other than footage of a Christian leader claiming to have open access to the White House and its decision-making processes, its most potent motif is a life-size cardboard effigy of George W. Bush, the ultimate American Idol: prayers are said for (to?) him, urging that he install 'righteous judges' – the youths chant the mantra 'righteous judges', over and over – who would conjure into being a truly Christian commonwealth. The fight for dominion, in short, gives yet further impetus to the fetishism of the law, and with it the judicialization of politics. Legality is the secular instrument by which civil society is to be remade in the image of the sacred.

Also *un*civil society – over the past decade or so, penitentiaries have become a major target of Christian movements in many countries (Burnside et al. 2005); in the USA, this initiative is associated primarily with PFM, the conservative Prison Fellowship Ministries founded in 1976 by Charles W. Colson, ex-Watergate conspirator and alumnus of an Alabama correctional facility. Neither Durkheim nor Foucault would have been surprised, of course, given their grasp of the constitutive relationship between the prison and the world, the disgraced and the disciplined. PFM's 'cultural commission' is to assist the Church in evangelizing inmates, to promote 'biblical standards of justice in the criminal justice system', and more broadly, 'to cultivate righteousness in society, strengthening the work of God's kingdom'.[39] In its Utopia, the Lord's Leviathan – about which Hobbes (1986, Pt III) himself would have felt distinctly queasy, given his belief that religious power ought always to be subordinate to civil authority – would be ruled by a seamless fusion of the Laws of Leviticus and the Laws of the Land. Again, the Protestant presence in prisons has a deep history: The Bishop of Norwich, Barry Unsworth reminds us in *Sacred Hunger*, owned one of England's more notorious houses of detention in the late eighteenth century (Unsworth 1992, 158). But there was less concern then for the promiscuous interpellation of Church into state. Ironically, as Governor of Texas, George W. Bush was sued by a convict for violating the Constitution by turning the pastoral care of the penitentiary over to PFM, hence to

38 So, of course, have liberal Christians in their struggles against injustice and inequality; they too have become much more adept at deploying the law. But that is beyond our present scope.

39 See 'Prison Fellowship Ministries/PFM/Chuck Colson', *MinistryWatch*, 22 February 2008, <www.ministrywatch.com/mw2.1/F_SumRpt.asp?EIN=620988294>, accessed 30 January 2009.

advantage evangelical Christianity over other faiths or no faith at all.[40] PFM has had to answer to the law on its own account as well: its InnerChange Freedom Initiative (IFI), partly funded by the state under President Bush's Faith Based Community Initiatives Program, was the object of a suit filed in Iowa in 2003 by Americans United for the Separation of Church and State. It 'is unconscionable', said the plaintiffs, for 'government to give preferential treatment to prisoners based solely on their willingness to undergo religious conversion and indoctrination'. The real controversy here, argued MinistryWatch, a Christian organization sympathetic to PFM and IFI, is about whether 'our nation's basic approach to solving social problems [is] secular humanism powered by big government and void of transcendent values [or] real and lasting social change ... effected by 'armies of compassion' working for true justice based upon unchanging principles.[41]

Critics of PFM accuse it of religious coercion, indeed, of theologico-lawfare. They point out that the evangelical Christian Ministry, committed to dominionism, has persuaded several states to make its programmes, paid for by tax dollars, a requirement of parole – and to give better carceral treatment to those who sign on.[42] As it turned out, the Iowa suit was successful. Both the lower courts and a federal appeals court, the second in late 2007, found that IFI *does* violate the constitutional separation of Church and state. Although the plaintiffs took the ruling to be 'a major setback for the White House's "faith-based initiative"', the IFI was banned *only* if it continued to operate with government funds.[43] In other words, as long as it is privately financed, it will continue to have access to prisons, and be free to press its convictions on convicts. At the time of writing, PFM was considering an approach to the ideologically stacked Supreme Court – in respect of whose composition President Bush *has* answered the prayers of the Jesus Campers – there to persuade the highest levels of the judiciary that government *should* pay for its work, and that the constitutional wall between Church and state, the sacred and the secular, ought to be re-aligned: again, the struggle continues. Nor only in the USA. In South Africa, where the constitutional protection for religious expression is much greater than it is in the USA, there is ongoing debate about the

---

40 'Lawsuits against Prisons: Texas Prisoners' Religious Rights Violated'. *North Coast Xpress*, <www.sonic.net/~doretk/Issues/01-03/lawsuits.html>, accessed 9 August 2005.

41 This quotation and the one in the previous sentence are from 'Prison Fellowship Ministries / PFM / Chuck Colson', *MinistryWatch*, 22 February 2008, <www.ministrywatch.com/mw2.1/F_SumRpt.asp?EIN=620988294>, accessed 30 January 2009.

42 For an acute, detailed critique of PFM in the public domain, see, for example, 'Court Rules against "Faith Based Coercion" Programs', by 'dogemperor', *Talk To Action*, 5 June 2006, <www.talk2action.org/story/2006/6/5/0566/59215>, accessed 30 January 2009.

43 The quote is from Debra E. Blum, 'Appeals Court Rules in Religious-Charity Prison Case', *The Chronicle of Philanthropy*, 4 December 2008, <www.philanthropy.com/news/updates/3564/appeals-court-rules-in-religious-charity-prison-case>, accessed 30 January 2009. This is one of a very large number of media analyses of the case published soon after the appellate decision.

place of faith in civil society and its governance, not to mention ongoing efforts on the part of religious parties to deploy the judiciary to extend their sovereignty.[44]

Similar things might be written about other faiths, other places. For example, the popularity of fundamentalist Judaism has grown strikingly over the past decades. In Israel, the role in government of the religious parties – in particular, their control over family law – has long posed a problem for the full accomplishment of a secular liberal democracy. With the occupation of Palestine and the expansion of settlements dominated by Orthodox Jews, the West Bank has become an archipelago of faith-based sovereign communities notorious for their aggressive self-assertion. Outside Israel, throughout the Jewish diaspora, ultra-conservative congregations have tended to be highly protective of their integrity, closing themselves off to the world and its interventions, settling disputes, enacting sociality, managing their public finances and negotiating their own moral economies – with rabbinical courts as the arbiters of order and propriety. Some time back, Channel 4 in the UK presented a television programme entitled 'Jewish Law' in its series *Faith and Belief*.[45] Focusing on just such a 'self-contained' community in Manchester, it showed scenes of religious authorities 'enforcing an array of intricate regulations' governed by biblical texts', rules that cover 'every element' of people's lives – and deaths.

The degree to which ultra-conservative Jews seek sovereign autonomy, and succeed in attaining it is highly variable, of course – as it is among other communities of conviction, be they evangelical Christians or orthodox Muslims, Mansions of Rastafari or ancestor-venerating Africans. But the overall trend seems clear. The sovereignty of difference, of ID-ology under the sign of culture or faith or the fusion of the two, is decreasingly a matter of indifference, increasingly the stuff of lawfare, ever more world-altering in its will to self-expression.

Note: World-altering

It is not simply that faith or culture are becoming more significant. In claiming sovereignty for culture and/or faith, the turn to ID-ology is having a fundamental impact on the very nature of political society. Nation-states may seek to subordinate these sovereignties to them; although, in the USA, it often seems the other way around. But, inevitably, they find themselves locked in a dialectic of mutual transformation, albeit an under-determined, as yet far from decided one. How so? Because assertions of sovereign difference, of policulturalism, seek to reconstitute the lineaments of the universe. Not only do they insist on a realignment of the relationship between the public and the private, the sacred and the secular, the empirical and the ineffable,

---

44 See special religion edition of the *Mail and Guardian*, 20–27 March 2008, pp. 12–23, and in particular Dennis Davis and Michelle Le Roux, 'My Rights versus Your Beliefs', ibid., pp. 12–13.

45 See <www.channel4.com/culture/microsites/C/can_you_believe_it/debates/jewishlaw.html> and <www.channel4.com/culture/microsites/C/can_you_believe_it/debates/jewishlaw3.html>, both accessed 30 January 2009.

and other founding oppositions at the core of liberal modern society. They also demand that the authority of the state – in respect of governance, legality, the means of violence, the fiscus and many things besides – no longer be cast as universal, that it be parsed rather along lines of difference, of *different* universalities: that is, those of god rather than government. This is similar to citizenship, whose rights and responsibilities are no longer to be defined purely in relation to the body politic, but to identities than nestle within it, transcend it, or transect its boundaries. Which returns us, full circle, to the historical shift of which we spoke earlier, the shift from a world built on vertical sovereignties to one erected on horizontal, partial ones.

Once again, the theory-work in all this for legal anthropology is to plumb the dialectic. It is a complex one, we reiterate, not one of winners or losers, domination and subordination, or even simple syntheses. It is one of translucent subtleties of substance, altering, as we have said, the political ontology of the lived world in such a way as to re-ground the future history of democracy, of law and governance, of our ways of being-and-knowing – of the Order of Things, *tout court*.

Could this be why so many people in so many parts of the world are concerned right now with order – and, conversely, with disorder? That is the question that points us finally, and very briefly, towards our third cardinal direction …

On the Metaphysics of Disorder, or Towards a Criminal Anthropology

We live, it seems, in an age of anxiety, an age of fear, an age of ambivalence. It is not the first, nor will it be the last. On the contrary, apprehension and uncertainty – at times acute, often just naggingly *there* – are the perennial undersides of social existence.

But what is notable about this age, if we tap into populist discourses across much of the globe, is the extent to which social *Angst* manifests itself in the gathering idea that criminality is almost everywhere out of control, everywhere excessive, everywhere a danger to life, limb, liberty, property (Comaroff and Comaroff 2004b) – even to society itself. Moreover, it is common cause, among many national publics, that the fight against lawlessness and disorder can no longer be won, except maybe in fiction, film, melodrama. Bertrand Russell's 'arduous journey', that great modernist march towards 'a social organization which curb(s) private violence and gives a measure of security to daily life' (Russell 1950, 143), appears to have ground to a halt. Moral panics have surfaced in many places: the Netherlands, Guatemala, Argentina, El Salvador, Haiti, Papua New Guinea, Japan, Australia. Brazil, we are told, lives with a culture of fear (for example, Caldeira 1996, 303f.; 2000). In sedate Sweden, citizens have come to see their country as 'a place of dark crimes and vicious psychopaths, of fractured families and a fraying society'.[46] In Britain, the 'rule of lawlessness' was a major issue in the 2001 national

46 Henning Mankell, Sweden's celebrated crime novelist (see above), quoted in Sarah Lyall, 'Brightening Thrillers with a Gloomy Swedish Detective', *The New York Times*, 13 November 2003, pp. B1, 5.

elections. At the time, England, which today has more students of criminology than students of sociology, was so vexed by the problem of social disorder that Polly Toynbee spoke of it as being on the verge of a 'nervous breakdown';[47] things have not improved appreciably since. In North America, where panics over crime peaked a little earlier, they have given way to a horror of terrorism, of warfare made criminal.

In sum, criminality has become a more or less global trope of undoing, of the imminent demise of civility, democracy, social order, just as economic meltdown, contagion, nuclear holocaust, moral decay, ecological catastrophe and other things have been in previous historical epochs. Seldom seen as political in its causes or effects – or, for that matter, as having anything at all to do with political economy – lawlessness is now, in vernacular imaginations, exactly what Durkheim's normative sociology long ago made it out to be: a human pathology that, unchecked, threatens the viability of modernist polities. Concomitantly, policing has come to 'stand for … order' in twenty-first-century notions of *governance* (Corrigan and Sayer 1985, 4). It – or, more generally, security – is now *the* state function *par excellence*. It is also a major criterion by which the strength of regimes is measured; hence its rhetorical significance when those regimes perform themselves for their citizens (Comaroff and Comaroff 2004b). This is in spite of the fact that, all over the world, the work of enforcement and incarceration is being ever more displaced into the private sector – or, more likely, because of it. There is good reason to believe that contemporary obsessions with disorder, themselves fed by a mass-mediation, are a corollary of the outsourcing of many of the operations of government, leaving the national citizen unsure of who or what might be the guarantor of life and death, of private property and public space. As Kevin Haggerty puts it, mass anxieties with lawlessness and punishment have more to do with 'the late-modern breakdown of a host of … social security systems' than with the brute fact of 'criminal victimization' (Haggerty 2001, 197). This, in turn, raises a number of questions, among them whether felony rates are *not* in fact rising precipitously, fed by the massive economic impact of upward flows of wealth and rising Gini coefficients, by the retreat of the welfare state and morphing labour markets. Some criminologists of both the left and the right have argued that they are. And crime statistics seem to bear them out, although the crime statistic is itself an inherently unstable knowledge-object (Comaroff and Comaroff 2006b). Whatever the 'truth' in this respect, there is a well-established *dis*proportion in many places, including the USA (see, for example, Garland 2001, 10f.) and UK,[48] between fear and risk:

47 Sarah Lyall, 'Soggy Pastures where All Things Crash and Burn', *The New York Times*, 7 April 2001, p. A4. Much the same thing was said by Paul Barker three years later; see 'Britain's Nervous Breakdown', *The Independent on Sunday*, 4 April 2004, p. 25.

48 See, for example, 'Fighting the Fear of Crime', *BBC Direct*, Newsletter, 6 February 2005, <www.rbkc.gov.uk/rbkcdirect/rdBehaviour/asb0502_story2.asp>, and Kathy Sutton, 'Fighting Fear of Crime', *New Statesman*, 1 August 2005, <www.newstatesman.com/200508010040>, both accessed 30 January 2009.

those who fear lawlessness most do not typically suffer it worst; those who suffer it worst do not tend to fear it most. In Cape Town, South Africa, for instance, where 350 murders occur in the poor black township of Khayelitsha for every one in wealthy, white Camps Bay, residents of the latter evince far greater concern with criminal violence. This disproportionality is why police departments often spend more these days on fighting the fear of crime than on fighting crime itself (cf. Haggerty 2001). It also points to something more general: that criminality is an ethical vernacular, a reflexive language in terms of which populations frame their discourses of deficit, arguing among themselves about what it is that stands between them and the good life. Which is why it always takes on a profoundly contingent, local content: such things as the alleged incapacity of the government of the day to deliver on its responsibility to it citizens, or worse yet, the corruption of its personnel; the inherent unruliness, incivility, violence of racialized others (a.k.a. young black men); the insidious presence of immigrants (a.k.a. 'illegal aliens'); the evil of those whose pious terror would wilfully destroy our civilization (a.k.a. Muslim fundamentalists). It is, conversely, by virtue of their translation into the argot of criminality that racism, xenophobia and their ilk may be spoken, and enacted, without being named.

Crime, to invoke Foucault, is productive: it is productive of emergent discourses of politics and law, of economics and ethics, of liberty, civility, sociality and religiosity – all of which it defines by its transgressions. As Durkheim (1938, xxviii) noted, Carol Greenhouse (2003, 276) reminds us, 'a society … free of crime would fall into chaos, since it would be bereft of the signs of its own existence *as* an authoritative order'. Like the African witch, in other words, the felon is a 'standardized nightmare' (Wilson 1951): an embodied figure by means of whom, as *camera obscura*, a civil order may conceive of itself – and, to the degree that nightmares are historical in their content, locate itself in its own contemporaneity. If, therefore, we are to interrogate law and governance at the dawn of the new century, if we are to understand the nature of its socialities and sovereignties, one way of doing so is to develop, within legal anthropology, an anthropological criminology that takes as its problem:

- what criminality and policing *mean*, what they convey and communicate in the here-and-now;
- how we read crime 'facts and figures', even fictions, as a species of political and social knowledge;
- what kinds of governmentality they bespeak;
- what sorts of world they conjure up.

We already have some extraordinary examples, of course: James Siegel's *New Criminal Type in Jakarta* is one. So, too, is Malcolm Young's *An Inside Job*. Each, in its own way, shows how it is that uncertainty and ambivalence, congealed in the spectre of lawlessness – in a *metaphysic of disorder*, so to speak – have come to haunt the present. Both underscore the contention with which we began: that a critical legal anthropology is foundational to the theory-work required to make sense of the twenty-first century.

This brings us to one or two words by way of conclusion.

Ends, Endings

Our three cardinal *topoi* – the fetishism of the law, ID-ology and anthropological criminology – converge. They are triangulated dimensions of the same thing: of the growing centrality of a culture of legality, broadly defined, in the post-Cold War (neoliberal?) era, in its politics and sociality, in its economics both moral and material, in its emergent forms of sociality, religiosity and citizenship, collective consciousness and subjectivity – in short, in world-making in the wake of the millennium. We have tried to take the measure of this 'legal turn', of its expression in such diverse things as the judicialization of political life, changing patterns of sovereignty, the rise of policulturalism and new faith-based movements, and spreading obsessions with lawlessness and disorder. But our primary objective has been more general, more programmatic. It has been to show *why* it is that a critical legal anthropology – one unafraid to take on Big Issues, even as it continues to interrogate small things – is so crucial to contemporary social theory at large, especially to theorizing the twenty-first century. In sketching one possible set of horizons for that anthropology, we seek to claim for it its proper place in the mainstream.

References

Ackerman, B. (1997), *The Rise of World Constitutionalism*, Yale Law School Occasional Papers, Second Series, no. 3.

Ahmed, A. (2006), *Adjudicating Muslims: Law, Religion, and the State in Colonial India and Post-Colonial Pakistan*, PhD Dissertation, University of Chicago.

Anderson, D. (2005), *Histories of the Hanged: The Dirty War in Kenya and the End of Empire*, London and New York: W.W. Norton.

Arendt, H. (1998 [1958]), *The Human Condition*, 2nd edn, Chicago, IL: University of Chicago Press.

Benda-Beckmann, F. von (2002), 'Who's Afraid of Legal Pluralism?', *Journal of Legal Pluralism* 47: 37–82.

—— and Benda-Beckmann, K. von (2006), 'The Dynamics of Change and Continuity in Plural Legal Orders', *Journal of Legal Pluralism and Unofficial Law* 53/54: 1–44.

Benjamin, W. (1978 [1921]), 'Critique of Violence', in P. Demetz (ed.) and E. Jephcott (trans.), *Reflections: Essays, Aphorisms, Autobiographical Writings*, New York: Schocken Books, pp. 277–300.

Beyer, J. (2006), 'Revitalization, Invention and Continued Existence of the Kyrgyz Aksakal Courts: Listening to Pluralistic Accounts of History', *Journal of Legal Pluralism and Unofficial Law* 53/54: 141–76.

Burnside, J. with Adler, J., Loukes, N. and Rose, G. (2005), *My Brother's Keeper: Faith-based Units in Prisons*, Cullompton, UK: Willan Publishing.

Caldeira, T.P. (1996), 'Fortified Enclaves: The New Urban Segregation', *Public Culture* 8(2): 303–28.

—— (2000), *City of Walls: Crime, Segregation, and Citizenship in São Paulo*, Berkeley, CA: University of California Press.

Comaroff, J. and Comaroff, J.L. (2003) 'Reflections on Liberalism, Policulturalism, and ID-ology: Citizenship and Difference in South Africa', *Social Identities* 9(4): 445–74.

—— and Comaroff, J.L. (2004a), 'Criminal Obsessions, after Foucault: Postcoloniality, Policing, and the Metaphysics of Disorder', *Critical Inquiry* 30 (Summer): 800–824.

—— and Comaroff, J.L. (2006a), 'Figuring Crime: Quantifacts and the Production of the Unreal', *Public Culture* 18(1): 209–46.

Comaroff, J.L. (2002), 'Out of Control: An Afterword', in D.J. Cohen (ed.), *Democracy, Law and Social Control in Classical Athens* [*Demokratie, Recht und soziale Kontrolle im klassichen Athen*], Munich: Verlag Oldenbourg für Historisches Kolleg, pp. 189–92.

—— and Comaroff, J. (2004b), 'Criminal Justice, Cultural Justice: The Limits of Liberalism and the Pragmatics of Difference in the New South Africa', *American Ethnologist* 31(2): 188–204.

—— and Comaroff, J. (2006b), 'Law and Disorder in the Postcolony: An Introduction', in J.L. Comaroff and J. Comaroff (eds), *Law and Disorder in the Postcolony*, Chicago, IL: University of Chicago Press, 1–56.

—— and Comaroff, J. (2009), *Ethnicity, Inc.*, Chicago, IL: University of Chicago Press.

—— and Roberts, S.A. (1981), *Rules and Processes: The Cultural Logic of Dispute in an African Context*, Chicago, IL: University of Chicago Press.

Corrigan, P. and Sayer, D. (1985), *The Great Arch: English State Formation as Cultural Revolution*, Oxford: Basil Blackwell.

Derrida, J. (1994), *Specters of Marx: The State of Debt, the Work of Mourning, and the New International*, trans. P. Kamuf, New York: Routledge.

Durkheim, E. (1938), *The Rules of Sociological Method*, 8th edn, trans. S.A. Solovay and J.H. Mueller, ed. G.E.G. Catlin, New York: The Free Press.

Eckert, J. (2006), 'From Subjects to Citizens: Legalism from below and the Homogenization of the Legal Sphere', *Journal of Legal Pluralism and Unofficial Law* 53/54: 45–75.

Elkins, C. (2005), *Imperial Reckoning: The Untold Story of Britain's Gulag in Kenya*, New York: Henry Holt.

Evans-Pritchard, E.E. (1940), 'The Nuer of the Southern Sudan', in M. Fortes and E.E. Evans-Pritchard (eds), *African Political System*, London: Oxford University Press for the International African Institute, pp. 272–96.

Garland, D. (2001), *The Culture of Control: Crime and Social Order in Contemporary Society*, Chicago, IL: University of Chicago Press.

Geschiere, P. (2006), 'Witchcraft and the Limits of the Law: Cameroon and South Africa', in J.L. Comaroff and J. Comaroff (eds), *Law and Disorder in the Postcolony*, Chicago, IL: University of Chicago Press, pp. 219–46.

Gibson, J.L. (2004), *Overcoming Apartheid: Can Truth Reconcile a Divided Nation?*, New York: Russell Sage.

Greenhouse, C.J. (2003), 'Solidarity and Objectivity: Re-reading Durkheim', in P.C. Parnell and S.C. Kane (eds), *Crime's Power: Anthropologists and the Ethnography of Crime*, New York: Palgrave Macmillan, pp. 269–93.

Haggerty, K.D. (2001) *Making Crime Count*, Toronto: University of Toronto Press.

Hansen, T.B. and Stepputat, F. (2005), 'Introduction', in T.B. Hansen and F. Stepputat (eds), *Sovereign Bodies: Citizens, Migrants, and States in the Postcolonial World*, Princeton, NJ: Princeton University Press, pp. 1–37.

Hobbes, T. (1986), *Leviathan*, ed. C.B. Macpherson, London: Penguin.

Keefe, P.R. (2007), 'Letter from Jaipur: The Idol Thief', *The New Yorker*, 7 May: 58–67.

Leslie, S. (2008), 'Dominionism and the Rise of Christian Imperialism', *Moriel Ministries*, <www.moriel.org/articles/discernment/church_issues/dominionism_rise_of_christian_imperialism.htm>, accessed 18 March 2008.

Maine, Sir H.J.S. (1919), *Ancient Law*, London: J.M. Dent & Sons.

Mankell, H. (2003), *One Step Behind*, London: Vintage Books.

Merry, S.E. (1988), 'Legal Pluralism', *Law and Society Review* 22: 869–96.

Moore, S.F. (1978), *Law as Process*, London: Routledge & Kegan Paul.

Oomen, B. (2005), *Chiefs in South Africa: Law, Power and Culture in the Post-Apartheid Era*, New York: Palgrave.

Peleikis, A. (2006), 'Whose Heritage? Legal Pluralism and the Politics of the Past: A Case Study from the Curonian Split (Lithuania)', *Journal of Legal Pluralism and Unofficial Law* 53/54: 209–37.

Pirie, F. (2006) 'Legal Complexity on the Tibetan Plateau', *Journal of Legal Pluralism and Unofficial Law* 53/54: 77–99.

Rancière, J, (1999), *Disagreement: Politics and Philosophy*, trans. J. Rose, Minneapolis, MN: University of Minnesota Press.

Roberts, S.A. (1998), 'Against Legal Pluralism: Some Reflections on the Contemporary Enlargement of the Legal Domain', *Journal of Legal Pluralism* 42: 95–106.

Russell, B. (1950), *Unpopular Essays*, New York: Simon & Schuster.

Schneiderman, D. (2000), 'Constitutional Approaches to Privatization: An Inquiry into the Magnitude of Neo-liberal Constitutionalism', *Law and Contemporary Problems* 63(4): 83–109.

Siegel, J.T. (1998), *A New Criminal Type in Jakarta: Counter-revolution Today*, Durham, NC: Duke University Press.

Tebbe, N. (2008), 'Inheritance and Disinheritance: African Customary Law and Constitutional Rights', *Journal of Religion* 88(4): 466–96 .

Tilly, C. (1985), 'War Making and State Making as Organized Crime', in P.B. Evans, D. Rueschemeyer and T. Skocpol (eds), *Bringing the State Back In*, Cambridge: Cambridge University Press, pp. 170–91.

Torre, G. Dalla (1998), 'A Strong Moral Conscience for a Culture of Legality', *Jubilaeum*, 'Tertium Millennium' (1998) 1, <www.vatican.va/jubilee_2000/magazine/documents/ju_mag_01021998_p-8_en.html>, accessed 30 January 2009.

Turner, B. (2006), 'Competing Global Players in Rural Morocco: Upgrading Legal Arenas', *Journal of Legal Pluralism and Unofficial Law* 53/54: 101–39.

Unsworth, B. (1992), *Sacred Hunger*, London and New York: Norton.

Waterman, A.M.C. (1991), *Revolution, Economics and Religion: Christian Political Economy, 1798–1833*, Cambridge: Cambridge University Press.

Wilson, M. (1951), 'Witch Beliefs and Social Structure', *American Journal of Sociology* 56: 307–13.

Young, M. (1991), *An Inside Job: Policing and Police Culture in Britain*, New York: Oxford University Press.

Chapter 3
Private Military Companies and State Sovereignty: Regulating Transnational Flows of Violence and Capital

Diana Sidakis

> Frankly, I'd like to see government get out of war altogether and leave this whole field to private industry. (Heller 2004 [1961], 259)

Introduction

The International Peace Operations Association (IPOA) website opens with the image of a sleeping lion, a map of the world and the slogan 'Businesses worldwide. United for peace.' The IPOA is the lobbying organization for private military companies. The language of human rights and the language of corporate branding are spliced seamlessly together in the materials available on the website, making it frighteningly easy to imagine an army of Lieutenant Milo Minderbinders eternally fighting a war for peace. Private military companies are taking on an increasingly large role in defence activities and engaging in a violence that is traditionally understood as the state's unique prerogative. Private military companies are a prime example of an actor engaging in an activity which the state once claimed as its reserve. Interestingly, private military companies are positioned as both subjects and producers of governance. As subjects, private military companies fall under and between various forms of governance – primarily, national and international law, and the contracts that determine their work. Yet private military companies also produce forms of governance. First, they produce governance as they exert violence to establish and maintain control in their areas of operation. Second, they generate codes of conduct and others standards in order to regulate the growing industry. However, as both subjects and producers of various modes of governance, the most striking quality of private military companies is their ability to evade legal responsibility, liability and accountability.

The ability of human rights to critique violence and to challenge inequality is neutralized as human rights language is co-opted in the legitimization of the industry. The ability of the state to regulate and to control these companies' activities is thrown into question as these companies and the individuals working for them evade prosecution for crimes ranging from rape to murder. In 'Representing In-between: Law, Anthropology, and the Rhetoric of Interdisciplinarity', Riles (1994) puts forth a model of interdisciplinarity that works between normative argument and reflexive consideration, drawing on both law and anthropology to illuminate each other and the social trends they inhabit. This chapter will apply this type of normative and reflexive analysis to the development of private military companies by drawing on both legal material and anthropological analysis. After analysing the relationship between sovereignty and violence that led to the outlawing of mercenarism in the twentieth century, we will examine the legal, economic and political conditions that produced the proliferation of private military companies in the twenty-first century. Finally, several modes of governance will be examined for their ability to regulate the industry. International law, national law, and industry generated codes of conduct are the three primary modes of governance for private military companies. This chapter will argue that none of the three currently provides a structure capable of regulating the flows of violence and capital generated by private military companies.

The Evolution of Today's Mercenaries and the Department of Defense

In a 2002 article entitled 'Transforming the Military', Donald Rumsfeld sets forth his vision for a new American military. The article highlights many of the recommendations found in the Department of Defense's *Quadrennial Defense Review Report* (QDR) that was published in the weeks following 11 September. Both pieces use a language of urgency, drawing on the 11 September attack to justify 'the transformation of US forces, capabilities, and institutions to extend America's asymmetric advantages well into the future' (Department of Defense 2001, 6). Both the QDR and Rumsfeld's article attach the urgent necessity of the transformation of the military in response to the 11 September attack. The most radical recommendation found in the QDR is that:

> only those functions that must be performed by DoD (Department of Defense) should be kept by DoD. Any function that can be provided by the private sector is not a core government function… over the last several decades, most private sector corporations have moved aggressively away from providing most of their own services. Instead they have concentrated efforts on core functions and businesses, while building alliances with suppliers for a vast range of products and services not considered core to the value they can best add in the economy… aggressively pursuing this effort to improve productivity requires a major change in the culture of the Department. (Department of Defense 2001, 53)

This passage creates a contradictory position for the DoD. The use of outsourcing by the private sector is first generalized into a successful trend for increasing productivity and then recommended as a strategy for the DoD. The report does not analyse what makes outsourcing a more profitable or efficient structure; it simply alludes to the market truism of competition creating efficiency and value in a free market. Presumably, by focusing on its 'core function' a business can streamline its operations and create greater profits for itself, the economy and society as a whole. There is also no further analysis of how of what is lost in the transformation to outsourcing.

Applying that business advice to a government department is fraught with problems. It requires conceptualizing the DoD as a business, operating in competition with others in the pursuit of profit and market efficiency. This conceptualization fails. The DoD's aim is not the creation of wealth or efficiency. It is the provision of security and defence. Furthermore, the DoD is not operating in competition with other providers. The privilege of the sovereign state to have a monopoly on coercive violence is a tenet of modern statehood that will be addressed further below (Weber 1964, 154). For outsourcing to be effective, it has to occur in a market with multiple firms competing for opportunities. The DoD is not operating in such an environment. Strictly speaking, the DoD was created in 1947, when the National Security Act. The War Department, the Navy Department and the newly created Department of the Air Force were merged in to the Department of Defense to be led by the Secretary of Defense. An analogy to a private company at the time would have been wildly out of place; the DoD would never be in competition with other similar organizations competing in the market. The DoD was constructed to unify the military establishment under a single authority appointed by the President.

The 2001 QDR elaborates on three types of DoD activities. First, there are 'functions directly linked to warfighting and best performed by the federal government' (Department of Defense 2001, 53). Warfighting and the pressures of coercive violence are not addressed as the tools of a sovereign state; rather, they are described in the market language of a 'core function'. By not addressing the authority of the sovereign state as the justification for violence, the QDR reconstructs the DoD in the operation of the market as opposed to the operation of the state. Therefore, concerns of legitimacy and authority are removed to the consideration of concerns of efficiency and profitability. Second, the DoD performs 'functions indirectly linked to warfighting capability that must be shared by the public and private sectors' (Department of Defense 2001, 53). This type of ambiguous activity is not further delineated. There are no clear demarcations between 'functions indirectly linked to warfighting'. This categorical ambiguity will be capitalized on by private military firms that offer an evolving range of skills and services in competition for government contracts. Thirdly and finally are 'functions not linked to warfighting .... DoD will seek to privatize or outsource entire functions or define new mechanisms for partnerships with private firms' (Department of Defense 2001, 54). It is difficult to construct a strict border around functions not linked to warfighting that are performed by the DoD. Management, infrastructure maintenance and other non-battlefield activities are intrinsic to the type of work performed by the DoD. The recommendation for outsourcing assumes that warfighting can be achieved in a vacuum, without a supporting web of functions and services. However, it is impossible to clearly delineate what constitutes warfighting and what constitutes support. The argument for outsourcing is made even more complicated by Rumsfeld's vision of a DoD that does not focus its main activities on the battlefield, but rather on deterrence.

The DoD's role is at once expanded and constricted. It is expanded in the sense that its work needs to operate in new arenas. Rumsfeld elaborates further on the changing type of work in his *Foreign Affairs* article. He writes of 'a new "capabilities-based" approach – one that focuses less on who might threaten us, or where, and more on how we might be threatened and what is needed to deter and defend against such threats' (Rumsfeld 2002, 24). This approach does not emphasize 'warfighting' capabilities. Yet the 2001 QDR emphasizes that warfighting is the core function of the DoD, to the exclusion of other activities. The DoD's role is put into a contradictory position: at once expanded by the new type of post-Cold War defence work, yet restricted by an emphasis on core functions and the move towards outsourcing. This ambiguous positioning creates a market opportunity for private military companies to flourish. Private military companies allow the flexibility sought by the DoD's new vision of work varying from intelligence to security, while simultaneously supporting the trend towards outsourcing.

Historical Background

A March 2003 article in *The Economist* refers to the Iraq War as 'the first privatized war'.[1] This article was written in the first week of the invasion of Iraq, yet accurately predicts how the war would be waged in the following years. At the start of the Iraq War, there were 10 civilian contractors for every 100 servicemen in the Middle East – which already represented a tenfold increase since the first Gulf War. A July 2007 *Los Angeles Times* article reported that the number of private contractors in Iraq now exceeded the number of American servicemen.[2] The article puts the number of civilian contractors at 180,000, in comparison to an estimated 160,000 American troops. However, the estimated figure of 180,000 civilian contractors clarifies as much as it obscures. It does not include contractors working for the State Department, the US Agency for International Development or other US government employers. It does not include private security contractors – civilians who are 'hired to protect government officials and buildings'. The use of labels such as 'civilian contractor' and 'private security contractor' developed with the growth of the industry, and indicates how the success of such firms depends on skilful branding and the fragmentation of the government and military market. However, before addressing the current position of private military companies, it is important to see the historical structure from which they developed.

Many articles and books on the topic refer to the proliferation of private military companies as a unique and new development in war. However, if private military companies are understood as the capitalist reincarnation of mercenaries,

1 'Military-industrial Complexities', *The Economist*, 29 March 2003.

2 C.T. Miller, 'Private Contractors Outnumber US Troops in Iraq', *LA Times*, 4 July 2007.

their heritage and position as political and economic actors is broadened. Janice Thomson's outlines how states achieved a monopoly on violence based on territorial boundaries. Written in the mid-1990s, before the proliferation of private military companies, Thomson argues that a transformation of violence occurred with the emergence of the dominant sovereign nation-state framework in the twentieth century. She frames this transformation in terms of a shift away from 'the heteronomous system of the medieval period in which violence was democratized, marketized and internationalized' (Thomson 1996, 4). Before the twentieth century, non-state violence was the norm. She traces the use of large-scale private armies in Europe during the fourteenth and fifteenth centuries to mercenary armies used by European states in the eighteenth century, and the development of mercantile companies from the sixteenth to the nineteenth centuries. She argues that these non-state actors were officially sanctioned by the state to help achieve its goals. In the case of mercenaries and large-scale private armies, the power of violence was bought on the international market. Mercantile companies were granted sovereignty from their sponsoring states. In both instances, private entities, whether individual or corporate, were employed by the state and granted state-like powers. The use of non-state actors allowed a reduction in cost and a measure of plausible deniability – two factors that also come into play with the use of private military companies in Iraq. However, Thomson also highlights that 'it is impossible to draw distinctions between the economic and political, the domestic and international, or the non-state and state realms of authority when analyzing these practices. All lines were blurred' (Thomson 1996, 41). Non-state actors profited while allowing states to gain military dominance, territorial control and profits from foreign territories. There is no strict boundary between the realms of authority and the actors employed by the state.

Thomson argues that the twentieth century saw the construction and hegemony of a nation-state system. This saw violence 'shift from the non-state, economic, and international realms of authority into the state, political, and domestic realms of authority. It [violence] was dedemocratized, demarketized, and territorialized' (Thomson 1996, 4). Violence is at once a means and an end to the construction of the sovereign state. The connection of the state to the monopoly on authorized violence draws directly on a Weberian understanding of the state (Weber 1964, 154). Thomson argues that mercenarism ended because of the international law developed in the nineteenth century regarding neutral states: 'A neutral state has a passive duty to not provide assistance to either belligerent and an active duty to prevent the use of its territory for hostile acts' (Thomson 1996, 55). This development corresponded to a changing understanding of military service that brought political concerns into the picture.

Anti-mercenary legislation was codified in the US Neutrality Act of 1794, which prevented 'citizens or inhabitants of the United States from accepting commissions or enlisting in the service of a foreign state' (Fenwick 1948, 46). Thomson sees this as a 'watershed' moment in the delegitimization of mercenarism. Instead of ensuring neutrality through temporary bilateral treaties or proclamations, the US codified its rights and duties as a neutral state in municipal law. Thomson (1996, 81) argues that this became the standard among nations, as between 1794 and 1938, 49 states enacted laws controlling their citizens' foreign military service. These laws assert that only the sovereign state has the authority to use violence in the international system. Thomson links the delegitimization of mercenarism with the growth of inter-state relations. Neutrality as an international practice required the state to assert control over its subjects' use of violence. A neutral state could not be considered as such if its subjects were engaged in the conflict. Although earlier states benefited from mercenarism, the development of an international norm against mercenarism increased state power by making it the sole authority for international violence.

This argument is complicated by the proliferation of private military companies in the decade since the publication of Thomson's book. Furthermore, private military companies often hire the services of third-country nationals, again complicating Thomson's argument. Thomson addresses twentieth-century mercenarism in three forms: the permanent employment of foreigners in a state's regular army (either with or without their home state's complicity), the temporary employment of foreigners for use in a particular conflict, and finally, when a state pays another state for the use of its troops (Thomson 1996, 90). Private military companies do not fit neatly into any of these three categories. Civilian contractors work for a company, often owned by a larger multinational enterprise which contracts with the government, either directly or through a subsidiary. In the case of third-party nationals, the private military company often recruits these individuals through a complicated system of sub-contracts and subsidiary companies. Therefore, the state is not directly employing the individual into its standing army. This crucial difference throws up a number of legal problems, which will be addressed below. In the final instance, when contracting with private military companies, the state is not contracting with another state for the use of its troops. Private military companies operate independently of the state.

Thomson's construction of twentieth-century mercenarism misses the development of twenty-first-century mercenarism when she states that 'today real states do not buy mercenaries' (Thomson 1996, 96). This statement is not strictly false, however. In the first instance, mercenarism as it existed prior to the dominance of the nation-state no longer exists. The United States do not straightforwardly hire the services of a third country to wage war. However, as seen in the construction of the Coalition of the Willing, foreign aid, beneficial trade agreements and mutual defence pacts can stand in for a straightforward cash exchange. The contracts developed between various US departments and multinational enterprises for the provision of security and defence services in Iraq are not representative of 'mercenarism' as it was practised in the nineteenth century. Alternatively, it can be argued that private military companies are mercenaries reincarnated in the parameters of a capitalist nation-state. Perhaps the flaw in Thomson's incorrect prediction of mercenarism in the twenty-first century rests in her qualification of 'real' states not buying mercenaries. To qualify a state as such is to draw on a classical theory of sovereignty that the modern existence of mercenaries undermines.

Thomson argues that the state's monopoly on violence came about with the evolution of sovereignty; the ownership of the means of violence changed from the non-state to the state (Thomson 1996, 143). Previously, the market allocated violence; then the state gained the authority and power to control violence away from the market. The argument hinges on the power of law and sovereignty. The shift back towards mercenarism in the form of private military companies indicates that the market is exerting more power over controlling international violence than the sovereign state. This puts pressure on the classic model of a sovereign nation-state. At the heart of the issue is the construction of violence as a market commodity that can be controlled by the sovereign power. Connecting sovereignty to the elimination of mercenarism draws on a theory of sovereignty in which the sovereign derives its authority from the citizenry. In this model, the state cannot separate itself from its citizens' actions in international conflicts. Legislation controlling the actions of its citizens to prevent a market in mercenarism protects state sovereignty in international affairs. However, with the rise of multinational enterprises acting as contracting parties for the provision of defence services, the power of the sovereign is redefined and reallocated to the market. The state claimed control and responsibility for its citizens' actions in international violence with the outlawing of mercenarism in the early twentieth century. However, by the early twenty-first century, private enterprises appear as the bodies capable of generating international violence, as opposed to private individuals. The ability of 'real' states to control this violence is as limited as the classical model of sovereignty in explaining it.

Roberts addresses the contested meanings of sovereignty in his article 'The End of Occupation: Iraq 2004' (Roberts 2005). He analyses to what extent sovereignty can be found in occupied Iraq after the official 'transfer of sovereignty' in June 2004. Roberts sees sovereignty as the 'proposition that, within a given area of the globe, a particular constitutional and governmental structure has the prime responsibility for reaching and implementing decisions, including in response to internal and external pressures' (Roberts 2005, 40). The ability of the Iraqi government to practise this type of sovereignty is negated not only by internal violence, but also by the occupation. The increasingly private composition of these occupying forces draws sovereignty into question not only for 'weak' states like Iraq, but the 'real' states that occupy them.

Thomson ends her book by stating that a shift in sovereignty 'would entail an end to or at least significant erosion of the state's monopoly on the authority to deploy violence beyond its borders. It is not at all clear to me that this is occurring' (Thomson 1996, 153). The power of multinational enterprises in setting up private military companies may be the first sign of this erosion. Although these companies work at the request of and through the funding of the state, they are blurring the boundaries between the legitimate use of military violence as embodied in international law and national legal frameworks such as the Uniform Code of

Military Justice. In the most obvious instance, the deployment of private security guards without the authorization of the US government in post-hurricane New Orleans indicates a significant shift in sovereignty and the authority to use violence (Scahill 2007, 321–40).

The Modern Establishment of Mercenaries

In the 2006 QDR, private contractors are classified as an official part of the US war machine. The concept of 'Total Force' includes the DoD's 'active and reserve military components, its civil servants, and its contractors [that] constitute its warfighting capability and capacity. Members of the Total Force serve in thousands of locations around the world, performing a vast array of duties to accomplish critical missions' (DoD 2006, 75). The transformation recommended in the 2001 Quadrennial Defense Review is fulfilled by this report. The DoD is at once expanded to include a host of private contractors and restricted in its core functions.

The DoD issued a protocol delineating policy and procedures regarding contractors accompanying US Armed Forces in October 2005 (Krieg 2005). The protocol was written by Kenneth Krieg, the Under Secretary of Defense for Acquisition, Technology and Logistics. The protocol calls for contractors to be armed when necessary. It also requires the creation of a joint database of all contracting personnel with details such as company contact information and sponsoring military unit information. The database would provide a degree of accountability and visibility in the contracting process. Furthermore, the protocol calls for all contracting personnel to process through a joint reception centre organized by the local commander. However, both of these tracking requirements are qualified by the right of Under Secretary Krieg to waive them. The instructions were premised on a need for accountability and visibility of contractors operating on the battlefield; however, since both the relevant requirements are subject to be waived by the Under Secretary, the contractors are granted continued invisibility.

In terms of sovereignty, the power to assert international violence is contracted away from the government. Armed contractors operating on the battlefield in support of the US Armed Forces demonstrate a blurring of government authority and private sector activity. Procedurally, the DoD delimits itself from tracking the private actors engaged on the battlefield. The waiver from Under Secretary Krieg can be understood in two ways. First, it may strategically allow the DoD a measure of plausible deniability, maintaining a separation between the actions of private contractors and the US Armed Forces. Alternatively, the lack of an updated database tracking the contracts indicates that the power of the private contractors has exceeded the capacity of the DoD to control and administer their actions. This was seen when a December 2006 Government Accountability Office report could not determine how many contractors were operating in Iraq (GAO 2006).

The fluid structure of private military companies and the complex contracts that determine their work make it impossible to maintain an accurate database of contractors operating in Iraq. This is not a flaw in the system that the companies or the government are trying to address; rather, it is an inherent structural advantage that is in both the companies and the government's interest to maintain. Newspaper articles and books on the subject refer to private military companies as operating in a 'shroud of secrecy' (Kinsey 2006, 1). However, this shroud of secrecy is maintained even as human rights instruments with benchmarks of accountability and transparency are absorbed and deployed. It could be argued that this is a limitation of human rights language: its ability to be translated and deployed for political and financial gains. In this instance, the human rights language of private military companies demonstrates the branding potential of human rights rather than a genuine commitment to their values. This tension is addressed further below. The combination of legitimacy and secrecy is not only a product of the legal framework of private military companies; it is a quality intrinsic to their structure.

As noted above, private military companies seized on the trend of privatizing government functions. Definite numbers are hard to come by, but it is estimated that private military companies generates $100 billion in annual revenue, with operations in over fifty countries (Kinsey 2006, 2). However, the large and growing scale of these companies is not the distinguishing quality of these mercenaries in modern form – their constitution as companies is what grants them a structural advantage. Previously, mercenaries operated largely on an *ad hoc* basis. Profit was measured on the individual basis, with personal motives and gains generating individual action. The corporate identity of modern mercenaries translates the profit motive into a broader institutional structure. This allows private military companies to 'make use of complex corporate financing – ranging from the sale of stock shares to intrafirm trade – and engage in a wider variety of deals and contracts … for [private military firms] it is not the people who matter but the structure they are within' (Singer 2001/2002, 192). By emphasizing the power of the structure over the power of the individual, the agency of mercenaries is redefined. It is not the individual with a gun that challenges the sovereignty of the nation-state or the legality and justness of war. Rather, it is the corporate structure that is both legitimized and supported by the state that affects sovereignty.

Timothy Spicer, the founder of Sandline and the Chief Executive Officer of SCI, explains private military companies as 'structured organizations with professional and corporate hierarchies … we cover the full spectrum – training, logistics, support, operational support, post-conflict resolution'.[3] The mercenary is reconstructed into a corporate structure that provides both legitimacy and opportunity. However, the permanence of the corporate structure is tempered by the fluidity allowed by the structuring of subsidiary companies, personnel

---

3 A. Gilligan, 'Inside Lt Col. Spicer's New Model Army', *Sunday Telegraph*, 22 November 1998.

databases, and networks. The permanence of the corporate structure is a marker of legitimacy for the companies; however, the distinctive trait of private military companies is their ability to regenerate and reinvent themselves.

Both Kinsey and Singer set up typologies for defining the different types of private military companies. Kinsey organizes the companies along two spectrums – one measuring the use of lethal force, and the other measuring whether work is of a public or private authority. For instance, Kinsey distinguishes private security companies from private military companies, in that security companies are 'generally concerned with crime prevention and public order' (Kinsey 2006, 16), while military companies provide 'military expertise, including training and equipment' (Kinsey 2006, 14). However, as 'private security companies' take on new business by, for example, offering humanitarian support as ArmorGroup does in de-mining Kosovo under the authority of the British government (Kinsey 2006, 18), the clarity of these labels is diminished. Singer (2001/2002, 200) organizes different types of companies according to the type of service and force levels they provide, ranging from military provider to military consulting to military support firms. However, firms continually change the services they offer in order to win contracts. These typologies obscure matters, given that the type of work performed by private military companies is rapidly changing, not only from contract to contract but also in day-to-day operations. The market rewards flexibility and reinvention – traits that private military companies capitalize on.

Kinsey describes the structure of private military companies:

> as a corporate body, PMCs generally have a Board of Directors. The composition of these Boards generally includes former military officers … the personnel structure of PMCs is not always clearly identifiable since the companies usually retain only a very small permanent staff to run the office and manage the contracts. The majority of their workforce is drawn from networks of ex-service personnel, whose details are held on a database … a further characteristic of PMCs is their ability to transform themselves from state to state, establishing parent companies, or operating subsidiary companies. (Kinsey 2006, 15)

This description of private military companies' structure echoes Teubner's construction of an anonymous matrix. Private military companies are able to structure and re-structure themselves in order to take advantage of tax laws, evade prosecution, and most importantly, maintain control over their profits and operations. This generates a 'new living law of the world [that] is nourished not from stores of tradition but from the ongoing self-reproduction of highly technical, highly specialized, often formally organized rather than narrowly defined global networks of an economic, cultural, academic, or technological nature' (Teubner 1996, 5). The networks of personnel managed by a small number of transferable staff that make up private military companies demonstrate one instance of the generation of the 'living law of the world' described by Teubner. The living law they create exists in both national and international frameworks, as seen in legislation, court decisions, UN conventions and the self-issued codes of conduct and protocol issued by the companies. We will now turn to these legal instruments in order to examine the capability of the law in regulating transnational flows of violence and capital.

Law: International and US Regulation

The DoD's 'Contractors on the Battlefield' guide referenced above discusses various legal instruments relevant to private contractors operating on the battlefield. This guide generates a procedural understanding of the law and protocol surrounding contractors. It is drawn from over sixty previous documents issued by the DoD in regard to the status of contractors on the battlefield. Within the DoD, it creates an understanding of the private contractors as operating under the same protections as the Armed Forces. By placing the contractors within a national and international legal framework, the guide legitimizes their status. The guide argues that under the 1949 Geneva Convention Relative to the Treatment of Prisoners of War, if contractors are carrying an 'appropriate identification card', they are entitled to prisoner of war status when captured. The right for civilian contractors to carry arms and use them on the battlefield is asserted in terms of a right to self-defence. The Geneva Conventions' binary of combatant and civilian, which has already been blurred by the development of 'unlawful enemy combatant', is not addressed within the guide, although arguably, an armed contractor not in uniform and not operating under the military's chain of command is in unclear legal territory.

In addition to claiming protection under the Geneva Conventions, the guide also refers to several pieces of national legislation. The Military Extraterritorial Jurisdiction Act of 2000 (MEJA), establishes federal jurisdiction over offences committed by 'persons employed by or accompanying the Armed Forces'. The guide also references the Uniform Code of Military Justice (UCMJ). It states that contractors may be subject to prosecution under the UCMJ, and that commanders have limited authority to take disciplinary action against contractors on the field. Placing contractors under the UCMJ was solidified in the 2007 Defense Spending Authorization Bill. Placing civilians under a military code reveals the inherent tension of having private entities perform public duties. Finally, the guide claims that contractors are subject to domestic criminal laws of the host nation. This assertion is meaningless in light of the Coalition Provision Authority's Order 17, which made all contractors operating in Iraq immune from the Iraqi legal process. The inability of both international and national laws to effectively regulate and prosecute private military companies indicates a failure of state-generated law to regulate the transnational flows of capital and violence generated by private military company. Potentially, the only mechanism capable of controlling these flows may be the protocols and procedures generated by the industry itself.

International Regulation: The Geneva Conventions

The DoD claims that the Geneva Conventions protect contractors as both civilians and as supporting members of the Armed Forces. This interpretation demands a particular reading of the text and the legal categories it constructs. The Geneva Conventions exclude mercenaries from their protection,[4] and the UN passed a 1989 Convention that outlaws mercenaries.[5] Mercenarism has been definitively outlawed by international law. However, both legal documents adopt a restrictively narrow definition of 'mercenary' that cannot be applied to the civilian contractors operating in Iraq. The shift from 'mercenary' to 'contractor' demonstrates how legal categories operate. By reframing mercenaries as contractors, the DoD is able to argue for their legal protection and status. It draws on the ambiguity regarding the categories of civilian and combatant that are essential to the Geneva Conventions. These categories are impossible to demarcate on the modern battlefield, and depend upon interpretation for their meaning and application. To interpret the Geneva Conventions as covering contractors demonstrates that legal interpretation is politically motivated, especially when seen in contrast to other instances where Geneva protections have been denied to combatants with ambiguous legal status that operate in opposition to the dominant (military and interpretative) power.

The 1949 Geneva Conventions do not define 'civilian', although the protection of non-combatants is a key aim of the document. The 1977 Protocols establish a definition of 'civilian' through negation: civilians are not members of armed forces or organized militias.[6] The Protocols grant extensive protection to individuals 'unless and for such time as they take direct part in hostilities'.[7] The place of contractors in relation to these Protocols hinges on the understanding of the word 'direct'. Contractors providing security, logistics or other types of support are engaged in varying levels of direct action in hostilities. Rumsfeld premised his argument for outsourcing military work on the notion that the DoD would benefit from focusing solely on 'warfighting'. This seemingly excludes contractors from taking 'direct part in hostilities'. However, as civilian contractors bear arms, protect key military and political figures, and take a dominant role in the reconstruction of Iraq, it is hard to sustain the argument that contractors are not playing a 'direct' role. The DoD constructs its legal argument by interpreting legal ambiguity to its advantage. The separation between combatant and civilian is essential to humanitarian law – its purpose is not only to limit civilian causalities but to reflect the fact that soldiers operate on behalf of the state.

The relation of civilian contractors to the state is revealed by analyzing whether or not contractors qualify for prisoner of war status. The DoD guide asserts that

4 Article 47 of Protocol Additional to the Geneva Conventions.

5 United Nations International Convention against the Recruitment, Use, Financing, and Training of Mercenaries.

6 Protocol Additional to the Geneva Conventions, Article 43.

7 Ibid., Article 51.

they do, as does Judge Advocate Joseph Perlak's opinion in a *Military Law Review* article (Perlak 2001). Perlak argues that 'prisoner of war status is accorded to persons who accompany the armed forces without actually being members thereof, such as … supply contractors (and) members of labor units … provided they have received authorization, from the armed forces which they accompany, who shall provide them for that purpose with an identity card' (Perlak 2001, 111). Instead of analysing the ambiguous legal and military role the contractors play, Perlak reduces the issue of legal identity and protection to the provision of an identity card. For the DoD and a military judge, a US-issued identity card is all that is necessary to be granted protection in an ambiguous position.

However, the identity and role of the civilian contractors in action is much more complicated. Scahill describes the Blackwater security guards protecting the head of the CPA, Paul Bremer:

> Blackwater's men brought a singularly Yankee flair to the Bremer job and, by most accounts, embodied the ugly American persona to a tee. Its guards were chiseled like bodybuilders and wore tacky, wraparound sunglasses. Many wore goatees and dressed in all-khaki uniforms with ammo vests or Blackwater T-shirts with the trademark bear claw in the cross-hairs, sleeves rolled up … their haircuts were short, and they sported security earpieces and lightweight machine guns. They bossed around journalists and ran Iraqi cars off the road or fired rounds at cars if they got in the way of a Blackwater convoy. (Scahill 2007, 71)

In this instance, the corporate logo replaces the military uniform. While the DoD guide recommends a processing centre that would issue identification cards for the contractors upon arrival in Iraq, this requirement is conditional to the Under Secretary's approval. Contractors are not regularly vetted and processed through any administrative or legal channels. The legal categories in the Geneva Conventions are reinterpreted by the DoD in order to take advantage of the protections they provide without clarifying the legal status of the contractors or their legal obligations. The state is thus able to protect its interests through its authoritative interpretation of the law. However, the private companies are also able to deploy the legal categories to their benefit. By at once side-stepping the international laws regarding mercenarism and the national protocol regarding processing and tracking, the private sector operates in a vacuum of law.

This vacuum can be understood in two ways. First, it can be argued that no law could have the power to effectively outlaw, or even to regulate, the private military companies. The flows of capital, profit, and violence move too quickly among transnational players to make effective regulation possible. Any regulation would need to be self-generated by the discourse of the private companies themselves. Alternatively, it could be argued that law does have the power to regulate, and if necessary limit, the activities of private military companies; however, the state lacks the motivation and political will to do so. In either interpretation, the validity of the law is dependent on the authority of greater (political or economic) actors.

Ultimately, it is the construction of legal categories that is vital to how the Geneva Conventions are deployed. Article 43 of Protocol I of the Geneva Convention provides that 'armed forces will be subject to an internal disciplinary system that, inter alia, shall enforce compliance with the rules of international law applicable in armed conflict'. This requirement reveals a key assumption of the Geneva Convention's civilian-combatant categories. Civilian contractors do not work in uniform or under the direct control of the military chain of command.[8] Prisoner-of-war status is granted to those operating on behalf of and under the authority of the state. Civilian contractors are operating on behalf of the state, yet they are not regulated as such. None the less, the state constructs their position so that they can receive legal protection denied to other ambiguous actors.

The category of 'unlawful enemy combatant' has been applied to actors resisting American occupation as a justification for the denial of Geneva protections. The state is able to authoritatively interpret international law and apply it to protect its interests. Baxi addresses this in his analysis of the war on terror and its effects on international law:

> At the technical juridico-political level, the foundations of the 'new' international law are being laid through a complex mosaic of the individual and collective right to 'preemptive' self-defense, justifications for the use of UN unsanctioned use of force for the violent achievement of 'regime change', and the equally violent disregard for the hitherto relatively settled norms of international humanitarian law. (Baxi 2005, 35)

Agency in changing international humanitarian law in each instance is framed in terms of the absolute power of violence. When Baxi refers to the 'individual and collective right to preemptive self-defense', he is referring to the invasion of Iraq on a broad scale; however, this 'justification' echoes the DoD guide, which allows the use of arms by civilian contractors for unspecified self-defence purposes. The 'use of UN unsanctioned force' can likewise be read as applying to both the general invasion of Iraq and the specific usage of civilian contractors, whose status as would-be mercenaries is outlawed by the UN. Finally, the 'violent disregard … of international humanitarian law' is seen in the states' reinterpretation of the Geneva Conventions.

A military law analyst observed that 'legally speaking, [military contractors] fall into the same grey area as the unlawful combatants detained at Guantanamo Bay' (Singer 2005, 126). By granting civilian contractors working for the US protected status while simultaneously denying protection to other actors in equally ambiguous legal positions, the DoD interprets and applies international law to solidify its occupation of another state. However, in seemingly strengthening and protecting its own interests, it creates a power that is incapable of being regulated

8 Recent legal changes to place contractors under the Uniform Code of Military Justice will be addressed further below.

by the state. As we will see by analysing US national legislation with regard to private military companies, the power to regulate these companies may exist only on the international level. However, instead of international law providing that regulation, it may be the market.

US Legislation: MEJA

The Military Extraterritorial Jurisdiction Act of 2000 grants the US jurisdiction over contractors in certain instances. Contractors accompanying or employed by the Armed Forces outside the United States can be tried in US courts for offences that would be punishable by more than one year of imprisonment. However, since its passage seven years ago, 'prosecutors appear to be reluctant to pursue such cases' (Chesterman and Lehnardt 2007, 252). Judge Advocate Perlak writes that 'there is a dearth of doctrine, procedure, and policy on just how this new criminal statute will affect the way military does business with contractors' (Perlak 2001, 95). While business with contractors has increased drastically since the passage of the act, legal prosecution of contractors remains rare. Federal prosecutors have not yet used MEJA for any alleged misconduct of contractors operating in Iraq (Peters 2006, 367).

Douglas Brooks, the President of the International Peace Operations Association (IPOA),[9] referenced this lack of prosecution under MEJA at a Congressional hearing: 'It is important to highlight the value and the potential of MEJA .... MEJA has been challenged by critics, primarily for the small number of prosecuted cases. IPOA members believe that MEJA can work, but would support improvements and expansions as we have in the past.'[10] Brooks, on behalf of the firms represented by the IPOA, supports the expansion of MEJA. Instead of addressing criticisms of why the Act has not produced prosecution, Brooks aligns his interests under the authority of the state to regulate the industry. The question of whether the state's legal apparatus is capable of regulating the industry is not addressed. Brooks is able to claim legitimacy by supporting government regulation although that regulation cannot be meaningfully enforced.

MEJA operates on the dichotomy between public and private that is essential to modern governance and business. The IPOA takes advantage of the public–private dichotomy by placing itself on both sides. MEJA regulates felony misconduct of contractors by placing them under US jurisdiction. In this instance, private military companies and the contractors they employ are liable as private entities to US laws. Simultaneously, the IPOA constructs its position as a public entity serving the military, and therefore immune to prosecution. The language of regulation

9 The IPOA is the private security/military firm's lobbying and regulatory body.

10 US House Committee on Government Reform: Subcommittee on National Security, Emerging Threats, and International Relations, *Congressional Testimony by Doug Brooks*. Hearing, 13 June 2006, p. 4.

is deployed to gain legitimacy, while actual prosecution is avoided by claiming government immunity.

In a recent case, the families of three US soldiers killed in the crash of a Blackwater plane in Afghanistan sought compensation from Blackwater in a wrongful death suit (*McMahon et al.* v. *Presidential Airways Inc. et al.* 2006[11]). Blackwater[12] argued that it is immune from tort litigation under the Feres Doctrine, which 'grants the government sovereign immunity from tort suits for injuries to servicemen where the injuries arise out of or are in the course of activity incident to service' (Scahill 2007, 251). Blackwater argued that the men died in service to the DoD, and therefore their families could not sue for wrongful death compensation. While Judge Antoon denied this application of the Feres Doctrine, he noted that 'the extent to which for-profit corporations, performing traditional military functions, are entitled to protection from tort liability is an area of interest to the political branches'.[13] The court rejected the claim for immunity; however, it also indicated the need for legislative clarification on the relationship between for-profit corporations and the typically state functions they perform that are granted prosecutorial immunity.

As noted above, the 2006 Quadrennial Defense Review classifies private military companies as part of the 'Total Force' of the US Armed Forces. MEJA places civilian contractors under US jurisdiction as private entities. In both cases, private military firms are able to evade prosecution by claiming they are alternatively public or private entities. While the companies benefit from the legitimacy afforded by US regulation, the individuals operating on the battlefield and those affected by their actions are left in a legal vacuum.

US Legislation: The Uniform Code of Military Justice

Article 2 of the UCMJ allows jurisdiction over 'persons serving with or accompanying an armed force in the field', but only 'in time of war'. Although the global 'war on terror' is constantly invoked by American politicians in justifying the invasion and occupation of Iraq, Congress has yet to formally declare war in Iraq, and has not done so since the Second World War. This exempted civilian contractors from the UCMJ, until Senator Graham inserted an amendment to the National Defense Authorization Act for Fiscal Year 2007 which expanded the UCMJ to cover civilians accompanying the force in a 'declared war or contingency operations'.[14] This expansion of the UCMJ creates a number of legal

11 No. 05-CV-1002, 2006 WL 194175 (MD Fla. 24 January 2006).

12 The Chair of the IPOA's Board of Directors is Chris Taylor, who also serves as the Vice President of Blackwater.

13 Judge Antoon, Order denying Blackwater's motions, 27 September 2006.

14 National Defense Authorization Act for Fiscal Year 2007, 109th Congress, 120 STAT 2217, *Public Law*, 17 October 2006,: 109–364.

questions. First, it is not clear whether this provision applies to civilian contractors not working for the Defense Department. More importantly, it radically expands a legal framework narrowly designed for individuals operating under the military chain of command who have explicitly relinquished their constitutional rights in joining the Armed Forces. The expansion of the UCMJ is further complicated by the increasing recruitment of third-country nationals by private military companies. Applying the UCMJ to non-American private citizens is a radical expansion of its use. The UCMJ is not designed to be applied to private individuals. Campbell writes that expanding the UCMJ to cover civilians is an 'egregious suspension of the supremacy of civilian constitutional authority', and is 'tantamount to an admission by the political leadership that it has reduced the military to a point which requires the creation of a true, contracted "Shadow Military"' (Campbell 2000). The outsourcing called for in the 2001 Quadrennial Defense Review successfully reduced the military. However, its corresponding legal framework cannot be outsourced as seamlessly.

Writing before the expansion of the UCMJ, Peters argues for 'courts-martial jurisdiction over a very narrow class of government contractors' (Peters 2006, 371). Peters argues that the Supreme Court's standard of precluding military jurisdiction over civilians except when war has been declared by Congress is 'outdated and misunderstood' (Peters 2006, 372). Peters cloaks his argument in divisive and provocative language, referring to the invasion of Iraq as 'the war against Islamist terrorism' (Peters 2006, 372). Peters writes:

> in a dark time, when the jurisdiction of military tribunal is decried even over unlawful foreign combatants captured in a theater of battle – whose stated aim remains the massacre of as many American citizens as possible – any courts-martial option for civilians, however limited the category, is likely unthinkable for some. (Peters 2006, 398)

The expansion of the UCMJ is masked in a language of fear. The political role of civilian contractors is obscured by Peter's dramatic language of massacred Americans and terrorism. Instead of analysing contractors' dual role as private civilians performing public duties, Peters grants them political authority as a part of the broad and undefined 'war on terrorism'. For the UCMJ to be applied to civilians outside of wartime also erodes Congress's powers in the oversight of war. It expands the executive branch's power over war, and blurs the separation of powers by placing an expanded judicial mechanism under the executive branch.

The expanded UCMJ has a number of implications that undermine the traditional separation of powers and threaten the rights of private citizens. However, the lack of prosecution under MEJA foreshadows the difficulty of prosecuting contractors under the UCMJ. Supreme Court and military court precedents demonstrate the difficulty of prosecuting civilians under the UCMJ. In *Reid* v. *Covert*,[15] the

15 354 US 1 (1957).

Supreme Court held that the Fifth and Sixth Amendments protect US citizens abroad, precluding military prosecution which is based on trial without a jury. In another seminal case, *United States* v. *Averette* (1970),[16] the Court of Military Appeals held that 'the words "in time of war" mean … a war formally declared by Congress'. Averette was a civilian contractor working at a US Army Camp in the Republic of South Vietnam accused of a plot to steal government-owned property. He was tried and convicted under the UCMJ. However, the appeal found that the military trial court has no jurisdiction over the civilian defendant. The prosecution of a civilian under the UCMJ would be unconstitutional and in opposition to precedent. Eugene Fidell, the President of the National Institute of Military Justice, says of the expansion of the UCMJ: 'ultimately, if this power is used, it will create a substantial issue that would likely reach the Supreme Court, and it will put us at odds with contemporary international standards' (Stockman 2007).[17] Accountability for contractors and their employees will likely not be found in domestic (civil or military) legal frameworks. To take one example, charges have yet to be filed against the Blackwater contractors involved in the September 2007 shooting in which 17 unarmed Iraqis were killed. Although this incident has received the most media attention and generated awareness in the general public, there has been no meaningful legal action to hold those responsible for the deaths accountable. Furthermore, in May 2008 Blackwater had its contract with the State Department renewed, after which Patrick Kennedy, the Under Secretary of State for Management, explained to the *New York Times* that 'if contractors were removed, we would have to leave Iraq'.[18] Through outsourcing, the state has become completely dependent on private military companies. In doing so, the state has simultaneously outsourced regulation of these companies as the state's legal mechanisms have proven incapable of providing accountability.

Contracts and Codes of Conduct: Self-generating Regulatory Mechanisms

One inherent contradiction of placing civilians under the UCMJ is the problem of the chain of command. Private military companies can abandon or suspend operations if the work becomes too dangerous or unprofitable. Their employees can choose to walk off a job. While soldiers must obey the military chain of command, contracts are the governing force between the civilian employees, private military firms, and the government. These contracts frame the flows of capital and violence managed by the private military firms. Contracts are the product of interaction between supplier firms and the government. There are many instances of fraud, corruption and abuse stemming from the allocation and fulfilment of contracts in

16 19 CMA 365 (1970).

17 F. Stockman, 'Contractors in War Zones Lose Immunity', *Boston Globe*, 7 January 2007.

18 'Blackwater's Impunity', *New York Times*, 16 May 2008.

Iraq. In a transparent competitive market, these instances of abuse and fraud would taint the reputation of the company and limit its future opportunities. However, the market for contracting opportunities in Iraq developed quickly and without the transparency and competition necessary for an efficient, fully functioning market. Furthermore, it is disingenuous to place fraud, corruption and abuse outside the provision of the contract and the contracting procedure. Private military companies are motivated by profit. What would be considered inefficient or corrupt for the government or the military can be considered legitimate and necessary in the private sector. The regulation generated by the industry will not be regulation in the sense of providing transparency and accountability for the greater good of the public. Rather, regulation will be generated in accordance with the production of profit.

The absorption of human rights language by the IPOA does not reflect a commitment to the greater good envisioned by human rights documents. Rather, it reflects the business opportunity of the profitmaking potential of corporate social responsibility. Friedman (1962) wrote that a corporation's only responsibility is to maximize profits for its shareholders; to act otherwise is to undermine the functioning of a market economy. However, in this instance, the language of corporate social responsibility legitimizes the actions of an industry operating on morally and legally ambiguous territory. By incorporating principles of international law and pushing for national regulatory legislation that have no meaningful application, the private military industry at once creates and legitimizes the market in which it profits. This symbiosis between human rights and business is reflected in an article by Mary Robinson (2007). Robinson relates several articles of the Universal Declaration of Human Rights to the business interests they protect. Robinson translates equality, the right to own property, the right to freedom of thought and other basic human rights principles into market advantages for businesses willing to respect them. While human rights were traditionally constructed as state obligations, the absorption of human rights language by various industries and their growing power to protect or abuse human rights indicates a shifting agency. Instead of the traditional 'vertical' obligation from the state, human rights are being deployed by a range of private transnational interests.

Conclusion: Transnational Flows of Violence and Capital

Teubner (2006) analyses to what extent human rights can be applied to private transnational enterprises. The principle of 'state action doctrine' binds private actors to human rights obligations if 'the private actors perform some public functions' (Teubner 2006, 329). Teubner argues that this type of public-to-private outsourcing is more evident on the domestic level. On the transnational level, 'the State influence on private actors is more indirect, more distant, so that the doctrine of state action has only a limited scope of application' (Teubner 2006, 329). He calls for a new conception of human rights, away from the divisional vertical–

horizontal application model which cannot easily be applied to the fluid, shifting power structures of transnational enterprise. Teubner elaborates on this model:

> Society's internal divisions should be understood … as resulting from the interrelations of communicative networks with their environment. Actual people are not at the centre of these networks, nor can they get back inside them. People are the *environment* for communicative networks, to whose operations they are exposed without being able to control them. (Teubner 2006, 333)

This evokes Singer's description of private military companies quoted above.[19] The structure, or the network, generates the action of individuals. Human rights are used internally by the structures in order to legitimize their market and claim to power. However, the purpose of human rights is not the pursuit of profit; it is the protection of equality and dignity. Teubner argues that for human rights to function in this sense, they must 'transcend the boundaries of communication – a simultaneously impossible and necessary task' (Teubner 2006, 333–4). The human rights obligations of non-state actors cannot be determined in a strictly juridical way. In the case of private military companies, the role of the state has been to shield the industry from meaningful human rights obligations. The state blocks the application of human rights law, while simultaneously the industry absorbs human rights language to legitimize its status.

For the most part, this chapter argues that the flows of violence and capital generated by the private military industry are not being regulated by the government. National legislation is emptied of prosecutorial power, while the relevant international regulation is interpreted in such a way as to diminish its regulatory capabilities. This can be normatively understood as a failure of state power in the face of an increasingly powerful private sector or as the intentional outsourcing of state responsibilities. In either analysis, traditional understandings of the state are thrown into question. The state loses its brief monopoly on the legitimate use of international violence. The foundational assumption of sovereignty has to be analysed in relation to the implication of privatized warfare. To echo the framework proposed by Riles (1994) at the beginning of the chapter, an alternatively normative and reflexive analysis of these trends reveals the foundational assumptions of the modern sovereign state. Ultimately, the rise of private military companies occurs on the back of capital. While mercenarism was outlawed in the twentieth century through the regulation of individuals, mercenarism in the twenty-first century will only be outlawed through the regulation of enterprise and capital. Sovereignty must be reframed to include not only the legitimacy it derives from its individual citizens and its ability to regulate their behaviour, but also from its ability to regulate the surrounding flows of capital. Whether the state lacks only the political will or the actual power to enforce such regulation remains to be seen.

19 'As for [private military firms,] it is not the people who matter but the structure they are within'; Singer (2001/2002), 192.

References

Baxi, U. (2005), '"The War *on* Terror" and the "War *of* Terror": Nomadic Multitudes, Aggressive Incumbents, and the "New" International Law', *Osgoode Hall Law Journal* 43: 8–43.

Campbell, G. (2000), 'Contractors on the Battlefield: The Ethics of Paying Civilians to Enter Harm's Way and Requiring Soldiers to Depend upon Them', paper presented at Joint Services Conference on Professional Ethics, Springfield, VA, 27–28 January 2000.

Chesterman, S. and Lehnardt, C. (2007), *From Mercenaries to Market: The Rise and Regulation of Private Military Companies*, Oxford: Oxford University Press.

Department of Defense (1997), *Quadrennial Defense Review Report*, 19 May.

—— (2001), *Quadrennial Defense Review Report*, 30 September.

—— (2006), *Quadrennial Defense Review Report*, 6 February.

Fenwick, C.G. (1948), *Neutrality Laws of the United States*, Washington, DC: Carnegie Endowment for International Peace.

Friedman, M. (1962), *Capitalism and Freedom*, Chicago, IL: University of Chicago Press.

Government Accountability Office (GAO) (2006), 'Military Operations: High-level DOD Action Needed to Address Long-standing Problems with Management and Oversight of Contractors Supporting Deployed Forces', GAO-07-145, December.

Heller, J. (2004 [1961]), *Catch-22*, New York: Simon & Schuster.

Kinsey, C. (2006), *Corporate Soldiers and International Security*, New York: Routledge.

Krieg, K. (2005), 'Contractor Personnel Authorized to Accompany the US Armed Forces', Department of Defense Instruction Guide 3020.413, October.

Perlak, J. (2001), 'The Military Extraterritorial Jurisdiction Act of 2000: Implications for Contractor Personnel', *Military Law Review* 169: 92–140.

Peters, W.C. (2006), 'Courts-martial for Civilian Contractors Misconduct', *Brigham Young University Law Review*: 367–414.

Riles, A. (1994), 'Representing In-between: Law, Anthropology, and the Rhetoric of Interdisciplinarity', *University of Illinois Law Review* 3: 597–650.

Roberts, A. (2005), 'The End of Occupation: Iraq 2004', *ICLQ* 54: 27–48.

Robinson, M. (2007), 'The Business Case for Human Rights', *Visions of Ethical Business*, <www.unhchr.ch/huricane/huricane.nsf/view01/E47D352DEDC39697802566DE0043B28E?opendocument>, accessed 30 January 2009.

Rumsfeld, D. (2002), 'Transforming the Military', *Foreign Affairs* May/June: 20–32.

Scahill, J. (2007), *Blackwater*, New York: Nation Books.

Singer, P.W. (2001/2002), 'Corporate Warriors: The Rise of the Privatized Military Industry and its Ramifications for International Security', *International Security*, Winter: 186–220.

—— (2005), 'Outsourcing War', *Foreign Affairs*, March/April: 119–32.

Teubner, G. (1996), 'Global Bukowina: Legal Pluralism in the World Society', in G. Teubner (ed.), *Global Law without a State*, Brookfield: Dartmouth Publishing, pp. 3–28.

—— (2006), 'The Anonymous Matrix: Human Rights Violations by "Private" Transnational Actors', *Modern Law Review* 69(3): 327–46.

Thomson, J. (1996), *Mercenaries, Pirates, and Sovereigns*, Princeton, NJ: Princeton University Press.

US House Committee on Government Reform: Subcommittee on National Security, Emerging Threats, and International Relations, *Congressional Testimony by Doug Brooks*, Hearing, 13 June 2006, <http://ipoaonline.org/en/gov/ipoa-shays.pdf>, accessed 30 January 2009.

Weber, M. (1964), *The Theory of Social and Economic Organization*, trans. A.M. Henderson and T. Parsons, New York: Free Press.

Chapter 4

Laws of Suspicion: Legal Status, Space and the Impossibility of Separation in the Israeli-occupied West Bank[1]

Tobias Kelly

On the northern fringes of Jerusalem, between an airport and a refugee camp, stands Qalandia checkpoint. Before the start of the second *intifada* in late September 2000 there was no permanent Israeli military presence at Qalandia. However, as the *intifada* progressed, a newly created checkpoint turned from a few concrete blocks to a sprawl of turnstiles, watch-towers, offices and loading bays. In order to pass through, people had to show identity cards and permits, as well as often have their bags and vehicles searched. Although the checkpoint is one of the busiest in the West Bank, it is merely one of scores that have been set up in the region by the Israeli military over the last few years in an attempt to separate Israelis and Palestinians in the name of Israeli 'security'. Qalandia presents a particular problem, as there are areas of the Israeli municipality of Jerusalem and the West Bank to the north and south of the checkpoint. As a result, Israeli and West Bank identity card holders live on both sides of the checkpoint. The soldiers stationed there are therefore faced with the complex task of deciding who is and who is not allowed to pass. The checkpoint is often the scene of fierce and sometimes violent arguments between soldiers and people seeking to pass, as they debate the meanings of implications of particular identity cards, permits, documents and regulations. Despite its particularities, Qalandia reflects wider processes that can be found across Israel/Palestine.

This chapter explores how Israeli security policies since the start of the second *intifada* have been produced particular configurations of legal status and insecurity. A system of control has been created that has attempted to codify the populations of the West Bank and control their movement through an understanding of 'security' threats rooted in irreconcilable ethnic difference (Zureik 2001; Kelly 2006a). Security strategies are therefore aimed at containing Palestinians and segregating them from Israelis. At the same time, however, these attempts at segregation run up against the legacy of other Israeli security policies, namely the dependency of Palestinians on the Israeli economy and the creation of Israeli settlements across

1 I would like to thank Julia Eckert for her insightful comments, which have helped to clarify and develop the arguments in this chapter.

the West Bank. In this context, checkpoints, patrols and barriers try to separate Israelis and Palestinians who live and work within sight of each other. Attempts to manage whole populations through the regulation of space can themselves never be complete. Not only are classifications always partial (Bauman 2001), but space itself is also only given significance through constantly shifting social relations (Lefebvre 1991). The result is an uneasy relationship between spatial control, categories of person and perceptions of danger, as perceived threats constantly seep into 'zones of safety'. Rather than creating a straightforward mapping of legal status and suspicion, the legal infrastructure of Israeli security in the West Bank creates its own forms of insecurity. Faced with the inability to make legal status and location map onto one another, the security regime is forced to rely on ever more violence methods to keep people in place.

The first section of this chapter explores the logic behind Israeli 'security' policies in the West Bank, and how the tensions inherent in this logic have driven the legal regime developed by the Israeli military in the region. The second section explores how throughout the 1980s and 1990s, the tensions inherent in this regime saw the reordering of the system of legal control, with often violent outcomes, eventually resulting in a model of 'punitive segregation'. The final and longest section examines how these processes worked out in the context of one small area of the West Bank centred on the checkpoint at Qalandia.

Punitive Segregation: Management of Space and People

The proliferation of identity documents and checkpoints across the West Bank can be seen as part of a process of 'punitive segregation' (Garland 2001). Since the early 1990s, and particularly since the start of the second *intifada* in September 2000, there have been attempts to physically separate Palestinians from Israelis, based on the assumption that Palestinians are irredeemably hostile to Israel, and present a fundamental threat both to individual Israelis and the Israeli state. According to this logic, Palestinians cannot be reformed or persuaded, and the only solution is separation. The stress is put on the incapacitation, punishment and segregation of a 'dangerous' population. The focus is on excluding potentially disruptive actions, rather than transforming behaviour, with the focus on whole populations rather than individuals. As part of this concern to reduce the risks represented by such dangerous populations, numerous techniques are developed in order to identify and separate potentially dangerous subjects. The mapping of legal status onto space plays a central role in such attempts at punitive segregation. Through the regulation of movement across space, zones of relative safety can be created for 'responsible citizens' (compare, in another context, Merry 2001; Feeley and Simon 1992).

The notion of 'punitive segregation' has of course been developed in the context of the criminal justice systems of North America and Northern Europe. In the West Bank, the policy of separation has to be understood within the broader context of the policies of the Israeli military. However, as Armstrong and McAra (2006) point out, the boundaries between criminal justice and militarization are often porous. In particular, the 'security' policies of the Israeli military have largely followed a 'criminological' model (Hajjar 2005). Whilst in the early years of the twenty-first century the actions of the Israeli military, in the shape of assassinations and the deployment of tanks, increasingly looked like those of open warfare, the use of mass arrest, imprisonment and trials have historically been the dominant approaches. The Israeli military has by and large sought to treat Palestinian nationalism as a 'law and order' issue.

Crucially, however, attempts at punitive segregation never exist in isolation, but always take place alongside alternative models of social control. The sedimented history of security policies on the West Bank often works against the desire for separation. After the 1967 occupation, Palestinian labourers were encouraged to work in unskilled and semi-skilled positions in agriculture and construction inside Israel. At the same time, the Palestinian economy was suffering from massive under-investment, and was left uncompetitive by the new taxation systems introduced by the Israeli military (Bornstein 2002). By the 1990s, thousands of Palestinian men were going to work in Israel on a daily basis. This flow of Palestinians into the Israeli economy would only be reversed in the mid-1990s, first with the creation of the Palestinian National Authority (PNA) in 1994, and later with the start of the second *intifada* in September 2000.[2] This integration of the Palestinian population into the Israeli economy gave Israeli employers a much-needed source of cheap labour, and for the Israeli military played an important 'security' role by maximizing the cost of any resistance to Israeli rule. At the same time, scores of Israeli settlements were built across the West Bank, motivated by a mixture of perceived security considerations, a messianic return to the land, and the need for cheap housing. By the late 1990s there were nearly 400,000 Israeli citizens living in the West Bank in over 150 settlements. The consequence of this was that thousands of Israeli citizens lived within a stone's throw of Palestinian areas and used the same roads as Palestinians as they made their way around the West Bank. The Israeli army and hundreds of thousands of Israeli settlers share the same space as the Palestinian population of the West Bank. Attempts to separate Palestinians and Israelis therefore come up against the economic and territorial integration of the two populations.

2 These restrictions in access to the Israeli economy have seen the Palestinian economy collapse. By 2001, a UN report estimated that over 40 per cent of the West Bank and Gaza's population has experienced 'economic distress' since the start of the *intifada*, with unemployment rising to 38 per cent (United Nations Special Co-ordinator for the Occupied Territories 2001, 10–11).

The Legal Infrastructure of Rule

The 1967 occupation of the West Bank by the Israeli military created a contradiction between territorial presence and the control of a potentially hostile population. Israeli control over the newly occupied Jordan valley, as well as the hills of the West Bank, was seen by the Israeli military as crucial for Israeli 'security' (Shlaim 2000, 256). Furthermore, many people inside Israel saw the presence of Israeli troops in the West Bank, and Jerusalem in particular, not as an occupation, but as the 'liberation' of historic Israeli territory. However, these claims to the territory of the West Bank faced the problem of what to do with the Palestinian residents of the area. To annex the West Bank to Israel and to give them citizenship would have undermined the Jewish majority in Israel, which was a central tenet of mainstream Zionism. On the other hand, to annex the West Bank and not to grant the Palestinian residents citizenship would have contradicted the claim that Israel was a democracy. The result of this tension has been the construction of a 'dual legal system' (Benvinisti 1990), through which the West Bank was not formally annexed to Israel, but the protection of Israeli law and the Israeli state was extended to Israeli citizens in the West Bank. Under this legal regime, one system of law covered Israeli citizens, and another covered the Palestinian 'residents' of the region (see Kelly 2006b).

Through a succession of legislative developments, Israeli courts and Israeli law have been given concurrent jurisdiction over the West Bank. Using the legal State of Emergency that had existed in Israel since 1948 (Hofnung 1996, 49), the Israeli government issued a number of regulations that extended Israeli law to Israeli citizens in the West Bank.[3] Although these laws were, in theory, concurrent with the laws in force in the West Bank and did not replace them, in practice Israeli courts became inclined to assume jurisdiction wherever there was the slightest link between the case and Israel or Israeli citizens (Shehadeh 1994, 20). Crucially, the Palestinian 'residents' of the region were excluded from this extra-territorial coverage of Israeli law, as the legislation explicitly excluded those not registered on the Israeli population registry.[4] In this process, the West Bank was not formally annexed to Israeli, but Israeli citizens were covered by Israeli law by a form of personal jurisdiction that followed them across the West Bank.

Palestinians, on the other hand, were governed under a mixture of the existing laws of the West Bank, which became frozen after the occupation, and the ever-growing system of military law and regulation. The Defence (Emergency) Regulations, which dated back to the British Mandate, gave military commanders the right to abrogate many legal rights, as well as allow detention without trial and the use of collective punishments such as house demolition. Hundreds of

---

3 Emergency Regulations (Areas Held by the Defence Army of Israel – Criminal Jurisdiction and Legal Assistance) 1967.

4 Israeli Emergency Regulations (Judea, Samaria and Gaza-Adjudication of Offences and Legal Aid, 5727–1967).

further regulations were passed by the Israeli Military Administration in the West Bank. These regulations gave local military commanders extensive powers to declare areas closed military zones and to detain 'suspects'. At the same time, the Jordanian criminal law that was in force before the Israeli occupation remained in place, and nominally covered non-security-related criminal acts. However, the military courts increasingly prosecuted 'ordinary' criminal issues as well (Hajjar 2005).

The distinction between the two different levels of rights and responsibilities inherent in the dual legal system was enforced through the creation of an elaborate system of identity cards and permits (Kelly 2006a; 2006b). Israeli citizens and those entitled to Israeli 'residency' were issued with blue identity cards. Palestinians who lived in the West Bank and were on the West Bank population registry were given orange identity cards. In 1988, after the outbreak of the first *intifada*, green identity cards were issued to those Palestinians who had previously been detained by the Israeli military. The presentation of identity cards was critical in order to pass through checkpoints or obtain access to many resources. It was also an offence not to present an identity card when requested to do so by a member of the Israeli military.

The Contradictions of Occupation

Although the dual legal system went some way to mitigating the tensions between economic, territorial and social integration on the one hand, and political exclusion on the other, it was not without its own contradictions. In this context, the system of rule developed in the West Bank has gone through several changes. In late 1987, civil disturbances broke out across the West Bank and Gaza Strip, marking the start of the first *intifada.* The long-term effect of this violence was to create increased calls from inside Israel for the physical separation of Israelis and Palestinians. In the short term, however, the Israeli military, originally caught off guard by the extent of the civilian uprising, responded with the full array of powers established by the military legal regime that had been developed over the previous twenty years. In response to then Minister of Defence Rabin's famous call to use 'might, force and beatings' to suppress the uprising, the Israeli military begun to deploy more widely, to implement the regulations that already existed more forcefully, and to pass a whole new set of regulations. Mass arrest, deportations, curfews and closures became ever more common. Particular use was made of the ability to declare curfews and create closed military zones in order to control the movement of people around the West Bank. Hundreds of thousands of people were also detained under administrative detention, and nine detention centres were set up across the West Bank, Gaza and Israel.

The first *intifada* had created a strategic quandary for the Israeli military. Although the occupation of the West Bank had given it 'strategic depth' by expanding the territory it controlled, it has also meant that it now had to deal with a hostile and largely unwanted population in the shape of the Palestinian residents of the West Bank. The presence of Israeli settlements across the West Bank, partly justified originally for 'security' reasons, also raised questions about how the Israeli Military could protect the Israeli citizens who lived within them. Calls increased across the Israeli political spectrum for harsher action against the uprising and for economic and political separation between Israelis and Palestinians. The 1988 general election, for example, saw the extreme-right Moledet party, which advocated the 'transfer' of Palestinians, winning seats in the Knesset. Less extreme voices called for greater administrative and economic separation between Israelis and Palestinians. The first move towards this was seen in 1991, with the cancelling of the collective permit which Palestinians had used in order to enter Israel, and the setting up of permanent checkpoints along the Green Line (which separated the West Bank from Israel proper) for the first time since 1967.

The tensions between territorial integration and economic dependency on the one hand and the call for political separation on the other were partially, if temporarily, eased by the Oslo Peace Process of the 1990s. Under the Oslo Agreements between the Israeli government and the Palestinian Liberation Organization, the newly formed Palestinian National Authority (PNA) was given partial control over many areas of Palestinian life in the West Bank. Crucially, however, the Israeli state did not give up its claim to the territory of the West Bank. In many ways, the Oslo Accords merely formalized processes that already existed, by allowing the regulated flow of Palestinian labour into the Israeli economy and the continued expansion of Israeli settlements in the West Bank, but strengthening political separation.

In the absence of clear territorial boundaries, the Oslo Accords attempted to make forms of legal status the basis of the distinctions between the jurisdictions of the Israeli state and the PNA. At a territorial level, the West Bank was divided into three areas, A, B and C. Most of the large centres of Palestinian population stood in Area A. Area B was mostly made up of Palestinian villages. The areas in between, making up most of the West Bank, fell in Area C. In Area A, the PNA was responsible for civil matters and policing. The PNA was also given civil control over areas such as education and health, and some security responsibilities were shared with the Israeli military in Area B. In Area C, the Israeli army maintained both security and civil jurisdiction. Crucially, a divided jurisdiction over persons cut across and effectively overruled this divided territorial jurisdiction. The PNA would be responsible for West Bank identity card holders in the West Bank, and the Israeli government would be responsible for Israeli identity card holders. Israeli identity card holders were due the protection of Israeli law and Israeli courts, no matter where they were in the West Bank. PNA law and the PNA courts covered West Bank identity card holders in the West Bank.[5]

The Oslo Accords were above all a 'security' agreement. Indeed, the Israeli delegation that negotiated the main details of the Accords was headed by an Israeli

5 Gaza Strip–Jericho Agreement 1994, Protocol Concerning Legal Matters, Article III.4.

army general. Under the Accords, the PNA was responsible for combating 'terror' in the areas under its jurisdiction. Throughout the mid-1990s, the PNA set up its own security courts, using a mixture of PLO Revolutionary Law and the same Emergency Regulations that the Israeli military had used to establish its own security apparatus. Up to a dozen branches of the PNA police force were established, with the American-trained *Amin Waqa'i* ('Preventive Security') leading the way in the detention of those who opposed the Oslo Process. However, although some partial responsibility for the policing of Palestinians had been handed over to the PNA, the main hallmark of the Oslo Accords was that it allowed the Israeli military to retain overall 'security' control in the West Bank. In particular, Oslo left the infrastructure of military laws and regulations intact.[6] Although the Israeli military relied on the PNA for the detention of many perceived 'security' threats, thousands of Palestinians remained in Israeli jails, the Israeli military retained control over movement around as well as in and out of the West Bank, and continued to conduct military operations, increasingly in the shape of assassinations.

In late September 2000, tensions over the failures of the Oslo Peace process erupted into the violence of the second *intifada.* The Oslo Accords were supposed to be an interim agreement that would eventually lead to final-status negotiations. In the intervening years between the original signing of the Accords and the collapse at Camp David, life in the West Bank had changed considerably. Although Israeli troops were now absent from the centre of Palestinian towns, at the same time there had been nearly a doubling of the number of Israeli settlers in the West Bank, and the standard of living of many Palestinians had decreased dramatically. The second *intifada* started out as clashes between stone-throwing Palestinians and Israeli soldiers on the edges of Palestinian towns, but had slowly descended into shoot-outs between Palestinians and Israeli troops. Whereas previously the Palestinian security forces, with a few notably exceptions, had co-operated with the Israeli military, many sections of the Palestinian police were now actively involved in attacks on the Israeli military, or had gone into hiding, fearing arrest or worse at the hands of Israeli soldiers.

Once again, in the wake of the escalating violence there were increasing calls from inside Israel to physically separate Israelis from Palestinians. In 2000, the then Israeli Prime Minister Barak argued that collapse of the Oslo Peace Process was the result of an 'irrational and intransigent' response by the Palestinians to a reasonable and just offer from the Israelis, and the only option available to the Israeli state was to 'go it alone' (Rabinowitz 2003, 221). The institutional structures produced by Oslo created administrative divisions, but they had also left important issues around the relationship between space, security and legal status unanswered. Furthermore, physical separation was made increasingly difficult by the territorial and economic integration that had developed over thirty years of

6 Article VIII.9 of the Gaza–Jericho agreement states that 'all laws and military orders in effect in the Gaza Strip and Jericho Area prior to the signing of this agreement shall remain in force …'.

occupation. Not only did many Palestinians depend on jobs in Israel in order to make a living, but also hundreds of thousands of Israeli citizens lived across the West Bank in settlements that overlooked Palestinian towns or villages, and had to use the same roads as Palestinians as they made their way to and from work.

The Israeli military responded to this call for physical separation in the face of economic and territorial integration by setting up a complex system of closures, checkpoints and permits, in an attempt to micro-manage the movement of populations that were increasingly seen as irremediably hostile. The long-standing policy of encouraging Palestinians to work in the Israeli economy was reversed, as physical separation was seen as the greatest priority. All Palestinian permits to enter Israel, which had only been intermittently issued over the last six years, were cancelled. Furthermore, checkpoints were established on the edges of all Palestinian towns and villages, controlling access in and out. Trenches were dug, mounds built and roads redirected in an attempt to control where Palestinians could and could not travel, and in doing so keep them away from Israeli citizens. An estimated 47 permanently staffed checkpoints were established across the West Bank (B'Tselem 2004). Some areas were declared closed military zones, where Palestinians, but not Israeli citizens, were prevented from entering. West Bank identity card holders were also banned from using many roads, and increasingly they needed permits in order to pass through the hundreds of checkpoints that were established across the region. In the absence of clear borders, the whole of the West Bank was turned in to an indeterminate border zone.

The limitations of a model of separation built on hundreds of checkpoints and bypass roads was implicitly recognized in the 2002 announcement that a 'security fence' or 'Wall' was going to be built across the West Bank. Importantly, the Wall is seen in some quarters as a form of punishment, not just a means of defence. In this context, the Wall is based on a notion that only through forceful separation can Israel have 'security'. There has also been a partial realignment of Israeli political parties through debates over the necessity of a physical separation between Israelis and Palestinians. The Kadima party was created by Ariel Sharon, bringing together elements of the Likud and Labour parties, with the express aim of creating a lasting and final separation between Israelis and Palestinians. The building of the Wall, alongside the 2005 withdrawal of Israeli troops and the dismantling of Israeli settlements in the Gaza Strip, was part of this process.

The system of governance and 'security' that developed in the West Bank following the Israeli occupation was an attempt to mitigate the tensions of the occupation. A complex system of laws and regulations developed in order to legally separate two deeply integrated populations. Throughout the 1990s, as the tensions between economic dependency and political separation became greater, there was a gradual if incomplete, at least on the Israeli side, economic disengagement. However, the tensions between territorial integration and political separation remained. These became particularly important during the second *intifada*, when, based on the notion that Palestinians represented a violent threat to lives of Israeli citizens, a complex system of spatial control was developed, based primarily on checkpoints and identity cards, in order to try to physically separate the Israeli and Palestinians populations of the West Bank. However, these attempts at physical separation have had to deal with the legacy of previous Israeli security polices that encouraged Palestinian dependence on the Israeli economy and the territorial integration of Israeli and Palestinian populations. The next section of this chapter will explore how this spatialized form of governance developed in one particular area of the West Bank around the Qalandia checkpoint to the north of Jerusalem, and the tensions between citizenship, security and suspicion that this created.

The Organization of Space and Legal Status in Northern Jerusalem

Qalandia checkpoint lies to the south of a refugee camp by the same name, to the north of the Palestinian village of Ar-Ram and the industrial estate of Atarot, and to the east the Israeli settlement of Giv'at Zev. Much, but not all, of this area falls within the disputed Israeli municipal boundaries of Jerusalem. Jerusalem, of course, has an added historic significance within both Palestinian and Israeli national histories. The critical event that marked the start of the second *intifada* was, after all, Ariel Sharon's walk across the Haram as-Sharif and his declaration that Jerusalem was an eternal part of Israel sovereignty. Furthermore, Jerusalem is also an important transport, commercial and cultural centre for both Palestinians and Israelis. Although it is a small area with a very particular political significance, the issues of population and spatial control that it raises are illustrative of much wider processes.

Following the Israeli occupation of the West Bank in 1967 the Knesset declared that it had unified Jerusalem, and extended the boundaries of the municipality of Jerusalem deep into the West Bank. Although the effective annexation of Jerusalem has remained unrecognized by the international community, it was reiterated in 1980 when the Knesset passed the Basic Law: Jerusalem, Capital of Israel. After the annexation of Jerusalem to Israel, the Palestinian residents of the area were given Israeli identity cards, but did not become Israeli citizens. These Israeli identity cards gave the holders the right of residence, but could be taken away at any time if the Israeli Ministry of the Interior decided that the holder's 'centre of life' was no longer in Jerusalem.[7] Those Palestinians who lived outside the newly declared borders of Jerusalem were given West Bank identity cards. The Palestinian residents of Jerusalem and the West Bank were originally Jordanian citizens, but after 1988 Jordan rescinded its claim to Jerusalem and the rest of the West Bank, and all the Palestinian residents of the area became stateless persons.

It is important to note that the newly declared municipal boundaries of Jerusalem did not correspond with an administrative unit that had previously existed, and were far larger than the municipal boundaries of Jerusalem under

7 This would happen with increasing frequency, and according to some estimates over 6,000 people have lost their residency rights in this way.

the British Mandate and the Hashemite Kingdom of Jordan (Lustick 2000). Instead, the new boundaries were a compromise between including as much land as possible and excluding as many Palestinians as was feasible. In the north of Jerusalem, the boundaries jutted out in a long arm. The principal aim of this part of the boundary was to include the area of Atarot. Not only had Atarot been the site of a Jewish settlement prior to 1948, but it also included an airfield. The area around the airfield, however, included the refugee camp of Qalandia, made up of the refugees who had been forced to flee the villages to the west of Jerusalem that fell under Israeli control in 1948. The villages of Ar-Ram, Beit Hanina and Bir Nabala also lay on the road between Atarot and the rest of Jerusalem. In order to include Atarot, but to exclude as many Palestinians as possible, the borders of the new municipality snaked up the main road out of Jerusalem, cutting the villages of Ar-Ram and Beit Hanina and the camp of Qalandia in two.

For much the 1970s and 1980s, the existence of the newly redrawn municipal boundaries would have relatively little impact on the lives of the residents of the area.[8] Both people who lived within the new municipal boundaries of Jerusalem and who lived in the West Bank, and therefore people with Israeli and West Bank identity cards, went to work inside Israel. Many went to work in the newly created industrial estate at Atarot, just to the south of the airport. At the same time, new Israeli settlements were being built across East Jerusalem and the nearby areas. To the south of Atarot, the neighbourhoods of Pisgat Ze'ev and Neve Ya'akov were built, acting as a buffer between the residents of Ar-Ram and Qalandia and the main commercial heart of East Jerusalem. To the west was a settlement called Giv'at Zeev, which although within the West Bank, acted as a commuter suburb for Israelis who could not afford the high rents inside Jerusalem. By 2000 there were nearly 35,000 settlers in Pisgat Zeev, 23,000 in Neve Ya'acov and 12,000 in Giv'at Zev. In East Jerusalem as a whole, by the year 2000 there was an almost equal number of Jews and Arabs, at just under 200,000 in each community.[9] At the same time, new roads were also built that led directly between the new Jewish settlements and bypassed the Palestinian communities.[10] The building of Jewish settlements across East Jerusalem was part of a plan, in the words of the former Israeli mayor, to 'Judaize Jerusalem'.[11] Many Palestinians also saw the placement of Israeli settlements within areas of Palestinian residence as an attempt to break up the feasibility of Jerusalem as a continuous Palestinian city. The Palestinian residents of the area around Qalandia were therefore increasingly surrounded by

8 Perhaps the major difference was that holders of Israeli identity cards were entitled to access to the Israeli social security system.

9 *Statistical Yearbook of Jerusalem* (2000).

10 According to the Master Plan for these roads, their aim was to 'bypass the Arab population'; Ministry of Agriculture and the Settlement Division of the World Zionist Organization (1983), 27.

11 *Ha'aretz*, 2 June 2000.

Israeli settlements and dependent on the Israeli economy, but were not granted full political and civil rights by the Israeli state.

The first *intifada* in the late 1980s and the first Gulf War in the early 1990s saw major changes to the spatial management of the area around Atarot. The collective permit to enter Israel was cancelled, and West Bank identity card holders had to apply for a permit on an individual basis. These permits became increasingly difficult to get hold of, and often they were cancelled completely when the Israeli military declared a 'closure' on the West Bank, usually in apparent response to 'security warnings'. New permanent checkpoints were also established for the first time between Israel and the West Bank. However, the immediate area around Atarot remained largely unaffected. Although the area was within the municipal boundary of Jerusalem, no checkpoint was established on its northern border where Jerusalem gave way to the West Bank town of Ramallah. Instead, a checkpoint was established several kilometres further south, near the village of Beit Hanina and the Israeli settlement of Pisgat Zeev. Although the area around Atarot was formally inside Jerusalem and therefore Israel, in terms of the security policies of the Israeli military, it was for the time being effectively treated as part of the West Bank. The area to the north of the new checkpoint, although technically within Jerusalem, was made up of the homes of Palestinians who held Israeli identity cards, whereas the area to the south was made up of large concentrations of Jewish Israelis. The industrial estate of Atarot could therefore continue to operate as normal, and West Bank identity card holders could continue to go to work there without the difficulties of applying for permits and passing through checkpoints. The largely Israeli owners of the factories that had been established in Atarot benefited from the fact that, in practical terms, their West Bank employees did not have to apply for a permit, and they could therefore avoid paying tax and social security. At the same time, many West Bank identity cards holders settled in the area and married residents with Israeli identity cards, although legally they were not allowed to enter Jerusalem. However, the effective treatment of Attarot as part of the West Bank by the Israeli military meant that those residents of the area who held Israeli identity cards faced the difficulty that if they wanted to travel to the commercial centre of East Jerusalem or the Old City, they had to pass through an Israeli checkpoint that lay to the south.

With the start of the second *intifada* in the late summer of 2000, the area around Atarot became the scene of frequent clashes. Within a few days a checkpoint was set up just to the south of the entrance to Qalandia, on the southern tip of the airport. At first, the checkpoint was made up of a series of concrete blocks, but it slowly developed into a more permanent structure. The road that led through the checkpoint became especially busy following the Israeli military's closure of several other roads in and out of the Palestinian town of Ramallah to the north. Although the checkpoint at Qalandia was often closed, and was blocked permanently at night, there were initially other small back roads that could be taken in order to bypass the Israeli checks, usually taking the small, winding tracks through the refugee camp. With the optimism of the Oslo Accords in the mid-

1990s, a new road was planned that would pass through Atarot, as it connected Tel Aviv directly to Amman. The western section of the road linked to the main Tel Aviv–Jerusalem road, known as Highway 443. With the closing of the other roads, many of the residents of villages to the west also started to use the half-completed Tel Aviv–Amman highway in order to get to their homes. Often, however, the soldiers at the checkpoint would prevent all cars from passing through, only sometimes allowing cars with yellow Israeli plates to pass.

Clashes between school children and Israeli soldiers were common, and there would be running battles as children and soldiers would duck between the cars queuing to get through. Due to the clashes, which often turned into gun battles, the airport remained closed, and was eventually taken over by the Israeli military for use as a base. The placing of the military base on the edge of the refugee camp meant that the area became the scene of frequent violence, and by 2003 over 30 people from the 10,000 residents of the refugee camp Qalandia had been killed by the Israeli military. The roads around Atarot also became the site of several hit and run attacks on Israeli cars trying to get to and from the industrial estate, resulting in several deaths and injuries. Several Israelis were killed on Highway 443, which ran to the west of the area. According to the Israeli military, the assailants then escaped through the Atarot area back to Ramallah.

In a series of moves that the Israeli military argued were designed to 'prevent excessive friction between Israelis and Palestinians', the movement of Palestinians on the roads of the area was severely restricted.[12] The Israelis declared the area around the airport a closed military zone and banned all West Bank identity card holders from travelling on Highway 443.[13] Earth mounds and trenches were also built on the edges of the villages of Beit Hanina and Bir Nabala, in an attempt to prevent them accessing the road or the nearby Israeli settlements. However, as these villages were potentially isolated from schools, hospitals and a means to make a living, checkpoints were set up which allowed the residents to move back and forth across areas that were nominally reserved for Israeli citizens. The Israeli military also began to require permits from West Bank identity cards holders if they wanted to move through some of the major checkpoints in the area, as well as for travel on the road that lead to the entrance of Atarot industrial estate.[14] At the same

12 Letter from the Israeli Defence force Spokesmen to the office of B'Tselem, 21 June 2004, quoted in B'Tselem (2004): 4fn.

13 The closure of the roads to West Bank identity card holders was carried out under verbal orders rather than written regulations. The issuing of verbal orders was made possible by the Order Regarding Defence Regulations (no. 378), 5730–1970, Section 88(a)(1), which gives the local military commander the power to 'prohibit, restrict, or regulate the use of certain roads or establish routes along which certain vehicles or animals or vehicles shall pass, in either a general or specific manner'.

14 These were known as 'Special Movement Permits at Internal checkpoints in Judea and Samaria'. To obtain one, the holder also needed a magnetic card, which was only issued to West Bank identity card holders with a 'clean' security record.

time, Israeli citizens who lived in Giva'at Zeev or worked in Atarot were allowed to travel freely on the road. Furthermore, Israeli identity card holders and foreign passport holders were formally banned from entering areas nominally under the control of the PNA.[15] As the checkpoint at Qalandia was not at the administrative boundary between Jerusalem and Ramallah, this order could only be intermittently enforced.

In August 2002, the Israeli government made the decision to extend the Wall that it was building in the northern part of the West Bank to the Jerusalem area. The Wall was made up of a mixture of concrete slabs, fencing and barbed wire. It was also punctuated by surveillance towers and access roads. The route of the Wall around Jerusalem was particularly problematic, as Israelis and Palestinian populations were so integrated. In the summer of 2002, the Israeli Ministry of Defence issued an order for the construction of the Wall under the Defence (Emergency) Regulations, giving it the power to confiscate land earmarked for the construction. The original route of the Wall would have run east from the settlement of Giv'at Zev until it reached the airport at Atarot and then headed south, excluding the refugee camp of Qalandia and cutting the village of Ar-Ram in two, before finally heading east again to include the largest Israeli settlement in the West Bank, known as Maale Adumim. As this route did not follow the municipal boundaries of Jerusalem, West Bank identity cards holders were also included on the Israeli side of the Wall. In order to circumvent this problem, a further Wall was proposed by the Israeli military which would enclose Bir Nabala and its adjacent villages. There would then be a series of gates and roads to allow the residents of these enclosed villages to have access to the schools and hospitals of Ramallah. As elsewhere in the West Bank, West Bank identity cards holders who wanted to enter this area would have to provide a special permit which proved that they were 'residents'.[16] However, following an appeal to the Israeli Supreme Court, the route of the Wall was changed, and it was now planned to go to the south of Bir Nabala.

By the spring of 2006, the checkpoint at Qalandia had developed from a few small concrete blocks of a collection of buildings and hangers, complete with X-ray machines and turnstiles that to all intents and purposes resembles an international border. There are even plans to introduce a system to enable the electronic checking of biometric identity cards, which the Israeli military has boasted will 'eradicate the need for face-to-face contact'. However, the model of separation built into the new Qalandia checkpoint and the Wall is incomplete. In particular, as Route 443 approaches Qalandia, it goes to the north of the Wall, away from the 'Israeli side'. As Israeli citizens drive between Giva'at Zeev and the settlements further east, they will now have to pass away from the 'secure' side of the wall. Furthermore, many Israeli identity cards holders will be left on the 'wrong' side. The residents

---

15 Order Regarding Defence Regulations (Judea and Samaria) (no. 378), 5730–1970, Declaration Regarding Closing of Area (Prohibition of Entry or Stay) (Area A).

16 Ibid., Regulations Regarding Permanent Resident in the Seam Area Permit.

of Kufr Aqab and Qalandia who live on the far northern tip on the municipality of Jerusalem and hold Israeli identity cards will be on the 'wrong' side of the wall, and as such will be cut off from their hospitals, schools and jobs. Although they pay taxes as Israeli residents, they will be cut off from the services of the Israeli state.

The territorial integration of the population makes the separation of Israelis and Palestinians promised by the builders of the Wall impossible. Given that Palestinians and Israelis will continue to live on both sides of the Wall, and that access through the Wall and around the West Bank will continue to be controlled through a system of permits and checkpoints, it remains to be seen what impact the Wall will have. Indeed, a Israeli State Comptroller's report on the Wall argued that checkpoints have been ineffective in stopping Palestinian 'terrorists', as the majority of suicide bombers actually moved through checkpoints, not around them (State Comptroller 2002, 10–12). The Wall will increase the number of checkpoints and forms of legal identification, as it will have numerous gates and gaps to allow Israelis and Palestinians to pass through. In its attempts to ignore the social and economic causes of conflict, the model of punitive segregation also ignores the ongoing social and economic relationships that make such separations impossible.

Conclusion

The attempts by the Israeli military to map legal status onto space in the West Bank, and thereby separate Israeli citizens from Palestinians, have ended up producing new forms of uncertainty and disorder. Rather than creating security, the policy of punitive segregation has created its own insecurities. A sedimented history of often contradictory security policies has created a situation where Israelis and Palestinians are territorially integrated, economically dependent, but legally segregated. The central tension of Israel security policy has been how to deal with a Palestinian population that lives in the same territory, but is perceived as an irreconcilable threat to both the Israeli state and to individual citizens. In order to mediate these tensions, the Israeli military produced an infrastructure that sought to combine different forms of personal status with a shifting spatial order. Models of security based on the economic dependency of the Palestinian population and the territorial presence of Israeli settlers and the Israeli military, have been overlaid with a policy of segregation that has sought to physically separate Israelis and Palestinians. This is seen most evidently in the presence of hundreds of checkpoints, bypass roads and the wall being built across the West Bank. However, the Wall has left many of the fundamental issues of the relationship between persons, space and legal status unresolved. West Bank and Israeli identity card holders continue to live within close proximity to one another. The creation of such physical boundaries does not separate populations who continue to live on both sides. Furthermore, attempts to police this physical separation through the constant checking of legal status also have to come to terms with the uncomfortable fit between the ability to hold an Israeli identity card and notions of ethnic difference (Kelly 2006a). Put simply, many Palestinians hold some form of Israeli identity card.

The people who live near the checkpoint at Qalandia are testament to the problems inherent in trying to map perceptions of danger, legal status and physical presence. They were caught between the contradictory processes of economic dependence, territorial integration and legal separation. Since 1967, they have become increasingly dependent on the Israeli economy, and have been surrounded on three sides by Israeli settlements. Many of them have also received Israeli identity cards as a result of living within a newly expanded Jerusalem municipality border. However, at the same time, they have been partially cut off from their economic and social relationships by a form of spatial control designed to separate Palestinians from Israelis. As a result, on a daily level as the residents of Qalandia try to provide for their families, they are forced to negotiate numerous checkpoints and identity checks, arguing whether they have the right pass, causing friction, anger and resentment.

It is perhaps useful here to ask what lessons the particular experience of the Israeli occupation of the West Bank has for the global 'war on terror'. The system of 'anti-terror' laws developed in the West Bank by the Israeli military has one of the longest institutional histories in the world. At the same time, the governments of Ariel Sharon and Ehud Olmert have also been very successful in their campaign to link their policies with those of the American 'war on terror', arguing that 'Arafat is our Bin Laden' or that 'Hamas is our Al-Qaeda.' Indeed, according to some commentators, Israeli policies have provided a model for the United States (Hajjar 2005, 243). This is not the time or the place to trace the institutional and personal links between American and Israeli 'security' practices. However, whilst there are of course important differences in the ways in which the figure of potential danger relates to imaginations of space and identity, there are important similarities in the implicit downplaying of the social causes of violence and the creation of systems of laws and regulations that are used to handle perceived threats.

In the wider context of a 'global war and terror', threats to both individual bodies and collective life are increasingly perceived in terms of irreconcilable cultural and racial difference. Threats to 'our way of life' and to life more generally are seen as stemming from 'uncivilized', or at least fundamentally different, political and social formations. The result is attempts to categorize whole populations, produce distinct forms of legal status based on perceived security threats, and create 'zones of safety' for 'responsible citizens' (Merry 2001). In this process, the movement of people is increasingly subjected to regulation through border controls, passports, checkpoints and visas in order to manage who can be where at particular times. However, such attempts at 'punitive segregation' always exist alongside other forms of social control that encourage economic and territorial integration. Zones of safety and danger, responsible citizens and dangerous populations are always seeping into one another. On one level, European and US economic policy towards the Middle East increases the flow of commodities and labour. At another level, there has been an expansion of a near-permanent military presence of American and European armies across the Middle East in order to try and control 'unruly' populations. Attempts at punitive segregation must therefore constantly work against practices that would bring populations together. The tensions between these two processes create the violence and inequality that can be seen at checkpoints and border controls all over the world, from Qalandia to Heathrow. As regimes of legal separation come up against economic and social integration, they must resort to ever more violent means to try and keep people in place. The lesson is that security polices based on notions of irreconcilable difference and punitive segregation deny both the dynamism of social life and the social origins of conflict, and therefore seem destined to create their own forms of disorder.

References

Armstrong, S. and McAra, L. (eds) (2006), *Perspectives on Punishment: The Contours of Control*, Oxford: Oxford University Press.

Bauman, Z. (2001), 'The Quest for Order', in P. Beilharz (ed.), *The Bauman Reader*, Oxford: Blackwell.

Benvinisti, E. (1990), *Legal Dualism: The Absorption of the Occupied Territories into Israel*, Boulder, CO: Westview Press.

Bornstein, A. (2002), *Crossing the Green Line between the West Bank and Israel*, Philadelphia, PA: University of Pennsylvania Press.

B'Tselem (2004), *Forbidden Roads: Israel's Discriminatory Road Regime in the West Bank*, Jerusalem: B'Tselem.

Feeley, M. and Simon, J. (1992), 'The New Penology: Notes on the Emerging Strategy of Corrections and its Implications', *Criminology* 30(4): 449–74.

Garland, D. (2001), *The Culture of Control: Crime and Social Order in Contemporary Society*, Oxford: Oxford University Press.

Hajjar, L. (2005), *Courting Conflict: The Israeli Military Court System in the West Bank and Gaza*, Berkeley, CA: University of California Press.

Hofnung, M. (1996), *Democracy, Law and National Security in Israel*, Aldershot: Dartmouth Press.

Kelly, T. (2006a), 'Documented Lives: Fear and the Uncertainties of Law during the Second Palestinian Intifada', *Journal of the Royal Anthropological Institute* 12(1): 89–107.

—— (2006b), *Law, Violence and Sovereignty among West Bank Palestinians*, Cambridge: Cambridge University Press.

Lefebvre. H. (1991), *The Production of Space*, Oxford: Blackwell.

Lustick, I. (2000), 'Yerushalayim and al-Quds: Political Catechism and Political Realities', *Journal of Palestine Studies* 30(1): 5–21.

Merry, S.E. (2001), 'Spatial Governmentality and the New Urban Social Order: Controlling Gender Violence through Law', *American Anthropologist* 103(1): 16–29.
Ministry of Agriculture and the Settlement Division of the World Zionist Organization (1983), *Master Plan for Settlement of Samaria and Judea, Plan for Development of the Area 1983-1986*, Jerusalem.
Rabinowitz, D. (2003), 'Borders and their Discontents: Israel's Green Line, Arabness and Unilateral Separation', *European Studies: A Journal of European Culture, History and Politics* 19(1): 217–31.
Shehadeh, R. (1994), 'Questions of Jurisdiction: A Legal Analysis of the Gaza–Jericho Agreement', *Journal of Palestine Studies* 23(4): 18–25.
Shlaim, A. (2000), *The Iron Wall: Israel and the Arab World*, London: Penguin.
State Comptroller (2002), *Audit Report on the Seam Area*, Report no. 2, Jerusalem.
United Nations Special Co-ordinator for the Occupied Territories (2001), *The Impact on the Palestinian Economy of Confrontations, Mobility Restrictions and Border Closures, 1 October 2000–31 January 2001*, Gaza: UNSCO.
Zureik, E. (2001), 'Constructing Palestine through Surveillance Practices', *British Journal of Middle Eastern Studies* 28(2): 205–27.

Chapter 5

Ritual and Rule in the Periphery: State Violence and Local Governance in a Peruvian *Comunidad*

Monique Nuijten and David Lorenzo

Introduction: State Power and Citizenship in the Periphery

'A mother that rejects her children' is how the villagers of Usibamba, a community in the Andean highlands of Peru, refer to the state. Although they belong to the Peruvian nation-state, they receive no attention or services from the government. They have often demanded to be treated as full-fledged citizens, to have their territorial rights restored and receive the same agricultural extension programmes, education and health services as other citizens do. Yet different populations in the same nation-state are not equal before the law. They are treated unequally and granted different entitlements. They live under what Inda (2005, 13) calls a system of 'variegated citizenship'.

Drawing on historical and ethnographic research conducted between 2003 and 2008 in Usibamba in the central highlands of Peru, this chapter seeks to further examine the nature of state power and citizenship in the periphery. As we will demonstrate, Indian peasant populations in the Andean highlands of Peru live in a *relation of exception* to the nation-state, the extreme form of relation by which a population is 'included solely through its exclusion' (Agamben 1998, 18). We argue that these 'excluded' populations in the margin are ruled not so much through practices of governmentality, but rather through territorial control based on sovereign power and physical violence. Moreover, we explore the local forms of governance and citizenship that exist in the absence of government administration and show how these local regimes of order mimic state rule by imitating and magnifying state rituals and symbols. We discuss the meaning of this mimicry of state rule in relation to the villagers' claims to national citizenship.[1]

1 The authors express their thanks to Luisa Steur for several useful suggestions.

The Co-existence of Different Modes of Power

Our theoretical framework starts from Foucauldian ideas on power and governmentality. According to Foucault, European societies used to be based on a juridical model of governance, in which the law supported sovereign power, based on physical force and repression. Since antiquity, however, new mechanisms for the exercise of power developed in Western societies, founded on the discipline of the body and attempts to influence everyday life and regulate the population. Foucault called these new mechanisms of rule 'bio-power', and demonstrated how they involved the imposition of a new system of administration, regulation and inspection. According to Foucault, modern society hence came to be characterized by a disciplinary order based more on normative, regulatory mechanism than on physical constraints.

The subject in modern society thus operates in the context of regulated practices according to which his or her own ideas are formed. These processes of subjectivization tie individuals to their own identity and consciousness, but simultaneously to an external power. This is Foucault's notion of governmentality, defined as the constitution of distinct subjectivities through discursive rituals and administrative practices. According to Foucault, techniques of governmentality form part of the liberal art of governing, and result in a feeling of freedom for the subjects as they always have the option to act otherwise. This is in contrast to coercive power and surveillance. Governmentality as the central form of rule of the modern state thus focuses on the versatile equilibrium between people's construction of the self and technologies of state domination (Foucault 1988; 1993; Dean 2001).

Governmentality approaches based on Foucault's ideas have several limitations, which have been widely discussed in the literature. They have, for instance, been criticized for a 'tendency to overemphasize the symbolic dimension of state activity' and 'the unity of the state, domination, and its consequences' (Dean 1994, 151). Foucault's work has also been rebuked for situating different modes of power in chronologically separate historical eras. As Nelson points out, 'discipline does not displace the power to take life in a progress narrative of history' (Nelson 2005, 221). In his work *Homo Sacer*, Agamben convincingly argues that Foucault's work remains unclear about the point at which the two faces of power – sovereign power and bio-political power – converge. In other words, it is not made explicit how the processes of governing which produce subjectivities based on self-regulation become articulated with external powers and states of domination (Agamben 1998, 5).

Contrary to the Foucauldian idea of separate stages, we assume that in any regime of governance, different modes of power operate at the same time. We maintain that even under 'modern' administrations, characterized by bio-political control, other modes of power operate, including sovereign power in which control over people is exercised through control over territory (Dean 2001). Several authors have persuasively argued that 'territorial sovereignty and the foundational violence that gave birth to it, still remains the hard kernel of modern states' (Blom and Stepputat 2005, 1). In his book *Suffering for Territory*, Moore (2005) convincingly shows how competing practices of spatial discipline, sovereignty and subjection all co-exist. Following a similar line of reasoning, Mathews (2005) – in his study of the national agency regulating forest fires and deforestation in Mexico – argues that Foucauldian analyses of governmentality have over-emphasized the ability of the state to produce forms of rule through the creation of subjectivities. Mathews shows that official state programmes and discourses often have little effect upon popular beliefs, and are ultimately backed up by coercion (Mathews 2005, 815; 816).

In addition to understanding that different modes of power co-exist, it is also important to remember that they often apply to different parts of the population. As Ong (2000) argues when analysing the case of Indonesia, 'different sectors of the population' have become 'subjected to different technologies of regulation and nurturance'. Nation-states often apply particular regulations and forms of government to specific parts of their population. Nation-states can use the art of liberal government for most of their citizens, while using authoritarian forms of coercion for gypsies, prisoners, slum dwellers, illegal immigrants or rebellious peasants:

> The result of such differential technological treatment has been to endow different populations with different kinds of rights, caring and protection. It has been to create a system of uneven distribution, or of 'variegated citizenship', in which some subjects are nurtured and afforded rights and resources, while others are largely neglected. (Inda 2005, 13)

As Li points out, 'authoritarian forms of government are often reserved for sections of a population deemed especially deficient and unable to exercise the responsibility of freedom. So, the freedom of some is predicated on the unfreedom of others' (Li 2005, 387). States can also exercise coercive forms of government towards populations who refuse to play the 'game' of liberal government. Excluded from full citizenship, they are 'the target of schemes for heightened surveillance, extending at times to enforced discipline …' (Li 2005, 388). Measures 'are applied to certain populations held to be without the attributes of responsible freedom' (Dean 2001, 46). Their 'political identity is defined as without citizenship, state, or even means of subsistence, that is, merely by the fact that they are living' (Dean 2001, 52).

Every society – even the most modern – decides who its 'sacred men' will be (Agamben 1998, 139). According to Agamben, in the state of exception – during evictions, dispossession and brutal bodily violence – authority places itself outside and above the law. It is not self-evident that the state will protect the lives of all its subjects. In fact, 'there is nothing obvious or natural as to who may or may not be protected as a citizen' (Petryna 2005, 164). Coercive power by the military almost always turns against marginal people even if implemented in the name of protecting them. Accepting this line of argument involves the acceptance of the excluded as integral to the constitution of society (Moore 2005). Agamben calls this extreme relational form by which people are included solely through their exclusion the *relation of exception* (Agamben 1998, 18). Das and Poole, following Agamben's analysis, call people in the state of exception 'killable bodies' as they can be eliminated without punishment (Das and Poole 2004, 12).

So we can distinguish different types of citizens with different entitlements within the same national border. These 'citizen categories' and the claims they include are not, however, fixed. They are the object of continuous contestation, struggle and change.

The Peruvian *Comunidad Campesina*: Controlling People by Controlling Space

The history of Indian communities in the Andean highlands of Peru shows how territorial control formed the basis on which the state claimed authority over people and defined people's political identities as citizens (Vandergeest and Peluso 1995, 385). In distinct historical periods, during colonialism and independence, authorities strategically used control over the territory to steer and manipulate the Indian population in the highlands and keep them in a position of 'inclusive exclusion' (Agamben 1998).

Under the colonial regime (1530–1821), the Indian population in the Andes lost much of its land to colonial administrators and *hacendados* because land rights were granted to Spanish settlers as a reward for their loyalty to the Spanish Crown (Faron 1985, 30). This forced the Indians to move towards the highest and poorest regions in the mountains (Del Castillo 1992, 39). However, in the central highlands, where Usibamba is located, Indian communities managed to maintain a higher degree of liberty and independence from haciendas than in the southern Andes (Manrique 1988a [1987]).

After Peru's independence from Spain, in 1821, the highland communities came under the political jurisdiction of valley towns, for which they had to perform a variety of services (Roberts and Samaniego 1978; Smith 1989). Usibamba belonged to Mito, one of the biggest communities in the Mantaro valley.[2] In addition to their duties for Mito, the villagers of Usibamba also had to carry out many tasks – from agricultural activities to construction work – for the hacienda 'Cónsac', which bordered their village. In exchange for this work the Usibambinos were allowed to let their cattle graze on the extensive hacienda pastures.

State territorialization strategies in this period were focused on securing the Indian labour force for the haciendas and the valley towns. By taking their land

2 We are much indebted to two officials in charge of the División de Comunidades Campesinas y Nativas of the Ministry of Agriculture in the city of Huancayo for helping us to gain access to the official archives. We are grateful for their invaluable assistance, sense of humour and willingness to co-operate.

away and pushing them up the hills, the Indian people were forced to offer their labour in exchange for access to pasture lands. Through these territorialization measures, the Peruvian state supported the interests of large landholders and town elites. In the central highlands, however, the communities fiercely defended their rights and entered into numerous lawsuits (Manrique 1988a [1987]).

Because of the continuing Indian claims for restitution of their territory, the Peruvian state issued a new law in 1828, which recognized ancestral claims and declared Indians to be the owners of the land they occupied. Other legal mechanisms protected indigenous communities against new encroachment by haciendas. However, the laws were not seriously implemented and rural rebellions in the Andes grew in force.

In 1919, a constitution was issued that provided for the registration of all Indian community lands, attributing special rights to indigenous groups who had controlled their landholdings uninterruptedly since pre-Hispanic times (Dobyns 1970, 11). According to the new legislation, the state would also expropriate private estates in order to grant land to communities with land scarcity. Special offices were established with the task of processing and approving petitions for the recognition and official inscription of 'indigenous communities'.[3]

The villagers of Usibamba actively participated in these struggles for land and recognition. In 1896, they won a lawsuit against the Lozano family of Mito and were granted the property rights to part of the land. In 1907, they bought an additional tract of land from the Lozano family. Next, the Usibamba started the procedure to be officially recognized as a *Comunidad Indigena* ('Indigenous Community') by the Ministry of Agriculture, which succeeded in 1939. At that time, the population consisted of 492 persons.[4]

During the 1940s, 1950s and 1960s, peasant demands and invasions of haciendas continued. This was accompanied by negative publicity about Indian rebels in the media. In fact, 'the categories of Indian, Communist and rebel overlapped considerably' (Orlove 1994, 84). The accounts did not, however, represent the uprisings as violent acts committed by the population against abusive authorities, but rather as the kind of savage acts that Indians were supposedly prone to (Orlove 1994, 83).

Through designating and demarcating areas as *Comunidad Indigena* and issuing special legislation for these institutions to operate, the Peruvian state was again orchestrating territorial control. It created spatialized zones within which certain practices were permitted based on the explicit or implicit allocation of

3 In 1962, there were 1,600 such officially recognized communities in Peru (Dobyns 1970, 12). Today, there exist approximately 3,312 officially recognized communities in the highlands (Paerregaard 2002, 56).

4 Expediente relativo al Reconocimiento e Inscripción Oficial de la Comunidad de Indígenas de Usibamba, del Distrito de Aco, de la Provincia de Jauja, del Departamento de Junín. Dirección de Asuntos Indígenas. Sección Administrativa. Minsterio de Salud Pública, Trabajo y Previsión Social.

rights, restrictions and control (Vandergeest and Peluso 1995). Through these policies, the state tried to pacify and govern the highland population.

However, the new laws and government programmes aimed at the restitution and protection of Indian property rights failed to put an end to serious land disputes between *latifundistas* and *comuneros*, and did not lead to the promised outcomes. Even though hundreds of villages throughout the *sierra* spent much time and money trying to recover their lands, their efforts were largely in vain. In practice, the agrarian offices and courts gave little support for regaining community lands. The highland Indian population thus shared a deep-seated resentment against the Peruvian state and felt exploited by a political system that continued to support large landowners (Handelman 1975, 34). Because of the state's failure to respond to the grievances of Indian communities, conflicts between communities and haciendas continued, as did land seizures and invasions. Establishing territorial control in this sense proved to be 'a process without closure, where claims to political/social space are constantly being brought into play (and constantly being questioned)' (Wilson 2004, 530).

To summarize this brief historical exploration of territorial control, we can say that after independence, the central authorities in Peru continued to use territorialization to support haciendas and valley towns in their demand for an Indian labour force, but in the course of the nineteenth and early twentieth centuries, began partial withdrawal of this support when Indian protests intensified. From the early 1920s on, the state started changing its territorial strategies further, and issued new laws to pacify an impoverished and angry Indian peasantry. It formally recognized Indian communities and their communal land tenure regimes in addition to promising the expropriation of large landholdings and the restitution of Indian territories. Yet, in reality, the landowning elite continued to receive the necessary political and legal support to fight of Indian claims to land.

Land Reform and Governance in the Periphery

The Revolutionary Government of the Armed Forces of Velasco (1968–75) decided to respond to the increasingly violent demands for serious land reform and the abolishment of haciendas. One of the most important reforms of the Velasco regime was to introduce a new agrarian legislation, including an agrarian reform law and a new statute for *comunidades*. Large-scale cattle haciendas were expropriated and the land and equipment handed over to highland communities. Whereas in the past indigenous identity and ancestral links to the territory had been decisive factors for land entitlement, the land reforms of the 1970s talked about changing the unequal distribution of land and creating productive associative enterprises. For the Peruvian state, the land reform was part of its modernizing project (Nuñez 1995, 36). Indian communities were considered to be ancient institutions that were to be replaced by modern co-operatives (Nuñez 1995, 36). Expropriated hacienda lands were therefore not handed over to Indian communities directly, but rather to a so-called Agrarian Association of Social Interest (SAIS), of which Indian communities then had to become members.

The official reason behind this was that, because of the economies of scale, production factors would be used more effectively by such an association. Another argument was the supposed lack of management capacity of the peasants, and the consequent need for state institutions to support the administration and organization of the agrarian associations. The land reform of the 1970s thus put Indian communities under state tutelage on the grounds of Indian peasants being uneducated, undeveloped and lacking in management skills. The Peruvian state tried to modernize the agrarian production system in the highlands by converting backward Indians (superstitious and lazy, almost by definition) into modern peasants (effective and dynamic entrepreneurs, commercially oriented farmers).

This state objective clearly clashed with the aim of *comuneros*, who saw the agrarian reform as an opportunity to recover communal lands stolen by haciendados – in other words, as a way to achieve the restitution of their rights (Renique 1994, 226). The Indian population felt utterly betrayed by the fact that they were forced to become members of a landholding association run by external officials (Sánchez 1989). In fact, the new associative enterprises reproduced many of the oppressive traits of the former haciendas (Renique 1994, 241). Several analysts pointed to the 'hidden' state objective that 'by taking the "associative" option, the government sought to preserve the administration and assets of the expropriated estates while at the same time defusing and controlling peasant demands for land' (Renique 1994, 227). It was also mentioned that by not returning the land directly to the Indian population, the state aimed to eliminate the land base of Andean Indian communities (Martínez-Alier 1973, 41).

Usibamba became one of the 16 member communities of the SAIS Túpac Amaru (SAIS TA), which was established through the expropriation of 19 haciendas.[5] The SAIS TA is managed by a team of directors – engineers and other professionals – that is accountable to the general assembly. The general assembly is the highest authority, and can vote to remove the directors from office and alter SAIS policies and budgets. Each member community sends a representative (delegate) to the general assembly, who holds office for two years.

In theory, this system gives member communities considerable power in the general assembly of the SAIS. In practice, however, several mechanisms conspire to reduce their control. Directors first of all try to secure the loyalty of the delegates by providing them with benefits and material compensation in the form of reimbursements, cheap products and food. As a result, the delegates work less in the interest of their communities than in that of the managers. But even if delegates actually want to defend the interests of their communities, there is little

5 We are much indebted to two officials in charge of the División de Comunidades Campesinas y Nativas of the Ministry of Agriculture in the city of Huancayo for helping us to gain access to the official archives. We are grateful for their invaluable assistance, sense of humour and willingness to co-operate.

possibility for them to participate effectively in decision-making. The directors make use of the existing divisions among the member communities to play the delegates off against each other.

Moreover, serious tensions exist within the communities, as the SAIS usually employs persons from the member communities as *huacchis*, shepherds who tend the large herds of sheep and cattle of the SAIS. In addition to herding the cattle, the *huacchis* are also charged with preventing *comuneros* invading the lands of the SAIS. For that reason, their role is much resented. Stories abound of the ill treatment of *comuneros* by the *huacchis*, and their abuse of women and children.

The relations the Usibambinos maintain with the SAIS TA today are very similar to the feudal relationships they had with the haciendas in the past. For example, member communities are not allowed to herd their animals on the extensive SAIS pastures, and are fined if they do so. Again we see how, through the definition of areas as owned by the association and with limited use rights for the member communities, techniques of territorialization are used to control the highland peasant population. Another popular territorial strategy used by the SAIS TA is that of the 'living frontiers', whereby the SAIS deliberately lends land to member communities in such an awkward way that communities fight among themselves rather than against the SAIS.

Officially, the member communities share in the yearly proceeds of the SAIS according to percentages laid down in the internal regulation of the SAIS TA. Yet, after payment of the directors, administrators and labourers, little money remains for the member communities.

From the day the SAIS Túpac Amaru was established, the member communities have fought for its dismantlement and the division of the territory among themselves. As the formal procedures for closing down the SAIS are systematically frustrated by the directors, the member communities have started invading and incorporating SAIS lands. Land invasion for them equals the recuperation of their own land. The feelings of injustice, of not having been taken seriously by the Peruvian state during the Land Reform of the 1970s, laid the grounds for further episodes of violent struggle over territory.

The Period of the Shining Path

In the 1980s, the Shining Path (*Sendero Luminoso*) Maoist guerrilla movement became active in the Andean region. The Shining Path was initiated by intellectuals in the city of Ayacucho, from where it spread to other Andean regions and to the capital of Lima (Degregori 1996). Being a remote area populated by impoverished peasants, the Andean highlands were ideally suitable for the Maoist insurgents. The Shining Path propagated a revolutionary agenda directed against 'the enemies of the people', among whom they included all authorities, but in particular those of the state (Degregori 1996; Fumerton 2001). The abolition of the SAIS as a state-run enterprise and the restitution of the land to the highland communities fitted the Shining Path's political agenda well. In the department of Junín, six SAISes were established under Velasco's regime, and all six were still operating when the Shining Path became active in the 1980s.

During the years of subversion, SAIS member communities were uncomfortably positioned between the revolutionaries and the establishment. Either attracted by the Shining Path's propaganda or 'moved by the threat of force, dozens of peasants participated in the massive attacks on the associative enterprises and in the sacking of goods and livestock which took place after the armed attacks' (Renique 1994, 235). In an event in 1989 that is still often recounted in Usibamba, the *senderistas* forced villagers to kill SAIS bulls in the main square and divide the meat among themselves. Later that same day, the army arrived and accused the *comuneros* of having stolen the bulls from the SAIS. The military took the meat and left. A few days later, two *comuneros* who had supposedly been involved in this action were taken away by soldiers driving a SAIS truck and never returned.

The worst years for Usibamba were 1989 and 1990. Don Rafael, who was President of the Executive Committee of the *Comunidad* of Usibamba in the years of strong subversion, 1990 and 1991, recalled that period as follows:

> The *senderistas* … told us very clearly, 'We are going to knock down the SAIS for you.' They went together with other *comunidades* to Cónsac to kill, burn, destroy … That's no good. Who wants to do this?
>
> We did not go from our own free will. That was not how it went. We were obliged by the subversives at gunpoint [*a punta de cañon*]. The entrance was not peaceful, they entered to kill. The company [SAIS] had the support of the government, the army and the police. What can a *comunero* do when faced with the army? … The ideas of *sendero* were good in theory, but they were not here when the army came. Their ideas were good, they tried to help the *campesino*, but in practice they only pushed us to destroy things.[6]

As Manrique (1998b, 209) points out, 'while not all comuneros of the region approved of the destruction of the SAIS, for the majority the measure provided a way out of the impasse provoked by the intransigence of the state bureaucracy that controlled the large SAIS units of the central sierra'. All SAISes in the Andes were violently attacked by *senderos*, and many of its directors killed. Three of the six SAISes in the region were closed down and their lands distributed to member communities, as well as to neighbouring communities that had not formerly been members. Being one of the largest associations, Túpac Amaru received a lot of support from the national military and the police. In this way, it survived despite suffering many *sendero* attacks, in which a total of 11 people were killed: six employees, one military officer, one delegate, two wives of delegates and one community leader.

6 All interview fragments and texts from Spanish sources are our own translations.

Usibamba, like other communities, used this time of political unrest and attacks on the SAISes to intensify pressure on state authorities to redistribute the land. For example, in a letter written by the authorities in Usibamba to the Director of the Ministry of Agriculture in 1987, they argued the following:

> we are overpopulated in the little village where we live, with only 3,810 hectares of land to support 2,840 inhabitants ... this is a continuing problem which we try to resolve through your respected intervention, ... an extension of 12,000 hectares, which corresponds to us as member of ... the SAIS Túpac Amaru.

The 12,000 hectares that the communal authorities refer to are those of the former hacienda 'Cónsac', which is part of the SAIS TA, but according to the Usibambinos, belongs to them.

In 1988 and 1989 – the years of severe violence in the region – Túpac Amaru responded by transferring first 230 and then 570 hectares to Usibamba. But it transferred only the use rights of the land, retaining official ownership. Although the *comuneros* perceived this as a strategic move by the SAIS in order to appease them, they were none the less pleased to receive the land 'in their own hands'. Yet, they were not appeased for long. In 1990 they sent another letter, this time to the administration of the SAIS, requesting the dismantling of the SAIS given the non-fulfilment of the aims for which it had been created and the repression and violence against *comuneros*.

> 11/01/1990 to the Administration of the SAIS TA by Community Authorities of Usibamba
>
> With this letter we, as community authorities of Usibamba, want to make the following claims:
>
> - The enterprise SAIS TA is not fulfilling the stated aims and objectives for its community members, in particular Usibamba.
> - Last year, 1989, on several occasions Police Forces arrested community members, some up to four times, their houses were searched and personal belongings, such as clothes or electronic devices were stolen.
> - On four different occasions Armed Forces have been stealing our cattle in 1989, 1990, with a total of 9 sheep stolen or even killed in front of us.
> - All these abuses by the army and police have become part of our daily life.
> - We want an explanation from the people at the SAIS TA who are responsible for labelling us as terrorists (subversives) about the grounds of such accusations. Once arrested, our community members are tortured and humiliated in the Police station in Pachacayo without any clear accusation and reason for this ill-treatment.

Instead of protecting us as a member community of the SAIS TA that Usibamba is, workers of SAIS TA accuse us of being terrorists and give our names to the army or police forces. Their workers say that we work hand in hand with the Shining Path as comrades [*compañeros*] and take part in the attacks on the different production units of the SAIS TA.

- Due to the reasons explained above, in an assembly of all its members the Community of Usibamba decided that it is time to carry out the specifications of the Agrarian Reform Law. … There is no longer any reason for us to continue being a member of the SAIS TA since we are treated as terrorists and subversives. Not only does the SAIS TA not protect us as members, but we are even accused of being its enemies. Taking this into account, what is the point in continuing being a community member of the SAIS TA?

Communities involved in land claims were labelled pro-*sendero* by the SAIS, and therefore treated as potential 'terrorists', or *terrucos*. Although some villagers did indeed participate in the Shining Path's activities, most *comuneros,* fearing military retaliation, tried to keep a safe distance from the violent conflict. In the next document, the Usibambinos complain about the violence used against them by the army.

[Undated letter] directed to the General Brigade responsible for the National Security of the Central Highlands

As authority of the Community of Usibamba, I express the following formal complaint. In the name of the community I represent, I would like you to throw light on the detention of 12 community members on Saturday 10th of this month between 7–8 p.m. At that time a military raid took place in the territory of our Community …. The soldiers searched every single house and violently drove out the owners. Those who couldn't identify immediately were arrested without any further explanation. They were taken to the military headquarters in Huancayo. … When we went to the headquarters nobody gave us a clear and definitive explanation. We only received evasive answers to our questions. We only knew that our community members were in isolation. In addition, I want to firmly complaint about the existence of people with connections to Top Army Officials that extorted us with exorbitant amounts of money of more than 200 intis for any information. This is excessive for peasants like us. … As Peruvians, we are aware about the difficult political climate our country is going through. We praise everything the army and police are doing in order to eradicate the curse of subversion. At any time we are willing to give our support to the democracy our Constitution recognizes. Until this point we fully agree but there is a big difference …. What we do not want is to continue being treated as the thrash we are considered today. If the situation does not improve, we will write a formal complaint to the President of the Republic and the Ministry of

> Defence. In a political programme on the radio … a General of the Peruvian armed forces stated the following: 'Peruvian Highland Communities have to regain confidence in the Peruvian Army by being involved in development and social support programmes; this is the only way, commonly organized, they can fight against the subversive elements.' What the army is doing with peasant communities such Usibamba, in my opinion, doesn't correspond to the spirit the Ministry of Defence preaches.

In Usibamba, seven *comuneros* disappeared during the worst years of violence at the end of the 1980s. Two of them were employees of the SAIS. Their bodies were found in the central square of Usibamba with a notice around their necks saying: 'This is the way in which informants of the SAIS die.' Everybody in Usibamba agrees that the Shining Path were responsible for these two killings. As the two men were from Usibamba and worked at the SAIS, they could easily provide the SAIS with firsthand information about subversive *comuneros*. Three other killings are also attributed to the Shining Path. One of them concerned a well-known cattle thief who posed as a terrorist in order to steal cattle from the peasant population. The notice hanging around his neck said: 'In this way cattle thieves die who pose themselves as "comrades" in order to steal cattle.' The other two Sendero victims in Usibamba were community members who refused to take part in the attacks on the SAIS that the terrorists promoted. In these cases, the notice on their dead bodies read: 'In this way people die who do not support the Sendero Political Party.'

Relatively few people were killed in Usibamba, and no local authorities were sacrificed by the Shining Path. For that reason, other communities accuse Usibamba of having collaborated with the Maoists. This type of accusation is still used today in conflicts within and between communities.

As we saw, the SAIS TA also used violence against *comuneros* who were suspected of supporting the Maoists. For example, two *comuneros* were taken away in November 1989 and never returned.

This event was mentioned in a letter by the communal authorities to the SAIS:

> We, community authorities of our Peasant Community of Usibamba, are surprised by the disappearance of two of our active members under strange circumstances on 17 November 1989. Both of them were violently driven out of their homes by so-called soldiers and forced to get into a truck of the SAIS TA. This is all we know until today.
>
> Usibamba, 11 December 1990

As the men were taken away in a truck of the SAIS TA – the Usibambinos call this event 'the revenge of the association'. They feel the SAIS wanted to punish the Usibambinos for supporting the terrorists.

On 15 July 1990, Usibamba together with 16 other communities in the region made a pact with the military and committed themselves to organizing civil defence committees (*rondas campesinas*) (Manrique 1988b, 207). A national army base was established in the region, and the heads of the *rondas* were trained by the military. Although officially the army came to protect the people against the Shining Path, in many instances they turned against those whom they had been sent to defend. As a *comunero* put it: 'The *terruco* betrayed us, the armed forces betrayed us and the police betrayed us.'

In 1991, the army began the massive distribution to Andean peasants of more than 10,000 shotguns (Starn 1995, 553). Usibamba figured among the first communities of the country to receive a donation of arms from President Fujimori in person. In 1992, the leader of the Shining Path, Abimael Guzmán, was captured by the Peruvian army and life in the Andes became more peaceful. In 1996, the self-defence committees ceased functioning in the region.

The SAIS TA survived the years of violence because of much military support, but relations between the association and its member communities, already uneasy, had now been further disrupted. The balance had shifted in the communities' favour. As several *comuneros* from Usibamba said: 'it is only since *sendero* that the SAIS started to respect us' (Nuijten and Lorenzo 2008).

Many innocent *comuneros* and *comuneras* lost their lives at the hands of *senderistas* or the state military. During the period of the Shining Path, they were invariably labelled by the government as communists and terrorists. One could argue that during this period the state declared the Andean highlands a *state of exception*, where order was to be re-established. For the duration of this episode, no laws were effective and many peasants were brutally killed. Being areas of exception drawn to subversive ideologies made the Indian highland population a source of fear for dominant parts of society, and for that reason physical *violence* could be used against them. However, the Shining Path refrained from protecting the *comuneros* when they were assaulted by the police or army. For that reason, *comuneros* also felt betrayed by the Shining Path. In this historical period, they were *Homo sacer* (Agamben 1998), or 'killable bodies' (Das and Poole 2004), for the state as well as the Shining Path.

Mimicry of the State

*Comunidad*es like Usibamba, are known for their strict local practices with respect to land tenure and jurisdiction and firmly established institutions of labour exchange, communal work, reciprocity and festivities (Paerregaard 1987). *Comunidades campesinas* developed into 'local republics', true disciplinary regimes in which *comuneros* have to obey countless rules and fulfil numerous responsibilities and functions in order to have certain rights (Yambert 1980). It is the *comunidad* that fulfils the role of public authority and takes responsibility for the organization of the many civic works for the entire village, such as cleaning roads, building bridges, taking care of the local burial ground and so on. The *comunidad* draws on the *comuneros* to carry out these many public tasks during communal work parties (*faenas*). These local systems, with their own rules, authorities and procedures, 'managed to survive through the centuries in a politically subordinated condition' (Yrigoyen 2000, 197). According to most authors, the continuation and strengthening of these local disciplinary regimes of governance has been a response to the absence of state administration. Other authors, however, have pointed out that these disciplinary communal regimes are perhaps not so much a reaction to the absence of the state, but rather to the forms in which the state intervened. As Stepputat argues, these forms of order and discipline can also be 'interpreted as a way of coping with modernity, not least with the emasculation, inherent in racialising and ethnicising forms of state formation' (Stepputat 2004, 254, 255).

Within certain limits, the Peruvian state permitted peasant communities to have some autonomy with respect to governance and jurisdiction within their territorial boundaries. The Peruvian state followed a pragmatic strategy: as long as Indians did not interfere with the rest of society, the state was not bothered with their particular systems of authority and customary law. Yet when their rule affected the interests of established classes, serious clashes developed in which Indian people were depicted as 'barbarian savages'. An important function of the highland population continued to be to serve as an obedient and cheap labour force for the owners of large landholdings living in the valley cities. A famous example is the case of Espinar in Cusco in 1931, when the police received an order to arrest several Indian peasants accused of rustling livestock from haciendas (Orlove 1994). One of the peasants tried to escape and was killed. The enraged villagers then killed two of the five policemen. In their turn, the police took several prisoners and set the village on fire. The media presented the killing of the police officers by the peasants as an example of the violent and savage Indian. The police had to act out of fear of Indian attacks. However, as Orlove describes, 'the key economic issue was the division between a small mestizo landholding elite and a large Indian peasantry, with conflicts between the two over the control of land and labor' (Orlove 1994, 67). Not situating the violence within its political context, the public debate depicted the Indian as 'barbarous by nature' and fed into narratives about Indian crimes and the state's responsibility to protect its citizens against the violent Indian (Orlove 1994, 78). As Yrigoyen points out, this leads to the 'criminalization of cultural differences' (Yrigoyen 2000, 197).

In this context of a highly contentious relation with the state, it is striking to see the high degree of mimicry of national symbolism in the *comunidades*. For example, one finds Peruvian flags in every house in Usibamba. During important festivities, local authorities sometimes even oblige some inhabitants to paint their houses in the national colours. Every local festivity starts with the hoisting of the national flag and the singing of the national anthem. Before starting the monthly meeting in the *comunidad*, all *comuneros* put their right hand on their heart and shout 'Viva Perú!' This is followed by 'Let's sing our national anthem as the good

Peruvians that we are.' Then they take off their hats and sing the national anthem together.

The central moment of every official celebration is the march by the local authorities. The authorities of the *comunidad*, the municipality, the schools, the medical posts and other institutions all participate in the march. They rehearse the movements days before, and discuss the clothing that will be worn by each of them. It is important to march 'sturdy as a man', showing resoluteness and firmness in every step. As they used to say: 'Feminized steps don't count.' These preparations take place with much discipline and discretion, as the group with the best performance will be awarded a prize, which is a great honour. Being present at these events for the first time caused a strange sensation, and made us wonder why the Andean villagers march like the military, even more disciplined, when in these regions the state has been largely absent, and if present, only in the form of repression by the military and the police. In other words, why does the Indian population imitate their oppressors?

How should we analyse this phenomenon of republics in the margin mimicking the state? Das and Poole argue that both political anthropologists and postcolonial and subaltern theorists have tended, until recently, to either emphasize resistance to the state or stress the development of relatively independent local legal and economic institutions in these areas in the margins (Das and Poole 2004, 6). However, they argue that the mimicking of state procedures and rituals shows another way in which communities in the margin position themselves in relation to the nation state. They argue that we should see these forms of mimicry of the state as a way of claiming economic and political citizenship (Das and Poole 2004, 11): 'The mimicry of the state … might be read as instituting the state as a fetish, but it also attests to community allegiance to the idea of state-instituted law and thus manages to claim citizenship for these communities' (Das and Poole 2004, 23).

In some terms, the appropriation of symbols of the state is a way to participate in the nation-project from the margin and create spaces for citizenship. In a similar vein, Orlove (1982) argues that the use of the Peruvian flag may convey their membership of the Peruvian nation and the desire they have that the government act on their behalf. In addition, the flag as national symbol lends force and legitimacy to local events through this reference to higher levels of administration (Orlove 1982, 258–9). As Eckert points out, this mimicry can be analysed as a form of claiming citizenship from a regime that does not rely so much on the law in governing them (Eckert 2006). In the next section, we will discuss how local rule relates to state law and further inquire into the possible meaning of this mimicry of the state.

State Rule and Citizenship

Over the centuries, the Peruvian nation-state has demonstrated little interest in the part of its population living in the Andean highlands, which is still by far the poorest area of Peru. The highland population receives few state services, protection or support. In other words, they are not treated as 'worthy citizens'. As we saw, in situations that might threaten the interests of regional or national power holders, the state has not hesitated to use intense violence against the highland population.

The sparse initiatives by the Peruvian state, activists or NGOs to try to 'develop' the highlands usually come in the form of programmes that fail to relate even minimally to the lives and interests of the population. For that reason, '[a]ctivists, state officials, and NGOs are often surprised and disappointed by the rejection of their efforts at advocacy' (García 2005, 10). A famous example is the latrines that have been placed in many highland communities as part of hygiene programmes. They stand out in the Andean landscape as sad symbols of 'abandoned development'. Highland people are used to answering nature's calls in the extensive pastures, and don't see much point in using the latrines. What they do want is for their territorial border problems with large landowners to be resolved – instead, however, they are subjected to a land registration and surveying programme implemented by the state under pressure from the World Bank. Moreover, villagers in the highlands want engineers from the Ministry of Agriculture to bring them the benefits of agricultural extension. As one of the *comuneros* in Usibamba said when he was cleaning his plot: 'What I would like most is an engineer from the Ministry who would come and tell me what fertilizer I should apply in order to increase my potato yield.' They want roads and clinics, but instead receive a bilingual multicultural education programme, implemented by the state under pressure from the international human rights agenda (García 2005). What the Indian highland population asks for is the restitution of their ancestral lands, an end to discrimination and being treated as worthy citizens through the delivery of infrastructure and public services.

The contentious relation between the state and the highland people becomes painfully clear during the visits of state functionaries, for example during election time. In Peru, voting is obligatory and the failure to do so is punished with a fine.[7] For the highland population this is awkward, as many of them are registered in another region, meaning that they have to travel and spend much time and money in order to 'fulfil their public duty'. For that reason, many highlanders do not vote, and during election time officials of the National Office of Electoral Processes visit the communities to remind the population of their duty to assert their rights as 'good Peruvian citizens'.[8] In a private talk with one of the officials about the fact that many villagers don't vote, she remarked about the highland population: 'There is no civic conscience, they don't know how to exercise their rights as citizens, they don't know how to be citizens.' In public, she addressed the communal assembly in Usibamba in the following way:

7 In 2005 the fine for not voting was 132 Nuevos Soles (approximately 31 US dollars).

8 This concerned the referendum for the creation of macro-regions held on 9 October 2005.

> Why do we in Peru still have fines? Because we are not aware of the value of our vote. We wait for others to decide for us. … just because this is a remote, far-away area, that doesn't mean you don't have capacities. Now it is time that you decide about your own future and not let others decide for you. (Meeting in Usibamba, 9 October 2005)

In her speech, she indirectly labelled the people as lazy ('you have the capacity, but you don't do it …'). In the remainder of her talk, she indirectly depicted them as uncivilized ('your hand is not used to holding a pencil') and backwards ('you have to break away from these old schemes of thinking'). However, at the local level, the Usibambinos actively use their voting right during elections and know very well how to behave as 'good citizens'. In this respect, it is interesting to take a closer look at the yearly elections of the communal authorities.

According to the national law of peasant communities (Ley de Comunidades Campesinas), a new executive committee has to be elected every two years. However, as fulfilling a position in the executive committee is a heavy responsibility and very time-consuming, the *comunidad* of Usibamba changes its authorities every year. As these yearly elections go against national law, this complicates formal registration at the Ministry of Agriculture in Huancayo, which is essential in order for the new executive committee to get access to public resources. For that reason, the change of executive committee is usually presented by the Usibambinos as a voluntary resignation. Even at the local meeting in Usibamba, everything is organized so as to look like the resignation of the executive committee, though everybody knows that it is simply the standard yearly elections taking place.

Another friction between the national Ley de Comunidades Agrarias and local reality is that according to national law, people with first- or second-degree blood kinship are not allowed to appear on the same election slate. This is problematic because in these small villages many people are related to each other. Another difficulty is how to establish these kinship relations. In the revision of slates, the officer of the Ministry of Agriculture – who has to give his or her approval – looks for kinship relations merely by checking surnames. This is awkward, as some people with the same surname are not related at all, while people with different names can be close kin.

In Usibamba, the slates that participate in the election are carefully checked in this way before they are sent for approval to the Ministry in Huancayo. The following dialogue occurred during a meeting (10 December 2005) discussing a local slate that included two men with the same surname who were not closely related:

> *Comunero* A: 'The Ministry of Agriculture already looks at us with suspicion because of our yearly change of the executive committee. Let's make sure there is no blood kinship!'

> *Comunero* B: 'Let's not fall in the trap of bureaucrats. Let's do the things in our own way. We have to separate the two. Vidal and Samuel [the men in the slate with the same surname] are distant in terms of blood kinship. We have to be firm with the government. How can we have different second names? The majority in Usibamba are Damian [the most common surname in Usibamba].'

Yet people in Usibamba know that the Ministry of Agriculture will not accept slates that include persons with the same surname, so another candidate was appointed.

In the event that two people whose second names are not the same but who do have close kinship relations appear on the slate, the Usibambinos themselves demand that one of the two withdraw. Although a slate including close relatives with different surnames would not cause problems with the Ministry of Agriculture, *comuneros* want to obey the official rule that individuals with close kinship relations cannot appear in the same slate.

The elections for the executive committee are always carefully prepared. In order to be entitled to vote, *comuneros* have to have all their duties and payments straightened out with the various local institutions. They receive official clearance from each authority in the form of a stamp on their document. So election time is the time of the year when all outstanding debts have to be paid. Yet the payment of debts to receive 'clearance' to vote is not so much about money, but rather about the evaluation of one's status as local citizen. For example, people who have problems with a divorce or who are not sending their children to school won't receive the clearance from, respectively, the local judge or the school director. Only if one receives clearance from all local institutions is one considered a worthy citizen and entitled to participate in the elections. On the other hand, people who fail to pay their debts or are for other reasons not cleared and registered as voters can be punished and even disqualified as *comuneros*. Thus, the clearance procedures for the yearly elections function as a process of 'purification of local citizenship' in the *comunidad.*

So, unlike during national elections, when many Usibambinos do not, for practical reasons, fulfil their duties as citizens of the Peruvian nation-state, during local elections in the *comunidad*, fixed scripts of order and discipline are followed. During local elections, *comuneros* have to prove their value as citizens through extensive administrative procedures. We argue that in copying national election rituals and in amplifying governmental forms of discipline and order, Usibambinos not only want to prove themselves to be good *comuneros*, but also worthy citizens of the Peruvian nation-state. This obsessive mimicking of state discipline can even be interpreted as a more insubordinate statement of the Usibambinos that their village is just as much – or even more – a community of justice and civilization as the official state is.

Conclusion: State Power, Citizenship and the Relation of Exception

The question that inspired this chapter is: 'What is the nature of state power in the periphery and what are the implications of this for notions of citizenship?' We discussed a population in the periphery that hardly notices any presence of the state with regard to government administration and programmes. So hardly any mechanisms of governmentality exist in terms of disciplinary processes of subjectivization that bind the individual to his own identity and consciousness, and at the same time, to state power. The Peruvian state apparatus does not influence or structure the day-to-day lives of its Andean population.

The Andean highland population rather experiences state domination through sovereign power in the form of laws governing their land and via direct physical violence. It is particularly the struggle over territory that has shaped the relationship of Indian people to the Peruvian state and their status of 'inclusive exclusion' or – in the words of the Usibambinos themselves – of 'a child that is rejected by its own mother'. For a long time, the Peruvian state used territorialization strategies to secure an Indian labour force for the haciendas and valley towns. Under the colonial regime (1530–1821), land rights were taken away from the Andean population and granted to Spanish settlers. This forced the Indian peoples to move towards the highest and poorest regions and to offer their labour in exchange for access to pasture lands. Military interventions and killings happened during fights over territory with large landholders and valley towns. In contrast to the southern Andes, Indian communities in the central highlands were more successful in defending their interests and maintaining a certain independence from the large landholdings.

At a later stage, when claims by the Andean population for restitution of their territories became increasingly forceful, the Peruvian state started to formally recognize *comunidades indigenas* by issuing special agrarian laws and granting them land rights. Subsequently, during the land reform of the 1970s large landholdings were expropriated, but rather than returning the land to the communities, state-led associations, SAISes, were created to manage the hacienda lands. Police and military intervention was common against *comuneros* who demanded the dismantlement of the SAIS and the return of the land in their own hands.

Although the Indian population always received little state care, laws were completely put aside when the state deemed the 're-establishment of order' in the Andean region necessary. The highlands and their population were at that time turned into a 'state of exception', where chaos was said to reign and where the state could suspend the validity of the law (Agamben 1998). This clearly happened during the civil war in the 1980s, when the Shining Path was active in the highlands but refrained from protecting the *comuneros* when they were under attack. During this period, the highland people were *Homo sacer* (Agamben 1998), or 'killable bodies' (Das and Poole 2004), for both the state and the Shining Path.

So the Andean highland population is included in the Peruvian nation-state through exclusion, and one could even say that they are a type of 'refused' citizens. They are seen and treated as second-rate, backwards, ignorant peasants or Indians. Like the paupers of Europe, highland populations are racialized and pathologized: they are regarded as both different and deficient. In Peru, the state has divided the population according to ethnic or spatial lines, leaving the *mestizo* urban population to find their way in a regime of liberal freedom while designating the highland population as static bearers of tradition, unworthy of state attention.

In this context of being kept in a relation of exception and lacking state care, highland communities have developed a high degree of autonomy in governance and jurisdiction, and turned into small peasant republics. Local state-like structures came into being, with written rules, extensive registration, formal procedures and a set of strict punishments. Within the *comunidades*, techniques of government have become part of a ritualized world of administrative practices that support a local system of governance. In this sense, we find forms of governmentalization in local rule. This reality sharply contrasts with the depiction of Indian people as barbarian savages. It is important to stress that these local disciplinary regimes have not developed endogenously, but have been shaped in relation to a violent outside world of discrimination and exclusion.

It is remarkable that in this local regime, national symbols of state power play such a central role. *Comuneros*, for example, commonly march in similar fashion to military parades during communal festivities, and the Peruvian flag and national hymn play a pivotal role during community ceremonies. This mimicry of the state can be interpreted in different ways. On the one hand it can be seen as a call for inclusion and a desperate desire and claim to be incorporated in the national project as 'worthy citizens' (cf. Das and Poole 2004). On the other hand, it can be analysed as a defiant statement that Usibamba is just as much a community of law and order as the official state is.

References

Agamben, G. (1998), *Homo Sacer: Sovereign Power and Bare Life*, Stanford, CA: Stanford University Press.

Blom, T. and Stepputat, F. (2005), 'Introduction', in T. Blom and F. Stepputat (eds), *Sovereign Bodies: Citizens, Migrants, and States in the Postcolonial World*, Princeton, NJ and Oxford: Princeton University Press, pp. 1–36.

Castillo, L. del (1992) 'Tienen Futuro las Comunidades Campesinas?', *Debate Agrario* 14: 39–53.

Das, V. and Poole, D. (2004), 'State and its Margins; Comparative Ethnographies', in V. Das and D. Poole (eds), *Anthropology in the Margins of the State*, Oxford: James Currey, pp. 3–33.

Dean, M. (1994), *Critical and Effective Histories: Foucault's Methods and Historical Sociology*, London and New York: Routledge.

—— (2001), '"Demonic Societies" Liberalism, Biopolitics, and Sovereignty', in T. Blom and F. Stepputat (eds), *States of Imagination; Ethnographic Explorations of the Postcolonial State*, Durham, NC and London: Duke University Press, pp. 41–64.

Degregori, C.I. (ed.) (1996), *Las Rondas Campesinas y la Derrota de Sendero Luminoso*, Lima: Instituto de Estudios Peruanos.

Dobyns, H.F. (1970), *Comunidades Campesinas del Peru*, Lima: Editorial Estudios Andinos.

Eckert, J. (2006), 'From Subjects to Citizens: Legalism from Below and the Homogenization of the Legal Sphere', *Journal of Legal Pluralism* 53/54: 45–75.

Faron, L.C. (1985), *From Conquest to Agrarian Reform: Ethnicity, Ecology, and Economy in the Chancas Valley, Peru, 1533 to 1964*, Pittsburgh, PA: University Press.

Foucault, M. (1988), 'The Ethic of Care for the Self as a Practice of Freedom', in J. Bernauer and D. Rasmussen (eds), *The Final Foucault*, Boston, MA: MIT Press, pp. 1–20.

—— (1993), 'About the Beginnings of the Hermeneutic of the Self', transcription of two lectures in Dartmouth on 17 and 24 November 1980, *Political Theory* 21(2): 198–227.

Fumerton, M. (2001), '*Rondas Campesinas* in the Peruvian Civil War: Peasant Self-defence Organizations in Ayacucho', *Bulletin of Latin American Research* 20(4): 470–97.

García, M. (2005), *Making Indigenous Citizens: Identities, Education, and Multicultural Development in Peru*, Stanford, CA: Stanford University Press.

Handelman, H. (1975), *Struggle in the Andes: Peasant Political Mobilization in Peru*, Austin, TX: University of Texas, Institute of Latin American Studies.

Inda, J. (ed.) (2005), *Anthropologies of Modernity: Foucault, Governmentality and Life Politics*, Oxford: Blackwell Publishing.

Li, T. (2005), 'Beyond the State and Failed Schemes', *American Anthropologist* 107(3): 383–94.

Manrique, N. (1988a [1987]), 'Las Comunidades Campesinas en la Sierra Central en el Siglo XIX', in H. Bonilla (ed.), *Comunidades Campesinas: Cambios y Permanencias. Chiclayo: Centro de Estudios Sociales Solidaridad*, 2nd edn, Lima: Consejo Nacional de Ciencia y Tecnologia, pp. 115–33.

—— (1988b) 'The War for the Central Sierra', in S. Stern (ed.), *Shining and Other Paths: War and Society in Peru, 1980–1995*, Durham, NC and London: Duke University Press, pp. 193–223.

Martínez-Allier, J. (1973), *Los Huacchileros del Perú: dos Estudios de Formaciones Sociales Agrarias*, Paris: Ruedo Ibérico, and Lima: Instituto de Estudios Peruanos.

Mathews, A. (2005), 'Power/Knowledge, Power/Ignorance: Forest Fires and the State in Mexico', *Human Ecology* 33(6): 795–820.

Moore, D.S. (2005), *Suffering for Territory: Race, Place and Power in Zimbabwe*, Durham, NC and London: Duke University Press.

Nelson, D. (2005), 'Life during Wartime: Guatemala, Vitality, Conspiracy, Milieu', in J. Inda (ed.), *Anthropologies of Modernity: Foucault, Governmentality and Life Politics*, Oxford: Blackwell, pp. 215–47.

Nuijten, M. and Lorenzo, D. (2008), 'Duenos de Todo y de Nada! (Owners of All and Nothing): Restitution of Indian Territories in the Central Andes of Peru', in D. Fay and D. James (eds), *The Rights and Wrongs of Land Restitution: Restoring What Was Ours*, London and New York: Routledge.

Nuñez, P. (1995), *Law and Peasant Communities in Peru (1969–1988)*, Wageningen: Wageningen Agricultural University, PhD thesis.

Ong, A. (2000), 'Graduated Sovereignty in South-East Asia', *Theory, Culture and Society* 17(4): 55–75.

Orlove, B. (1982), 'Tomar la Bandera: Politics and Punch in Southern Peru', *Ethnos* 47(3–4): 249–61.

—— (1994), 'The Dead Policemen Speak: Power, Fear and Narrative in the 1931 Molloccahua Killings (Cuzco)', in D. Poole (ed.), *Unruly Order: Violence, Power, and Cultural Identity in the High Provinces of Southern Peru*, Boulder, CO: Westview Press, pp. 63–96.

Paerregaard, K. (1987), *Nuevas Organizaciones en Comunidades Campesinas: el Caso de Usibamba y Chaquicocha*, Lima: Pontífica Universidad Católica del Perú, Fondo Editorial.

—— (2002), 'The Vicissitudes of Politics and the Resilience of the Peasantry: Contesting and Reconfiguring Political Space in the Andes', in L. Engberg and N. Webster (eds), *In the Name of the Poor: Contesting Political Space for Poverty Alleviation*, London: Zed Press, pp. 52–77.

Petryna, A. (2005), 'Science and Citizenship under Postsocialism', in J. Inda (ed.), *Anthropologies of Modernity: Foucault, Governmentality and Life Politics*, Oxford: Blackwell, pp. 158–77; reprint from *Social Research* 70/2 (2003): 551–78.

Renique, J.L. (1994), 'Political Violence, the State, and the Peasant Struggle for Land (Puno)', in D. Poole (ed.), *Unruly Order: Violence, Power, and Cultural Identity in the High Provinces of Southern Peru*, Boulder, CO: Westview Press, pp. 223–46.

Roberts, B.R. and Samaniego, C. (1978), 'The Evolution of Pastoral Villages and the Significance of Agrarian Reform in the Highlands of Central Peru', in N. Long and B. Roberts (eds), *Peasant Cooperation and Capitalist Expansion in Peru*, Austin, TX: University of Texas Press, pp. 241–63.

Sánchez, R. (1989), 'Las Sais de Junín y la Alternativa Comunal', *Debate Agrario* 7: 85–101.

Smith, G. (1989), *Livelihood and Resistance; Peasants and the Politics of Land in Peru*, Berkeley, CA: University of California Press.

Starn, O. (1995), 'To Revolt against the Revolution: War and Resistance in Peru's Andes', *Cultural Anthropology* 10(4): 547–80.

Stepputat, F. (2004), 'Marching for Progress: Rituals of Citizenship, State and Belonging in a High Andes District', *Bulletin of Latin American Research* 23(2): 224–59.

Vandergeest, P. and Peluso, N.L. (1995), 'Territorialization and State Power in Thailand', *Theory and Society* 24(3): 385–426.

Wilson, F. (2004), 'Towards a Political Economy of Roads: Experiences from Peru', *Development and Change* 35(3): 525–46.

Yambert, K. (1980), 'Thought and Reality: Dialectics of the Andean Community', in: B. Orlove and G. Custred (eds), *Land and Power in Latin America: Agrarian Economies and Social Processes in the Andes*, New York and London: Holmes and Meier Publishers, pp. 31–54.

Yrigoyen, F.R. (2000), 'The Constitutional Recognition of Indigenous Law in Andean Countries', in W. Assies, G. van der Haar and A. Hoekema (eds), *The Challenge of Diversity: Indigenous Peoples and Reform of the State in Latin America*, Amsterdam: Thela Publisher, pp. 197–222.

Chapter 6

Government, Business and Chiefs: Ambiguities of Social Justice through Land Restitution in South Africa

Anne Hellum and Bill Derman

Introduction

South Africa's law and governance structures are rapidly changing in the country's endeavour to unmake race, class and gender injustices deriving from apartheid's racialized land policy. The land restitution process, like many other reform processes launched by the current ruling party of South Africa, the African National Congress (ANC), contains unresolved tensions between three overlapping policy frameworks that are currently in use to change deep-rooted race, class and gender inequalities. These are

- the human rights-based approach;
- the political economy of poverty, and the necessity for land redistribution;
- a market-led approach emphasizing property rights and market access.

This study of the land restitution process and the return of, or compensation for, land taken for racial reasons since 1913 explores how the ANC government balances the search for economic growth and undoing historical and social injustices underlain by efforts to balance universal citizenship with recognition of difference. Land restitution, the third leg of South Africa's land reform, has entered a critical phase, with the planned restoration of hundreds of highly developed commercial farms to claimant communities in the face of substantial landowner resistance and government over-commitment. According to the current Director General of Land Affairs, Tozi Gwanya, 94 per cent of all claims are settled, with 4,898 unsettled. Of those remaining, 2,585 were prioritized for settlement in 2008.[1] According to

1 This is the number provided by Tozi Gwanya on 11 March 2008 to the Portfolio Committee on Agriculture and Land Affairs. 'Settled' does not mean that communities have received and are operating farms. It means only that an agreement has been reached between the government and the landowners. The aim was to have all claims settled by end of March 2008, but this goal has not been attained.

the Director General, South Africa's land restitution programme is a big success story.[2]

Limpopo Province, which is the site of our study, now has 70 per cent of its total land area under claim. The province's commercial farms are an important contributor to South Africa's land-based export economy, through production of fruit, nuts, vegetables and timber, employment and other economic opportunities. The combination of productive land, substantial export revenues, pervasive restitution claims and past disappointments has led the government to embrace a new model of restitution. Successful claimant communities will form a joint venture company with a private entrepreneur, with a small share reserved for farm workers. In this strategic partnership (SP) model, the entrepreneur – 'the strategic partner' – invests working capital and retains control of farm management decisions for a period of ten years or more, with the option of renewal for a further period. The benefits to the claimant communities comprise rent for use of the land, a share of the profits, employment, and training opportunities for community members.

This new modified business model raises a series of fundamental questions about how the South African government balances its responsibility for providing economic and social development while achieving social justice. A related question is how it equalizes the three sources of inequality: race, gender and class. To claim land, communities had to demonstrate their possession of rights to land and removal from the land for racial reasons after 1913. In Limpopo, this has mainly been through documenting chiefdom or tribal boundaries, ancestral grave sites and locations of ritual activities. Thus, initial legal criteria lean on past socio-political organization, but now must respond to present imperatives, including economic sustainability, class and gender justice. The process thus epitomizes the ambiguities of restitution as a means of social justice in a post-apartheid context.[3] The government, rather than promoting devolution and the direct return of land to claimants, has opted for a joint venture model whereby private farm management companies are entrusted with many of the post-restitution responsibilities in terms of competence and institution-building. This is a novel institutional approach to the dilemma of how to turn over highly sophisticated farming operations to inexperienced rural communities. Viewing the homelands as underdeveloped regions needing modernist policies, the business model has now married social justice with economic development through a contract between government, claimant communities and strategic partners.[4]

In the following, we explore how this new governance model changes the role of law, the role of the state, the market and the community. We ask whether the

2 *Mail and Guardian*, 21 November 2007.

3 The history of land reform and the changing models of delivering land have been well summarized by, among others, Hall (2003; 2004); Lahiff (2005); Walker (2005a; 2005b; 2006; 2007).

4 See Mbeki (2004) for the articulation of this perspective, and Cousins's thoughtful response (Cousins 2007).

interests of the strategic partner and the community's right to restitution, ensuring equity and fairness between groups and individuals within the claimant community, are compatible.

To examine this process, we have read legislation, policy papers, court records and empirical studies of the implementation of restitution settlements in different parts of the country. Community claims lodged with the Regional Land Claims Commissioner (RLCC) in Limpopo and constitutions of the communal property associations (CPAs) formed by the claimant communities are key sources. With a focus on Levubu, we have visited claimant communities in the former homelands, farms that are the object of joint ventures, met with representatives of the farm management companies, communal property associations and chiefs, and examined draft settlement and shareholders' agreements. Through the archives of the Nkuzi Development Association,[5] the non-governmental organization (NGO) that has assisted the claimants in lodging claims and providing farm workers on the farms that are under claim with legal assistance, we have had access to information about the process over a longer time span.

The article is organized into ten sections, including this Introduction. It begins by outlining the goals of land restitution, the place of race, ethnicity and gender in the process, and the changing laws and policies of implementation in the second and third sections. We then explore the formation of new institutions, laws and policies to meet the competing objectives of historical redress and contemporary economic and social development. In the fourth and fifth sections we provide a more detailed consideration of land restitution in Limpopo Province, with a focus on the making of the strategic partner model. The next three sections analyse how the contradictory terrain of mixing a business model with social justice is negotiated in the intersection of state law, contract and custom. Among the paradoxes highlighted in the Conclusion is how chieftainship is re-emerging within this new partnership model.

The Right to Restitution in Constitution, Law and Practice

The Freedom Charter of the African National Congress of 1955 set out to return the land to the tiller: 'Restrictions of land ownership on a racial basis shall be ended, and all the land redivided amongst those who work it to banish famine and hunger.'

South Africa's land laws are slowly changing in its endeavour to undo race, class and gender injustices deriving from apartheid's dual land-holding system made up of freehold and communal land. Underlying this legal dichotomy is the racialized countryside, with privately owned white commercial agriculture, and the

5 Nkuzi started operating early in 1997, and now has full-time staff and volunteers working throughout the Limpopo Province, northern parts of Mpumalanga Province, and with farm residents in Gauteng Province.

impoverished state-owned homelands, held communally by one third of the black population with communal tenure security. This dual property system corresponds to the legal division between the received Roman Dutch common law that applied to the white settler population, and African customary laws that applied to the black population in the former homelands.

The South African Constitution of 1994 is premised on evidence that establishment of legal monism – a single, unified system – through abolishment of customary law and customary tenure does not work. In the spirit of international human rights principles embodying both the right to be equal and the right to be different, the Constitution puts customary law on a par with general law, customary tenure on a par with freehold tenure, and the right to culture on a par with gender equality. The property clause in Article 28 of the Constitution balances existing rights with redress for racial injustice. In line with international law, existing owners are entitled to fair compensation when the land is subject to restitution or redistribution. It extends the state's obligation to protect, respect and fulfil those rights in land that lacked recognition and protection under apartheid. The aim is to broaden protection of basic livelihood resources by extending ownership rights to users and occupiers who suffered discrimination because of the nature of property rights under apartheid. A cross-cutting constitutional concern is to undo the gender hierarchy embedded in both freehold and customary land law.

The Constitution provides that a person or community dispossessed of property after 19 June 1913 as a result of past racially discriminatory laws or practices is entitled, to the extent provided by an Act of Parliament, either to restitution of that property or to equitable redress (25.7). The Restitution of Land Rights Act (RLRA), no. 22, establishes a legal framework for the restitution process. Under the Act, the cut-off date for lodging claims was December 1998.

How to link restitution, which looks at past injustices, with contemporary race, class and gender inequalities has been a recurrent problem. In making a restitution claim, the starting point is whether the claim is that of an individual dispossessed of a right to land, or of a direct descendant, or relates to a deceased person's estate. If it is a community or part of a community dispossessed of a right to land, the community as a whole becomes a legal person, and all potential individual claims are now subsumed into that. If the claim is successful, the ownership of the land will be vested in one entity that will hold the land on behalf of the community – in practice, a communal property association, or less frequently, a business trust.

In line with the well-documented complexities on the ground, Article 1 of the RLRA gives a broad definition of property rights to compensate for the multiple forms of dispossession that took place in the apartheid years after 1913. According to this:

> Right in land means any right in land whether registered or unregistered, and may include the interest of a labour tenant and sharecropper, a customary law interest, the interest of a beneficiary under a trust arrangement and beneficial occupation for a continuous period of not less than 10 years prior to the dispossession.

What it means to be dispossessed of 'a right in land' has given rise to contestation – for example, whether existence as a tribe since 1913 has to be proved, rather than just land use. To fulfil this requirement, groups that were dispersed – particularly farm workers who have worked on different farms and integrated into different communities – have had difficulty demonstrating that they existed either as a tribe or members of the community that is making the claim. In Levubu, where we are working, farm workers have established claims only as members of chieftaincies or communities, but not as farm workers or farm dwellers, despite the existence of large numbers of such people on the farms after 1913.

Although chieftaincy retains formal recognition in the Constitution, chiefs were not formally included in the restitution process.[6] While equal under the RLRA, tribal groups are in practice in a far better position than, for example, religious groups or dispersed farm workers to organize and document their claims.[7] In Limpopo Province, the lodging of community claims has primarily been through efforts to prove tribal identity. The relatively recent date of removal, the relative proximity of many communities to their ancestral lands, and the continuity of community identity have all contributed to the strong demand for repossession of original lands rather than compensation or alternative lands. In the settlement of the Levubu claims, the Regional Land Claims Commissioner chose the boundaries of chieftainship. This was done partly because chiefs had been instrumental in lodging land claims, and because they claimed to be the only legitimate landowning authority. It was also seen as the most sustainable option, as the user-based approach would lead to the break-up of already existing farms. Furthermore, chiefs in this area are recognized as the ultimate owners of land, or at least the legitimate custodians of land rights.

The Communal Property Associations Act of 1996 was enacted to create new and fair group property-holding institutions to replace tribal structures left over from the apartheid era. The Act applies to both restituted and redistributed land. Communal Property Associations (CPAs) became the primary local organizations to receive land on behalf of claimant communities from the Department of Land Affairs (DLA) and the Regional Land Claims Commissioner (RLCC) (see below). In line with the principle of gender equality, women hold individual membership and women's participation on the CPA board is mandatory. Rural women's restitution claims are accommodated as part of group claims. As Pienaar points out, the legal content of membership and the rights of members in a group claim

6 Chiefs have been given both political and judicial power under the Traditional Leaders Act of 2003. The court's use of this term differs from that of the legal anthropologist B. Oomen (2005), who demonstrates variations dependent on the background of the different chiefs rather than a uniform practice. The Communal Land Rights Act of 2004 (not yet implemented) empowers chiefs to hold land on behalf of people in the communal lands, and will, if it passes the constitutional test, affect restitution.

7 C. Louw, 'Claims Now Require Proof of Tribal Identity', *Farmer's Weekly*, 24 June 2005; James (2007).

has not been accomplished prior to the transfer of land.[8] This lack of legal clarity is particularly problematic from the perspective of married women, who do not have equal property rights under customary law.

The intersection of individual women's rights to equality on the one hand and protection of a group's right to culture on the other is a site of political and legal contestation, culminating in legislative and constitutional battles. By enacting the Communal Land Rights Act (CLRA) in 2005, the ANC government veered in the opposite direction from the CPA Act, giving traditional authorities the right to hold communal land on behalf of the community. Women in several rural communities are, with the assistance of human rights NGOs, challenging the constitutionality of the CLRA on the basis of the equality principle in the Constitution. The government, on the other hand, refers to the Traditional Leadership and Governance Framework Amendment Act of 2003, which requires at least one third of the members of a traditional council to be women. In the *Bhe* case, which was lodged by two rural women, the Constitutional Court struck down the prevailing customary inheritance law with reference to the equality principle in the Constitution.[9] Striking down discriminatory aspects of the written customary law, the Constitutional Court also made reference to the dynamic and changing customary law.

The re-regulation of land that is taking place through land reform in general, and land restitution in particular, is a conflict-ridden and contradictory process. The restitution process, by turning to the customary laws of past communities and the use of tribal criteria, is facilitating the re-creation of a dual property system that resembles apartheid's chiefly rule. Without any legal definition of the rights of the individual members within a group claim, the property relations within successful claimant communities is likely to reflect existing divisions of status and power. In the following sections, we examine in greater detail the outcomes to date of the restitution process.

The Restitution Process: Rights, Discretion and Development

Consonant with the Constitution, the RLRA sets out a procedural framework to deal with the gross historical injustices of land dispossession that took place throughout the colonial and apartheid era. The RLRA established new legal and administrative institutions to restore land, to find appropriate new lands or to pay appropriate compensation. The chief actors, aside from the community, are the Chief Land Claims Commissioner, the Regional Land Claims Commissioners and the Land Claims Court.[10]

---

8 Pienaar (2007), 37; he argues that unless CPAs specify what rights members have to CPA-owned resources and shares in those resources, community members exist in a 'rightless sphere'.

9 *Bhe* v. *Magistrate, Khayelitsha and Others*, Case CCT 49/03.

10 RLRA, 1994, s. 4 (1).

The Land Claims Court was established to grant restitution orders contemplated in section 123 (3) of the Constitution and to determine conditions which must be fulfilled before rights to land can be restored.[11] The RLRA prescribes the procedures to be followed in lodging, investigating and settling claims by individuals or groups.[12] Owing to the slow progress in handling claims, amendments to the RLRA in 1999 shifted the approach from a judicial to an administrative one. The Land Claims Commissioner was given delegated power to facilitate settlements. Only claims that are not resolved through agreement between the parties take the judicial route through the Land Claims Court. The administration is now empowered to settle claims on its own when the claims are not contested. The shift from a judicial to an administrative model gives the Ministry of Agriculture (through the Department of Land Affairs), with the assistance of the Land Claims Commissioner, wide discretionary power to implement the right to restitution.

The scale of land claims, the high value of the farms involved, combined with fragmented and dispersed communities lacking agricultural experience due to labour migration and deprivation of arable land, have taken law and policy makers by surprise. In an effort to make rights real and match rights and state obligations, a series of development interventions has been imposed on claimant communities through court decisions and settlement agreements in order to ensure sustainable and equitable use of resources. A recurrent tension within the implementation process resides in balancing a community's right to restitution with principles of equity and fairness. The White Paper on Land Policy of 1997 states: 'Restitution policy is guided by the principles of fairness and justice. At the heart of this is the recognition that solutions must not be forced on people.' Yet it also states: 'The principles of fairness and justice also require a restitution policy that considers the broader development interests of the country and ensures that limited state resources are used in a responsible manner. To be successful, restitution needs to support, and be supported by, the reconstruction and development process.'

A standard condition linked to settlement agreements between the Department of Land Affairs (DLA) and the claimant community is the formation of a legal entity that will become the owner of the land. The Communal Property Associations Act of 1996 forms the legal backdrop for this condition. In accordance with section 2(1), the provisions of the Act shall apply to a community which:

> by order of the Land Claims Court is entitled to restitution under the Restitution of Land Rights Act, where that Court has ordered restitution on condition that an association be formed in accordance with the provisions of this Act.

11 Ibid., s. 36.

12 In each province, a Regional Land Claims Commissioner is established to investigate the validity (s. 12) of the claim and to mediate competing claims (s. 13). To assess the feasibility of the claim, the Regional Land Claims Commissioner shall request a Certificate of Feasibility (s. 15) from the Minister (DLA).

The Communal Property Association is a legal entity that can own the land and has the capacity to sue and be sued under section 8(6)(a). Registration as a CPA requires the drafting of a constitution regulating issues pertaining to membership and decision-making. Among the principles to be accommodated in the constitution, in accordance with section 9(1), are fair and inclusive decision-making processes and equality of membership.

How to distribute property between different groups or individuals within the community is unspecified, despite the obligation under section 35 of the RLRA to 'ensure that all the dispossessed members of the community shall have access to the land or the compensation in question on a basis which is fair and non-discriminatory towards any person, including a woman and a tenant'. The requirement that a certain percentage of the CPA committee members should be women is the only legal measure taken to ensure fair and non-discriminatory access.

For a number of communities that successfully claimed their land back, the post-restitution process has posed problems and conflicts unforeseen by community members, NGO activists, law-makers and policy-makers and the administration. In the planning process, local communities were seen as undifferentiated, with similar interests, therefore no account was taken of their complexity (Pienaar 2006). The restitution process was, to a large extent, based on romanticized notions of self-sufficiency and self-regulating agricultural communities. The post-restitution experiences of bringing dispersed, impoverished and highly diverse groups of people together speak to the need for a more comprehensive property system, balancing group rights and individual rights (Pienaar 2007).

The records of the Land Claims Court are illustrative of the post-restitution scenario, where impoverished communities struggle to make a living for themselves as they move onto commercial farms that have been left by the previous owner and stripped of equipment and agricultural input. The court records also reflect escalating conflicts within dispersed communities which, without adequate resources, are trying to manage run-down farms while forming new institutions, rules and practices pertaining to sharing common resources (Dodson 2006; 2007; Pienaar 2006). In the *Kranspoort Community* case, the Land Claims Court responded to the post-restitution crisis and conflicts by demanding changes from the claimant community, the RLCC and the DLA. The court found that without government assistance and planning, the CPA could not assume its responsibilities. The case illustrates how the court has widened the legal obligations of these government agencies.

Between State and Market

Faced with the enormous scale of developmental responsibilities involved in the demand for a just and sustainable post-restitution process, the government has altered the land restitution process, at least in the case of relatively high-value farms. In adopting a market-based model, claimant communities, as a condition for the return of their land, are required to form strategic partnerships with agribusiness corporations for a minimum period of ten years. The strategic partner and the CPA from the claimant community form a new operating company which will receive and distribute benefits. It will also serve as the training ground in farm business for the CPA. The benefits to the claimant communities comprise rent for the land, a share in the profits based on their 50 per cent share in the new company, and employment and training opportunities for community members.

The factors contributing to the emergence of the strategic partnership model can be summarized as follows:

- a constitutional imperative to return land to communities that were dispossessed on racial grounds in a fair and equitable manner;
- an economic imperative to maintain the productivity of farms and minimize the impact on employment and the local economy, while ensuring a transition to new owners;
- a developmental imperative to ensure long-term benefits to claimants (over and above the symbolic value of the return of the land), and to ensure that farms remain businesses, and are not used for livelihood (or subsistence) purposes;
- a political imperative to demonstrate how government and its ruling party, the ANC, can succeed in bringing development to rural areas; in addition, to preserve South Africa's reputation as a secure place for investment.

This policy option has emerged on an *ad hoc* basis through individual settlements in Limpopo Province. There is no policy document, and there is no evidence of consultation through political conferences, parliamentary debates or consultation with civil society, much less a White Paper.[13] The model was pioneered through a successful joint venture between the Bjatladi Communal Property Association and Henley Farm Properties Ltd concerning the management of the state-owned Zebediela Citrus Estate, although there have been other experiences with equity-sharing arrangements in Kwazulu-Natal and the Western Cape which form part of the pattern of business-oriented land reform.

The settlement agreements mainly regulate the relationship between the strategic partners and the CPAs. They are accompanied by a series of agreements pertaining to the organization of the operating company. The operating company is a shareholding company, run by a board of directors elected by the shareholders: the strategic partner, the CPA, the workers' trust[14] and the DLA. The strategic partner model is not accompanied by any overarching guidelines from the RLCC and the DLA to ensure fairness and representativeness of community members on the board of directors and on the executive of the CPA.

13 In general, prior to major policy shifts, the government has written a White Paper to be discussed with all interested parties.

14 These had not yet been formed at the time of writing (June 2008).

It bears emphasizing that there are significant limits to the market dimension of the restitution process. CPAs are not permitted to either sell or mortgage the land to anyone in perpetuity. Such a restriction will also be part of the Communal Land Rights Act as it is implemented. While this is an attempt to protect CPA members from once again losing their land, the full implications of maintaining a separate land tenure system for communal areas remains highly contested.

Having created the precise manner in which restitution cases are to be handled, it seems that how government will continue to be involved has been unresolved. There seems to be a transition period in which the RLCC purchases the land on behalf of claimants, negotiates the prices, and facilitates the transfer. Initially, government sought to withdraw from the process to let the private sector manage the restituted farms. However, the withdrawal of one strategic partner from Levubu and the severe economic difficulties of the other strategic partner have had the result that government cannot withdraw. Having pushed communities to accept the SP model, the claimant communities have pressured government to assist them in these times of increasing difficulty. We discuss below how the state is changing its engagement in the restitution process.

Land Restitution through Strategic Partnerships in Limpopo Province[15]

The Upper Luvuvhu Catchment, the site of our field research, is one of a number of pockets of high-value irrigated land in Limpopo Province. It lies between the towns of Makhado (also known as Louis Trichardt) and Levubu, which is approximately 60 kilometres to the east.

Limpopo Province remains South Africa's most rural province, with high rates of poverty and unemployment. Its population is 5.6 million (Statistics South Africa 2006a), of which 37,349 are full-time farm workers and 27,053 are casual and seasonal workers, with approximately 10,000 agricultural jobs in Makhado Municipality (Statistics South Africa 2006b).

We chose this site because it is water-abundant, highly productive, has several agro-processing factories and lumber mills, and is involved in international marketing. The Levubu area reveals the complex processes involved in transferring highly capitalized agriculture to claimant communities.[16] This area is the site of one of the largest transfers of farms from white to black owners. Our research entails a longitudinal study of this transitional process, including the interactions among strategic partners, NGOs, government ministries, claimant communities and different segments within the claimant communities.

15 The discussion of strategic partners and communal property associations in this section draws heavily upon Derman, Lahiff and Sjaastad (2006). Lahiff (2005) critiques the willing seller/willing buyer model.

16 The original site selection was conducted in collaboration with Dr Edward Lahiff.

Prior to 1898, the military strength of the local Venda tribes, and the presence of malaria, meant the area was not occupied. Substantial numbers of white settlers arrived in the 1920s and 1930s, with government support (Lahiff 2000; Mulaudzi 2000). Because of continued agricultural failures, the government established an irrigation scheme from 1935 to 1937 for poor white farmers, which also failed. The African population of the area, mainly Venda and Tsonga speakers, were gradually and forcibly removed from the prime irrigated land and adjacent hillsides, which became tree plantations. This occurred as the new owners increased labour obligations and reduced areas for grazing and cultivation (Harries 1989; Nefale 2000). The government built the Albasini Dam in the 1950s to improve and intensify agriculture for the white farmers, who until that point had done quite poorly. Following the Nationalist Party's electoral victory in 1948, black South Africans were forced on the basis of ethnicity into 'homelands' created for them by the apartheid state (Platzky and Walker 1985).

The relatively recent date of removal, the relative proximity of many communities to their ancestral lands and the continuity of community identity have all contributed to the extraordinary extent of restitution claims in Limpopo, claims which, unlike in other parts of the country, contain a strong demand for repossession of original lands, not compensation. And government has acceded to these demands.

The Levubu claim has 350 farms totalling around 10,000 hectares of irrigated agricultural land (more than 80 have already been purchased). There are nine claimant communities for these farms. In addition, all the land adjoining these farms, including private and public forests, is under claim. Transferring such a large resource to a new set of owners presents enormous practical challenges for the Regional Land Claims Commissioner's office, which has limited staff and technical resources. A precipitous transfer could be disruptive of the local economy in terms of productivity, farm employment, upstream and downstream industries, and property values. These concerns not only affect those directly involved, but have also been voiced by political leaders across the political spectrum and by business interests in the province. Strong opposition to the restitution process is evident among some landowners, while others accept the constitution and law. A few farmers who accepted restitution constituted the Group of 23 in 2000/2001 and attempted to become a strategic partner. The original proposal by members of the farmers' organization, Agri SA, was turned down. The group was renamed Mavu Management Services, and it became a strategic partner, only to pull out in August of 2007 after seven years of engagement with the restitution process.

The failure of some restitution projects and the underperformance of others added to the pressure on the Provincial Land Claims Commissioner to provide solutions that preserved the productive capacity of the farms in question, and ensured a reasonable degree of material benefits for the claimants over time. This model comes neither from the claimants nor from the previous landowners, but has been politically and administratively driven. It partly derived from the Provincial Department of Agriculture. The SP model coincides with the provincial vision of agriculture as expressed by the MEC for Agriculture – that it was to be a business, and only a business.[17]

In practice, traditional leadership has a strong presence in the process. The claims that were lodged on behalf of the claimant communities follow the boundaries of pre-colonial and colonial chieftainships. Such claims can invoke historical conflicts between chiefdoms and chiefs and sub-chiefs. A testimony accompanying the Ratombo land claim, where the community had been dispersed as a result of forced removals, speaks to the significance of chieftainship in the land restitution process as seen by those articulating the voice of the community:

> I am resettled at Nzehele present under headman Tshitumi, who is always fighting me. I am acting as the right hand of chief Ratombo. Our Community was taken by forced removal. We were never compensated for the loss of our land. People are scattered all over Venda. Other people are fighting against my people. I am suffering at Tshitumi. I am unable to practice my chieftainship. They referred me to my original tribal land. I am unable to make rituals for my ancestors because the whites forbid me to enter the area. The royal community is unable to meet because we do not have a place. The community wants land to cultivate their food. People have no land to cultivate.[18]

Because of the emphasis on land being returned according to chiefly boundaries, there exists the possibility of intensifying intra- and inter-ethnic conflict. In part, this is due to competing claims by different communities for the same farms, some of which remain unresolved. Moreover, there are claims by some communities against others for loss of grazing land, loss of agricultural land and so on, when communities were forced to accept those being forcibly removed from designated white areas.[19]

The Strategic Partnership Model in the Making

The SP model represents the reliance of government on a partial market approach to make land restitution work. While not relying directly on any specific law, like the other new institutions in the restitution process, it is based on contract. Strategic partners have been inserted into the restitution process through a contractual construction fashioned through the discretionary power of the DLA and the Regional Land Claims Commissioners.

---

17 Budget Speech 2005 by Honorable MEC for Agriculture, Limpopo Province, Ms D.P. Magadzi.

18 Written statement by Acting Chief of Ratombo, 1998, in the archives of Nkuzi.

19 There is as yet no estimate of the numbers of these cases.

The current arrangements in each of the major clusters of restitution claims on high-value land in Limpopo – Levubu, Magoebaskloof[20] and Hoedspruit – are that a small number of commercial companies are pre-selected by the Regional Land Claims Commissioner (working with the provincial Department of Agriculture and other agencies) and then recommended to the particular claimants. Initially, it appeared that the existing landowners could be included as potential partners, but this was abandoned since this would make it appear as though no real change had taken place. It was later proposed by the Limpopo RLCC that a single strategic partner would be selected for all the claims in the Levubu valley. The strategic partner in question was to be South African Farm Management (SAFM), a company controlled by a mix of established white operators in the agricultural sector and newer black partners. SAFM had a close working relationship with the provincial Department of Agriculture. Under pressure from claimants at Levubu, some of whom were reluctant to accept this lack of choice, the Commission undertook a process to select other potential strategic partners, at which point the newly formed company, Mavu Management Services (Mavu), was added to the list of potential strategic partners selected. Eventually, SAFM ended up as the selected strategic partner for approximately 70 per cent of the claimants at Levubu, and Mavu as the strategic partner for the remaining 30 per cent. There are former landowners in Mavu. However, the landowners among them have sold their land, and SAFM is managing at least some of the former farms owned by them.[21]

Under the strategic partnership model, the claimant community, organized in a communal property association or a trust, takes outright ownership of the land, which is directly transferred to it on the following conditions: that the community cannot sell or mortgage the land, and that the community (a) forms an operating company with the strategic partner to run the farm, and (b) agrees to lease the farm to the new operating company for an extended period, typically 10 or 15 years. In cases where there are permanent farm workers on the land who are not themselves members of the claimant community, farm workers may also be included as shareholders in the operating company as members of a workers' trust, yet to be formed.

20 Mashile Mokono, the Regional Land Claims Commissioner, has found that the land claims by the Makgoba community were prima facie valid. These claims are against 168 prime agricultural farms, comprising almost 200,000 hectares, in the Hoedspruit and Blydepoort areas of Tzaneen, about 70 kilometres from Polokwane (formerly Pietersburg).

21 In interviews with their senior management personnel in 2007, they cited the following major issues: their substantial expenditure of monies to rehabilitate the farms, the short duration of their contracts, and the amount of time that would have to be spent negotiating with claimant communities in the absence of full managerial control of the restituted farms. When government delayed paying Mavu for its expenses in running its farms, Mavu withdrew, and has been replaced by another agribusiness company, Umlimi Ltd, with headquarters in Stellenbosch but seeking to expand in Limpopo Province. Their contracts are for 15 and 20 years respectively, while Mavu's had been for ten.

Early proposals suggested that farm workers might be granted as much as 10 per cent of the shares, but at Levubu this has been diluted to a token 2 per cent.

This first phase of land restitution in Levubu has involved the transfer (in freehold title) of approximately 5,382 hectares of private land in 63 parcels, purchased at a total price of R219 million.[22] Strategic partners have asked for and received additional monies to restore farms that have been degraded due to the time lag between when the owners left and when they began operating them. They have also requested monies for farm development and new orchards. The government provides a series of grants to claimants to assist them in utilizing these restored lands. However, in Levubu, these grants have been given to the strategic partners to reimburse them for the costs of farm rehabilitation. Unfortunately, the government gave these monies to the strategic partners without the knowledge and agreement of the CPAs, thus causing further mistrust.[23]

The state has been drawn in to new negotiations due to the difficulties with the strategic partners on the one hand, and the unmet expectations of claimant communities on the other. They will be expected to restore the grants to communities and to commit further resources to the strategic partners. Simultaneously, there continue to be national discussions about whether or not land reform is on the right track and whether or not CPAs are the best form of organization for claimant communities. The role and place of government will be fluid and uncertain in the near future.

The Relationship between Strategic Partners and Communal Property Associations

The settlement and shareholder agreements regulate the relationship between the parties to the agreement, the strategic partners and the claimant communities by the CPAs. Shareholding in the operating companies has been a matter of considerable negotiation and contestation in some cases. How difficult the process has become is reflected in the fact that it was not until December 2007, after a full year of negotiations and the strategic partners running the farms (Derman, Lahiff and Sjaastad, 2006), that a contract was signed by Umlimi (the replacement for Mavu) and SAFM. The shift from restitution as a development and social justice issue to a business venture challenges the role of the state and the role of state law. The shareholding agreement makes reference to company law, while discrimination law, labour law and social welfare law, which have a bearing on the operation of the company, are not referred to. The role and responsibility of the Department of Land Affairs and the Regional Land Claims Commissioner in overseeing that the

22 All monetary values are in South African Rand (R).

23 The total grants given to the five SAFM Levubu claimant communities were R49 million, of which R30 million was given directly to SAFM without consultation; personal communication, 29 July 2008.

principles of non-discrimination, gender equity and fairness have been absent to date.

Under current agreements, the strategic partners hold 48 per cent of shares, the community 50 per cent, and workers 2 per cent. The share allocated to strategic partners is, in theory, based on the value of working capital to be provided by the strategic partner, along with the expertise that it will provide.[24] The allocation of shares was determined in the contractual negotiations between the parties, with government in the end deciding that the boards of directors should not be controlled by the strategic partners. Each CPA selects its own representatives to the boards of directors. There are three from each CPA, and they have been drawn from the executive committees and those who have been active for several years. The strategic partners are represented by three delegates, one of whom serves as the board chair for the first three years. The Umlimi boards have two independent observers: one selected by the CPA, the other by the strategic partner. Lastly, there are two government representatives who are non-voting. There are no requirements that a certain percentage of the Board of Directors be women or other segments of the claimant community in order to ensure fair and non-discriminatory representation.

Communities are to be compensated for the use of their land through the payment of rent, set at 1.5 per cent of land value, determined by the purchase price the government paid to acquire the land, paid per annum and indexed to inflation. This is below the market value of farming land, which implies that the community's share of the operating company is thus based not, as might be expected, on the land itself, but on other (non-land) assets that they can contribute. This typically includes the infrastructure and permanent crops on the farm, plus any capital grants they might receive as part of the restitution settlement, and again is not being fully quantified. In other words, the division of shares is pre-set, and cannot be related directly to the actual levels of investment by the various parties.

According to the SP model, claimant communities will benefit through a combination of rent paid on the land, a share in profits, training opportunities provided by the strategic partner, and preferential employment opportunities in the enterprise. Although the full value of these benefits, with the exception of rent, has not generally been specified during the negotiation phase, community members are expecting significant material benefits from the restoration of their land and their involvement in the business ventures.

It is widely understood, and explicitly stated in settlement agreements, that the claimants will take over the running of the farms at the end of the ten- to twenty-year period when management is the primary responsibility of the strategic partners. At present, there is no model as to how the handover will take place. Communities must therefore build up resources over the initial contract period

24 A major complaint by all CPAs has been that the strategic partners have brought no working capital to the table: in short, they have not invested their own capital in these new companies.

to buy out the shareholding of the strategic partner, and acquire the skills and experience to allow them to take over the running of the company. Since the restitution programme does not pay for moveable property, most farms no longer have productive equipment, including tractors, trucks and so forth. These now have to be obtained by the strategic partners and then be purchased by the joint operating companies. This points to a clear tension between the need for communities to accumulate capital to invest in the company in the longer term, and the need to distribute income (from dividends and rental) to members over the lifetime of the strategic partnership agreement. In addition, the CPAs lack capital, and will be under exceptional pressure from their communities for direct benefits driven by the large number of members, and their relative poverty. We thus have the issue of a large, poor community owning a valuable asset, and lacking the working capital and expertise to make them work. Whether and how they can influence the board of directors, and thereby the strategic partners, to balance investing in the future and providing direct benefits to claimants remains to be seen. In addition, to date, the training and education components remain unspecified and unfounded.

For the strategic partner, the benefits lie in the management fee, a share in the profits of the company, and control of upstream and downstream activities, with potential benefits exceeding that of the farming enterprise itself. Also, by entering into partnerships with multiple communities in a specific area, across numerous farms, strategic partners have the possibility of consolidating and rationalizing production in a way that was not generally open to the previous owner-occupiers. The divergent interests of communities and strategic partners, and the potential for strategic partners to maximize their profits at the expense of their community partners, remain likely. The formal operation of the new joint venture companies began in 2008. The boards of directors have now had two meetings (as of August 2008), and most farms are operating at a loss. Thus, the initial expectations of CPAs bringing significant economic benefits will, at the least, be delayed. Claimant communities have increasingly been active in visits to their new farms, meetings with the strategic partners and involvement with hiring, disciplining and firing farm workers. In short, there has been substantial active participation by claimant communities, or at least their leadership.

On behalf of government, the Limpopo Department of Agriculture has the responsibility to ensure the feasibility of business plans, the capacity of the strategic partner and the operations of the new joint-venture companies by its staff attending board meetings as non-voting participants. RLCC staff also attend, but its role is less defined. They are partly there to ensure that the Settlement Agreements are adhered to.

How broader justice and development issues will be considered in the rules emerging from decision-making, disputes and board of trustee resolutions will depend on how the bargaining power of the different parties in the process is balanced. In so far as the CPAs depend for economic and legal know-how on the strategic partners (who also have a major business interest in the company), there will be conflicting interests. The business vision of agriculture dominates this model. Broader questions of who speaks on behalf of the CPAs on the board of directors and in the CPA committee are shelved in favour of intensifying business. It is not unreasonable to predict that there will be efforts by local elites to capture the boards, and increased conflicts over monies as they begin to flow. Partly, this is due to lack of regulations ensuring fair representation of different segments of the claimant communities, combined with the non-specification of CPA members' rights and shares in the new companies. In this unequal partnership, CPAs have requested the assistance of the government and the Nkuzi Development Association that originally assisted communities in their land claims. Whether or not they can perform this role depends on their responsiveness to broader CPA concerns, and the mandates and resources given to them towards these ends.

Communal Property Associations, Traditional Councils and Chiefs

Although CPAs were supposed to be the mechanism to change the status of communal dwellers from subjects under a landowning chief to an association of free and equal citizens that hold land in common, this has, in reality, not occurred. In Levubu, the RLCC hired a national NGO, Nkuzi Development Association, to assist the communities in this process. Nkuzi, which was already assisting the claimant communities in the claims process, acted as a broker between state, civil society and claimant communities. Through workshops, they facilitated the drafting and adoption of the required constitution regulating issues pertaining to membership and decision-making.

The communal property association added a new layer to already existing local structures dealing with communal property. It was an intervention that took the chiefs, who in most of the claimant communities had initiated or taken the lead in the process, by surprise. According to information we have obtained from chiefs, committee and community members, the responses were varied. The Tshakuma opposed a communal property association and formed a trust, which was led by the chief, who was the former Minister of Agriculture in the homeland of Venda. According to those board members we met with, the chief owned the land, and the people living on it were all his subjects. According to one board member, the Tshakuma opposed a communal property association where 'any boy could be elected leader and run off with the money'. The Masakona chief told us that he had understood and learnt to work with the CPAs after being 'workshopped' by the Regional Land Claims Commission and Nkuzi. The chair of the Shigalo Communal Property Association saw the CPA as an important supplement to existing structures. He emphasized: 'The land belongs to the community and not to the chief. The chief leads the community. The CPA brings the people together.'[25]

While state law is apparently accepted and adopted through the CPA constitutions and confirmed by the settlement agreement between the Department of Land Affairs,

25 Interview, 10 August 2007.

the Regional Land Claims Commissioner and the claimant community (represented by the CPA), the new rules and the new institutions are re-negotiated and reinterpreted in the context of already existing norms and institutions. The composition of the CPA committee reflects the significance that traditional leaders and their families place upon them in the wider struggle over property rights. In all Levubu claimant communities, chiefs have been active in support of the land claims and are among the initiators of them. In three of the CPA committees, the acting chief or headman is also chair of the CPA. In one, the chief is chair of the trust. In another two, the acting chief and secretary of the tribal council are chairs of their respective CPAs. In all the CPAs, several members of the royal family are members. The most active and powerful female members are those who come from the royal family. The overlap between the initial land claim committees, the royal council, the tribal authority and the CPA committee puts chiefs in a powerful position.

Strategic Partners, CPAs, Chiefs and Farm Workers

Among the unresolved issues in the process of land restitution is what to do about existing farm workers and farm dwellers that are (or were) living on the farms to be restituted. In the wider political economy, commercial farms have been significantly reducing their labour force (Wegerif et al. 2006). The National Evictions Survey found that from 1994 to the end of 2004, 2,351,000 people have been displaced, and 942,000 evicted from farms. National and provincial government ministries have been lax in enforcing the laws that guarantee farm worker protections[26] and farm dwellers' home security.[27] But the declining numbers of farm workers can also be attributed to the withdrawal of agricultural subsidies and the formalization of farm workers' status, including much higher minimum wages, unemployment insurance and pension payments (Atkinson 2007; James 2007). Moreover, there has been a striking absence of unions assisting farm workers to protect their jobs.

Since November 2007, when the strategic partners began managing the farms, the greatest benefit for claimant community members has been employment on the farms. Several hundred members have now been hired as permanent and seasonal farm workers. Moreover, there are the further promises of education and training. The employment opportunities of members of the claimant community are, in principle, limited by the existing workers' rights as farm workers, labour tenants or farm dwellers. As part of the agreement between strategic partners and CPAs, they were not to lay off any farm worker or employee. Only as workers and employees retire or quit are they to be replaced by members of claimant communities. The existing farm workers' primary leverage came from possessing the functional and operational knowledge of a farm, but that required hiring only a few of the best workers. The farms now owned by claimant communities and being managed

26 Land Reform Labour Tenants Act (LTA), no. 3 of 1996.

27 Extension of Security of Tenure Act (ESTA), no. 62 of 1997.

by SAFM and Umlimi had no processes or procedures in place to record farm workers (permanent and seasonal) at the time the farms were purchased by the Land Claims Commission on behalf of the claimant communities from the farm owner. No procedures were installed to pay or keep farm workers in place, especially when there was a delay in the process and the former owner left before the strategic partners took over management (which was the typical case, not the exception). The Land Claims Commission had no mandate, nor was it interested in meeting and consulting with farm workers. In sum, there has been no protection for farm workers in the transition. Neither government departments nor NGOs are willing to step into the breach.[28]

The shareholder agreement acknowledges, and to a certain degree seeks to even out, short-term social and economic differences between the strategic partner company on the one hand and the claimant community on the other. The hiring prerogative in the shareholder agreement is an effort to increase the benefits for claimant community members. Yet the prerogative gives rise to conflict between the dispossessed community members' right to restitution on the one hand and the right to livelihood and work without discrimination for those outside the community on the other. The hiring prerogative is likely to have far-reaching implications for the job opportunities of those outside the claimant community in a situation where most of the jobs in the area are in the agricultural sector. Whether creating this form of positive discrimination to redress past social injustices of members of one group can be justified in the light of the South African Constitution's protection of the right to non-discrimination is a question that is yet to be considered.

Unlike in the past, when it was difficult to meet with farm workers on the farms, claimant communities have been more willing to let us conduct interviews. However, when we have done so, representatives from the 'royal' family have accompanied us. It appears to be standard practice that the workers are subject to discipline by chiefs as well as by their employers, the strategic partner. If a farm supervisor or manager has difficulty with a worker, the case is often referred to the chief for further action. It is uncertain how farm workers will respond to working on their own land. In our most recent interviews, farm workers from non-claimant communities report having multiple difficulties with the 'new owners' of the land. It is too early to draw hypotheses or conclusions on emergent conflicts, except to signal that they are quite likely to occur.

The Communal Property Association: Gender, Group Rights and Individual Rights

The Communal Property Associations were created through the CPA Act of 1996 to facilitate new, fairer and accountable property-holding institutions. In turn, the

28 A policy brief will shortly be written concerning the steps needed to protect existing workers in the transition.

CPAs throughout Limpopo Province have become the new landowners through the purchase of land from private landowners on their behalf. It is government, then, that grants them the land and land title and sets the conditions for the transfer.

While there is a national law on CPAs and several land claims court cases have taken place, we have found that in practice, the CPA constitutions are interpreted in the light of the prevailing customary norms. The membership status of children of sons and daughters who marry outside the claimant community is, according to key informants in the CPA, not the same. Unlike sons, daughters who marry non-community members cannot pass on membership. While mandating internal democratic principles of participation and decision-making, CPA constitutions are vague or silent in relation to sustainable use of resources, individual use rights and allocation of benefits that will flow to the community from rent, profits from the new company or grants from government. While not specifying individual use rights or individual shares, the constitutions make reference to ill-defined or undefined principles of fairness and equity. One (typical) example is the Ratombo Constitution, which in one statement mandates fairness and equity, and in another limits it:

- powers of the association and committee shall be interpreted and implemented at all times in accordance with the principle of fairness and equity;
- nothing hereinfore contained or implied shall preclude the Association or Committee from entering into arrangements involving differentiation between individual members, provided that a bona fide attempt is made to avoid ostensible disparity, and to ensure broad equity and fairness between affected members.

How the eventual benefits flowing to the community from the business enterprise are to be distributed and expanded will be subject to extensive negotiation and ongoing research. On paper, the decisions will be made by the CPA's committee in consultation with the members of the association. As required for the registration of the CPA, a certain number of committee members must be women. The Shigalo Constitution set a minimum of four female members out of 15 on the committee; the Masakona and Ratombo Constitutions specified that four out of nine members should be women. The Tshakuma formed a trust, not a CPA. The board has 11 members, one of them a woman. In two of these communities, women were committee secretaries. None of the female committee members had been elected chair.

Given the complexity of the terrain and the uncertainty of commercial agriculture, it is unclear how the flow of benefits, if any, will be redistributed within the claimant communities. The CPAs will have to make difficult decisions as to whether rent for land should be reinvested or given back to the community. It will be up to the company, not the CPA, to determine benefits to the CPA. If benefits are given, the CPA committee will follow the procedures laid out by their constitutions. The communities involved in the SP model have not reached this stage in the process.

Interviews with CPA members of Ratombo, Shigalo, Ravele and Masakona reflect tensions as to how a fair balance between communities, households and individuals may be reached.[29] Out of the 69 members interviewed, 36 per cent favour individual and/or household benefits alone. In this grouping, a majority of women favoured the individual, whereas the men preferred household payments. Twenty per cent of respondents favour dividing the benefits between individuals and households and the community. Once again, there was a gender difference, with only two women supporting this division. Those who thought that the community alone should receive the benefits were 29 per cent of the total, of whom three-quarters were men. Women were far more supportive of individual benefits, whereas men supported household or community ones. In any event, decisions are already being made by CPA committees (the small groups that manage CPA affairs). The first monies to be given to CPAs are rental monies for the land and for the farmhouses on community land. These monies are being used to purchase large four-wheel-drive double-cab pickup trucks, office equipment, and in one case, furnishing a chief's home. While it is understandable that the CPA executive committees need equipment to function, decisions about how to use the money were made by a small group of individuals without broader discussion in the CPA as a whole.

A group interview with Shigalo women illustrates how difficult it is to achieve justice through investment in common goods.[30] Emphasizing internal differences between community members in terms of age, education and participation, many women were in favour of cash transfers to households. The group interview we held with Masakona women (June 2007) emphasized differences between the women who got individual benefits through jobs on the farms, and themselves, who were not employed. These women wanted benefits that could be distributed in the community. They wanted money to start income-generating programmes and money for a water pump. Where membership is dispersed through two or more communities and members living in urban areas, reconciling these differences may pose new and unforeseen challenges.

In the context of the SP model, where different segments of the community are differently positioned to access information and exert their influence on the operating companies, internal CPA conflicts are likely to occur. There are no transparent procedures for the election of directors or the employment of managers, technical personnel and workers. The processes are, as we have witnessed, informal. For example, available jobs are often allocated through a communication from the management company to the chair of the CPA or the chief who makes the selection. Only one group has appointed two women to the boards of directors, and two groups have chosen women to be in administrative positions on the farms. A royal family

29 These results are from a more general interview schedule for members of successful claimant communities, focusing upon their backgrounds and expectations from the restitution process.

30 Field notes, June 2007.

dominates one CPA, but their dominance is increasingly contested. Another group cannot agree on its leadership and has become non-functional for the time being. Even the Trust has become split between two factions in its community. These are early indications of significant variations among communities in responding to the strategic partnerships and farm ownership.

Conclusions

South Africa's law and governance structures are changing in response to conflicting claims and unresolved tensions between economic growth and undoing historical and social injustices. This is underlain by efforts to balance democratic universal citizenship with recognition of difference. Thus, South Africa has adopted a set of detailed new laws to legislate democracy and undo past injustices while protecting property. To accomplish these goals, it has developed a modified market model, assuming that social justice can be matched with economic growth. As a result, tensions between state and non-state institutions, between new democratic structures and chiefly power, and deep social differentiation that characterizes poor rural communities have all been refashioned. Our analysis of how these regulations are translated into practice highlights a series of paradoxes in the multiple overlapping regulatory processes that are shaping this mixed model. Moreover, these changing structures will have very different consequences for the entrenched gender, class and racial inequalities.

One paradox is how the re-institutionalization of chiefs that is taking place at the interface of the Restitution of Land Rights Act and the Communal Land Rights Act is likely to have South Africa divided again by two primary systems of land tenure: communal land and freehold land. What the consequences will be for the rights of the community members will depend on the background and attitude of the chief, and the power relations between the chief and the community. There are, as we have seen, distinctions between the communities in terms of how they view the returned farms – as, ultimately, chiefly ownership or community ownership. In rights debates surrounding communal land law, one question concerns how this re-emerging division can be reconciled with the constitutional equality imperative through a dynamic and responsive living customary law. An emerging challenge that we have found is that in the claimant communities' practice is not in accordance with the state court version of a more egalitarian customary law, as expressed in the *Bhe* case, for example. In the Masakona and Shigalo claimant communities, the membership status of children of sons and daughters who marry outside the claimant community are not the same. In their interpretation of their respective CPA constitutions, patrilineal customs trump the equality principle in the South African Constitution. The official customary law, which is considered defunct by higher courts, is the living law according to CPA members in the claimant communities.

Another paradox emerges whereby privileged social structures are recreated through the combined effects of the business model and affirmative action. According to the contract between the strategic partner and the CPA, members of the claimant community will be given preference in future hiring. So far, farm employment, given the need for reinvesting profits and paying off debts, is the only certain economic benefit that individual CPA members will receive in the near future. Preferential hiring means that a real business model in terms of job competition and individual consideration cannot be implemented. It also means that non-community members will be deprived of jobs in the farming sector, where most jobs are located in Limpopo. Whether creating this form of positive discrimination to redress past social injustices can be justified in the light of the South African Constitution's prohibition against discrimination is a question that needs to be considered carefully.

This new model constitutes a mixed and multi-sited governance structure based on law, administrative discretion, contract and custom. While chiefs figure neither in the Communal Property Act nor in the agreements, they are playing a significant role in negotiating workers' rights and determining hiring practices and the use of potential profits, as they are considered by most members of claimant communities to be the ultimate owners of the land. The living law on the new farms will depend on how the bargaining power of the different parties in the process is balanced between strategic partners and CPAs, within each CPA, and between farm workers and the new company.

Underlying this model is the notion of common community interest. Our findings, however, are that there is a highly gendered, and to a certain extent classed, response to how benefits, when they come, should be distributed. Women favour individual benefits, recognizing that if benefits are given to the community or to household heads, they are unlikely to obtain them. The CPA leadership favours community distribution, and they are already gaining benefits not available to others. This reinforces Pienaar's call for specifying the rights of beneficiaries in CPAs which would work to the benefit of women and the poorer members.

The initial SP model sought to distance government from the operational management of the new farms in order to reduce the need for post-settlement support. However, it appears that this new structure will require sustained government engagement, but how this will be carried out remains to be seen. The record to date of government support for more democratic and inclusive CPAs has been weak, as they have focused on farm business and the strategic partners. Whether the concerns of claimant communities as a group and those of individuals within the community such as women, children and youth will be adequately protected through representation in the process of negotiation between and within these new institutions remains highly uncertain. It is in the implementation of the Communal Land Rights Act and the Communal Property Act that one might see a greatly intensified conflict between traditional authorities and the ANC-dominated government. We are not assured that the modified business model will support more democratic structures and a focus upon poverty and gender justice in the claimant communities.

Acknowledgements

This research has been funded by the Research Council of Norway in co-operation with Noragric, the Norwegian University of Life Sciences, the Institute of Women's Law, University of Oslo, and the Programme of Land and Agrarian Studies, University of the Western Cape. Most recently, Bill Derman has benefited from a grant from the Norwegian Centre for Human Rights in collaboration with PLAAS. We would like to thank Franz von Benda-Beckmann for his insightful and useful comments, along with Ben Cousins and Malcolm Langford. In this chapter, we have built upon the work of Edward Lahiff on restitution in Limpopo. We especially want to acknowledge Tshililo Manenzhe, who has worked with us for the past two years and who has been generous in sharing his knowledge and experiences based on his work at Nkuzi Development Association. None the less, we take full responsibility for the analyses and conclusions.

References

Atkinson, D. (2007), *Going for Broke: The Fate of Farmworkers in Arid South Africa*, Pretoria: Human Sciences Research Council Press.

Cousins, B. (2007), 'Agrarian Reform and the "Two Economies": Transforming South Africa's Countryside', in L. Ntsebeza and R. Hall (eds), *The Land Question in South Africa: The Challenge of Transformation and Redistribution*, Cape Town: Human Sciences Research Council, pp. 220–45.

Department of Land Affairs (1997), *White Paper on South African Land Policy*, Pretoria: DLA.

Derman, B, Lahiff, E. and Sjaastad, E. (2006), 'Strategic Questions for Claimant Communities, Government and Strategic Partners: Challenges and Pitfalls in South Africa's New Model of Land Restitution', paper prepared for the conference 'Land, Memory, Reconstruction and Justice: Perspectives on Land Restitution in South Africa', Cape Town, 13–15 September 2006.

Dodson, J. (2006), 'Unfinished Business: The Role of the Commission [Land Claims] on Restitution of Land Rights after Restoration', paper presented at the conference 'Land, Memory, Reconstruction and Justice: Perspectives on Land Restitution in South Africa', Cape Town, 13–15 September 2006.

—— (2007), *Unfinished Business: The Role of Governmental Institutions after Restoration of Land Rights*, Consultant's Report for the Belgian Technical Cooperation, Commission for the Restitution of Land Rights and the Department of Land Affairs.

'Draft Shareholders' Agreement, MAVU and SAFM Template', 2006/2007.

Hall, R. (2003), *Evaluating Land and Agrarian Reform in South Africa,* Occasional Papers Series, Belville, Cape Town: Programme of Land and Agrarian Studies.

—— (2004), *Land and Agrarian Reform in South Africa: A Status Report 2004*, Research Report no. 20, Belville, Cape Town: Programme of Land and Agrarian Studies.

Harries, P. (1989), 'Exclusion, Classification and Internal Colonialism: The Emergence of Ethnicity among the Tsonga-Speakers of South Africa', in L. Vail (ed.), *The Creation of Tribalism in Southern Africa*, Berkeley and Los Angeles, CA: University of California Press, pp. 82–117.

James, D. (2007), *Gaining Ground? 'Rights' and 'Property' in South African Land Reform*, Abington and New York: Routledge.

Lahiff, E. (2000), *Apartheid Oasis? Agriculture and Rural Livelihoods in Venda*, London: Cass.

—— (2005) *From 'Willing Seller, Willing Buyer' to a People-driven Land Reform*, Belville, Cape Town: PLAAS Policy Brief.

Mbeki, T. (2004), 'Two Worlds: Two Economies', *South Africa Labour Bulletin* 28(2): 10–11.

Mulaudzi, M. (2000), *U Shuma Bulasi' Agrarian Transformation in the Zoutpansberg District of South Africa, up to 1946*, PhD Thesis, University of Minnesota.

Nefale, M. (2000), *The Politics of Land in Levubu, Northern Province c. 1935–1998*, MA Thesis, University of Cape Town.

Oomen, B. (2005), *Chiefs in South Africa: Law, Power and Culture in the Post Apartheid Era*, London: James Currey.

Pienaar, K. (2006), 'Having a Second Bite at Fixing Elandskloof and Other Dysfunctional Sets of "New" Land Reform, Group Land Holdings and Management Arrangements', paper presented at the conference 'Land, Memory, Reconstruction and Justice: Perspectives on Land Restitution in South Africa', Cape Town, 13–15 September 2006.

—— (2007), *A Review of Institutional Arrangements for Land Reform, Community Land Hold and Land Management*, Consultant's Report for the Belgian Technical Cooperation, Commission for the Restitution of Land Rights and the Department of Land Affairs.

Platzky, L. and Walker, C. (1985), *Surplus People: Forced Removals in South Africa*, Braamfontein: Ravan Press.

Prinslo, F. and Schlesinger, E., 'Levubu Claim, A Proposal by Group 23'.

Statistics South Africa (2006a), *Mid-year Population Estimates, South Africa*, Pretoria: Government of South Africa.

—— (2006b), *Survey of Large Scale Agriculture (Preliminary)*, Pretoria: Government of South Africa.

Walker, C. (2005a), 'Misplaced Agrarianization? Reflections on Ten Years of Land Restitution', *Social Research: An International Quarterly of Social Sciences* 72(3): 647–70.

—— (2005b), ‘Women, Gender Policy and Land Reform in South Africa’, *Politicon* 32(2): 297–315.

—— (2006), ‘Delivery and Disarray: The Multiple Meanings of Land Restitution’, in S. Buhlungu, J. Daniel, R. Southall, J. Lutchman (eds), *State of the Nation: South Africa 2005–2006*, Cape Town: HSRC Press, pp. 67–92.

—— (2007), ‘Redistributive Land Reform: For What and for Whom?’, in L. Ntsebeza and R. Hall (eds), *The Land Question in South Africa: The Challenge of Transformation and Redistribution*, Cape Town: Human Sciences Research Council, pp. 132–51.

Wegerif, M., Russell, B. and Grundling, I. (2006), *Still Searching for Security: The Reality of Farm Dwellers Evictions in South Africa*, Pretoria: Nkuzi Development Association and Social Surveys.

Chapter 7

Re-scaling Governance for Better Resource Management?

Melanie G. Wiber and Arthur Bull

Introduction

Around the world, vital resource stocks are disappearing or are under significant stress, with concomitant increases in global poverty and food insecurity. A recent report published in *Science* (Worm et al. 2006) predicts that not only will the global stocks of commercial fishing species be extinct by 2050, but many other species will have disappeared as well, with severe consequences for the health of our global ecosystem. This is particularly amazing when put in the context of governance institutions and theory. The fisheries sector has received billions of research dollars, has produced reams of research reports touting numerous management theories, and has more governance institutions at regional, national and international levels than any other resource stock. And yet, around the world, vital fish stocks are disappearing or have already disappeared. There is little difference between North and South in terms of the broad management outcome, which may be explained by the globalizing effects of the epistemic community that has been guiding fisheries management for over thirty years (Wiber 2005). Many people who depend on marine resources for their livelihood blame centralized, bureaucratic, top-down management regimes that are largely impervious to democratic processes and that fuel the 'democratic deficit' at all levels of the governance chain (Haas 2004). And as the fisheries sector falls under the ecological gun of stock collapse and habitat decline, bureaucratic managers increasingly isolate themselves from those most directly affected, so government management plans ignore local needs and realities.[1]

Thus, despite international agreements such as the 1992 Earth Summit, where signatory nations agreed to seek participatory governance of natural resources[2] (see Agenda 21, ch. 23.2), it would appear that most states have not acted to re-scale governance structures. In this chapter, we will argue that the

1 For other examples, see Cole (2002); Fung and Wright (2001); Rhodes (1997); Schneider (1999); Swyngedouw (1997).

2 As Spaeder notes, participatory governance is said to enable local users to play a role in management over resources on which they depend while government realizes the 'benefits of reduced social conflict, and greater user compliance' (Spaeder 2005, 166).

Canadian experience is illustrative. Under pressure from environmental groups and fisher organizations, the Canadian government passed the 1996 Oceans Act, which explicitly recognized the importance of involving local communities in the management of coastal resources. In 2002, Canada announced its Oceans Strategy as a response to Agenda 21, and again promised to create institutional arrangements (specifically mentioning community-based management) whereby all stakeholders would be involved in designing, implementing and monitoring coastal and ocean management plans. In setting this direction, it was clear that the law was seen as the tool to facilitate devolving powers, roles and responsibilities to the grassroots level. But we shall argue here that the law has more often been deployed in ways that block participatory governance of resource management. Unless and until the political will exists to shift the real barriers to participatory governance, significant changes to governance structures will not emerge.

This chapter explores some case material from the Canadian context, drawn from an ongoing multidisciplinary project[3] that is gathering comparative examples from both the North (mostly Canada) and the South (international examples). In this project, we have examined examples of governance (the mechanisms and processes by which power and decision-making are allocated among different actors), in order to explore impacts on management (the decisions about use patterns as well as about transforming the resource by making improvements) (Schlager and Ostrom 1992; Ostrom, Gardner and Walker 1994; Béné and Neiland 2004). In three annual workshops from 2005 to 2007, this project brought together 'learning communities' from Canada's three coasts to discuss how they have pursued horizontal and vertical linkages,[4] to broaden the level of engagement, and to democratize both governance *and* management (Kearney and Wiber 2006). For these workshops, learning communities were defined as place-based, resource-dependent groups that have developed shared values and effective problem-solving techniques through iterative, practice-based learning (see also Davidson-Hunt and O'Flaherty 2007). The participating communities were rural native and non-native communities. Each community initiative discussed at these workshops formed in a different way, with more or less inclusiveness as to membership. They have all engaged with many barriers, and have responded

3 Funding for this project and related work has come from the Social Sciences and Humanities Research Council (Research Development Initiative Grant, Community University Research Alliance Grant, Workshop Grant), and from the International Development Research Center (IDRC Learning Network Funding). This work links academics and community members into a Canada-wide participatory research network. The authors of this chapter are an example of the community-academic research collaborations that have been generated through the network.

4 Horizontal linkages connect communities in the same region or ecological zone together for integrated or ecological-based management, while vertical linkages connect communities with other scales of government. For examples, see Kearney and Wiber (2006) and Goetze (2005).

to, and in some cases generated, specific legal frameworks in order to overcome barriers. Comparing their experiences suggests that the role of the law in adapting state resource management to the needs of such communities has been uneven, especially as relates to incorporating local rules of access to and withdrawal from a resource into state management regimes. In Canada, a few promising scenarios come from northern aboriginal communities (but see Goetze 2005), while other communities (both native and non-native) have faced more barriers, as this chapter will demonstrate.

Much recent literature on community-based management relies on certain indicators to assess whether or not viable community-based management institutions exist (Bradshaw 2003; Gibson and Koontz 1998; Singleton 2000; Zanetell 2001). But, following Tsing (2005), we argue that various agents are continuously in the process of developing political projects with respect to any resource stock, and that these will often run at cross-purposes to each other. The resulting friction must be a continuing challenge for community-based management, especially in cases of what have been described as 'complex, multi-level, multi-scale systems', such as are required for attempts to integrate management across ecological regions (Janssen, Anderies and Omstrom 2007). Community-based management is thus an iterative political project of learning, of struggle, of accommodation and of conflict, and is best analysed from this perspective (McCallum, Hughey and Rixecker 2007).

Recently, members of the multidisciplinary governance project discussed above published a paper in the journal *Coastal Management* (Kearney et al. 2007). That paper surveyed the situation with respect to integrated coastal management in Canada, and concluded that in order to make the Oceans Strategy effective, nine initiatives would be needed, including: shifting paradigms, overcoming bureaucratic 'turf protection', ensuring compatibility of goals, promoting sufficiency of information, addressing internal community stratification, making cross-scale linkages, creating a participatory policy environment, building community capacity for governance, and monitoring of participation and resilience. That conclusion was based on a recognition that participatory democracy and community-based management are ongoing processes, not end points (Feit and Spaeder 2005; Spaeder 2005). In this chapter, we will examine one Canadian case study to further illustrate the importance of several of these nine initiatives, and to discuss when and how the law is involved in derailing many of them.

This case study documents a political struggle over integrated management. Integrated management is generally viewed as the bringing together of bureaucratic and civil society organizations to collaboratively address multiple management goals, including ecological protection, economic development and disaster management (Isobe n.d.). As examples from the learning community workshops illustrated, integrated management in Canada often involves dealing with conflicting notions of access and management rights drawn from First Nation communities, non-native communities, and federal and provincial bureaucracies.

Integrated Coastal Management Case Study: Annapolis Watershed Resource Committee

In the Annapolis Watershed region of Nova Scotia (see Figure 7.1, Area 18), integrated management is facilitated through a local organization called the Annapolis Watershed Resource Committee, which is a multi-stakeholder management board. The committee provides a platform for both vertical and horizontal linkages. Vertical linkages include co-ordinating with national and provincial administrators, and meeting with municipal authorities on issues such as sewage disposal and water quality. Horizontal linkages are facilitated by member organizations that include two regional clam harvester associations, the Annapolis Basin Association (see Figure 7.1, Area 18) and the Digby Clam Diggers Association (see Figure 7.1).[5]

Other organizations include the Bay of Fundy Marine Resource Center, the Clean Annapolis River Project and the Bear River First Nation, all of which hold voting privileges. There are also representatives from the processing sector, but these are non-voting members of the committee. As shellfish beds along the intertidal zone are impacted by sewage treatment, agricultural land wash, leeching from dumpsites, siltation from hydroelectric developments and more, the clam harvester membership on the committee has often been critical of the lack of effective co-ordination of multiple use of the coastal zone.

The clam harvester members on the committee have proposed an Annapolis Clam Strategy to restore and enhance clam-flats in the area, through reseeding depleted clam-flats, transferring clams from above the power generation causeway to more productive beds below, and developing harvest management protocols and strategies for their membership.[6] For reasons that will become obvious, they have also supported a federal income stabilization programme for workers in the clam industry to pay clam harvesters to work on such stock recovery programmes. While the voting members of the Annapolis Watershed Resource Committee supported these objectives, the committee itself has struggled to be effective in the face of a regulatory environment that does not allow for a significant local voice in coastal resource management decisions. Through a closer look at the clam harvester situation, we will highlight the system of regulatory incentives and the lack of transparency in government management that together have enabled large-scale privatization of coastal resources. This in turn has undercut participatory integrated management.

5 Faced with expanding difficulties in accessing their resource, these two associations have since united into one organization.

6 We are grateful to Ken Weir of the Digby Clam Diggers Association for access to association records dating back to the early 1980s. These records show a history of harvester lobbying for habitat restoration, stock rebuilding and harvester regulation. The records also contain minutes of meetings of the association, of the Annapolis Watershed Resource Committee, and of government regional clam advisory committees, as well as court case records and correspondence with the government that were valuable to this analysis.

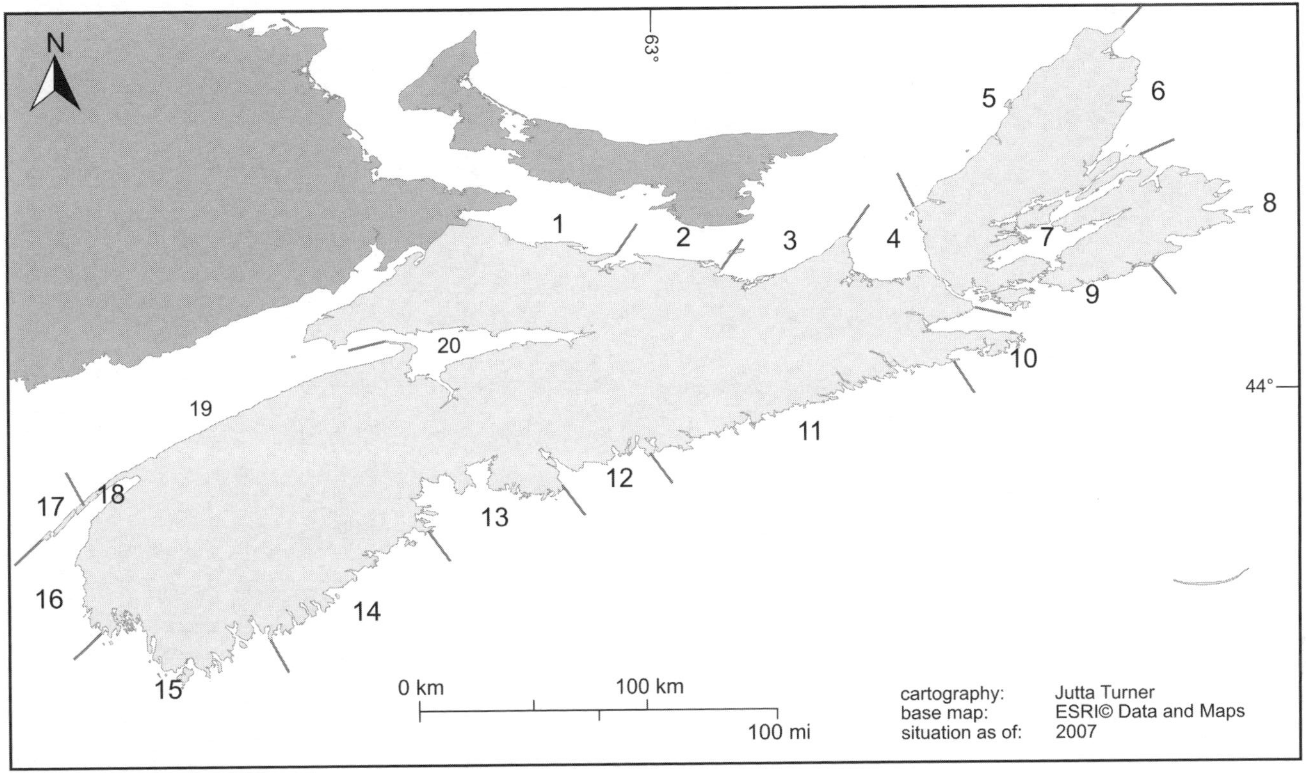

Figure 7.1 Shellfish production areas in the province of Nova Scotia, Canada (2007)

Shifting Paradigms or Privatization by Other Means?

Privatization has taken on the aura of dogma in fisheries management circles, in that this paradigm has proven extremely resistant to contrary data. Together with a wider administrative law context that was not designed with community-based management in mind, and a bureaucracy that resists both paradigm change and power sharing, the privatization of important coastal resources is severely challenging any attempt to foster community-based and integrated management. Under British common law, tidal lands have long been considered incapable of private occupation, cultivation and improvement, and therefore best reserved for public enjoyment. While the Crown generally holds title to lands below the high tide line, these lands have traditionally been open in Canada for public uses, including fishing and navigation.[7] In the Annapolis Basin and St Mary's Bay areas, the intertidal zone has long been a significant source of food and income for many aboriginal and non-aboriginal families, including those of the Bear River First Nation. However, in recent years, under the ubiquitous privatization paradigm that also tends to be 'authoritarian, paternalistic, and corporatist' (Nigh 2002), this historic pattern has been significantly eroded.

The largest corporate actor in the shellfish industry in the Annapolis Basin/St Mary's Bay area is Innovative Fisheries Products, Inc. (IFP). According to the company Website, it was established in 1988 and is now a major supplier of fresh, salted and dried seafood products with markets throughout North America, the UK, the Far East and Algeria.[8] Products for which IFP has been aggressively building markets are clams, including quahog (locally known as cherry stone) and soft shell clams, two species found in the Annapolis/Digby area. Local clam harvesters acknowledge that before the market for quahog was established, that resource was underexploited, with most clam digger income coming from soft shell clams.

In 1997, IFP was granted an aquaculture lease for 1,682 hectares of beach in St Mary's Bay, Nova Scotia.[9] This bay is said to contain the only commercially viable quahog clam stock in the Bay of Fundy. Granting this aquaculture lease was possible because of ministerial discretionary power under the Nova Scotia Aquaculture License and Lease Regulations (Section 3), which state that while

7 In Canada, arrangements vary between the provinces and the federal government in terms of jurisdiction over intertidal zones and over the degree to which private freehold title in land can include intertidal areas. In Nova Scotia, colonial land titles sometimes include beach areas to the low-water mark.

8 It is interesting that Industry Canada reports that this company only employs 30 people in its multi-million-dollar business: <www.ic.gc.ca/app/ccc/search/navigate.do?language=eng&portal=1&subPortal=&estblmntNo=123456104482&profile=completeProfile>, accessed 30 January 2009. We will return to this point later in the chapter.

9 There are questions about how this aquaculture site licence was granted, since there seems to have been little public notice or consultation with local users of the resource as is required under provincial regulation. From the local perspective, the St Mary's Bay clam-flats were first closed due to contamination, and then later the site licence was announced.

marine aquaculture lease sites shall normally be located 25 metres from the mean low-water level, the minister may issue an aquaculture lease for a marine area up to the high-water mark if in the minister's opinion the area is required for the aquaculture undertaking. The direct benefit to the province appears to be yearly lease fees and annual licensing fees that in this case could have generated a resource rent in the region of C$17,900 per annum.[10]

While the federal and provincial regulators ostensibly promote sustainability, a policy environment that explicitly favours privatization counters this putative goal. Under fisheries management regimes, the concept that resource stocks 'can be actively controlled through human intervention and maintained at a sustained yield remains foundational' (Spaeder 2005, 169). While Wiber has elsewhere critiqued the economic models that underlie justifications for privatization (Wiber 2000), including the perception that a private owner will better protect the resource for which they have an exclusive benefit stream, it is clear that management bureaucrats view the large corporate sector as the preferred partners in the drive towards sustainable yields. For example, the conditions for this aquaculture site licence include harvest rotation, minimum shell lengths, daily harvest monitoring, and active lease surveillance throughout the year to prevent 'illegal' harvesting activity. In addition, IFP has agreed to collaboratively fund research into the clam stocks. IFP and the federal Department of Fisheries and Oceans (DFO) have a co-operative agreement to evaluate the use of biological information and population modelling to optimize quahog harvesting on a long-term basis (Leblanc et al. 2005). The federal portion of the funding comes from support for research partnerships between aquaculture producers and DFO researchers. The programme enables scientific research projects to be conducted that are proposed and jointly funded by industry partners and the federal government. The three-year project with IFP has received C$189,400 in federal funding.[11]

The research is described on the DFO Website in the following way:

> Some species of bivalves, such as clams and quahogs, live within the bottom sediments. The specific characteristics of the sediment will influence the growth and survival of the bivalves. As well, it is difficult to ascertain how many bivalves are on a farmer's site as they are buried in the sediment. This project will use new technology to determine sediment characteristics and assess number of

10 While the regulations in effect at the time put the fee at C$10.65 per hectare, the 2000 lease signed between the province and IFP lists a fee of C$2 per hectare, but notes that this fee has been 'severed under section 21(1)(a)(i)(b) and (c)(i) and (iii)'.

11 Whether this is tax dollars well spent is an open question, as the published results we have been able to access (dating from 2002 onward) are all largely repeats of the same information.

> bivalves buried within the sediment. This information will be used in developing a production model for the management of the stock.[12]

We draw your attention to the use of the phrase 'on a farmer's site', which may be misleading as clam harvesters claim there is no available public record of seeding, growing out or maintaining habitat for clams on this site. Little farming appears to be going on, even in the aquaculture sense. Wiber has commented in a previous publication on the use of misleading representations in the contest over natural resources (Wiber 2004) – this example attaches the language of progress (farming and aquaculture versus clam diggers) to a decision that privileged a corporate actor over pre-existing resource users.

On 30 January 2007, a public meeting was organized by a local coalition that protested a plan, announced in late 2006 to enable leaseholders to apply for ten-year exclusive leases, followed by five-year renewal periods, in place of the annual renewals currently available. Federal and provincial representatives agreed to attend the public meeting to respond to questions posed by municipal officials and stakeholders. The evidence for sustainable aquaculture was raised during the meeting. IFP maintained that it was doing aquaculture, but as federal regulators admitted to monitoring *only* landed value, increased landings from leased sites could be accounted for by higher harvesting rates. When pressed for concrete evidence that private corporate management was more sustainable, the bureaucrats cited the privacy needs of a business that had made significant capital investments in the region, and refused to release further information.

We have only been able to find indirect evidence for the sustainability of the lease in St Mary's Bay, and this evidence suggests sustainable harvests are doubtful. For example, based on the collaborative research into quahog population dynamics in the Bay (Leblanc et al. 2005), the annual harvest since 1997 (the baseline year) has ranged between 95 and 370 tons, and extraction rates have increased dramatically over the period from 1999 to 2001. A federal bureaucrat later confirmed by email the percentage of change in landed value from leased sites, with dramatic landing increases until 2005, and some levelling off in 2006. But as quahog were not easily marketed before privatization, these percentages of increase in landed value are extremely misleading. Meanwhile, Leblanc et al. report that natural mortality among these clams is high, probably a result of ice scouring or other winter kill-off. It is unclear whether the natural reproduction rate of the clams can absorb the recent level of extraction/mortality (quahog are reportedly a very slow-growing species), especially as Leblanc et al. acknowledge that the stock in St Mary's Bay does not appear to recruit from outside populations.

What is more important from the perspective of integrated management is that one private-sector stakeholder has been allowed to effectively concentrate the benefits of the quahog clam harvest into their corporate hands. This has

---

12 <www.dfo-mpo.gc.ca/science/aquaculture/acrdp-pcrda/margulf/MG-01-09-003_e.htm>, accessed March 2007.

happened without any integrated management overview. Instead, two venues offered through the regulatory environment (aquaculture licences and public health restrictions) have been exploited to effectively privatize not only St Mary's Bay, but a large part of the Annapolis Basin as well. In the process, privatization has created several social and economic problems in the region that are resulting in considerable unrest and economic hardship. One aspect of this situation is the lack of transparency in government regulatory decisions and licensing arrangements that raise serious questions about how government bureaucrats view existing local users and their rights.

Addressing Internal Community Stratification or Granting a Monopoly via Health Regulation?

Unlike recent fears about contamination levels in farmed salmon and albacore tuna, the public has long been aware that shellfish are a marine-related food source with potentially serious health implications. Given the deadly risk from contaminated shellfish, identifying and classifying the sources of shellfish is very important. In Canada, there are several regulatory agencies involved in ensuring shellfish quality and safety through the Canadian Shellfish Sanitation Program (CSSP), which is administered co-operatively by the Department of Fisheries and Oceans (DFO), the Canadian Food Inspection Agency (CFIA) and Environment Canada (EC). This complex structure of shared jurisdiction requires a great deal of collaboration between these branches of the federal administration, plus co-operation with provincial departments.[13] The Fisheries Act, Management of Contaminated Fisheries Regulations, the Fish Inspection Act, and Fish Inspection Regulations provide the legal authority for the Canadian Shellfish Sanitation Program (CSSP).[14] These acts and regulations empower the departments to classify all shellfish growing areas on the basis of their sanitary quality and public health safety. This authority also empowers the responsible departments (the DFO and CFIA) to control many aspects of harvest, processing, transport and marketing:

> Sanitary surveys are used to classify coastal areas and include a bacteriological survey (to measure fecal material) and a shoreline survey (to identify and

---

13 Based on a February 1990 Memorandum of Understanding, Environment Canada is the lead agency with regards to water quality and classification of shellfish growing areas through comprehensive sanitary and bacteriological surveys of such areas, while the Department of Fisheries and Oceans (DFO) is the lead agency with regard to the controlled harvesting, transportation and cleaning of shellfish from classified areas. Under the authority of the Fisheries Act and Regulations, the DFO is also responsible for the enforcement of closure regulations and enacting the opening and closing of shellfish growing areas. The Canadian Food Inspection Agency is responsible for the handling, processing, marketing, import and export of shellfish, and for liaison with foreign governments.

14 All of these Acts are available online at <www.canadagazette.gc.ca/index-e.html>.

> quantify the pollution sources and to estimate their movement, dilution and dispersal in the environment). The resulting programme classifications include: *approved* where minimum counts of contaminants are found and harvesting and direct marketing is allowed; *closed* where direct harvesting is prohibited due to chemical or bacteriological contamination, and *unclassified* areas where the sanitary suitability for harvesting is undetermined and therefore not approved for harvesting at present.

Figures from 2004 published on the Environment Canada website show the percentage of beaches under each classification in the Canadian Atlantic region, including 33.5 per cent of beaches as closed and 65.2 per cent as approved.[15] The same source shows that closures have increased remarkably in this region since 1995, especially in the province of Nova Scotia.

Few consumers realize, however, that shellfish can be harvested from closed beaches and marketed under certain conditions. As the DFO website explains, shellfish from contaminated beaches must go through a depuration process which involves placing them in purified seawater for periods exceeding 24 hours.

> The effectiveness of the depuration process is influenced by temperature, salinity, dissolved oxygen, suspended particles and the degree of contamination in the shellfish. … shellfish contaminated with high levels of bacteria and viruses are not completely depurated during this period … [and] no shellfish are allowed to be harvested from grossly contaminated areas for depuration.[16]

Closed beaches are a resource, then, only for those with the capital to invest in depuration plants and other infrastructure that meets federal inspection guidelines for accessing, transporting, processing and marketing clams from contaminated areas. In the region from which this case study is drawn, IFP has the only depuration plant certified by federal inspectors. But more importantly, it appears that it would be difficult for any other fish processor to develop similar facilities, as IFP appears to have secured a right of first refusal for the best closed beaches in the area.[17] According to the federal bureaucrat who responded to questions at the 20 January 2007 public meeting, IFP was granted this right of first refusal in order to provide some stability for their capital investment in the depuration plant. However, with their aquaculture site licence, the right of first refusal on leased beaches and the depuration plant, IFP has effectively garnered a monopoly on the clam industry in this region of Nova Scotia.

---

15 See <www.atl.ec.gc.ca/epb/sfish/cssp.html>, accessed 30 January 2009.

16 <www.mar.dfompo.gc.ca/science/review/1996/AmarMenon/Menon_e.html>, accessed March 2007.

17 This is probably a result of the fact that as lease-holders, they were given the first option to apply for any commercial lease subsequently offered for that same site once their lease terminates (as indicated in Experimental Lease no. 8356, dated 23 February 2000).

The proposed ten-year exclusive leases designed to replace the annual renewals would entrench the IFP monopoly. This has raised questions about aboriginal rights to fish resources in the area, which include fishing for *both* food and ceremonial purposes and for commercial purposes. The adjacent First Nation of Bear River, for example, has a long history of fishing the clam-flats in both the Annapolis Basin and St Mary's Bay. Given the 1999 Supreme Court decision on the *Marshall* case,[18] it is now well established that such First Nation communities have a constitutional right to be involved in the commercial fishery (Wiber and Kennedy 2001). While their access to the clam-flats as part of their food and ceremonial fishery is constrained by health risks, their right to enter the commercial clam industry has not been recognized in the arrangements for ten-year exclusive leases.

'Innovative' Labour Relations

Clams are harvested from May to November, with a peak period from June to September. Digging with a hand rake for four hours during low tide is the sole harvesting method.[19] This is backbreaking labour, but in previous years it yielded a decent living for many clam harvesters. However, since the advent of privatization and given a recent decline in clam numbers, 2006 was one of the worst seasons on record for clam harvester incomes. Harvest rates from the open areas were said to be one quarter of what they have been historically. Clam harvesters reported having made less than one third of their normal income, and many harvesters were forced out of the region to seek employment elsewhere. Those that remained report that they were in dire financial straits – many were threatened with foreclosure on their homes and vehicles, and most had been unable to qualify for the weeks of employment required to file for federal Employment Insurance benefits.

While one difficulty was the closure of increasing numbers of clam-flats due to land-based contaminants, and the resulting pressure on those clam-flats remaining open, a more important problem, according to clam harvesters, was the artificially low price for clams offered by Innovative Fisheries Products, significantly lower than in adjacent Maritime Provinces or US states. Despite the increasing scarcity of the resource, clam prices offered by IFP continued to drop. Clam harvesters, for example, reported that quahog clam prices dropped from 75 Canadian cents a pound six years ago to 50 Canadian cents a pound in 2006.[20] That year, the

18 See *R.* v. *Marshall* SCR 1999[3]:456 and 533.

19 Clam harvesters have protested plans to introduce mechanical harvesting in the past.

20 According to an online report in 2007 (<www.seafoodbusiness.com>), clam prices had been relatively stable over the previous two to three years. Quahog fluctuated between a low of US$27 per bushel to US$30. Soft clam prices swung between US$90 per bushel in the winter to US$120 in the summer. There appeared, then, to be little reason for clam diggers to receive declining prices overall.

average income reported by one clam digger was C$550 per week for seven days' work. As a result of these pressures, the clam harvesters associations petitioned the government to reset the minimum annual income for qualifying for unemployment benefits to C$10,000.

The reported low prices for quahog and other clam types exacerbated the strained relations between labour and IFP management. But other practices imposed by IFP were more contentious from the harvester point of view. To dig in open areas, clam harvesters require an annual licence, to which are attached numerous regulatory conditions that are reviewed on an annual basis. To dig in closed areas, clam harvesters must work for IFP. When digging in open areas, clam harvesters are self-employed, with no benefits package or registered pension plan. Theoretically, they are free to sell clams sourced from open beaches to the highest bidder. However, for two reasons, no clam digger can make a living exclusively from open beaches; fewer and fewer productive beaches are classified as open, and those that are open have been hard-hit by the domino effect of stock collapse in the region. When the ground fish stocks collapsed, fishing effort was redirected into the scallop industry. As the scallop industry is now in decline, many former scallop fishers are turning to clam digging. It is estimated that one third of current clam harvesters are former scallop fishermen. The resulting increased pressure on the open clam beds has depleted the resource. As a result, clam harvesters must work at least part of the year on closed beaches.

However, to dig in the closed beaches requires that clam harvesters enter the IFP 'system'. For example, harvesters report that the company requires that anyone who works for them must first dig a 'quota' of 2,500 pounds of (largely soft shell)[21] clams from open beaches, which must then be sold to IFP at prices they dictate. Any clam harvester who sells clams from an open beach to a competitor will not be hired to work on closed beaches.[22] Furthermore, IFP maintains the fiction that clam harvesters working for them are independent contractors, and thus not entitled to any benefits packages or seniority. This is viewed as a fiction by IFP harvesters, since they must show up to work on closed beaches according to schedule, and are handed their licence to dig by the IFP regional managers. This licence must be turned in to the IFP manager at the close of digging each day.[23] This interpretation

21 Soft shell clams are more difficult to harvest, as they are found deeper under the surface of the sand.

22 Complaints about these practices were raised at the public meeting discussed above. Federal and provincial regulators responded that their regulatory powers did not extend to the labour practices of the private sector.

23 It is unclear whether the volume of licences granted to IFP to hand out to their workforce on a daily basis is a contravention of the federal 'owner/operator' licensing policy. This policy was developed to prevent concentration of the harvesting sector into the hands of the processing sector. Clam harvesters report receiving licences from the company with their name written in ink beside the company name. Clam harvesters also report questioning why company licences came without the normal list of annual conditions set by the regulators.

is supported by Leblanc et al. (2005), who write that IFP employs a 'maximum of 50 clam harvesters per tide where the mean harvest per day for a clam digger has been as high as 167 kg'. Recall that the company lists 30 employees on the Industry Canada registry. Since their depuration plant also employs staff, it would appear that they do not count clam harvesters as part of their workforce.

Clams are taken directly by IFP, and are sorted and weighed by the company. The diggers report receiving the volume count from the company with no independent check on volume or weight, and harvesters often complain that the company under-reports what harvesters have turned in. When harvesters complain to the company, they are told that many of their clams were too small or too big for marketing, and that they will not be paid for those. When harvesters request that these small and large clams be returned to the beach as seed stock, the company refuses to do this – so harvesters assume those clam meats are being sold without remuneration to the digger.

Furthermore, in order to access work on the closed beaches, clam harvesters must conform to company expectations in other ways. Clam harvesters report that IFP discourages their involvement in clam harvester associations or in boards set up to further integrated management. One area manager for IFP is said to appear at every fisheries or integrated management meeting held in the region. Clam harvesters report that this man undermines effort to undertake stewardship and conservation work, either directly or indirectly. For example, clam harvesters had suggested restocking of open beaches using seed stock from closed beaches. A second proposal from the clam harvesters was that in order to support sustainable harvest practices, a 'professionalization' process be followed for harvesters, with the management board producing a list of approved harvesters with appropriate training. While federal regulators supported the latter suggestion, the IFP representative has been able to frustrate both initiatives. The process employed appears to be rather effective, if blunt. Clam harvesters report being subject to harassment and job loss for being critical of company practices in management board meetings or in meetings with federal and provincial regulators, or for taking direct labour action.[24] Clam harvesters who serve on management boards or as executive members of clam harvesting associations have suffered intimidation firing. The director of the Digby Clam Diggers Association reports having been fired several times by the company after speaking out at management meetings and organizing a protest (see below).

As the effects of privatization and IFP labour practices work their way through the community, IFP has been criticized. Some clam harvesters, for example, organized a protest along a road to St Mary's Bay over low prices and the intimidation firing practices. Although the local police were informed of plans for a 'peaceful protest',

24 There is some evidence for these claims. In the 6 May 2004 minutes of the Southwest Nova Scotia Soft Shell Clam Advisory Committee, for example, an unnamed processor stated that they reserved the right not to hire harvesters previously involved in strike actions.

and despite the fact that this was not the only road into St Mary's Bay nor was the road blocked by the protest, the company was able to obtain a court order to end the protest. Furthermore, they filed legal actions against the leaders of the protest, claiming loss of income from the St Mary's Bay clam beds as a result of the protest. They also threatened to bring clam harvesters in from another shellfish zone to harvest, despite the fact that harvesting licences are specific to a particular harvesting zone and are non-transferable. Finally, the company may have given rise to local resentment through the manner in which it enforces its property rights in leased beaches. Local residents have been forced off beaches despite the fact that the lease states that the leaseholder does not have the right to 'exclude the general public from the leased area except for the harvesting of shellfish' (Lease no. 8356, 23 February 2000).

In an interview with one clam harvester, we were told that he felt that he had fewer rights than an illegal immigrant when it came to accessing natural resources or in speaking out against unfair labour practices. Some families are torn by the resulting tensions, with a few family members willing to abide by the company 'system' in order to remain employed in the industry, while others argue for participating in integrated management planning and lobbying with government to change the IFP 'system'.

Building Community Capacity for Governance? Ensuring Sufficiency of Information?

The heavy manual labour involved plus the minimal technology employed may be one reason that clam harvesters tend to be stigmatized by bureaucrats. While many families along the shoreline in this region of Nova Scotia have accessed clams for their own use, specialized clam harvesters have for generations made a living from the resource. Clam harvesting is a skilled activity, and has generated a significant portion of household income for families involved in the industry, yet many federal and provincial bureaucrats argue that clam harvesting is 'an employment of last resort', and subsequently have not treated clam harvesters as important stakeholders. Clam harvesters report a distinct lack of support when they turn to federal or provincial bureaucrats for assistance; for example, clam harvesters are finding their rights to public information severely curtailed. They report that it is difficult to get at accurate information about the company and its ownership structure. When they requested information on the St Mary's Bay aquaculture licence, they were told it was publicly available on the Web (it is not).[25]

While the province has mandated Regional Aquaculture Development Advisory Committees (RADACs) to work within communities to establish sites and resolve

25 While there are currently more than 380 aquaculture site licences in the province of Nova Scotia, the government Website on routine access records lists aquaculture site licences as among those records for which the government will provide confirmation only that a person (which includes a corporation) has a current licence, permit or approval; see <www.gov.ns.ca/fish/foipop.shtml>, accessed 30 January 2009.

potential conflicts among users of coastal resources, the St Mary's Bay case does not suggest the process is working well. The provincial Website refers to RADACs as 'community-based organizations', and argues that they:

> provide an important forum for interest groups to voice opinions and concerns about aquaculture projects proposed for their area. RADACS are an important source of information and feedback from communities to the provincial Fisheries Minister.[26]

The committee reviews aquaculture applications to determine whether they are suitable for the proposed site and whether there are any conflicts with other user groups. They then pass their recommendations to the minister, who makes the final decision on issuing a lease and licence. The province states on its Website that RADACs have been successful in introducing aquaculture into new areas and in resolving user conflicts. It states that RADACs give residents an opportunity to take control of aquaculture development in their area, and provide the department with much-needed local input. However, no RADAC process appears to have been followed with respect to the St Mary's Bay aquaculture lease, probably because of a highly contentious 1995 case over salmon cages in the region, in which the minister overturned the local RADAC recommendation.[27]

Another problem clam harvesters in this region confront is the difficulty of having a closed beach reclassified as open. The process is anything but transparent. For example, the clam harvesters' associations are finding it difficult to establish who is collecting the samples, how often they are being collected, and how the samples are being processed. If the regulators have partnered with the corporate sector to facilitate this work, clam harvesters feel that there is a significant conflict of interest, since IFP has an interest in keeping beaches closed in order to retain control over them. And these suspicions are difficult to eliminate so long as the relevant regulatory agencies refuse to release information about the survey process to clam harvester's associations or to the management committee. Clam harvesters report that regulators have refused to release survey data for particular beaches; regulators claim that harvesters will try to use the data to demand the opening of closed beaches.

Re-scaling Governance?

Haas has written:

> Decentralized information-rich systems are the best design for addressing highly complex and tightly-coupled problems. In short, centralized institutions

26 See <www.gov.ns.ca/Fish/aquaculture/faq.shtml>, accessed 30 January 2009.

27 This was documented in numerous stories in the *Digby Courier*, February–May 1995.

> are fundamentally unecological. They run counter to the ecological principle of requisite diversity or flexibility; inhibit random mutation, or policy innovation; and are easily captured by single powerful parties. (Haas 2004, 7)

While Haas is speaking of global levels of governance, one could easily extend his observations to the national and regional level. What is unclear in his and in other policy advice is how decentralization is to be moved forward effectively. How could or should communities respond to the sort of situation that these clam harvesters face every day? How is it that regulation and the law let them down? And what is the nature of the disconnect between them and government that makes this sort of thing more likely to happen? What systems of incentives and disincentives are in place to make bureaucrats more responsive to the corporate sector than to the regional constituencies? How can information-rich systems be created when information is clearly viewed as a dangerous resource to be carefully controlled? These questions are particularly valuable when asked about situations in the North, as it is all too easy to dismiss similar situations in 'developing countries' as part of a larger problem of a lack of real democracy, graft and corruption.

Much of the existing literature on decentralization, whether addressing the North or the South, retains a utopian flavour (see Janssen, Anderies and Ostrom 2007) without addressing many of the real, significant and deeply ingrained problems confronting effective decentralization, including: resistance to paradigm change, bureaucratic 'turf protection', undermining compatibility of goals, suppressing information, exacerbating internal community stratification, blocking cross-scale linkages, allowing the corporate sector to co-opt policy development, rejecting any community capacity for governance, and lack of effective monitoring for evidence-based management decisions. The situation facing the clam harvesters in the Digby area illustrates most of these problems. The privatization paradigm has proven a significant barrier to integrated management and to maintaining a public good, and despite concerted protest from two other levels of government (aboriginal and municipal), the provincial and federal bureaucratic managers have refused to consider alternative paradigms as valid options. Furthermore, bureaucrats collect and distribute insufficient evidence to base management decisions (such as long-term leases) on solid data (such as assessments of clam stocks subsequent to privatization). The information that is collected (such as volume and source of contaminant levels on beaches) is not made freely available to stakeholders.

Local communities are attempting to organize to address some of these problems. In order to constrain powerful local agents, for example, the Annapolis Watershed Resource Committee uncoupled the 'stakeholder' approach (much loved by bureaucrats) from local decision-making by including processors on the committee, but without voting privileges.[28] They also struggled to align management

28 A grassroots political backlash against the stakeholder approach is being experienced in many settings. The Center for International Forestry Research, for example, has developed what they call 'a simple tool' for determining the most relevant stakeholders.

goals by integrating information and decision-making across resource sectors and ecological zones, despite inadequate data. They have sought access to information that they need to assess the impact of management decisions on resources in their area. And in particular, they recommended the Watershed Committee as an appropriate local venue to assess the impact of the annual leases before extended clam leases were granted. But in all of these areas, politicians and bureaucrats failed to recognize the advantages of the committee as an integrated management organization, and further, have actively undermined committee efforts. This was amply illustrated at a meeting held between members of a coalition formed to demand public consultation over the ten-year extension of the clam beach leases and the provincial Minister of Fisheries.

The members of the coalition specifically critiqued the failure to consult with local stakeholders, and asked the minister to recognize the expertise of the Watershed Committee and its appropriateness to facilitate public consultation. As one example of the need for consultation, they asked the minister how leases would accommodate native commercial fishing rights as recognized in the *Marshall* decision. A representative from Bear River First Nation also raised the issue of aboriginal food and ceremonial rights to the resource. The minister responded by pointing out that aboriginal harvesters could not access clams on the affected beaches in any case, due to the contamination issue. When reminded that a native clam fishery could presumably include a native depuration plant, the bureaucrats at the meeting responded by asserting that they had consulted directly with the Chief of Bear River and did not need to rely on any other organization to address aboriginal access. In fact, the Chief of Bear River First Nation latter denied this assertion; he sent a powerfully worded letter of protest to the provincial government, and has stressed his faith in the aboriginal members of the Watershed Committee to represent Bear River's interests. In this, as in other discussions, however, government bureaucrats represented the Watershed Committee as irrelevant by suggesting that the important discussions and decisions were going on elsewhere.

While the provincial minister ended the above-mentioned meeting by stating that a final decision on the future role of the committee in public consultation on clam management was still pending, it was subsequently announced that longer-term leases had been granted, and that two further beaches in the area had been closed. However, there were some changes to the initial lease proposal as a result of the protests, for example:

- the areas could be opened if they were tested as clean;
- the Annapolis River lease is only for five years, rather than ten;
- the minister can force the company to co-operate with conservation work, and there will public access for non-clam harvesting use.

In this tool, dependency on the resource and a history of utilizing the resource are more important that capital investments; see <www.cifor.cgiar.org/acm/methods/candi.html>, accessed 30 January 2009.

None of these make a significant difference to the essential privatization of this resource.

Any further resistance to this privatization initiative will probably have to be through the courts and rely on aboriginal rights. But this resistance will have to confront powerful actors, some from the private sector and some from the public sector, many of them astute at using the law (and science) to move forward their particular agendas. Those people in local communities who find their access to natural resources denied in favour of new corporate investors rapidly discover that national promises of integrated management and of participatory governance are but lip service, as are ideals of liberal democracy. Combined with a thin veneer of transparency, this lip service gives the appearance of sound governance and management. When local people organize a protest, they find themselves stigmatized and marginalized. As we examine governance at the local level, then, such examples suggest that more recognition must be paid to the inherently political nature of the resulting interaction and to the ways in which law is a tool in local-level political struggles. Despite Canada's Oceans Strategy and the promise to create institutional arrangements whereby all stakeholders would be involved in designing, implementing and monitoring coastal and ocean management plans, the actual devolution of decision-making and of management roles and responsibilities to the grassroots level has met significant legal and bureaucratic barriers. The role of the law has so far been to block participatory governance of resource management. Unless and until the political will exists to shift the real barriers to participatory governance, significant changes to governance structures will not emerge. Those who would promote decentralization and sustainable resource use must work harder at understanding the real (rather than imagined) barriers and impediments.

References

Béné, C. and Neiland, A.E. (2004), *From Participation to Governance: Challenge Program on Water and Food*, Penang: World Fish Center and Challenge Program on Water and Food.

Bradshaw, B. (2003), 'Questioning the Credibility and Capacity of Community-based Resource Management', *The Canadian Geographer* 47(2): 137–50.

Cole, H. (2002), 'Contemporary Challenges: Globalization, Global Interconnectedness and that "There Are not Plenty More Fish in the Sea". Fisheries, Governance and Globalization: Is there a Relationship?', *Oceans and Coastal Management* 46: 77–102.

Davidson-Hunt, I.J. and O'Flaherty, R.M (2007), 'Researchers, Indigenous Peoples, and Place-based Learning Communities', *Society and Natural Resources* 20: 291–305.

Feit, H.A. and Spaeder, J.J. (2005), 'Co-management and Indigenous Communities: Barriers and Bridges to Decentralized Resource Management – Introduction', *Anthropologica* 47: 147–54.

Fung, A. and Wright, E. (2001), 'Deepening Democracy: Innovations in Empowered Participatory Governance', *Politics and Society* 29(1): 5–41.

Gibson, C.C. and Koontz, T. (1998), 'When Community is Not Enough: Institutions and Values in Community-based Forest Management in Southern Indiana', *Human Ecology* 26(4): 621–47.

Goetze, T.C. (2005), 'Empowered Co-management: Towards Power Sharing and Indigenous Rights in Clayoquot Sound, B.C.', *Anthropologica* 47: 246–65.

Haas, P.M. (2004), 'Addressing the Global Governance Deficit', *Global Environmental Politics* 4(4): 1–15.

Isobe, M. (n.d.), *A Theory of Integrated Coastal Zone Management in Japan*, vol. 2006, Department of Civil Engineering, University of Tokyo.

Janssen, M.A., Anderies, J.M. and Ostrom, E. (2007), 'Robustness of Social-ecological Systems to Spatial and Temporal Variability', *Society and Natural Resources* 20: 307–22.

Kearney, J. and Wiber, M.G. (2006), 'Learning Communities as a Tool in Resource Management', *Proceedings of the Halifax Workshop*, November 2005.

——, Berkes, F., Charles, A., Pinkerton, E. and Wiber, M.G. (2007), 'The Role of Participatory Governance and Community-based Management in Integrated Coastal and Ocean Management in Canada', *Coastal Management* 35(1): 97–104.

Leblanc, K., Ouellette, M.G., Chouinard, A. and Landry, T. (2005), 'Commercial Harvest and Population Structure of a Northern Quahog Populations in St. Mary's Bay, Nova Scotia, Canada', *Journal of Shellfish Research* 24(1) (January): 47–54.

McCallum, W., Hughey, K.F.D and Rixecker, S.S. (2007), 'Community Environmental Management in New Zealand: Exploring the Realities in the Metaphor', *Society and Natural Resources* 20: 323–36.

Nigh, R. (2002), 'Maya Medicine in the Biological Gaze. Bioprospecting Research as Herbal Fetishism', *Current Anthropology* 43(3): 451–77.

Ostrom, E., Gardner, R. and Walker, J. (1994), *Rules, Games and Common-pool Resources*, Ann Arbor, MI: University of Michigan Press.

Rhodes, R.A.W. (1997), *Understanding Governance: Policy Networks, Reflexivity and Accountability*, Buckingham: Open University Press.

Schlager, E. and Ostrom, E. (1992), 'Property Rights Regimes and Natural Resources', *Land Economics* 68: 24–62.

Schneider, H. (1999), 'Participatory Governance for Poverty Reduction', *Journal of International Development* 11(4): 521–34.

Singleton, S. (2000), 'Co-operation or Capture? The Paradox of Co-management and Community Participation in Natural Resource Management and Environmental Policy-making', *Environmental Politics* 9(2): 1–21.

Spaeder, J.J. (2005), 'Co-management in a Landscape of Resistance: The Political Ecology of Wildlife Management in Western Alaska', *Anthropologica* 47(2), 165–78.

Swyngedouw, E. (1997), 'Neither Global nor Local. "Glocalization" and the Politics of Scale', in K.R. Cox (ed.), *Spaces of Globalization. Reasserting the Power of the Local*, New York and London: Guildford Press, pp. 137–66.

Tsing, A.L. (2005), *Friction: An Ethnography of Global Connection*, Princeton, NJ: Princeton University Press.

Wiber, M.G. (2000), 'Fishing Rights as an Example of the Economic Rhetoric of Privatization: Calling for an Implicated Economics', *Canadian Review of Sociology and Anthropology* 37(3): 267–88.

—— (2004), 'Finding Common Ground in the Fisheries Field: Agency in the Ethnographic Encounter', *Zeitschrift für Ethnologie* 129: 49–70.

—— (2005), 'Mobile Law and Globalism: Epistemic Communities versus Community-based Innovation in the Fisheries Sector', in F. von Benda-Beckmann, K. von Benda-Beckmann and A. Griffiths (eds), *Mobile People, Mobile Law: Expanding Legal Relations in a Contracting World*, Burlington, VT: Ashgate Press, pp. 131–52.

—— and Kennedy, J. (2001), 'Impossible Dreams: Reforming Fisheries Management in the Canadian Maritimes after the Marshall Decision', *Law and Anthropology* 11: 282–97.

Worm, B., Barbler, E.B., Beaumont, N., Duffy, J.E., Folke, C., Halpern, B.S., Jackson, J., Loetze, H.K., Micheli, F., Palumbi, S.R., Sala, E., Selkoe, K.A., Stachowicz, J.J. and Watson, R. (2006), 'Impacts of Biodiversity Loss on Ocean Ecosystem Services', *Science* 314: 787–90.

Zanetell, B.A. (2001), 'Legislating Community-based Management: Lessons from the Venezuelan Freshwater Fishery', *Journal of International Wildlife Law and Policy* 4: 279–94.

Chapter 8

The Governance of Children: From Welfare Justice to Proactive Regulation in the Scottish Children's Hearings System

Anne Griffiths and Randy F. Kandel

This chapter explores the relationship between law and governance in the context of administrating access to, and provision of services to, vulnerable Scottish children. It explores the role law plays in shaping discourses of legitimacy for intervention into these children's lives in conjunction with the bureaucratic policies and procedures that frame the contexts for such intervention. Such law encompasses both the voluntary provision of services[1] as well as compulsory measures of supervision.[2] Our chapter, however, focuses on the latter in connection with children under 16 who are referred to the Scottish children's hearings system. It examines how law in this area has developed over time, drawing on different legal models that have fluctuated between a welfare-based paradigm, a more formal, rights-based paradigm, and a proactive, regulatory paradigm. Each model accentuates different features. Thus, the welfare model embraces a more discretionary form of process than a rights-based model that endorses a more formal and procedural process, while a proactive regulatory model actively seeks to promote legal intervention at an earlier stage in the process, thereby reducing the number of referrals for compulsory supervision. In our discussion of these models, we explore how those participating in or serving the system respond to them as they accommodate, resist or grapple with transnational law embodied in international conventions such as the United Nations Convention on the Rights of the Child (UNCRC), or the European Convention on Human Rights and Fundamental Freedoms (ECHR).

These developments have made the situation more complex by adding a tension between the rights of parents and children. Article 6 of the 1998 Act upholds everyone's due process right to a fair hearing in civil cases. Article 8,

1 Such services include accommodation such as daycare facilities for pre-school children under five, aftercare assistance for children aged 16–19 who are leaving care, and short-stay refuges. They also include assistance in kind, home helps, laundry facilities and cash (in exceptional circumstances).

2 The Children (Scotland) Act 1995, Part II, in conjunction with what remains of the Social Work (Scotland) Act 1968, sets out a framework to support children and their families in the community, emphasizing partnership between parents and local authorities.

dealing with respect for private and family life, supports family autonomy or freedom from state interference for both parent and child. Hence, the rights of all family members must be balanced. According to Norrie, this requires a shift in the hearings' mind-set so that they operate 'in a way that balances somewhat competing interests, rather than simply hold the child's interests to be paramount (by which was understood sole) consideration' (Norrie 2005, 5).

Phase One – Establishing Hearings: The Welfare Paradigm

When hearings were initiated, they represented a welfare model of justice that focused on a less formal, rights-based system in favour of a more 'informal', participatory model of justice. For, when they were introduced, they marked the culmination of a comprehensive process of juvenile justice and child welfare reform in Scotland. This represented a departure from earlier attempts at regulation, which were spread across four distinct types of juvenile courts, namely the Sheriff Court, the Burgh (or Police) Courts, the Justice of the Peace Courts and the specially constituted Justice of the Peace Juvenile Courts. This fragmentation represented different discourses of intervention and modes of practice that embraced both criminal and civil jurisdictions. These placed differing emphases on accountability that included both protective measures and punishment. Following the recommendations of the Kilbrandon Committee, published in 1964 and founded upon the Social Work (Scotland) Act 1968, the new system was set up to deal with all children in need of compulsory measures of care.[3] It permitted state intervention in the lives of children under 16 across a broad spectrum of circumstances, including neglected or abused children, as well as those children who had committed offences or who were 'beyond the control of a relevant person' or who failed 'to attend school regularly without reasonable excuse'.[4] In this system, no distinction was to be drawn between offenders and non-offenders, on the grounds that both sets of children required care and protection because their 'normal up-bringing process' had 'fallen short' (Kilbrandon 1964, para. 15).

Thus, at its inception, the children's hearings system had a number of distinctive characteristics that set it apart from previous attempts to regulate and assist children. Key to its operation was the concept that a unified welfare-based system was required, one which responded to children's needs rather than their deeds. As a result, the system endorsed a non-punitive focus where the welfare of the child was to be the hearing's 'paramount consideration' (now contained in s. 16(1) of the Children (Scotland) Act 1995). To achieve these goals, the new system was predicated upon diversion from the courts, with cases referred to a

3 This has been changed under the Children (Scotland) Act 1995 to 'compulsory measures of supervision'. The change in terminology is instructive. It was altered because the prevailing view was that the system did not really 'care' for children.

4 Under s. 70 of the Children (Scotland) Act 1995.

local official, the Reporter to the Children's Panel, to determine whether there was sufficient evidence to support the referral and whether there was a *prima facie* need for compulsory measures of care. This permitted the reporter to decide to take no further action, or to refer the case to a social work department for voluntary measures of care, or finally, if compulsory measures of care might be required, to refer the case to a children's hearing. So the first steps in dealing with children did not involve exposing them to formal proceedings.

Children's hearings themselves were also distinctive in a number of ways. First, the intention was to see an extra-judicial resolution of the problems; second, this was intended to be pursued on a relatively informal basis in discussion with parents and the child; third, the three members of the panel conducting the hearing were lay people drawn from the local community who were public volunteers, whose services were unpaid and who worked on a part-time basis. For the Kilbrandon Committee recognized that a court of law is not an environment which is likely to encourage a child to take an active or a helpful part in proceedings, and for that reason the determination of what, if any, measures of care or supervision should be imposed should be dealt with by a lay tribunal. Finally there was a separation of adjudication from disposal. If the reason or reasons for referral to the children's hearings (known as the grounds of referral) were not accepted by the child or parents, the case was adjudicated before a judge in the Sheriff Court and returned to the panel for disposal. In this way, the demands of formal legality – requiring determination of the facts with regard to due process – were kept distinct from a disposal of the case, so that intervention based on welfare could be kept separate from adjudication as to whether the grounds for referral were established.

All in all, the new system took a novel approach to dealing with children by diverting their cases from courts,[5] by promoting a unified welfare-based system for both offenders and children in need of protection, by fostering relative informality through non-adherence to formal rules of evidence or procedure of the type applicable in courts, by eschewing specialist legal personnel, and by promoting dialogue round an open table where all parties, including the child and his or her family, were encouraged to participate and reach a decision based on consensus about what was in 'the best interests of the child'. The discourse for intervention, regulation and provision of services was geared to welfare and participation.

However, it is important to note that although relatively informal in comparison with courts, panel members wield wide-ranging powers, including power to make a residential supervision requirement placing the child in a foster or local authority home, or even in secure accommodation. None the less, since its implementation, the children's hearing system in Scotland has been hailed as 'unique' (Norrie 1997, 1), 'an exciting innovation' (Morrison and Beasley 1982, 191) and as 'a vastly superior way of dealing with children and their problems than ever the old courts were' (Scottish Office, Education Department 1993, 24).

5 In extreme cases, children under 16 may be dealt with in the criminal courts, but such cases prove to be exceptional.

Phase Two – Bringing Rights Back In: Due Process Interventions

Inevitably, as weaknesses in the system became apparent, it became subject to scrutiny and criticism.[6] Much of this centred on the fact that hearings had been too focused on welfare and too lax in terms of respecting the child's and family's legal rights. The Kilbrandon Committee did acknowledge that its proposals might permit more or earlier compulsory intervention than a system of punishment would allow, and that compulsory supervision, education or training of children (beyond that universally required by compulsory schooling) was a direct invasion of parental control and autonomy. Over time, the growing awareness of transnational approaches to justice embodied in the European Convention on Human Rights and Fundamental Freedoms and United Nations Convention on the Rights of the Child, along with a desire to bring Scots law into line with their requirements (after lobbying by organizations such as the Child Law Centre and Childcare Scotland), led to changes in the system embodied in the Children (Scotland) Act 1995 and subsequent legislation, such as the Human Rights Act 1998.

It was during this period that we commenced our research on children's hearings in Glasgow.[7] This involved interviews with 40 of the 400 active panel members in the Glasgow area, 25 social workers, 25 safeguarders, 65 young people with experience of panels and 67 without, 25 parents and the observation of 34 hearings. At the time, it was clear that hearing personnel were having to take account of transnational standards in their daily practice. Our interviews with the 40 panel members together with attendance at initial and follow-up training sessions revealed that they were very aware of the above international standards and the impact these had on the system through changes brought about by the 'new' Act (as panel members referred to the 1995 Act). They, as well as reporters,[8] were also aware of changes that were imminent due to legislation contained in the Human Rights Act 1998 that was about to become law.

These changes primarily involved strengthening the due process rights of the child and family. In taking account of the provisions of Article 12 of the UNCRC, Scots law now provided that children must be given the opportunity to express their views in legal proceedings affecting them, and have them taken into account where they are sufficiently mature.[9] It enacted a presumption of maturity in favour

6 See The Clyde Report (Clyde 1992); The Kearney Report (Kearney 1992); The Finlayson Report (Finlayson 1992); Scottish Office (1990); Home Office (1993).

7 This formed part of a comparative research project from 1997 to 2000 on 'The Child's Voice in Legal Proceedings' in Scotland and the USA, funded by the Annenberg Foundation and the British Academy.

8 Unfortunately, we were unable to interview reporters, as they withdrew from the project and declined to be interviewed about the system and the impact that the 1998 Act would have on it. Any comments and observations made about reporters therefore come from our informal discussions with them before or after our observation of hearings.

9 S. 16(2) of the 1995 Act.

of children aged 12 or over. In keeping with Article 8, enshrining respect for private and family life and the autonomy of parents, the 1995 Act provided that there should be minimum intervention – a hearing should only make an order if it was better for the child to make such an order than to make no order at all.[10]

After the case of *McMichael* v. *UK*,[11] which went to the European Court of Human Rights, the Principal Reporter became obliged to make available to each parent[12] or 'relevant person' the social background reports that social workers prepare for the panel members. Previously, these reports were only for panel members, and the family were only entitled to a verbal account of their substance at the hearing. This still left children themselves without a statutory right to access reports concerning their own case, a position conceded in *S.* v. *Miller*[13] to be contrary to Article 6 of the ECHR. As a result, guidance has been issued by the Principal Reporter under which children over 12 are to be sent the same documents as panel members unless this is likely to cause significant distress or harm to the child, or to impede prevention or detection of a crime.[14] The need to meet the demands of procedural and substantive justice embodied in Article 6 which was also established in *S.* v. *Miller* led to hearings being required to appoint a child with legal representation in those cases where a young person was unable to effectively conduct his or her own case.[15]

Children and young people's participation at hearings has always been problematic. This was highly evident from the hearings we observed, and many of the children we interviewed observed that they found them 'scary', as 'it's frightening to have to go and talk in front of lots of people' (Griffiths and Kandel 2000). Panel members also observed that while it is essential to hear a child's story about the circumstances giving rise to a referral directly from the child, this is generally 'an uphill struggle' (Griffiths and Kandel 2001). For, as one panel member explained, 'it's important all the time, every day, every hearing, to hear the child's story right from the child. Whether you do or not is a different matter' (Griffiths and Kandel 2006, 136).

Part of the problem derives from the fact that however egalitarian panels attempt to be, they can never quite escape from the fact that there is generally a class divide between the panel members and the children and families that inhibits discussion.[16] Thus, the power position of the parties cannot be ignored, for it is not

10 S. 16(3). But note that where it is deemed to be in the child's best interests that an order be made, this does not mean that the intervention must be kept to a minimum. The test is rather what would be better for the child as against no order being made at all.

11 [1995] 2 FCR 718.

12 Children's Hearings (Scotland) Rules 1996, r. 5(3).

13 2001 SLT 531. For detailed discussion, see Griffiths and Kandel (2004).

14 SCRA Practice Guidance Note 24.

15 See Children's Hearings (Legal Representation) (Scotland) Rules (2002).

16 See Hallett and Hazel (1998); Waterhouse et al. (2000); Waterhouse and McGhee (2002).

only the panel members' social standing that is at issue, but their power to remove a child from the family home. Although such power is rarely exercised, children and families remain fearful that the outcome of the hearing will be to remove the child from his or her home. This fear is hard to allay. Three of the young people who had experience of panels expressed the view that 'they're just there tae put you in a residential home'. Even those who had no experience of panels expressed the view that they existed to deal with 'wee neds', or 'hard men', or children who were in some way 'bad'.

In order to enhance children's participation, the panel now has power under section 46 of the 1995 Act to exclude a 'relevant person' and his or her representatives from parts of the hearing in order to allow a child to express his or her views more freely, or because their presence is causing, or is likely to cause, significant distress.[17] This is a welcome change, allowing more scope for the child's expression of views in difficult circumstances. However, the substance of what is discussed in private must be revealed to those who have been excluded after their exclusion has ended.[18] This means that the child's views cannot be treated as confidential. The reason for this is to maintain an open process so that nothing is 'hidden' from the participants. This is in keeping with the principles of natural justice and the requirements of 'a fair and public hearing' set out in Article 6 of the ECHR. It is especially pertinent where the hearing may be making a decision that will have an impact on parents' rights protected under the Human Rights Act 1998.

These represent just a few examples of attempts to reorder the balance between welfare and rights. Thus, the discourse of legitimate intervention into children's lives must now factor in a more highly articulated repertoire of rights. Ironically, however, our research shows that attempts to promote a greater respect for rights may have unintended consequences of the kind that may lead participants to being more circumspect, rather than more open and transparent at hearings. So what is intended to be a more transparent, open forum becomes less accessible, as more of an emphasis on due process leads to a greater degree of formalization that not only makes for more bureaucratic control, but also makes the process less comprehensible to children because of the technical language that is involved. An example is provided by the provision of social background reports to children and families. This is intended to promote due process by making sure that all participants have the relevant information that is central to the decision-making process. However, a number of panel members observed that far from making the process more transparent, it may render it more opaque, as some social workers have become much less candid, if not vague, in what they write. In some cases, this results in social workers making statements such as that the family feel 'unable to co-operate', rather than revealing that lack of co-operation is due to a parent's drug addiction (Griffiths and Kandel 2006). As a result, panel members are left in the

17 S. 46(1).
18 S. 46(2).

dark about what is really going on in the child's life and find it difficult to make the best possible disposal for the child due to lack of information.

Another example involves conforming to the demands of a fair trial. This has led to a greater formalization of the process, with the grounds for referral and references to rights of appeal being presented in legal language at the beginning and end of the hearing. As a result, some children find the process less comprehensible because of the technical language that is used. Only four out of the 50 young people interviewed who responded to this question observed that they had had no difficulty in understanding the language. Others made comments like:

> They used too big words I think. When you're only young, I mean 12 or 13 I would sit and go through my report, I would be sitting in the children's panel and I would say what does that mean. What did this mean. I didnae have a clue what half the words meant cause its social work language. (16-year-old girl)

or

> I only understood a wee bit' but didnae ask them [panel members] nuthin' 'cos yer shy when yer talking tae other people. (12-year-old boy) (Griffiths and Kandel 2004).

It must be remembered that many young people try to make themselves as invisible as possible at hearings, so their nervousness and reluctance to be there affects their attitude to participation. None the less, complex technical language or jargon does not help. As one 16-year-old girl observed, 'I wisnae listening when they read out the Acts and all that rubbish I didnae have a clue.'

Even clearing the room to speak with the child alone under section 46 has its problems. For while the panel may clear the room to talk to the child on his or her own, they must disclose the substance of what is said to any excluded parties on their return to the hearing.[19] A number of panel members commented that having to disclose the substance 'defeats the purpose' of the section, making it 'relatively useless' or a 'false thing'. One long-serving panel member summed up the view of the majority, explaining that he had:

> [a wide] concern about the whole [1995] Act [because] the changes that have been introduced, on first reading, look to have given people more rights in terms of understanding and getting access to papers and so on. But in effect we have reinforced the rights of parents and of lawyers and we have created a slightly more adversarial system than we had before. I don't think we have done anything to enhance the rights of children because, at the end of the day, 80 or 90 per cent of the cases we get, the parents are in some way culprits in the problem that this child has got, and if we are reinforcing the rights of potential culprits then we

19 Ibid.

> are taking away our right and our duty of protecting the child. So I think we have gone the wrong way with this last bit of legislation, it has not been a good move. (Griffiths and Kandel 2006, 140)

This perspective on the system has led a number of panel members to engage in strategies that enable them to meet the legal requirements of due process, while simultaneously gathering information and managing the hearing to serve the child's welfare. They adopt a form of statutory interpretation that we have dubbed 'gisting' or 'loopholing' in order to manoeuvre their way round the section's difficulties to get the information they want (Griffiths and Kandel, 2009).

Attempts to bolster participants 'rights' in regulatory processes affecting children's welfare are constantly in tension with one another as, over the years, they have shifted back and forth along a spectrum from welfare to rights in attempts to maintain the right kind of balance between the two concepts' demands. For as Norrie has acknowledged, 'the children's hearing is a quasi-judicial tribunal which has many of the powers of a court and it must, therefore, for the protection of all those who appear before it, conform to the standards of procedural fairness required not only by natural justice but by international obligation' (Norrie 2005, 3). Hallett and Hazel, dealing with trends in juvenile justice and child welfare in an international context, note that 'recent decades have seen a retreat from welfare associated with a concern for the young person's access to formal justice and due process' (Hallett and Hazel 1998, vol. 2, i). In this context, they view welfare and justice in terms of the models outlined by Alder and Wundersitz (1994), with the former being:

> associated with paternalistic and protectionist policies, with treatment rather than punishment being the key goal. From this perspective, because of their immaturity, children cannot be regarded as rational or self-determining agents, but rather are subject to and are the product of the environment within which they live. Any criminal action on their part can therefore be attributed to dysfunctional elements in that environment. The task of the justice system then, is to identify, treat and cure the underlying social causes of offending, rather than inflicting punishment for the offence itself. (Alder and Wundersitz 1994, 3)

By contrast, the 'justice' model:

> assumes that all individuals are reasoning agents who are fully responsible for their actions and so should be held accountable before the law. Within this model, the task of the justice system is to assess the degree of culpability of the individual offender and apportion punishment in accordance with the seriousness of the offending behaviour, In so doing, the individual must be accorded full rights to due process, and state powers must be constrained, predictable and determinate. (Alder and Wundersitz 1994, 3)

As with all ideal types, these models are rarely found in a pure form, and the Scottish children's hearings system contains a mixture of both. However, as Hallett and Hazel (1998, vol. 2, iii) observe, 'there has been [a] clear trend in recent years towards greater responsibility and accountability for young offenders to accompany greater rights and legal process' (Hallett and Hazel 1998, vol. 2, iii). As a result, 'young people are encouraged to take a "mature" approach involving accepting guilt, co-operation with official agents and attempting reparation' (Hallett and Hazel 1998, iii). In Scotland, this has resulted in the Antisocial Behaviour etc. (Scotland) Act 2004, which empowers courts to impose anti-social behaviour orders on children (including electronic tagging) and to impose orders on parents who fail to co-operate in reforming their children's behaviour.[20]

Children's hearings have a role to play in dealing with these orders, but that role is not informed by panel members' expertise in identifying the child's welfare; rather, the purpose of the order is to protect others from the child's actions, so the focus no longer lies on 'needs', but 'deeds' – in other words, in disciplining the child's behaviour. Thus, Scotland now appears to be following a trend that has been apparent in English-speaking countries since the 1970s towards the procedural separation of young people accused of 'judicial' offences, and other children seen as in need of care and protection. This includes the provision of fast-track procedures to deal with children who are persistent offenders.[21]

Phase Three – Looking to the Future: Proactive Regulation

Part of this process of change has included a comprehensive review of the hearings system. This has been driven by debates surrounding persistent offending, a shift in grounds of referral from offence to non-offence grounds,[22] differential experiences of hearings due to local variations in support, practice and speed of delivery, and dissatisfaction with the failure to effectively implement hearings' decisions.[23]

As the Scottish Executive (2004) observed, since its inception thirty-three years earlier, the system has never been subject to 'a thorough review "although it has faced changes" in society, family structure and legislation'. The 1995 Act did

20 Such parenting orders are likely to mean that parents will be required to attend counselling or guidance sessions for a particular period (Edwards and Griffiths 2006).

21 Significant failure to implement the supervision requirements of hearings in 'ordinary' offender cases was noted by the Audit Scotland report (Audit Scotland 2002, paras 147–8). However, the Research Team (2005) pilot study observed that the use of this fast-track approach has to be regarded as 'not proven with regard to impact on offending'.

22 The figure rose from 16 per cent in 1976 to 60 per cent in 2002–2003. This position was maintained in 2004–2005, with 60 per cent of cases being referred for neglect or abuse, and only 40 per cent on offence grounds (SCRA *Annual Report* 2004–2005).

23 Research by Audit Scotland revealed that 25 per cent of young offenders on supervision did not get a service, and in cases of children on home supervision, a fifth had no social worker attached to the family for several months.

introduce changes, but these were principally of a procedural nature rather than presenting any fundamental challenges to the system's welfare orientation (Hallett and Hazel 1998, vol. 1).

The review process, with its emphasis on how to regulate and assist children more comprehensively, was thrown open to public consultation.[24] As part of its broader remit, the review examined the relationship between hearings and other organizations and professionals working with children to see to what extent the degree of overlap between hearings and these other bodies might be reduced to create a more streamlined and efficient provision of services. Thus, the hearings' review was undertaken within a much wider framework for dealing with children in general.

Along with the recognition of the rise of referrals on non-offence grounds comes the acknowledgment that child care policy in Scotland and the rest of the U.K. places a growing emphasis on developing effective prevention and family support provision for children in need (McGhee and Waterhouse, 2002). The need to integrate child protection policy with family support was a key finding of the Department of Health (1995) review that took the view that the division between child protection and child welfare was artificial (Little 1997). This led to a shift in perception that intervention was better conceived of in terms of a process along a continuum where varying degrees of protection and support might be required. Thus, the legitimacy for intervention became formulated in terms of whether or not to offer a service to the child and his or her family, regardless of whether such a child was the subject of a referral (Little 1997, 30).

At the same time, although referrals on offence grounds have fallen significantly, the figures reveal a small hard core of repeat or persistent offenders, with figures rising from 33 per cent in 2000/2001 to 37 per cent in 2003/2004. It is clear that as public anxiety about youth crime and unruliness (fuelled by media attention and government discourse on the subject) has grown in the last five to ten years, so hearings have increasingly come under scrutiny regarding whether the disposals available to them are sufficiently punitive to discourage the hard core of young delinquents, who reoffend with regularity until they move on to the adult justice system.[25]

---

24 Scotland has a long tradition of putting proposals for law reform out to public consultation. While in practice it is generally those who are experts in the area who respond, members of the general public are free to make their views known and lodge written responses to proposed legislation.

25 McAra (2002) compares the period 1968–85 as the 'high point of welfare in juvenile justice in Scotland' to 1995–2000, which she characterizes as a period of 'protective tutelage' when 'issues of juvenile justice have become increasingly caught up in the new Labour Government's social inclusion and social crime prevention agendas'. See also McDiarmid (2005); McAra (2006).

After consultation,[26] the Scottish Executive (2004) moved towards Phase Two of 'Getting it Right for Every Child', dealing with proposals for action. It modified its approach to reform while continuing to endorse a more proactive approach to dealing with children in general. Thus, it conceded that 'the vast majority of respondents felt strongly that the hearing system should remain focused on meeting the needs of individual children rather than balancing these with the needs of family members and the wider community'. It also acknowledged that there was strong support for maintaining the current system, where all children, whether offenders or abused or neglected, should be dealt with before a hearing made up of generalist panel members. Finally, it noted that there was little support for establishing specialized panels to deal with specific issues.

The new proposals for change are intended to operate in two ways: (1) by raising the threshold for referral to children's hearings, while (2) extending the proactive work of professionals dealing with children, such as social workers, school teachers, doctors and police, who will have formal legal duties placed on them to provide 'high-quality services', assisting children where required to 'overcome the social, educational, physical, environmental and economic barriers that create inequality'. This is to be achieved by providing for a more co-ordinated intervention, extending beyond those cases where children are in need of compulsory measures of supervision, one that requires a plan of action known as an Integrated Assessment Planning and Recording Framework (IAF). This plan will apply:

> to everyone working with children and young people, whether they are part of a universal service such as education, primary health care, or the police, or whether they are in a more specialist, targeted service, such as social work, school care accommodation service or secure accommodation services, acute/tertiary health services or the psychological services. (Scottish Government 2005, s. 3)

Thus, the remit for intervention is considerably widened in the move to regulate behaviour at an earlier stage in the child's development.

At the same time, under this model the number of cases referred to hearings is to be cut by introducing more stringent criteria for referral. Referrals will now have to meet two tests, namely 'significant need' and the 'need for compulsion'. The intention is for a more proactive engagement with children outside hearings, to be balanced by an increase in the hearings' powers over children who come before them, especially persistent offenders. They will now be empowered to make an interim supervision requirement in advance of their reaching a final decision. This means that a child can get help straight away even if all the papers or plans required to make a disposal are not ready. Hearings will also have greater powers of scrutiny, enabling them to call for a review on the grounds of a child's 'pattern of behaviour' or 'need'. Under these

26 The Executive received 732 responses; 70 per cent of those responding had some direct involvement in the hearings system.

circumstances, where a child is not responding, a hearing may 'adapt its procedures as appropriate', for example by inviting community representatives or victims to sit in on the hearing 'to reinforce [the child's awareness] that the behaviour [complained of] has an impact on others'. Given the impact that this will have on individuals' rights, a new duty will be placed on the Scottish Children's Reporter Administration (SCRA) 'to ensure legal representation for children, where this is necessary, under current criteria to protect their rights'.

Potentially Positive Aspects of the Proposed Model

Decreasing Caseload So that Hearings Focus on Children with the Greatest Needs

A more co-ordinated service for children will pre-empt unnecessary referrals to hearings, which should lessen the burden on the service. A number of social workers commented that in their view, too many children were being referred to hearings in circumstances where the panel would take no action. Having to write reports for such hearings, as one social worker observed, 'puts limitations on my time management, it takes time away from the constructive time actually visiting and spending time with clients'. By reducing the number of cases that come before hearings, not only will professionals, such as social workers, have more time to spend with their needier clients, but hearings will be freer to concentrate on a smaller number of children with severe problems.

Creating Good Citizenship through Unified Action Plans

The Executive's approach is in keeping with its broader aim to promote good citizenship. Getting children to behave appropriately is not only the goal of Anti-Social Behaviour legislation, but also permeates the provision of services to children across the board. The aim is 'to concentrate more on preventative educative programmes which help people to tackle their own problems'.

The proposed IAF action plan would assist children like the nine-year-old boy we observed at a hearing who had been referred because of his fire-raising activities. While all concerned commented on his inability to sit still and his difficulties in paying attention to what was being said (because he had a short attention span), none of those present seemed to pick up on the fact that this could be a case where the child suffered from Attention Deficit Disorder. When we raised this issue after the panel, the reporter observed that because the family moved so often between Edinburgh and Glasgow, he seemed to have 'slipped through cracks' in the system and escaped assessment, because it 'takes such a long time to set things up'. Under the new proposals, even if shunted from one agency to another, a unified plan would have to be drawn up, under which one agency would retain responsibility for its implementation.

Clearly identifying who has responsibility for a child is important. In our discussion with social workers and panel members, it became clear that there was an issue of accountability concerning who was responsible for dealing with children who are truants. Social work maintained that it was the responsibility of the Education Department, while Education maintained it was the responsibility of Social Work. In one hearing we observed, the social worker opposed the panel members' desire for a supervision order to deal with the boy's failure to go to school on the basis that, given his department's priorities, the boy was not 'appropriate for group work …. He doesn't fit the "care package" criteria … Prioritization is the name of the game … and [he] is not a priority' (Griffiths and Kandel 2005, 280). As one social worker explained:

> We deal a lot with education. They never come down to represent anything in the children's panel …. We're always saying to them this is not a social work problem this is an education problem, you need [the] education department and it's a multi-disciplinary collaborative approach of awareness. And then we end up finding the place [for the child] …. Education opt out and leave it very much for us to pick up. And panels are very happy as well. We end up taking the flak for everything and they [panel members] are very critical of social work. They are very focussed on what we can't provide and what we can't do.

To ensure and enforce compliance, the provisions in the Antisocial Behaviour (Scotland) Act 2004 to refer local authorities to the Sheriff Principal to compel action will be extended to cover *all* agencies identified in a supervision requirement. Thus, any action agreed to in the plan must be carried out. Not only that, but any changes to the plan can only be made if the hearing agrees to them. This should prevent the kind of situation arising that was brought to our attention by one panel member. In discussing the worst case he had had to deal with, he recalled a hearing where the panel had placed a young woman in a secure unit because of her drug addiction. A review hearing had been held before Christmas to consider whether to lift the supervision requirement. The panel declined to do so, but this was ignored by those in charge of the unit, who let her out for Christmas. She then died from a drug overdose. The panel member was so upset he tendered his resignation (which was not accepted), as he had sat on a number of panels dealing with this young woman and he felt that the hearings system had failed her. In theory, this failure to carry out a hearing's decision could not happen under this model.

Potentially Negative Aspects of Proposed Model

Interpretive Dilemmas: Extending Control Within and Beyond Hearings

Although aimed at reducing the caseload for hearings, much will depend on how reporters, who are gatekeepers to the system, interpret need and compulsion in practice. Under the new proposals, the emphasis moves from concrete events justifying intervention to the concept of need, so that 'in rewriting the grounds for referral to the Reporter we concentrate on the need rather than the incident'. An indicator of need would 'include a pattern of behaviour which gives rise to concern'. According to the Executive, this would be advantageous, as it 'would … allow action to be taken over behaviour which may not be significant in itself, but as apart of a pattern of behaviour gives rise to concern'. Taking account of such need would include an additional component – that of the need for compulsion to deal with the situation. So, where parents cannot provide adequate care for their children or a child's behaviour is causing serious concern and cannot be dealt with through voluntary co-operation with social services, the Executive envisage that 'this may require compulsory measures of supervision'. However, the focus on behaviour rather than discernible events as a trigger for referral might have the unintended consequence of widening rather than limiting the hearings' caseload.

Conversely, control will also be extended at the other end of the spectrum, where voluntary measures of assistance are in place. This is where most children end up, as only 11 per cent of children referred to reporters in 2004/2005 went on to appear before hearings. All the others were dealt with under voluntary measures of assistance. As the SCRA 2004/2005 *Annual Report* observes, 'it is in fact much more common for the Reporter to establish voluntary measures with the local authority, family or suitable diversion if possible' than to proceed to a compulsory referral.[27] In this situation, the new proposals will empower the reporters to refer the case to agencies to act on the Action Plan. This means that any professional working with a child will have to produce a plan of action that meets the requirements of the IAF, thus widening the net for intervention well beyond compulsory measures of supervision to anyone working with children, including professionals such as health care workers, doctors, police, educational specialists and social workers. It may also include non-governmental organizations such as Scottish Women's Aid where they are assisting mother and child, for example, in cases of domestic violence, or like the charity Barnardo's, which provides homes for children.

The Paradox of Rights in Differential Arenas

While 'rights' continue to inform hearings' discourse, especially in the light of more stringent powers vested in panels, they appear to be downgraded, if not invisible, within the more bureaucratic, regulatory sphere. This is because a child has no real choice about whether or not to participate in an action plan, nor the right to dispute it (other than in the forum which is assessing him or her). As a result, there is no clear avenue for addressing human rights issues, such as breaches of Articles 6, 8 or 12, in the proposals as currently framed. A child's options are either to proceed to more compulsory measures of care under the hearings system and

27 SCRA *Annual Report*, 40.

appeal there, or take the matter to court, an undertaking which requires knowledge, determination and money.[28] Although provision is made for accountability among professionals, something that was lacking in earlier inter-agency collaborations, no such accountability to child and family is provided for in terms of giving them clearly defined rights of appeal like those operating in hearings or courts.

Concerns about due process also extend to the source and quality of information on which action plans are based and which form part of an historical record that will follow the child up to adulthood. This record will not be easy to correct. While the child or his representative may make a request for disclosure of personal information under section 7 of the Data Protection Act 1998, the record can only be amended if factually inaccurate. Where a professional opinion is at stake, all that can be done is to note on the form that this has been challenged by the individual concerned. Such action does, of course, require knowledge of the procedures to be followed and an application to the UK office of the Information Commissioner. There are also issues about the use that may be made of such information by the supervising agencies, and about its confidentiality.

Balancing Welfare and Confidentiality among Professionals

Competing approaches to rights, involving their extension on the one hand and their retraction on the other, also encompass professionals' approaches to welfare and confidentiality. Although legislation for sharing child protection information has been passed under the Protection of Vulnerable Groups (Scotland) Act 2007, this does not deal with checking the sources of information that are used or the highly pertinent issue of confidentiality. The Act aims to place duties on relevant public organizations to disclose information when a child is at risk of harm. It leaves the details of how this is to be done to a code of practice.[29] The difficulty that arises is that legal duties placed on personnel from these institutions vary, so teachers, doctors, social workers and police may have very different ethics and views regarding confidentiality. For different professionals and agencies have different views about what constitutes confidentiality and when it may be breached in order to comply with child protection.

A code of practice is essential, but how well it will work in practice remains to be seen.[30] One of the positive features of the new proposals is the requirement for all parties to produce a co-ordinated action plan that attributes clear responsibility

---

28 Legal Aid may be available, but given the cutbacks in the system, it is not clear how much funding will be made available for challenges to the system at this level.

29 See *Sharing Information when a Child is in Need of Protections: A Draft Code of Practice*, April 2007, <www.rcn.org.uk/__data/assets/pdf_file/0006/165795/2007-08_Sharing_Information_When_a_Child_is_in_Need_of_Protection_-_A_Draft_Code_of_Practice.pdf>, accessed 30 January 2009.

30 After consultation, the Draft Code issued in April 2007 is being extensively rewritten.

to one particular body for its implementation. This development represents a response to a whole series of inquiries investigating children's deaths, most recently those of Victoria Climbié,[31] Caleb Ness[32] and Danielle Reid,[33] that have been highly critical of the lack of inter-agency co-operation or accountability. However, there is a very real problem in addressing this co-ordination, for the professionals involved engage in different discourses and practices which may very well come into conflict with one another. The current proposals say nothing about how this co-ordination is to be managed. The experience of interdisciplinary teams set up to deal with domestic violence, including police, social workers and health care specialists, has not been heartening.[34] Our research on children's hearings shows how what is intended to be an open and transparent forum may turn out to have a more opaque side due to the constraints imposed by the differing institutional and professional demands placed on panel members, reporters, social workers and safeguarders, who speak from different perspectives and with different priorities at hearings.[35]

Modelling Justice for Children: An Ongoing Process

The Scottish Government[36] has recently put the legislation implementing these proposals, The Children Services (Scotland) Bill, on hold as it engages in a wider process of consultation.[37] The question still remains, however, what type of model will provide the greatest justice for children. As we have demonstrated, the Phase One model, which focused on welfare and a participatory forum for dealing with children, was found lacking when it came to upholding their rights and those of their families. While the Phase Two model attempted to correct this imbalance through a greater degree of formalization, promoting a more highly articulated repertoire of rights, this had the unintended consequence of rendering hearings less transparent and accessible to the participants. For a greater emphasis on due process has not only led to a more bureaucratic control of proceedings, but has also made them less comprehensible to children because of the technical language that is involved.

31 Laming (2003).

32 Edinburgh and the Lothians Child Protection Committee (2003).

33 Herbison (2005).

34 Greenan (2004) discusses multi-agency work on domestic abuse, noting a lack of shared objectives, differing levels of resources, incompatible data sets and poor evaluation, and so on. See also Crawford (1997), especially ch. 4 on 'Partnerships, Conflicts and Power Relations'.

35 See Griffiths and Kandel (2006).

36 The Scottish Executive became the Scottish Government after a change of administration in Scotland that took place in May 2007.

37 See the First Minister's Address to the Scottish Parliament outlining the government's legislative programme for the year on 5 September 2007.

The Phase Three model, which seeks to address children's needs today, proposes to raise the threshold for referral to hearings while extending the circumstances in which professionals should engage in proactive work with children. However, the focus on general patterns of behaviour, rather than discernible events, as a trigger for referral might have the unintended consequence of widening rather than restricting hearings' caseloads, while the focus on action plans for every child may also widen the net for intervention in circumstances where the rights of children and their families are not adequately protected. There is a danger that those who are required to operate the system may find themselves buried under a morass of data and bureaucratic procedures that are far more wide-ranging than has previously been the case. Not only that, but reforms seeking to streamline services aimed at children, making them more efficient, accountable and productive, might have the opposite effect, by putting in place a system that in fact controls, coerces and exercises surveillance over its vulnerable citizens.

References

Alder, C. and Wundersitz, J. (1994), 'New Direction in Juvenile Justice Reform in Australia', in C. Alder and J. Wundersitz (eds), *Family Conferencing and Juvenile Justice: The Way forward or Misplaced Optimism?*, Canberra: Australian Institute of Criminology, pp 1–11.

Audit Scotland (2002), *Dealing with Offending by Young People*, <www.audit-scotland.gov.uk/docs/central/2007/nr_070823_youth_justice_update_km.pdf>, accessed 30 January 2009.

Clyde, J.J. (1992), *The Report of the Inquiry into the Removal of Children from Orkney in February 1991* (The Clyde Report), HC Papers 1992–93, no. 195.

Crawford, A. (1997), *The Local Governance of Crime: Appeals to Community and Partnerships*, Oxford: Clarendon Press.

Department of Health (1995), *Child Protection: Messages from Research*, Studies in Child Protection, London: HMSO.

Edwards, L. and Griffiths, A. (2006), *Family Law*, Edinburgh: Thomson/W. Green.

Edinburgh and Lothians Child Protection Committee (2003), *Report of the Caleb Ness Inquiry*, <www.edinburgh.gov.uk/internet/council/council_publications/cec_report_of_the_caleb_ness_inquiry>, accessed 30 January 2009.

Finlayson, A. (1992), *Reporters to the Children's Panel: Their Role, Function and Accountability* (The Finlayson Report), Edinburgh: HMSO.

Greenan, L. (2004), *Violence against Women: A Literature Review*, commissioned by the National Group to Address Violence against Women, Edinburgh: Scottish Executive, pp 73–75.

Griffiths, A. and Kandel, R.F. (2000), 'Hearing Children in Children's Hearings', *Child and Family Law Quarterly* 3: 283–99.

—— (2001), 'Working towards Consensus: Children's Hearings in Scotland', in P. Foley, J. Roche and S. Tucker (eds), *Children in Society: Contemporary Theory, Policy and Practice*, London: Palgrave Macmillan, pp. 121–32.

—— (2004), 'Empowering Children? Legal Understanding and Experiences of Rights in the Scottish Children's Hearings System', in S. Halliday and P. Schmidt (eds), *Human Rights Brought Home: Socio-legal Perspectives on Human Rights in the National Context*, Oxford and Portland, OR: Hart Publishing, pp. 231–55.

—— (2005), 'Localizing the Global: Rights of Participation in the Scottish Children's Hearings System', in F. and K. von Benda-Beckmann and A. Griffiths (eds), *Mobile People, Mobile Law: Expanding Legal Relations in a Contracting World*, Aldershot: Ashgate, pp. 277–95.

—— (2006), 'Children's Confidentiality at the Cross Roads: Challenges for the Scottish Children's Hearings System', *Journal of Social Welfare and Family Law* 28(2): 135–50.

—— (2009), 'Half-told Truths and Partial Silence: Managing Communication in Scottish Children's Hearings', in F. and K. von Benda-Beckmann and A. Griffiths (eds), *The Power of Law in a Transnational World: Anthropological Enquiries*, Oxford: Berghahn Books.

Hallett, C. and Hazel, N. (1998), *The Evaluation of Children's Hearings in Scotland*, 2 vols, Edinburgh: The Scottish Office Central Research Unit.

Herbison, J. (2005), *The Independent Review into the Circumstances Surrounding the Death of Danielle Reid*, <http://www.protectinghighlandschildren.org/dr-pdfs/dr-finalreport-8thsept-bkmarked.pdf>, accessed 30 January 2009

Home Office (1993), *Police Reform: A Police Service for the Twenty-first Century*, Cm. 2281, London: HMSO.

Kearney, B. (1992), *The Report of the Inquiry into Child Care Policies in Fife* (The Kearney Report), HC Papers 1992–93, no. 191.

Kilbrandon, L. (1964), *Report of the Committee on Children and Young Persons* (The Kilbrandon Report), Cmnd. 2306, Edinburgh: HMSO.

Laming, W.H. (2003), *The Victoria Climbié Inquiry: Report of an Inquiry by Lord Laming*, Cm. 5730, London: SO.

Little, M. (1997), 'The Re-focusing of Children's Services: The Contribution of Research', in N. Parton (ed.), *Child Protection and Family Support: Tensions, Contradictions and Possibilities*, London: Routledge, pp. 25–38.

McAra, L. (2002), 'The Scottish Juvenile Justice System: Policy and Practice', in J. Winterdyk (ed.), *Juvenile Justice Systems: International Perspectives*, 2nd edn, Canadian Scholars Press, pp. 441–75.

—— (2006), 'Welfare in Crisis? Youth Justice in Scotland', in B. Goldson and J. Muncie (eds), *Comparative Youth Justice*, London: Sage, pp. 127–45.

McDiarmid, C. (2005), 'Welfare, Offending and the Scottish Children's Hearings System', *Journal of Social Welfare and Family Law* 27(1): 31–42.

McGhee, J. and Waterhouse, L. (2002), 'Family Support and the Scottish Children's Hearings System', *Child and Family Social Work* 7(4): 273–83.

Morrison, G. and Beasley, R. (1982), 'The Future of the Children's Hearing System', in F.M. Martin and K. Murray (eds), *The Scottish Juvenile Justice System*, Edinburgh: Scottish Academic Press, pp. 191–97.

Norrie, K.M. (1997), *Children's Hearings in Scotland*, Edinburgh: Thomson/W. Green.

—— (2005), *Children's Hearings in Scotland* (2nd edn), Edinburgh: Thomson/W. Green.

Research Team (2005), *Fast Track Children's Hearings Pilot: Final Report of the Evaluation of the Pilot*, Edinburgh: Scottish Executive, <www.scotland.gov.uk/Resource/Doc/54357/0013029.pdf>, accessed 30 January 2009.

Scottish Executive (2004), *Getting it Right for Every Child: Consultation Pack on the Review of the Children's Hearings System*, <www.scotland.gov.uk/consultations/education/chhp-00.asp>, accessed 30 January 2009.

—— (2005), *Getting it Right for Every Child: Proposals for Action*, <www.scotland.gov.uk/Resource/Doc/96074/0023275.pdf>, accessed 30 January 2009.

Scottish Government (2005), *Integrated Assessment Planning and Recording Framework*, <http://openscotland.gov.uk/Publications/2005/10/2191333/13350>, accessed 30 January 2009.

Scottish Office (1990), *Review of Child Care Law in Scotland*, Edinburgh: HMSO.

Scottish Office, Education Department (1993), *Scotland's Children: Proposals for Child Care Policy and Law*, White Paper, Cmnd. 2286, Edinburgh: HMSO.

Waterhouse, L. and McGhee, J. (2002), 'Children's Hearings in Scotland: Compulsion and Disadvantage', *Journal of Social Welfare and Family Law* 24(3): 279–96.

Waterhouse, L., McGhee, J., Whyte, B., Loucks, N., Kay, J. and Stewart, R. (2000), *Evaluation of Children's Hearings System, Volume 3: Children in Focus*, Edinburgh: Scottish Office Central Research Unit, The Scottish Office.

Chapter 9

Migration and Integration of Third-country Nationals in Europe: The Need for the Development of an Efficient, Effective and Legitimate System of Governance

Marie-Claire Foblets

Introduction

This chapter revolves around three basic questions: (1) who manages immigration and integration of third-country nationals (TCNs) in contemporary Europe, (2) what are the modes of governance behind that management, and (3), a question of a more critical nature, do these modes of governance produce comprehensive, consistent and sufficiently transparent regulation? In this chapter, I wish to investigate in particular the entanglements of national and EU (European Union) law in the European context, and some of the effects of the differences between Member States' policies in the field of immigration and integration of TCNs.[1]

One of the questions which this volume raises is whether new modes of governance processes increase, or on the contrary, lessen, the significance of law for governmental authority. This contribution highlights some of the paradoxes of Europeanization in the area of migration. In a recently published paper, Velluti (2007, 55) offers an interesting definition of governance within the EU: 'within the EU, governance signifies a shift from "government" to the establishment of a broader framework of regulation that goes beyond the legislative arena embracing also the political, social and economic spheres of public policy …'.

Her analysis takes into account a variety of actors as well as ideas and practices. What follows in this chapter builds on that premise: the EU system represents a multi-layered system of decision-making that seeks to achieve a compromise between those who are against any type of extension of the power of the EU institutions and those who, on the contrary, would support an increased role for them. Efforts made in the post-Treaty of Amsterdam period on the part of the EU

1 This chapter is part of a larger research project on the (in)consistencies of European migration law. The project was approved of by the Rockefeller Foundation and the German Marshall Fund Foundation with a view to the Bellagio Dialogues on Migration (18 June–16 July 2006).

institutions to shape a communitarian (EU) legislative framework in the fields of immigration and integration of TCNs is illustrative of some of the difficulties generated by multi-level governance: it shows a continuous tension between two systems – inter-governmental co-operation among the Member States on the one hand, and trans-governmental integration at EU level on the other. Despite the general recognition by most Member States today of the need for strengthening a Community-wide immigration policy, the EU has for many years been struggling to shape such policy. So far, it has achieved minimum harmonization, but no more. A truly Community-wide policy is difficult to achieve since Member States wish to maintain a wide margin of discretion in the areas of immigration and integration of TCNs.[2] There is even the (serious) risk that Member States may make use of the absence of an efficient system of governance at EU level to push through their own views on how to shape a regulatory framework for access to their territory and for integration of TCNs. Their first goal is keep a firm grip on things – with a focus on strengthening the control of immigration. One could see this patchy way of addressing issues of immigration on the part of Member States as an 'instrumentalization' of European migration law: national authorities make EU law an instrument of their own regulatory policies (Foblets and Vanheule 2007). As I will try to demonstrate, this is made possible by the unanimity requirement that has prevailed until recently in European migration law.[3]

We will specifically focus on two issues: the right to family reunification for TCNs, and the newly created status of TCNs who are long-term residents. The main justification for adopting a common policy in these two specific fields is that legislative instruments which address issues such as family reunification and the status of TCNs who are long-term residents can foster the protection of TCNs within the EU, thus facilitating their integration into European societies. In practice, however, as I will try to illustrate, Member States have so far employed the 'lowest common denominator' approach to convergence, which results in low minimum standards. They have given preference to a mode of governance that leaves a wide margin of discretion to the national legislators in the process of transposing EU rules within their own domestic legal systems: there is indeed substantial disagreement among the Member States regarding the question of which rights (that is, legal status) should be granted to TCNs.

Immigration and integration of TCNs appear to be particularly sensitive areas to regulate, since both issues have a number of core economic, social and cultural consequences which directly affect not only TCNs, but also EU citizens and, more

2 See, among others, De Bruycker (2003); Peers (2005) (annual overviews).

3 According to Article 67.1 of the EC Treaties, 'During a transitional period of five years following the entry into force of the Amsterdam Treaty, the Council shall act unanimously on a proposal from the Commission or on the initiative of a Member State and after consulting the European Parliament.' This provision was amended by the Treaty of Nice, and the Protocol and Declaration on Article 67 TEC in the Treaty of Nice (*Official Journal of the EU*, vol. 44, C 80, 10 March 2001).

broadly, civil society. This analysis endeavours simply to illustrate some of the effects of these disagreements among EU Member States. It does not purport to be exhaustive in any way. Ultimately, what the illustrations make clear is the urgent need at EU level for the development of more effective governance techniques that can help provide the basis for a coherent regulatory framework in the area of immigration and integration of TCNs. Ideally speaking, such a framework should entail a shift from primarily security concerns on the part of the Member States that keep TCNs in a position of inequality towards a more open and inclusive approach that promotes the integration of TCNs by protecting their basic rights. Two types of techniques may prove effective policy responses in this context. Further extension of the powers of the EU institutions is one option. Yet another, radically different, option is to advocate less rigid governance mechanisms that preserve the autonomy and diversity of the various actors involved in the decision-making process – political as well as social and cultural actors, both state and non-state representatives, international bodies and so on. I conclude this chapter by assessing both of these options. With the prospect of the entry into force of the Treaty of Lisbon of 13 December 2007, the dynamics characterizing the processes of European integration around the field of immigration make the Member States subject to an increasing interplay between the two options.

Developments towards a European (EU) Migration Policy: The Progressive Establishment of a Common Framework on Immigration, Integration and Asylum

One of the striking characteristics of recent developments in European (im)migration policy is the gradual shift since the early 1990s from a national issue – being dealt with at the level of each sovereign state – to a communitarian (EU) issue. Europe has become, progressively, the context for developing policies, setting the rules, and in some cases designing international (bilateral or multilateral) agreements that aim to balance security and facilitate human mobility for economic and other purposes on the one hand, and to protect civil liberties and basic rights on the other.[4]

This progressive shift of immigration and integration issues to Europe over the past few years is characterized by a growing legal complexity. This complexity is mainly due to profound differences in views among Member States as to what sort of regulations are needed, but also to the increasing impact of human rights protection in the fields of immigration and integration.[5] The EU has not undermined the significance of the domestic (national) legal systems and the political communities

4 See, for example, Guild (1996); De Bruycker (2003); Julien-Laferriere, Labaye and Edström (2005). The Treaty of Lisbon will eventually replace the term 'Community' with 'Union'. In this chapter, I use the two terms 'Community' and 'Union' interchangeably.

5 This is coupled with an extension of their application to the growing group of undocumented newcomers. See, for example, De Bruycker (2000); Bouckaert (2007).

that identify with them by making them become part of a broader framework of regulation (at EU level), even though territorial borders between Member States have become porous and flexible. In charting the contours of a common immigration and integration policy, the differences in views among Member States regarding how to shape policy in these fields prove a major handicap, since in effect they result in a lack of internal consistency among the regulations that apply. So far, the only mode of governance that has proven effective in overcoming the resistance of the Member States in ceding to the EU some of their decision-making power on immigration and integration issues has been the technique of instruments that are either in line with their own domestic regulatory policy or are simply not binding on them. Non-binding co-ordination is also the reason why the development of an EU immigration policy is so fragmented; some Member States resort almost exclusively to measures of controlling TCNs and restricting their immigration, while others rely more willingly on the enactment of positive measures aimed at guaranteeing TCNs the protection of their basic rights.

With the exception of a few common characteristics, migration issues in Europe have for years remained a terrain of national sovereignty *par excellence*, with competences that are therefore considered to fall exclusively under the control of the Member States.[6]

Meanwhile, at the international level, migration has continued,[7] including illegal forms such as through trafficking in human beings, unaccompanied minors, clandestinity (in growing numbers since the 1990s) and, last but not least, improper use of the asylum procedure. All of these forms are to be seen as the effect of demographic and economic inequalities in the world (Van Amersfoort 1995). However, since all of them are considered highly undesirable by the public authorities of the receiving countries, they have eventually led to more intense co-operation between States. Illegal migration at least partly explains, so to speak, why since the 1990s European Member States have begun to appear willing to collaborate more intensely with one another on issues of border controls and migration policy. The decisive step in the direction of a common European migration policy was taken with the Treaty of Amsterdam, which entered into force on 1 May 1999. The Treaty of Amsterdam introduced major changes in EU law, both by revising institutional provisions and by laying down the foundation for developing a common immigration policy. In its newly introduced Title IV on the free movement of persons, asylum and immigration, the Treaty of Amsterdam for the first time established considerable competencies for the EU regarding asylum and immigration: Articles 61 and 63 TEC[8] transpose these fields from inter-

6 These are limited, however, by human rights standards of protection (we will return to this issue).

7 The official figures for European countries provide, at the moment, along with asylum, for a few tens of thousands of new migrations per year. See, for example, Poulain, Singleton and Perrin (2006).

8 TEC is an abbreviation of Treaty of the EC, also referred to as the EC Treaty.

governmental co-operation to the realm of the Community method.[9] Migration (and asylum) now clearly relate to the general objective included in Article 2 TEC, namely, to maintain and develop an area of freedom, security and justice in Europe. This 'communitarization' has, since 1999, taken the form of a number of European directives and regulations that in the coming years will increasingly determine the immigration and integration policy of the Member States.[10]

After the Treaty of Amsterdam entered into force, the European Council, at a special meeting in the Finnish city of Tampere in October 1999, agreed that the separate but closely related issues of asylum and migration call for the development of a common European policy. The Tampere European Council declared that:

> The legal status of third country nationals should be approximated to that of Member States' nationals. A person, who has resided legally in a Member State for a period of time to be determined and who holds a long-term residence permit, should be granted in that Member State a set of uniform rights which are as near as possible to those enjoyed by EU citizens; e.g. the right to reside, receive education, and work as an employee or self-employed person, as well as the principle of non-discrimination vis-à-vis the citizens of the State of residence.[11]

The elements on which such a common policy should be based are also mentioned in the documents: partnership with the countries of origin, a common European asylum system, fair treatment of TCNs, and management of migration flows. The aim is thus fair treatment of TCNs residing legally in the territories of the Member States through an integration policy granting them rights and obligations comparable ('nearly equal') to those of EU citizens. To what extent has this ambitious political statement in favour of the inclusiveness of TCNs really taken effect?

The Wider Problem of Legitimacy

After the Tampere summit, the Commission started to implement the programme by developing what appeared at first sight quite a vigorous and astonishing legislative activity.[12] However, this active progress in the development of a European

---

9 Nevertheless, some special rules concerning the decision-making procedures (Art. 67 TEC), the limitation of preliminary reference proceedings (Art. 68 TEC) and opt-in or opt-out clauses for some Member States (Art. 69 TEC) have been necessary to find a consensus. On these special rules, see, for example, Kuyper (1999), 436–7ff.

10 Cf. note 1 above, and Velluti (2007), 55.

11 The Presidency Conclusions of the European Council in Tampere, Brussels, 4/5 November 2004, Annex I, para. 21 <www.europol.europa.eu/jit/hague_programme_en.pdf>, accessed 30 January 2009.

12 See, for example, De Bruycker (2003); Julien-Laferriere, Labaye and Edström (2005).

migration policy towards legal, and especially economic, migrants was suddenly and severely interrupted by the attacks of 9/11 in New York and Washington, DC. After 9 September 2001, the goals of the legislative programme as well as the majority of political activities in this area changed quite considerably.[13] Legal migration was no longer at the centre of legislative attention. Instead, all attention turned towards the fight against illegal migration and terrorism.[14] Only during the Greek presidency, in spring 2003, did the position of legal migrants return to the agenda:[15] the Thessaloniki European Council of 19 and 20 June 2003 reconfirmed the official call given at Tampere for the elaboration of a comprehensive policy on the integration of legally residing TCNs.

To date, ten major directives have been issued relating to migration and asylum.[16] Member States are under the obligation to transpose these directives into national law.[17] However, the directives afford the Member States a large margin of discretion in the way they retain or adopt national provisions in accordance with European migration law. The outcome is foreseeable: the policies of the Member States will not (easily) grow closer to one another. They will only do so in the case of the provisions that are 100 per cent compulsory for the national legislators of the Member States.

Basically, two reasons explain, at least partly, why attempts to harmonize legislative policies in Europe within the field of migration have so far missed their goal. The first reason is historical: as I have already mentioned in the Introduction, until recently migration fell within the near-exclusive competence of the 27 Member States. They wish to retain primary responsibility for the elaboration and implementation of their own (legal) migration policy. The second reason reinforces the first: to reach agreement at European level on the adoption of measures in the area of migration, unanimity in the Council was required, at least

---

13 On this change, see Brouwer (2002).

14 On this sudden change of orientation, Schneider makes the following comment: 'the EU Member States reached, in a few months, agreement on subjects which used to be highly controversial among them, and for which without the terrorist attacks years of negotiations would have been necessary' (Schneider 2005, 25).

15 For the Thessaloniki Council in June 2003, the Commission published its *Communication on Immigration, Integration and Employment*, COM (2003) 336 final, <http://ec.europa.eu/justice_home/funding/2004_2007/doc/com_2003_336_final.pdf>, accessed 30 January 2009.

16 The following analysis of legal texts will include only two directives concerning legal migration: Council Directive 2003/86EC on the right of family reunification, dated 22 September 2003, and Directive 2003/109/EC on the status of TCNs who are long-term residents, which was accepted by the Council in November of 2003.

17 In this regard, the special position of Denmark, Ireland and the United Kingdom has to be taken into account. These countries have opted out of the application of this part of the Treaty and have gone their own respective ways. See, for example, Kuyper (1999).

until 1 May 2004.[18] That requirement, which still applied at the time when the first major directives concerning TCNs were negotiated, is certainly the main reason why harmonization could not thus far be achieved: it made the final adoption of sensitive issues a rather complicated process. On the other hand, as I have already suggested, the advantage of minimum harmonization is that it facilitates the participation of the more reluctant Member States. Hence, to reach consensus on common objectives requires that Member States be allowed to participate in the realization of these goals, but not necessarily by completely common means. The wording of the European directives illustrates of the difficulties in reaching consensus on immigration and integration issues: this wording is to be seen as the result of subtle political compromises among Member States. When negotiating the directives on immigration, integration and asylum, some Member States managed to impose their views by making compromises on the part of other Member States the very condition of their further participation in the negotiations on and, eventually, their agreement to the setting up a European migration policy. This is probably one of the most striking paradoxes of the developments towards a European migration law so far: at first, Member States showed themselves willing to give up – within the framework of the EU – part of their sovereignty with a view to facilitating the harmonization of migration policy in Europe. For that purpose, they signed the Treaty of Amsterdam. But when some years later it came to giving concrete effect to the Treaty and negotiating the various legal instruments needed to implement it (the directives), they have appeared reluctant to do so, or even to decide eventually not to join the club.[19]

In effect, discrepancies between national legislations (and sometimes also between the various national/state regulations) on the position of TCNs encourage new patterns of cross-border mobility of people both within and from outside Europe. The benefits that one legal system offers to TCNs and that are not offered to them in the country of their habitual residence in some cases give people sufficiently strong reason to move, temporarily or definitively, to another Member State. What ultimately gives them the impetus to settle elsewhere is profit-maximization at an individual level. This type of mobility, when it occurs on a large scale, may constitute a serious challenge to the legislators of the different Member States that extends across different territories and levels of jurisdiction. Belgium and the Netherlands, for example, are currently facing the phenomenon of the so-called 'Belgium route' (Vanvoorden 2007): several hundred Dutch citizens – married to a TCN – have recently settled (on a temporary basis) in Belgium with a view to circumventing the recently amended – very restrictive – conditions

18 Since 1 May 2004, the Commission, under Article 67(2) of the EC Treaty, has the exclusive right of legislative initiative with regard to measures under Title IV of the Treaty, where the right of legislative initiative was previously shared with the Member States. But the unanimity requirement continues to exist for legal migration. See the section 'What Modes of Governance Lie Ahead?' below. See also note 42 below.

19 Cf. note 17 above.

imposed by Dutch legislators on family reunification. The Dutch regulation on family reunification with TCNs requires that the non-European spouse(s) speak sufficient Dutch and demonstrate basic knowledge of Dutch society *prior* to being granted to right to migrate to the Netherlands (Baldinger 2007; Groenendijk 2007; Lodder 2007). The Belgian legislation is far less severe with regard to the same situation: neither the language test nor any basic knowledge of Belgian society are made a legal condition for family reunification with TCNs (Vanheule 2007). The result is forum-shopping by spouses from the Netherlands, who move to Belgium in order to be granted the right to reunify with their partner from outside Europe. As soon as the latter has received permission to stay, the couple moves (back) to the Netherlands: the conditions placed on cross-border migration within the EU are more flexible.

Obviously, these practices bring EU law into disrepute and fuel public scepticism about the legitimacy and the desirability of the legislative process at the European level.

Two Illustrations: Family Reunification and the Newly Created Status of Long-term Resident

This article brings two illustrations of loopholes in the regulation on the migration and integration of TCNs in EU law that are the consequences of the failure so far to achieve a significant level of harmonization of these issues across the European Union. I would specifically like to highlight here the Council Directive on the right to family reunification (2003/86/EC) and the one on the status of TCNs who are long-term residents (2003/109/EC). Both instruments have direct consequences for the legal position of TCNs residing on the territories of the Member States and their integration. Not surprisingly, the first one has been challenged before the European Court of Justice (ECJ).

Directive 2003/86/EC and the ECJ Judgment of 27 June 2006 on the Right to Family Reunification

The ECJ Judgment of 27 June 2006[20] on the right to family reunification may serve here as an example of the difficulties that characterize the developments in those areas of European migration law that fall under the unanimity requirement. The case shows how, in the process of transposition by Member States of the European directives on migration and integration into national law, clashes may occur – discrepancies between Member States and the European institutions, but also between the European institutions themselves (*in casu*, *Parliament* v. *Council*).

20 ECJ, C-540/03 (*Parliament* v. *Council*), *Jur*. 2006, I-05769.

Yet, in order to evaluate the implications of the judgment of 27 June 2006 for TCNs and their families, it may be useful to give a few words of explanation of the instrument related to family reunification with regard to TCNs. That instrument is Directive 2003/86/EC of September 2003 on the right to family reunification, which provides for the conditions on the right of TCNs who are legal residents in an EU Member State to reunify with their families.[21] Within the directive, conditions for granting family reunification as well as the rights to be enjoyed by those covered by the directive are specified.[22] The provisions that are considered to be the most important elements of the directive include Article 4, which stipulates which family members (of TCNs) are eligible for family reunification, Articles 6, 7 and 8 dealing with the possible requirements to be imposed on TCNs for family reunification, Articles 13 and 14, which lay down the conditions for entry and residence of family members, and Article 15, providing rules on the acquisition of an autonomous residence permit.

Initially, the *Directive on Family Reunification* was envisaged in order substantially to improve the situation of TCNs residing legally in one of the Member States by establishing EU-wide rules on the right to family reunification. Yet the text of the directive that was eventually adopted by the Council on 22 September 2003 makes family reunification in the case of TCNs subject to a series of procedures and conditions which are more restrictive than those envisaged in the previous draft versions. The aim of the first draft was 'to establish a right to family reunification', while in the final draft it became 'to determine the conditions in which the right to family reunification may be exercised'. As a result of the many disagreements between the negotiating parties (the Member States) and the amendments which were imposed by some, the directive which had initially been conceived of as a framework of principles eventually became the lowest common denominator of laws already applying in the Member States. Carlier (2003, 576) speaks of a directive *against* family reunification. In fact, the directive gives Member States the right to reject the entry and residence of family members of TCNs in a number of situations. These include Member States' concerns related to public policy, domestic security or public health (Article 8), the sponsor's lack of sufficient and stable resources or adequate housing (Article 9), as well as the non-fulfilment of a period of residence in the country of up to one year (Article 10). Furthermore, from close scrutiny of the text of the directive in comparison with the individual national legislations of the Member States, the conclusion can be drawn that several of these national laws are already largely in compliance with the rules for family reunification, and in some cases even more favourable in granting rights to family members of TCNs (Groenendijk et al. 2007). Consequently, in these countries the transposition of the directive into national law will not lead to major improvements in the rights of TCNs and their family members. Some authors

21 See, for example, Cholewinsky (2002); Schaffrin (2005).

22 *Official Journal of the EU*, vol. 46, L 251, 3 October 2003.

(Schneider and Wiebrock 2005) have even expressed the fear that these Member States may use this opportunity to introduce more restrictive provisions.[23]

Undoubtedly, the directive contains several provisions that are highly controversial, since they might endanger fundamental human rights, especially the rights of children. Yet these concerns explain why the European Parliament eventually took action against it. This action was based on the existence of substantial doubts that the directive respects fundamental freedoms as guaranteed in the European Convention for the Protection of Human Rights and Fundamental Liberties (ECHR 1950).

The legal action was settled 27 June 2006. It had been introduced by the European Parliament (which was unprecedented) on 16 December 2003 in order to seek annulment of three provisions of the directive, since in its view these provisions did not sufficiently respect the guarantees of protection offered by the ECHR. The European institutions have a duty to respect these guarantees. In its action, the Parliament invoked in particular the right to respect for family life and the principle of non-discrimination.[24] It raised three questions: (1) who in Europe sets the standards when it comes to granting the right to family reunification to TCNs, (2) what are these standards, and (3) who has control over the implementation of these standards?

The three following provisions were challenged: Article 4(1) 2 of the directive, which provides that before authorizing entry and residence, Member States may require children aged over 12 years who are entering independently (that is, at a different and later time) from the rest of the family, to satisfy integration conditions that are provided for by the existing legislation of the Member State at the date when the directive enters into force. Minors may thus be required by the Member States to comply with certain conditions for integration in order to become eligible for family reunification under the directive. The provision was introduced into the text of the directive by the German government because a similar provision could be found in the Draft German Immigration Act 2002. The question raised in the action was whether it is justifiable – that is, without being in breach of Article 8 of the ECHR – to apply a condition for integration to children aged over 12 years arriving independently of the rest of the family, and to permit Member States to refuse entry and residence to these children if they do not comply with the integration test.

A second provision contested was Article 4(6) of the directive: Member States may require that applications for family reunification of children be submitted before the age of 15 (as provided for by their existing legislation on the date of the implementation of the directive). If the application is submitted after the age of 15, the Member States which decide to apply this derogation shall authorize the entry and residence of such children on grounds *other* than family reunification.

23 On this risk more generally, see also Schibel (2004, 399); De Cecco (2006).

24 In its action, Parliament also invoked a number of provisions of UN Conventions, in particular of the Convention on the Rights of the Child.

To Boeles (2001), the provision completely undermines the right of children over the age of 15 to live together with their family, as it offers 'not only less than the level of protection required by Article 8 and 13 of the European Convention for the Protection of Human and Fundamental Freedoms but [it is] also beneath the level required by Article 47 of the Charter of Fundamental Rights of the European Union'.

And finally, Article 8 of the directive was also challenged: Member States may demand a waiting period of two years' legal residence before entitling TCNs to be joined by family members. Moreover, if the legislation existing at the time of adoption of the directive takes account of reception capacity of the Member State, that state may introduce a waiting period of three years between request and grant of residence permit to the family member(s).

I will not enter here into the details of the arguments.[25] The Court finally dismissed the action by the Parliament, but that action provided the Court with the opportunity to clarify several important issues regarding the meaning of central provisions of the directive. What is of particular interest for the purposes of this chapter is the way the European Court of Justice was led, under EU law, to conduct a human rights review: the review concerns the question whether the contested provisions of Directive 2003/86/EC, in themselves, meet the criteria of respect for the right to family life, the obligation to have due regard to the best interest of the child, and the principle of non-discrimination on grounds of age.

Groenendijk (2006b, 7) identifies several reasons that make him foresee that in the years to come, the judgment will be referred to as a milestone decision in the establishment of a common framework in immigration and integration of TCNs in the EU.[26] First, the Court affirms that Directive 2003/86/EC grants a subjective right to family reunification, subject to certain conditions.[27] Second, it recognizes that the Convention on the Rights of the Child has to be taken into account in applying the general principles of EU law (para. 37 of the decision), and thus when applying the directives as well.[28] Third, the Court for the first time explicitly refers to the legal status of the EU Charter of Fundamental Rights.[29] Fourth, the Court reminds (in para. 107) those Member States that are bound by the European Social Charter or the European Convention on the legal status of migrant workers

25 See, for example, Bailleux (2006).

26 See also Groenendijk (2006a).

27 The right to respect for family life is not equivalent, in itself, to a right to family reunification. According to the case law of the European Court of Human Rights (Strasbourg; ECrtHR), it is sufficient that family life is possible, be it in the state of origin of the parties. A party need not necessarily be granted protection in one of the EU Member States.

28 The Court holds that Articles 9 and 10 of the Convention have a function in recognizing the principle of respect for family life (para. 57).

29 The Court stresses that 'the principle aim of the Charter as apparent from its preamble is to reaffirm "rights as they result, in particular, from the constitutional traditions and international obligations common to the Member States" …' (para. 38).

that the directive is without prejudice to more favourable provisions in those two instruments.[30]

However, notwithstanding the importance of the above-mentioned reasons, human rights watchers have expressed disappointment in the decision.[31] Not only did the Court affirm that in those cases where family members and their sponsor(s) do not have the subjective right to family reunification granted by Article 4(1) the Member States still have a margin of appreciation, but more importantly, it concluded that the exceptions allowed in the final sentence of Article 4(1), in Article 4(6) and in Article 8(2) of Directive 2003/86/EC – the three challenged provisions – cannot be regarded as running counter to the protection granted under fundamental rights.

One of the regrettable effects of the judgment is that it turns out to benefit those Member States that had taken a restrictive position during the negotiations on the directive and had managed to impose their view by taking their national legislation as the (minimum) standard and a condition of further collaboration. By so doing, the Court gave its approval to a process of competitive lowering, or 'downward harmonization', of the level of protection granted in the EU to TCNs when it comes to their right to settle with their kin inside the territories of the Member States.

The conclusions to be drawn from the Court's position are that differences among Member States in the way they show respect for the family life of TCNs thus remain possible. In each individual case, when making a decision on an application for family reunification, Member States are bound to take due account of the right to family life as guaranteed by Article 8(1) of the ECHR and of the case law of the European Court of Human Rights, but they are entitled to do so in different ways, with flexibility, or conversely, by keeping a firm grip on things. The directive explicitly preserves a 'margin of appreciation' in a number of situations. This way, the Member States ultimately keep control over the way they eventually implement the principles of EU law and their concrete application in the case of TCNs applying for family reunification. Schneider and Wiebrock conclude: 'Arguably, the Directive cannot be seen as harmonizing EU legislation on family reunification in a positive way. It merely provides for extremely low standards and leaves wide discretion to the Member States as to how they wish to deal with the issue of family reunification' (Schneider and Wiebrock 2005, 66).

Groenendijk exhibits more optimism, since to him the practical importance of the exceptions allowed in the last sentence of Article 4(1), in Article 4(6) and in

30 This consideration is relevant for six Member States that are party to the Convention (France, Italy, the Netherlands, Portugal, Spain and Sweden), since Article 12 of that Convention grants rights to family reunification to migrant workers that are more favourable than the rights under Directive 2003/86/EC, and considering the reciprocity principle in the Convention, in particular for workers from the two non-Member States having ratified the Convention: Turkey and Moldova.

31 See, for example, Bailleux (2006).

Article 8(2) of Directive 2003/86/EC is rather limited due to the standstill clauses in each of these provisions: those exceptions can in fact be relied on by a Member State only if at the time of the adoption or at the final date for the implementation of the directive (3 October 2005) a corresponding rule in the national legislation of the Member State was in force. In his view, therefore, the danger that, in the long run, standards of protection of the right to family life for TCNs will be lowered in those Member States where the rules in the directive are less favourable than the original national legislation should not be overestimated (Groenendijk 2006b, 7). The future will tell whether the Court in its judgment of 27 June 2006 has indeed laid down principles that will prove of importance for the interpretation and application of other directives on immigration and integration adopted by the Council on the basis of Articles 62 and 63 TEC as well.

Yet a second illustration of developments in the regulation of immigration and integration of TCNs in the EU that may serve as a case study of the entanglements of national and Community law in a European context, relates to the newly created status of TCNs who are long-term residents. I shall look critically here at the content and the scope of Council Directive 2003/109/EC of 2004.[32]

The Directive on Long-term Resident Status: Towards Equal Treatment?

I have already mentioned the European Council at Thessaloniki and the role it played in revisiting the open call given at Tampere to develop a comprehensive EU immigration and integration policy.[33] The Tampere milestones, as they have become known, heralded the beginning of the legislative programme of the EU regarding TCNs. The heads of state and government stressed that while primary responsibility for its elaboration and implementation remains with the Member States, a comprehensive EU immigration and integration policy should be developed within a coherent EU framework establishing common basic principles and standards that would reinforce policy co-ordination. The prominent role given by the Greek EU presidency to the development of such a framework has reopened discussions on the rationale for migration within and to the EU. Yet at the same time it also revived the struggle between security and liberty in the EU. On the one hand, there is the call of Member States for more security in an attempt to combat terrorism, illegal migration, human trafficking and so on. On the other hand, there is the growing consciousness that the EU is increasingly facing serious economic and demographic evolutions that need to be tackled urgently by, among other measures, opening and facilitating cross-border migration for TCNs within the EU as well as developing effective integration opportunities for them. In this scenario, the progressive establishment of a common framework on the status of TCNs who are long-term residents has become a key issue on the political agenda

32 *Official Journal of the EU*, vol. 47, L 16, 23 January 2004.

33 *Cf.* note 16 above.

of the EU. Council Directive 2003/109/EC concerning the status of TCNs who are long-term residents[34] is of paramount importance as regards its impact on the inclusion processes of immigrants inside the EU.[35]

The legal basis for the directive is to be found in Article 63(4) TEC. This provision stipulates that 'the Council shall adopt … measures defining the rights and conditions under which nationals of third countries who are legally resident in a Member State may reside in other Member States'.

After long discussions in the Council of Ministers and its working groups, the directive was eventually adopted in November 2003, but only after being significantly 'watered down' (Carrera 2005, 124), as had been the case with the *Directive on Family Reunification*.

The directive seeks to confer free movement and residence rights upon TCNs who are lawfully long-term residents inside the EU territory. Traditionally, under Community law, TCNs had residence or other related rights only in the Member State where they were first admitted. They did not have the right to move to a second Member State inside the EU unless they belonged to the group of privileged non-EU citizens who benefit from derived rights, for example through family ties with an EU citizen.[36]

To what extent does the directive truly guarantee free circulation to TCNs? Does it confer a set of rights and obligations comparable ('nearly equal') to those of EU citizens, as was envisaged at the Tampere summit?

One of the main critiques relates to the fact that the directive does not guarantee a homogeneous status of long-term residents throughout the EU. Following Article 4, Member States have to grant this status to those TCNs who have resided legally in that Member State for a period of five years immediately prior to the submission of their application. Regarding, on the contrary, the right for TCNs who have been granted the status of long-term residents to subsequently move to another Member State, it is not clear whether the directive indeed confers such a right. The reference to 'a right to reside' in other Member States has been omitted in the text of the directive that was formally adopted. The final text establishes that the directive will determine 'the terms of residence' in Member States other than the one that conferred the status of long-term resident on the TCN. The question of whether or not the directive confers such a right therefore remains open to interpretation.

In practice, solely those TCNs who meet all the conditions contained in the directive will hold a right to move and reside in the territory of Member States other than the one that granted them that status in the first instance. The directive indeed offers wide discretion to Member States to ask TCNs to comply with mandatory integration conditions. This requirement was not included in the initial

34 *Cf.* note 16 above.

35 See, for example, Handoll (2003; 2005); Peers (2004, 437); Boelaert-Suominen (2005); Carrera (2005); Gross (2005); Halleskov (2005); Urth (2005); De Heer (2007a; 2007b, 272–80, 281–8).

36 See, for example, Barnhard (2004).

text. It was included afterwards, during the Council negotiations. Article 5 now provides that 'Member States may require TCNs to comply with integration conditions, in accordance with national law.' It allows Member States to reject applications owing to failure to comply with 'integration conditions' under national law, without providing any limitations to the conditions that Member States may require. Indeed, no definition of integration is provided therein. The final interpretation and practical scope of these conditions will therefore be defined according to the variety of national immigration legislations and the political priorities of each Member State. They will also be the ones testing and scrutinizing whether TCNs are successfully integrated into the receiving societies. This way, the need to comply with integration measures may become a barrier to one of the main initial objectives of the directive – freedom of movement and residence of long-term residents in the EU.[37] The use of an obligatory integration test as a potential ground for refusal of the status of long-term resident has for that reason been strongly criticized by some authors.[38] Their fear is that Member States will place the emphasis on concerns about national public policy issues rather than on the integration of TCNs and their rights. The directive would therefore, in their view, end up maintaining inequalities between EU citizens and TCNs, rather than eliminating them.

In practice, much will depend on the applications the Member States will effectively make of the directive. Most of the restrictions in the directive – authorizations for the Member States to maintain or to introduce a less favourable legal situation for TCNs – are indeed optional. They are not binding European law. Member States are free to grant equal treatment if that is their regulatory policy. In practice, however, the prediction that most Member States will maintain the legal distinction between EU citizens and TCNs – even if the latter are long-term residents – is a plausible one. The directive adopted is not based on a comprehensive strategy for integration, but mainly upholds the existing differences in the treatment of TCNs. The status of long-term resident requires at least five years of legal residence and economic independence. Hence, it already assumes a certain proof of integration which then is rewarded with a better legal status by European law. Member States even have the possibility of introducing into their legal systems (if they do not yet have it) the requirement that TCNs who apply for the status of long-term resident cover the financial costs of the integration measures and programmes. By so doing, a process of inclusion of TCNs may instead become an effective process of exclusion (Carrera 2005, 133).[39] Behind such a policy, there is indeed the risk that one's ability to integrate will be linked to financial status. Moreover, cultural, religious and ethnic diversity may be endangered where

37 Article 15 of the directive provides that TCNs holding the status of long-term resident may be requested to (re-)pass a language test in the second Member State where they intend to move and reside in order to acquire equal rights and benefits.

38 *Cf.* note 35 above.

39 See also Groenendijk (2004).

'integration' becomes the litmus test by which an individual may – or may not – move from the category of 'them' to one of 'us'. The rationale for such an EU immigration policy is that Member States remain largely responsible for economic migration, as Caviedes (2004, 304) comments, and consequently, 'integration measures can also be drafted so as to perpetuate established lines of ethnic and cultural division'.

Eventually, the introduction of rigid conditions of integration in order to gain access to the status of long-term resident and the package of economic, social, cultural and political rights that goes with it may equally weaken the prohibition of discrimination and unequal treatment.[40]

Directive 2003/109/EC on long-term resident status could in these ways undermine, instead of facilitate, a process of integration of TCNs in the receiving societies. What it will encourage instead is the *im*mobilization of TCNs within the EU, or – another risk – push them into patterns of cross-border mobility similar to those I have signalled above and qualified as the 'Belgium route': whenever TCNs get a chance, they will do whatever they can to circumvent the rules that impose restrictive conditions and will evidently give preference to more liberal legal systems. Who would blame them?

In light of the aforementioned, it becomes clear that the provisions contained in the directive regarding integration conditions put the fair treatment regime promised at Tampere and the creation of 'nearly equal' opportunities for TCNs to participate fully in society at risk. This applies in particular to the legal conditionality (the lack of integration as a ground for refusal of the secure status) that is present in the wording of some provisions of the directive. These kinds of rules impede free movement and foster strategic behaviour on the part of TCNs. By failing to grant TCNs who are long-term residents the foundation necessary for their full integration – the right to equal treatment with nationals – Member States still consider them, even after they have resided and worked legally in a Member State for more than five years and fulfilled the conditions laid down in the directive, to be second-class citizens: 'Accordingly, the Community visions for "social cohesion and social justice" are little more than empty promises,' Halleskov (2005, 201) concludes. Any new rules at the EU level in this area must avoid such pitfalls.

Key to the success of the EU's internal market has been the firm commitment to free movement of goods, persons, services and capital. The engagement of

40 At the EU level, discriminatory practices are prohibited by Article 13 TEC. This provision was introduced with the Amsterdam Treaty. On this basis, two anti-discrimination directives have been adopted: the Council Directive implementing the principle of equal treatment between persons irrespective of racial or ethnic origin (the Race Discrimination Directive 2000/43; *Official Journal of the EU*, vol. 43, L 180, 19 July 2000) and the Directive on equal treatment in employment and occupation (Directive 2000/78; *Official Journal of the EU*, vol. 43, L 303, 2 December 2000). They are at the centre of the EU human rights framework on combating discrimination.

people in the success of economic development and integration was recognized from the start, and the principle of free movement of persons is maintained as a core objective until it becomes a reality. Today, it would be unfair – and unrealistic – to continue seeking the benefits of economic development and integration in the European Union if TCNs are excluded from the project. If TCNs cannot travel to find new markets for their needs, they cannot and will not fully benefit society. Thus, the EU must pursue policies and regulations regarding border management, economic migration and access to the EU for TCNs which enhance rather than hinder movement of persons. Closed EU borders for TCNs sit uneasily with objectives seeking to maximize the engagement of people in the success of economic development and integration. If the EU's agenda for the future is still aimed at providing employment and prosperity within the EU through participation, TCNs must be able to move freely within the EU to seek markets, and not be hindered by reciprocal restrictions which governments impose because the EU rules leave them discretion to create substantial obstacles for TCNs wishing to gain access to their territory.

What Modes of Governance Lie ahead?

Probably nothing could be easier for an expert in European migration law today than to point at the lacunae, the contradictions even, in the way(s) European Member States are developing a 'common' migration policy within the EU. The reasons for these lacunae and contradictions are linked to the fact that in the past, Member States have, each in their own way, developed a policy of admission and deportation of non-nationals to and from the national territory, and have therefore been unwilling to give up their sovereignty in these domains. Some Member States appear less willing than others.

The key question now is how these shortcomings and imbalances will be addressed in the years to come. The overall picture one gains when investigating the different attempts that have been made over the past few years at EU level to manage migration from outside Europe is one of tensions between, on the one hand, a security obsession and the firm will on the part of State authorities to keep control over access to their national territory and, on the other hand, the growing consciousness that in Europe, Member States will sooner or later have to overcome, collectively, these obsessions and prepare for fair treatment of TCNs. Some aspects of the ECJ Judgment of Justice of 27 June 2006 reinforce that picture – the more so since the action by the Parliament was eventually dismissed. What would be best? Further extension of the powers of the EU institutions is one option. Yet another possible mode of governance, which may be complementary to other modes, is the so-called open method of co-ordination (OMC) that preserves the autonomy of the various actors involved in the decision-making process, both state and non-state representatives.

The deadline set in the TEC for the achievement of the Tampere process was 1 May 2004. That day, the five-year transitional period concerning immigration and asylum law applied by the Treaty of Amsterdam came to an end.[41] The end of this period had several effects. First, the Commission obtained more or less a monopoly on *proposals* for EU legislation, thus no longer sharing that power with the Member States.[42] The second effect was that the number of issues subject to qualified majority voting (QMV) in the Council and co-decision for the European Parliament increased.[43] Moreover, Article 67(2) TEC gives the Council the power to change the decision-making rules applicable to all or part of EU immigration and asylum law after 1 May 2004. Co-decision along with QMV – instead of unanimous voting in the Council and consultation of the European Parliament – radically amend the *decision-making process* at EU level by changing the power relations between Member States and EU institutions: co-decision together with QMV indeed significantly weaken the position of the Member States and reinforce the role of Parliament. Moreover, the Council was equally obliged by Article 67(2) TEC to adopt a decision after 1 May 2004 adapting the provisions of the Treaty relating to the Court of Justice. Thus, when the Netherlands took over the presidency of the EU in July 2004, there was a major task ahead of them with respect to establishing a new mandate to follow the Tampere milestones. A core document that prepared this new programme for the next five-year period is the so-called Hague Programme.[44] This was initially incorporated into a Communication from the Commission dated 18 May 2004: the purpose was to further build on the achievements of the Tampere Programme. The multi-annual work programme agreed by the European Council in The Hague in November 2004 aimed to establish a new agenda for the next five years (2004–2009). It emphasizes the importance

41 *Cf.* note 3 above.

42 Article 67(2) TEC provides that after 1 May 2004, the Council shall take a decision with a view to providing for all or parts of the areas covered by Title IV to be governed by the co-decision procedure. Declaration 5 concerning Article 67 annexed to the Treaty of Nice provides assistance with the interpretation of this article. It contains a precise (political) commitment to change over to a co-decision procedure immediately after 1 May 2004 for the measures provided for by Article 62(3) and 63(3)(b) of the Treaty concerning respectively the free movement of TCNs for a maximum period of three months, and illegal migration and residence, including repatriation.

43 Measures concerning rules on a uniform short-term visa and the conditions for issue of short-term visas became subject to QMV in the Council and co-decision with Parliament; measures relating to administrative co-operation among Member States and between Member States and the Commission are from then on subject to QMV in the Council in consultation with Parliament. Internal border controls, external border controls, freedom to travel for TCNs, burden-sharing in the asylum field and immigration remained subject to unanimous voting in the Council and consultation with Parliament; Articles 62(1), 62(2)(a), 63(2)(b), 63(3) and 63(4) TEC.

44 See, for example, the Presidency Conclusions of 4–5 November 2004 (see note 11 above).

of developing a 'comprehensive approach, involving all stages of immigration, with respect to the root causes of migration, entry and admission policies and integration and return policies'.[45]

It would lead me too far a field here to survey the different initiatives that have been taken, at various levels since 1 May 2004, with a view to further developing a common framework for immigration and integration issues. What is of relevance here is to mention that the Hague Programme places significant emphasis on the human rights dimension of immigration and on the integration of TCNs, advocating not only respect for but also the active promotion of fundamental rights and an inclusive and participatory form of integration. The integration of TCNs has been given a separate chapter, emphasizing that this is a distinct policy area which requires a specific policy:

> Many different initiatives had already been taken at EU level with respect to integration, but so far the Justice and Home Affairs Council had only emphasized the need for exchanging information and best practices, and although the Member States already had committed themselves at the Thessaloniki European Council to establish a common framework for integration, they had never as such discussed or agreed on which basic principles such a common framework should be based. (Urth 2005, 176)

The Hague Programme is therefore a major step.[46]

The Dutch presidency finally managed to establish these principles, which were adopted on 19 November 2004 – very shortly after the Hague Programme.[47] The principles adopted state what the most important parameters of integration are: respect for the basic values of the EU, including the diversity of cultures and religions, and they identify access to employment, basic knowledge of the language, history and institutions of the host society as some of the key elements

45 Ibid., 7.

46 In addition, the Commission has adopted an Action Plan implementing the Hague Programme which identifies ten specific priority areas for intervention. See European Commission Communication *The Hague Programme: Ten Priorities for the Next Five Years. The Partnership for European Renewal in the Field of Freedom, Security and Justice*, COM (2005) 184 final, 10 May 2005. The ten priorities are: (1) fundamental rights and citizenship; (2) the fight against terrorism; (3) a common asylum policy; (4) migration management; (5) integration of migrants; (6) integrated management of external borders; (7) privacy and security in sharing information; (8) developing a clear concept of organized crime; (9) justice – guaranteeing an effective European area of civil and criminal justice; (10) sharing responsibility and solidarity for freedom, security and justice.

47 See Council Document 14615/04 of 19 November 2004, 16–24; see also *Communication on a Common Agenda for Integration: Framework for the Integration of Third-country Nationals in the European Union*, COM (2005) 389 final, <http://eur-lex.europa.eu/LexUriServ/LexUriServ.do?uri=COM:2005:0389:FIN:EN:PDF>, accessed 30 January 2009.

of successful integration. Finally, they provide suggestions as to the tools which are necessary to achieve successful integration by emphasizing the importance of ensuring participation in the democratic process, education, inter-cultural dialogue and seeing that integration measures are mainstreamed in all policies affecting immigrants. These principles serve to assist the Member States in formulating their own domestic integration policy, but at this stage they are non-binding. Nevertheless, 'they go further than ever before in specifying what integration means in the EU context'.[48]

The Hague Programme also restates a major concern with security, and specifies that the EU should take an effective, joint approach to problems such as illegal migration, human trafficking, terrorism and organized crime, as well as the prevention thereof. To Brouwer (2005), the Hague Programme hence seems to recast the (im)balance between promotion of fundamental rights on the one hand and security on the other, emphasizing the latter unduly.

Yet one way to acknowledge the shortcomings of the decision-making process at EU level in guaranteeing respect for fundamental freedoms and rights of TCNs is to further extend the powers of the EU institutions. Much will depend on whether the EU institutions will manage to strengthen co-operation between Member States at EU level in a way that overcomes the pervasive lack of trust among the Member States thus far towards an EU competence in the formulation and interpretation of a coherent regulatory framework for immigration and integration policy issues. It is foreseeable that the 'divided sovereignty' (Pernice 1999, 706) between Member States and EU institutions will continue to remain a major obstacle in the years to come.

The Treaty of Lisbon of 13 December 2007[49] – if it comes into force – envisages a series of innovations in the field of European co-operation on legal immigration and integration policies. In brief, policies related to legal immigration will finally benefit from QMV in the Council and the co-decision procedure. The new Article 79.4 of the Treaty on the Functioning of the Union (TFU) will provide the basis for developing common legislative measures to encourage and support the work of the Member States in the area of integration of TCNs, thereby formalizing the EU Framework on Integration into an open method of co-ordination through the application of ordinary legislative procedure (co-decision). In her above-mentioned article Velluti suggested re-launching the technique of OMC in developing an EU immigration policy. In her view, OMC offers an appropriate mode of management of both immigration and integration issues in order to solve shortcomings in the decision-making process at EU level so far:[50]

48 Ibid., 176.

49 Treaty of Lisbon amending the Treaty on the European Union and the Treaty establishing the European Community, signed at Lisbon, 13 December 2007 (*Official Journal of the EU*, vol. 50, C 306, 17 December 2007).

50 Velluti (2007); see also Urth (2005).

> The structure of this OMC, tailored specifically to the field of immigration … draws upon a transnational basis of self-regulation, consensus building, exchange of best practices and information and open participation in the framework of a multi-tiered framework of governance. … [T]he OMC in immigration policy is not intended to be merely a soft law instrument such as recommendations, resolutions, action programmes or guidelines but it is conceived as a 'process within the process', which fosters policy learning and innovation. (Velluti 2007, 71)

Among the examples she gives, she makes reference to the adoption by the Council of 'common basic principles' (CBPs) on integration which are meant to assist Member States in formulating integration policies by offering them non-binding guidelines against which they can assess their own measures and which complement existing legislation. That was under the Dutch presidency. Yet another example she gives is the *Communication on a Policy Plan on Legal Migration*,[51] which outlines a roadmap for the remaining period of the Hague Programme (2006–2009) and lists the actions and legislative initiatives for achieving a coherent development of EU legal migration policy.

OMC governance techniques involve a variety of social actors, such as social partners, NGOs and (migrants') organizations, with a view to promoting policy experimentation and identifying ways of furthering policy co-ordination. OMC techniques also allow for the use of pilot projects, research studies and dissemination of results, consultative meetings with experts, feasibility analyses and/or impact assessments, and so on. Velluti sees OMC as a complement to existing legislation, as well as part of a 'trend at EU level which promotes differentiation and flexibility and eschews traditional forms of decision-making whilst, at the same time, it maintains intact the sovereignty of the Member States in sensitive policy areas' (Velutti 2007, 77).

It remains to be seen whether, in the years to come, OMC will indeed prove a promising mechanism of governance at EU level that offers a valid complement to existing legislation. More recently, the EU has started experimenting with new techniques to establish a common framework for immigration and integration: a handbook on integration that identifies best practices; annual reports on migration and integration reports; national contact points have been established for the exchange of information on more political issues; a website must ensure involvement of the local level as well as civil society; a new Integration Fund gives financial support to Member States' actions, to mention only a few initiatives. Since these initiatives preserve the diversity of domestic (national) legal systems, they may indeed constitute appropriate instruments to help overcome Member States' reluctance to show (greater) co-operation in immigration and integration issues at EU level. However, as yet it is not clear how OMC mechanisms could play a decisive role in formulating

51 See *Communication on a Common Agenda for Integration*, 669 final.

a more inclusive regulatory framework that would effectively promote – EU-wide – the integration of TCNs rather than their exclusion.[52]

Conclusion

The fragmented development of EU immigration and integration policy highlights at the same time the objectives and the difficulties of a project that attempts to transcend divergences of views among Member States.

Can we speak of fair treatment of TCNs under EU law? Looking back at the conclusion of the European Council at Tampere, have the promises been fulfilled? The answer is clearly no. The requirements on family reunification according to Directive 2003/86/EC certainly do not fulfil the expectations raised by the Tampere conclusions. The same is true for the newly created status of long-term resident. The purpose of facilitating the integration of TCNs is mentioned in the preambles of both Directive 2003/83/EC on family reunification and Directive 2003/109/EC on long-term residents. However, in their provisions both directives clearly refer to the national integration duties of TCNs, either as a prerequisite or as a consequence of residence rights.[53]

I have limited the analysis here to these two illustrations. They make obvious that European Member States have difficulty handling cross-border mobility that is not strictly linked with the free circulation of EU citizens. A series of reasons explain this resistance on part of the Member States, the main one most probably being Member States' formal and territorial sovereignty, and their consequent concerns about preservation of the autonomy of national regulatory competence. There is a lack of trust in the EU institutions. So far, Member States have agreed to instruments of such a wide scope that their discretion in the areas of immigration and integration of TCNs is in fact only marginally restricted. In the end, Directives 2003/85/EC and 2003/109/EC provide merely for absolute minimum standards in the protection of TCNs, and fall short of the objective set at Tampere to assimilate the status of TCNs to that of EU citizens. The rights of TCNs are still far more restrictive than those enjoyed by EU citizens.

In the years to come, new forms of governance, which rely on OMC techniques, may help facilitate the development of a more consistent, inclusive and transparent EU policy in the fields of immigration and integration of TCNs, but OMC

52 Urth (2005) acknowledges some of the weaknesses of OMC, or obstacles, so to speak, in particular in dealing with integration issues.

53 The first alternative has been chosen in Article 5(2) of Directive 2003/109/EC and Article 7(2) of Directive 2003/86/EC, stating that the Member State may require, as a condition for obtaining the status of a long-term resident for purposes of family reunification, that TCNs comply with integration conditions in accordance with national law. The second alternative is found in Directive 2003/109/EC: according to Article 15(3), Member States may require TCNs to comply with integration measures, in accordance with national law.

mechanisms alone cannot solve problems of decision-making at EU level, hence it is reasonable to fear that soft mechanisms of governance will not suffice to bridge the gap between the concerns of national governments (of the Member States) and a supranational common objective – fair treatment of TCNs.

Assuming that the Treaty of Lisbon will sooner or later enter into force, the application of QMV would probably pave the way for a more formal action plan for a common approach to these issues, and would offer the possibility of adopting new legislation to solve this type of problem.

References

Amersfoort, H. van (1995), 'Migration, the Limits of Governmental Control', *New Community* 22(2): 243–57.

Bailleux, A. (2006), 'La Cour de Justice et les Droits de l'Homme: à propos de l'Arrêt. *Parlement c. Conseil* du 27 juin 2006', *Journal des Tribunaux*: 589–93.

Baldinger, D. (2007), 'The Family Reunification Directive: A Survey of Jurisprudence in The Netherlands', *Migrantenrecht* 22(7): 289–93.

Barnhard, C. (2004), *The Substantive Law of the EU: The Four Freedoms*, Oxford: Oxford University Press.

Boelaert-Suominen, S. (2005), 'Non-EU Nationals and Council Directive 2003/109/EC on the Status of Third-country Nationals who are Long-term Residents: Five Paces Forward and Possibly Three Paces Back', *Common Market Law Review* 42(4): 1,011–52.

Boeles, P. (2001), 'Directive on Family Reunification: Are the Dilemmas Resolved?', *European Journal of Migration and Law* 3(1): 61–71.

Bouckaert, S. (2007), *Documentloze Vreemdelingen. Grondrechtenbescherming Doorheen de Belgische en Internationale Rechtspraak vanaf 1985*, Antwerp and Apeldoorn: Maklu.

Brouwer, E. (2002), 'Immigration, Asylum and Terrorism: A Changing Dynamic. Legal and Practical Developments on Migration in the European Union', *European Journal of Migration and Law* 4(4): 399–424.

—— (2005), 'Effective Remedies for Third Country Nationals in EU Law: Justice Accessible to All?', *European Journal of Migration and Law* 7(3): 219–36.

Bruycker, P. de (ed.) (2000), *Les Régularisations des Etrangers Illégaux dans l'Union Européenne/Regularisations of Illegal Immigrants in the European Union*, Brussels: Bruylant.

—— (ed.) (2003), *The Emergence of a European Immigration Policy/L'Emergence d'une Politique Eeuropéenne d'Immigration*, Brussels: Bruylant.

Carlier, J.-Y. (2003), 'Conclusions', *Revue du Droit des Etrangers*, special issue, 'Le regroupement familial: à la croisée des droits belge et européen': 576.

Carrera, S. (2005), 'Integration as Process of Inclusion for Migrants? The Case of Long-term Residents in the EU', in H. Schneider (ed.), *Migration, Integration and Citizenship: A Challenge for Europe's Future*, vol. 2, Maastricht: Forum, pp. 109–38.

Caviedes, A. (2004), 'The Open Method of Coordination in Immigration Policy: A Tool for Prying Open Fortress Europe?', *Journal of European Public Policy* 11(2): 289–310.

Cecco, F. de (2006), 'Room to Move? Minimum Harmonization and Fundamental Rights', *Common Market Law Review* 43(1): 9–30.

Cholewinsky, R. (2002), 'Family Reunification and Conditions Placed on Family Members: Dismantling a Fundamental Right', *European Journal of Migration and Law* 4(3): 271–90.

Foblets, M.-C. and Vanheule, D. (2007), 'Editorial: Editorial Instrumentalization in the Realm of (European) Migration Law', *European Journal of Migration and Law* 9(3): 283–7.

Groenendijk, K. (2004), 'Legal Concepts of Integration in EU Migration Law', *European Journal of Migration and Law* 6(2): 111–26.

—— (2006a), 'Family Reunification as a Right under Community Law', *European Journal of Migration and Law* 8(2): 215–30.

—— (2006b), 'Note on Some Aspects of the Judgment of the Court of 27 June 2006 in the Case C-540/03 (*Parliament* v. *Council*) Concerning some Provisions on Directive 2003/86/EC', *ILPA European Update*, September.

—— (2007), 'Integration Tests abroad as a Condition for Family Reunification in the E.U.?', *ILPA European Update*, June.

——, Fernhout, R., Dam, D.P.L.M. and Van Oers, R. (2007), *The Family Reunification Directive in EU Member States: The First Year of Implementation*, Nijmegen: Centre for Migration Law.

Gross, T. (2005), 'Integration of Immigrants: The Perspective of European Community Law', *European Journal of Migration and Law* 7(2): 145–61.

Guild, E. (1996), *The Developing Immigration and Asylum Policies of the European Union: Adopted Conventions, Resolutions, Recommendations, Decisions and Conclusions*, The Hague: Kluwer Law International.

Halleskov, L. (2005), 'The Long-term Residents Directive: A Fulfilment of the Tampere Objective of Near-equality?, *European Journal of Migration and Law* 7(2): 181–201.

Handoll, J. (2003), 'The Status of Third-country Nationals Residing on a Long-term Basis', in P. de Bruycker (ed.), *The Emergence of a European Immigration Policy/L'Emergence d'une Politique Européenne d'Immigration*, Brussels: Bruylant, pp. 269–362.

—— (2005), 'The Long-term Residents Directive', in P. de Bruycker and J.-Y. Carlier (eds), *Immigration and Asylum Law of the EU: Current Debates*, Brussels: Bruylant, pp. 144–60.

Heer, C. de (2007a), 'De Status van Langdurig Ingezeten Derdelander (1): Achtergrond en Inhoud van Richtlijn 2003/109/EG2007', *Migrantenrecht* 22(5): 184–92.

—— (2007b), 'De Status van Langdurig Ingezeten Derdelander (1): Achtergrond en Inhoud van Richtlijn 2003/109/EG2007', *Migrantenrecht* 22(7): 272–88.

Julien-Laferriere, F., Labaye, H. and Edström, O. (eds) (2005), *La Politique Européenne d'Immigration et d'Asile: Bilan Critique Cinq Ans après le Traité d'Amsterdam/The European Immigration and Asylum Policy: Critical Assessment Five Years after the Amsterdam Treaty*, Brussels: Bruylant.

Kuyper, P.J. (1999), 'De Communautarisering van Visa-, Asiel- en Immigratiepolitiek Krachtens het Verdrag van Amsterdam en de Incorporatie van het Schengen Acquis', *Sociaal Economische Wetgeving, Tijdschrift voor Europees en Economisch Recht*: 436–42.

Lodder, G. (2007), 'De Gezinsherenigingsrichtlijn: Legitimering van of Keerpunt voor het Restrictieve Nederlandse Beleid?', *Migrantenrecht* 1/2: 26–31.

Peers, S. (2004), 'Implementing Inequality? The Directive on Long-term Resident Third-country Nationals', *European Law Review* 29(4): 437–60.

—— (2005), 'Key Legislative Developments on Migration in the European Union', *European Journal of Migration and Law* 7(1): 87–118.

Pernice, I. (1999), 'Multilevel Constitutionalism and the Treaty of Amsterdam: European Constitution-making Revised?', *Common Market Law Review* 36: 703–50.

Poulain, M., Singleton, A. and Perrin, N. (eds) (2006), *Towards Harmonised European Statistics on International Migration*, Louvain-la-Neuve: Presses Universitaires de Louvain.

Schaffrin, D. (2005), 'Which Standards for Family Reunification of Third-country Nationals in the European Union?', in J.-Y. Carlier and P. de Bruycker (eds), *Immigration and Asylum Law of the EU: Current Debates/Actualité du Droit Européen de l'Immigration et de l'Asile*, Brussels: Bruylant, pp. 91–143.

Schibel, I. (2004), 'Transposing EU Law on Legal Migration', *European Journal of Law and Migration* 6(4): 395–404.

Schneider, H. (2005), 'Towards a European Migration Policy: From Maastricht to Amsterdam, from Tampere to The Hague', in H. Schneider (ed.), *Migration, Integration and Citizenship: A Challenge for Europe's Future*, vol. 2, Maastricht: Forum, pp. 7–33.

—— and Wiebrock, A. (2005), 'The Council Directive on Family Reunification: Establishing Proper Rights for Third-country Nationals?', in H. Schneider (ed.), *Migration, Integration and Citizenship: A Challenge for Europe's Futures*, vol. 2, Maastricht: Forum, pp. 35–70.

Urth, H. (2005), 'Building a Momentum for the Integration of Third-country Nationals in the European Union', *European Journal of Migration and Law* 7(2): 163–80.

Vanheule, D. (2007), 'Gezinshereniging: een Belgisch Perspectief', *Migrantenrecht* 22(1/2): 17–25.

Vanvoorden, K. (2007), 'Stelt het Arrest Jia een einde aan de België-route?', *Tijdschrift voor Vreemdelingenrecht* 2: 72–84.

Velluti, S. (2007), 'What European Union Strategy for Integrating Migrants? The Role of OMC Soft Mechanisms in the Development of an EU Immigration Policy', *European Journal of Migration and Law* 9(1): 53–82.

Chapter 10
From the Revenue Rule to Soft Law and Back Again: The Consequences for 'Society' of the Social Governance of International Tax Competition

Bill Maurer

In the late 1990s, international standard-setting bodies, multilateral institutions and non-governmental organizations began to worry that, in a world of the free movement of money, governments would lose tax revenue to states that competitively lowered their rates to attract foreign investment.[1] 'Tax competition', it was feared, would erode the ability of states to provide needed social services to their citizens. Although market promoters around the world had been extolling the virtues of liberalization, even those institutions most associated with the promulgation of neoliberal reforms like the World Bank expressed alarm about the effect of those reforms on revenue collection as well as on the control and interdiction of financial crime and money laundering.

After a flurry of activity aimed at curbing tax competition worldwide, however, including the issuance of a series of 'blacklists' of countries deemed not to be in compliance with an emerging set of international fiscal norms, the effort was deemed a failure. Citing the hypocrisy of the large, wealthy nations behind the effort to curb tax competition, who would not subject themselves to the same level of scrutiny demanded of the tax havens, many small countries accused of tax competition demanded a 'level playing field'; that is, they made the centrepiece of their counter-campaign the call for universal rules of the tax game, so that large states would be subject to exactly the same forms and level of scrutiny as small states. Meanwhile, many of these same small countries struck individual deals in the form of Double Taxation Treaties with the big players like the United States.

1 Although not all of the jurisdictions targeted by these efforts are politically independent nation-states (many are dependent territories, like the British Virgin Islands), I will use the term 'state' or 'country' throughout this chapter for convenience. And although the term 'tax haven' is a highly charged one for those countries so labelled, I will employ it here in place of more convoluted locutions (such as 'countries or territories deemed not in compliance with the FATF's 40 recommendations' or some such), also for convenience. See Sharman (2006, 165, n. 1).

This, in effect, killed the multilateral effort for global tax regulation. What had begun as an effort at international governance through 'soft law' – non-binding guidelines, peer review, peer pressure and shaming – ended up reaffirming the sovereignty of individual jurisdictions, free to make treaties with each other and free to pursue their own fiscal policies (Sharman 2006; Rawlings 2007).

Viewed one way, the international effort against 'harmful tax competition' at the turn of the century can be seen as a story of the limits of social governance or multilateral regulation of the financial sphere. Spearheaded by the Organization for Economic Co-operation and Development (OECD), the effort to curb tax competition relied on consultation and peer review, which allowed other actors such as estate planning practitioners and representatives from tax haven countries to shape the normative deliberations of the OECD and ultimately to shift the discourse on tax competition itself. In striving to achieve a kind of epistemic governance (Marcussen 2004) based on persuasion rather than force, the OECD of necessity had to invite 'society' – here, in the form of NGOs and international organizations formed specifically to counter the OECD's initiatives – to the table. Once they became a part of the consultative process, they were able to use the power of words to transform it. The tax havens and their advocates were able to turn the language of the OECD against it, calling into question its 'reputation for impartial expertise' (Sharman 2006, 161). Relatively weak, small states like the British Virgin Islands and the Cayman Islands were able to trump the concerted efforts of the powerful OECD countries by using the very tools of organizations like the OECD: peer pressure, and the deployment of rhetoric about reputation and fairness in the context of new social networks that were created through the consultative process. Jason Sharman ends his compelling account of the global effort to co-ordinate tax regulation by noting the unpredictability of regulation through rhetoric. Given the double-edged nature of the tax havens' relative victory in this affair – small states won, but tax havens continued to operate – Sharman concludes that 'there is no reason to think that a more social view of politics and economics entails a world of greater harmony or justice' (Sharman 2006, 161).

There is a fascinating ambiguity in his statement, however. Sharman intends by a 'social view of politics and economics' to refer to analytical strategies for scholars, such as his own constructivist political economy. Yet the phrase could also be taken to refer to policy or regulatory strategies for political actors, like the OECD, which seek to lead policy discussions and governance programmes through social relations and social pressure. Indeed, there is an epistemological and pragmatic isomorphism between social science itself, and efforts to govern through or with 'the social'. That convergence can be traced back to nineteenth-century social thinkers like Comte, who sought a social science that would facilitate rule. But the rise of 'social' forms of governance through participation and consultation lends it a new cast. This chapter reflects on the implications for the anthropology of law. As anthropologists increasingly grapple with new forms of governance and new assemblages of politics, economics and ethics (Collier and Ong 2005), and as anthropologists turn to transnational and international legal processes (Merry

1992; 2006), the question of the 'social' takes on a particular salience and has the potential to create productive theoretical muddles. One of the lessons of those muddles is that every analytical, ethical or political position can be co-opted for other ends: the world, after all, is a pragmatic puzzle, not a grand theory. Discourses 'may contain elements of theory but they are not theoretical,' Nigel Thrift reminds us; rather, 'They are practically oriented orders bent to the task of constructing more or less durable social networks and they are constantly redefined in order to cope with the vagaries of that task' (Thrift 1996, 22). This chapter serves as a demonstration of Thrift's statement, and points toward a less linear, less causal account of the role of the 'social' in transnational, multilateral governance today. It proceeds by reviewing the notion of soft law and its incorporation/creation of a category of the social. It then analyses the OECD's effort to curb harmful tax practices as an initiative designed to incorporate 'society' into governance. It concludes by reflecting on the observation among legal anthropologists and law and society scholars that international legal processes resemble and contingently re-assemble something called 'society' in the process of trying to take society into account.

'Society' and allied terms like 'civil society' are used by many participants in the debates this chapter will outline. Among people on the ground, who are not experts in the offshore financial services sector and have little knowledge of the details of the regulatory process of the issues at stake, 'country' or 'territory' are more often invoked, especially together with words like 'voice' or 'say', as in wanting to make sure my country has a say in matters that affect it. From a social scientific perspective, one might easily dismiss such words as mere rhetoric, concealing other powerful interests which hide behind the cloak of legitimacy conferred by 'social' words. My argument in this chapter, however, like that of Thrift, Strathern and others who have examined the bureaucratic constitution of 'society' itself, is that the instrumentalization of 'the social' or 'society' is no longer as distinct from either the general social scientific concept of the social – indeed, they have the same origin point in modernist reconfigurations of human organizations of all types – or the nebulous entity popularly understood as 'society'. This means, too, that words are rarely 'just' words, and that rhetoric is a form of world-making.

Social Governance and Soft Law

Numerous scholars from a range of disciplines have drawn attention to the increasing role of so-called soft law in solving problems of international governance and regulation that cannot be addressed through the hard laws of individual sovereign states or by enforceable international treaties. As with all dichotomies, the boundary between soft law and hard law is indistinct, both analytically and in practice. Here, I use the term 'soft law' to refer to governance through peer review, consultation, peer pressure, shaming, and the creation of non-binding guidelines and recommendations. Soft law includes 'a variety of processes … which have normative content [but] are not formally binding' (Trubek, Cottrell and Nance 2006, 65). The sources of soft law are varied. They include multilateral international organizations like the OECD, as well as non-governmental organizations, private actors and civil society groups. In Europe, soft law has become the hallmark of the Open Method of Co-ordination (OMC) in the creation and maintenance of European integration (Trubek and Trubek 2005). Soft law is also a key component of the so-called 'new governance', based on participation, networked decision-making, diversity, consultation rather than the formal mechanisms or the centralized 'command and control' regime association with law and constitutionalism (see de Búrca and Scott 2006, 2–3). Mörth provides a convenient ideal-typical sketch contrasting hard law 'government' with soft law 'governance', the former based on public actors and state-centrism, the latter based on private actors and 'deliberative and societally based' processes and models (Mörth 2006: 121).

There is a good deal of ambiguity in the definitions of soft law offered by scholars and practitioners, and many have questioned the dichotomy between hard and soft law, positing processes through which the latter becomes legalized or formalized, or querying various hybrid or intermediate forms (Kirton and Trebilcock 2004). I do not intend to delve into the various debates about the concept of soft law in the academic literature (for a good starting point on these debates, see Mörth 2004). I am more interested in an early and recurrent question about soft law, which has to do with the degree and valence of 'social' forces operating through or within it (Abbott and Snidal 2000; Finnemore and Toope 2001). Thus, Finnemore and Toope state: 'Law is a broad social phenomenon deeply embedded in the practices, beliefs, and traditions of societies, and shaped by interaction among societies' (Finnemore and Toope 2001, 743). This is a point of connection between scholarship on soft law and legal anthropology and socio-legal studies more broadly, for which law has always been a social phenomenon, and shot through with social interests, processes, forms and forces. Seen through the lens of law and society scholarship, perhaps all law is always 'soft'. The level of degree, however, may very well depend on the impact of law and society scholarship itself on a specific legal domain or practice: one is reminded that Alternative Dispute Resolution, using mechanisms 'outside' formal law, has its genesis in anthropological accounts of dispute-settlement processes outside the West and in socio-legal efforts to bring the voices of the powerless to the legal table.[2] Therefore, any discussion of the relationship between society and law of necessity begs the question of which domain is inside or outside the other; indeed, it calls into question the very notion of there being such domains in the first place. As we will see, a good deal of the work involved in the debate over harmful tax competition was a kind of domain-work: the creation of groups and interests

2 Strathern (2004) discusses the analogous situation in science, where ethical review boards and the attempt to anticipate the unexpected led science to be imagined as 'inside' society, rather than society as something that could be rationally re-ordered in accordance with science.

as 'social' in themselves, and therefore owed by the OECD, due to its inclusive doctrine, a seat at the table.

Tax Competition and the Revenue Rule

The historical association between sovereignty and taxation precluded any direct interference in the tax policies of countries deemed to be participating in 'harmful' tax practices. Both by exacting revenue and by spending it, states stitch together taxation, sovereignty and citizenship, as the American Revolutionary War and the founding of the United States republic remind us (Einhorn 2006). The connection to sovereignty is also evident in the so-called 'Revenue Rule', Lord Mansfield's eighteenth-century dictum that 'no country ever takes notice of the revenue laws of another'. Cameron (2006, 236) traces the origins of the publicly financed, tax-based fiscal state to the rise of statistics and audit that developed in tandem with modern European money and trading systems. He notes that the 'overwhelming majority of modern fiscal states have only been in existence since 1945', and emphasizes the spatial dimension of taxation, since, in its redistributive capacity, it 'involves the transmission of money, goods, services and so on through space from one group to another' and also helps to suture together the 'social, political and economic citizen' with the 'norms and institutions of the state' (Cameron 2006, 237). The fiscal state of the twentieth century is thus the social welfare state, a state to serve 'society', in accordance with ideals of social democratic citizenship. This is also the vision of the state that has come under attack since the Thatcher/Reagan era and market-oriented neoliberal reform. The very idea of tax competition is in line with such neoliberal visions, and it conjures threats to the 'social' norms and institutions and the bounded fiscal territories of contemporary states. Indeed, Oxfam, the hunger relief NGO, joined the debate on tax competition by emphasizing the harm done to 'society' by tax haven jurisdictions:

> Tax is widely regarded as an essential component of a fair and efficient society. An essential principle underlying tax collection has been the liberal social obligation on companies and individuals to pay tax proportionately to their income in order to finance public goods and social welfare. (Oxfam 2000, 6)

If state sovereignty precludes one state's interference in the tax policy of another, however, then how could international organizations hope to counter tax competition? The answer came from a set of soft law initiatives put forward by the OECD (1998), which were followed closely by similar projects, sparked by slightly different concerns, by the Financial Action Task Force of the G7 (for example, FATF 2001), the Financial Stability Forum (FSF) and NGOs like Oxfam. Seeking to 'name and shame' countries into compliance with international financial norms, these initiatives, in the process, created those norms, but not exactly as they might have pleased. The impetus behind the actions of each was slightly different. For the OECD, the focus was on tax competition. For the FATF, the issue was money laundering. For the FSF, the emphasis was on international financial stability in the wake of the Asian financial crisis. Countries on the receiving end of these efforts experienced them as of a piece, however. Nearly all countries initially named on so-called 'blacklists' of non-compliant or non-co-operating jurisdictions – including almost all of the world's tax havens – complied, often rather quickly. In some cases, compliance came even before the blacklists were issued, pre-empting international 'shaming' through what were called 'advance commitments'.

Tax competition itself, meanwhile, is a product of an imagined future inspired by economic theory (Webb 2004, 795), and thus a fine example of the way economic theory performs, rather than describes or predicts, the economy (after Callon's 'performation' of the economy by economic theory; Callon 1998, 22). Rather than describing an actually existing condition whereby the lowing of tax rates in one jurisdiction in fact spurs a race to the bottom in revenue regimes elsewhere, tax competition is the logical but not empirically observable outcome of a particular economic theory.[3] In calling for an end to tax competition, Oxfam argued that tax competition saps revenue from poor countries when their wealthy elites squirrel their money offshore. That phenomenon, however, is not necessarily linked to tax *competition* so much as the mere presence of lower-tax jurisdictions, not a process of competitive lowering of rates internationally. It would occur regardless of whether the race to the bottom predicted by economic theory took place. That 'tax competition' names a phenomenon of dubious ontological status makes the debate about it an interesting object for anthropological investigation – like Evans-Pritchard's (1937) ensorcelled granaries, or the divine.

In another publication, I have discussed some of the debates in tax haven countries sparked by the OECD initiative, as well as the procedures that offshore financial centres put into place in its wake (Maurer 2005; see also Sharman 2006). Chief among these are due diligence and 'Know Your Customer' (KYC) policies to collect and maintain information on clients. I argued that due diligence is a specific kind of ethical regulation based on qualitative assessments of virtue. I also argued that due diligence and its critique fold into one another and obviate certain conventional forms of academic analysis (Maurer 2005). This chapter fills in another piece of the ethical puzzle of offshore financial services by focusing not on the procedures, but on specific form of governance attempted by the OECD, a kind of social governance effected through peer review and pressure, moral suasion, and the creation of new epistemic communities. This form of governance

3 Webb (2004) makes the most sustained argument that the OECD's harmful tax competition initiative was based on and shaped by norms rather than actual revenue crises or rational policy decisions independent of the predictions of liberal economic theory. On the question of whether competition among states to attract investment leads to a taxation race to the bottom, the evidence is contradictory at best. As Webb (2004, 788) puts it, 'governments certainly behave as if tax competition has increased', but the empirical evidence does not always support the contention.

can be seen as a scaling-up of due diligence, for it proceeds in much the same fashion and through many of the same forms of review and pressure. Rather than taking the form of a dictate from powerful states interfering with the revenue laws of other states, and thereby challenging sovereignty and violating the revenue rule, the OECD would proceed through its signature method of consultation and multilateral co-ordination. Here was a case where the social nature of OECD soft law governance seemed perfectly suited to address the threat to 'society' posed by tax competition.

Creating 'Participating Partners'

The OECD campaign against harmful tax competition generated intense debate. Tax haven countries saw it as heavy-handed, imperial and unfair. Being blacklisted evoked old colonial forms of domination, surveillance and control. Countries so targeted felt sidelined and caught off guard. OECD members with histories of bank secrecy like Switzerland and Luxembourg vociferously opposed the OECD initiative. But the possible damage to offshore jurisdictions' reputations by being blacklisted quickly led them to seek to minimize the damage. Most sought to get themselves off the blacklists by adopting best practices proposed by the OECD and FATF or by issuing press releases committing themselves to compliance. Jason Sharman, Gregory Rawlings and others have all amply documented this process (Webb 2004; Maurer 2005; Rawlings 2005; Woodward 2005; Sharman 2006). All the while, a discursive war raged over the OECD's concepts and definitions. The main parties opposed to the OECD were the Society for Trust and Estate Practitioners (STEP), a professional association of tax planners; the Center for Freedom and Prosperity (CFP), a Washington, DC think tank, and the International Tax and Investment Organization (later renamed the International Trade and Investment Organization, ITIO), a multilateral body of tax haven countries that was established with the assistance of the Commonwealth Secretariat, explicitly modelled on the OECD itself as a consultative body made up of representatives from its own member states as well as entities with observer status.[4]

The logic of the OECD demanded that the ITIO be incorporated into its own process of consultation as a participating partner. The result was the creation of the Global Forum on Taxation, which would meet every two years under the auspices of the OECD. The Global Forum consisted of OECD and non-OECD members, including the ITIO membership. The discourse of harmful tax competition very

4 The members of the ITIO are: Anguilla, Antigua and Barbuda, Bahamas, Barbados, Belize, British Virgin Islands, Cayman Islands, St Kitts and Nevis, St Lucia, St Vincent and the Grenadines, Turks and Caicos Islands, Panama, Cook Islands, Samoa, and Vanuatu. The observers are the Commonwealth Secretariat, CARICOM Secretariat, Caribbean Development Bank, Eastern Caribbean Central Bank, and the Pacific Islands Forum Secretariat.

quickly shifted to 'principles of transparency and effective exchange of information for tax purposes' (OECD 2003). Furthermore:

> The focus of the meeting was on how to achieve a global level playing field and how to improve further the process by which this initiative can be taken forward based on the widely accepted principles of equity and shared responsibility. (OECD 2003)

The ITIO quickly issued its own press release, headlined, 'It's Official: OECD Tax Project Depends on Level Playing Field' (ITIO 2003). The chief outcome of the first Global Forum meeting was the creation of a 'Level Playing Field Joint Working Group'. The 'level playing field' slogan has by now made its way into the title of nearly every major report by the OECD and other parties in the tax competition debate, including the title of the OECD's own report on the 2005 Global Forum meeting and a 2007 report by the Commonwealth Secretariat titled *Assessing the Playing Field* (Stoll-Davey 2007).

The effect of the inclusion of the ITIO into the Global Forum has been a kind of politics by press release (after Rawlings' phrase, 'compliance by press release'; Rawlings 2007, 59). At the close of the 2007 Global Forum meeting and the release of the Commonwealth Secretariat report, the ITIO issued a press release headed:

> LITTLE DIFFERENCE BETWEEN ONSHORE AND OFFSHORE, NEW ANALYSIS OF OECD DATA REVEALS
>
> 'End stigmatization and let us into treaty network', say small countries
>
> Commonwealth calls for fair play

The release concludes:

> Big countries operate through clubs and use organizations that they control (OECD, FATF, IMF, FSF, and so on) to establish and promulgate rules, standards of practice and intended norms. They call these 'international standards' and impose them on weaker states. Small and developing states feel unfairly pressured to apply standards not uniformly applied by those countries which are applying the pressure or by other more powerful competitor countries.
>
> In his introduction to the ITIO report, Ransford Smith, Deputy Secretary-General of the Commonwealth Secretariat, states: '*In the global arena the lack of representation and effective participation of small vulnerable economies in international standard setting bodies and processes is one of the major drawbacks. The small states have limited opportunities to make inputs into the development of measures that are critical for the efficient functioning of the*

> *sector, as well as for their development. Yet their compliance is expected within given timeframes.*' (ITIO 2007, 6; italics in original)

The press release echoes the discourse of much of the tax competition debate, framing the issue in terms of weak versus strong states and calling into question the universality of rules and practices devised by the few and the powerful. This is a profoundly post-colonial rhetoric as well, drawing on legacies of imperial rule and touting the principles of liberty, equality and fairness. It also draws on the post-colonial network of expertise embodied in the Commonwealth Secretariat (which had earlier issued another volume in support of small states' 'fiscal sovereignty'; Biswas 2002). What was the effect of the incorporation of new participating partners and their discourse of the level playing field?

Soft Law or Hard Imperial Power in the HTC Debate?

Allow me to present a series of quotations from various observers of and parties to the debate over harmful tax competition:

> In the end, the OECD juggernaut was brought to a halt by the resistance of some of its other members – Switzerland, Luxembourg and Liechtenstein in particular – who refused to go along with the demands of their more strident sister states in the OECD for fear of the harmful effect on their vital financial services sector.[5]

> The failure to note widespread US derelictions in permitting anonymously owned companies is a significant shortcoming in the [OECD's 2006] Report. If illicit companies with secret ownership merely migrate out of the tax havens and into the United States, what is the point of the OECD project? (Hay 2006, 5)

> [The] OECD initiative has really run out of steam … the initiatives have really got diverted from their main goals …. (Guernsey interviewees of Gregory Rawlings, quoted in Rawlings 2005, 299)

> [T]he jury is still out on whether the OECD's attempt to define and neutralize harmful tax practices by 'naming and shaming' tax havens as renegade states in the international tax regime will be successful. (Eden and Kudrle 2005, 124)

> Without US support or the creation of a level playing field the OECD project is stalled. (Woodward 2005, 212)

---

5 Roland M. Sanders, 'Europe Eyeing Tax Havens Again', *Caribbean News*, 11 September 2006.

> OECD officials engaged in serious efforts to consult and pacify business opponents, and made concessions to those business criticisms that resonated most strongly with liberal economic ideology. … [T]his is the equivalent to consulting with the fox about policies to protect the henhouse. (Webb 2004, 812)

> [T]he OECD-sponsored campaign against 'harmful' tax competition has been unsuccessful because regulative norms have severely constrained the means legitimately able to be employed. (Sharman 2006, 143)

> OECD countries embarked on a difficult challenge when we commenced our work on countering harmful tax practices and this report reflects the success we have had in bringing about change. In 2000, we identified 47 potentially harmful preferential tax regimes in OECD countries. Of those regimes, 19 regimes have been abolished, 14 have been amended to remove their potentially harmful features, 13 were found not to be harmful and only one has been found to be harmful. This Report, along with the report recently issued by the OECD Global Forum on Taxation on the transparency and exchange of information practices in 82 economies, shows that we are making real progress in addressing harmful tax practices. (Ciocca 2006)

> 35 jurisdictions have made commitments to transparency and effective exchange of information and are considered co-operative jurisdictions by the OECD's Committee on Fiscal Affairs. (OECD 2006)

These assessments of the OECD initiative come from a number of academic political scientists, as well as a former ambassador of the Caribbean commonwealth of Antigua and Barbuda (Sanders), a professional consultant for the firm Stikemann Elliott, one of Canada's top seven corporate law firms (Hay), the Chair of the Organization for Economic Co-operation and Development's Committee on Fiscal Affairs (Ciocca) and the interviewees of an anthropological colleague (Rawlings). The diligent reader will detect the rhetorical shift, presaged in the quotations above, from competition to co-operation, as well as the use of the prepositional phrase 'toward a level playing field'. The point of contention between the first seven and the last two quotations above is whether the OECD initiative has been a success or a failure (and, in case the point is unclear somehow, only the OECD itself judged its effort a success!).

Different actors caught up by the OECD's initiative had different views on it. To many of the small states targeted by the effort, it was a neo-colonial imposition by an undemocratic alliance of powerful, rich countries on the smallest and weakest players in the international political arena. Caribbean leaders complained that the OECD campaign was 'nothing less than a determined attempt to bend other countries to [the OECD's] will', 'a form of neo-colonialism in which the OECD is attempting to dictate the tax economic systems and structures of other nations for the benefit of the OECD's member states'.[6] They accused the OECD of 'bullying' (Julian Francis, Bahamas Central Bank) and called its actions a threat to the islands' 'economic sovereignty' (Ambrose George, Dominica Finance Minister).[7] In the United States, both the Bush administration and the Congressional Black Caucus came out against the initiative, in the name of defending the sovereignty of small nations against powerful and non-democratic global entities. To conservative Washington, DC think-tanks, meanwhile, the OECD initiative was an effort by global institutions with world government aspirations to quash the free market and trample on American sovereignty. Others argued that the OECD held double standards, as several of its member states would not be deemed in compliance with its own recommendations on tax competition. The Bush administration, for its part, advocated for an information-sharing regime rather than the reduction of tax competition itself, in line with security concerns born of the post-9/11 climate, but just as importantly, based on its ideological commitments to both low taxes and surveillance.

As already noted, the OECD effort also sparked the consolidation of existing professional networks of estate and tax planners (mainly through the Society for Trust and Estate Practitioners, or STEP) as well as the formation of new multilateral organizations (for example, the ITIO).[8] These new networks and organizations significantly reshaped the OECD's discursive and regulatory regime. The emphasis on tax competition shifted to tax co-operation and the establishment of a 'level playing field' – that is, a commitment to securing compliance of OECD member states before forcing non-members to do the same. And the emphasis on ending tax haven abuses and thereby reallocating revenue wealth back to countries in which it is owed shifted to information-sharing. These discursive and practical shifts led to charges that the effort was ultimately a failure.

Indeed, by now, most proponents and critics of the initiative concur that the exercise has been meaningless: small states initially targeted have issued letters of commitment, but nearly all make a condition of that commitment OECD member states' own compliance. In other words, they demand a 'level playing field' before bringing their own practices into compliance. The result, commentators claim, is a stalemate. Or, as Ronen Palan argues, the result has been a shift from curbing tax haven abuses to ensuring that tax havens 'play by the rules of the advanced

6 Ronald M. Sanders, 'The OECD's "Harmful Tax Competition" Scheme: The Implications for Antigua and Barbuda', address to the Luncheon Meeting of the Antigua and Barbuda Chamber Commerce, 27 March 2001.

7 Catherine Kelly, 'Don't Count on Friends in the New Global Economy', *The Punch*, 17 July 2000; Government of Dominica, Budget Speech 2000/2001, 'Stabilization, Consolidation and Diversified Growth – Foundations for a Sustainable Recovery'. See James (2002) for a further discussion of these comments.

8 The FATF's distinct initiative also encouraged the formation of new regional multilateral organizations concerned with combating money laundering, such as the Asia/Pacific Group (APG).

industrial countries that by and large represent – let us have no illusions – business interests' (Palan 2003, xvi). Indeed, Palan notes, the liberalization of onshore regulatory regimes demonstrates more than ever the importance of the offshore to contemporary global political economy (Palan 2003, xix). And, because of the initiative – not despite it – offshore activity and onshore activity that takes the same form as offshore arrangements is growing at a fine clip: there are now 'huge incentive[s] for companies and individuals to open multiple businesses in various havens in the hope that if an investigation occurs, it will drag on endlessly' (Palan 2003, xvii).

The problem with the consensus that the OECD initiative has failed is that so much activity has taken place in the mean time, and so much work, paper, and argument continues to be generated by it and that so many new social networks have been created and sustained by it (not least networks of scholars!). If we consider the actual effects of the initiative separate from its stated goals, then what comes into view is, first of all, the massive generation of documents and discourse, especially press releases, commitment letters and a discursive regime organized in terms of the 'level playing field', information sharing, and 'tax co-operation'. Second, we see the consolidation and enlargement of professional societies – STEP being the primary example, but also the creation of scholarly networks of those studying the phenomenon as well as, and sometimes at the same time, consulting on or contributing to it. We also see the expansion – regardless of how we ultimately evaluate it – of what scholars of the OECD have called 'normative deliberations' or 'epistemic governance': the use of peer consultation and review among participating countries and territories to generate, redefine and promulgate knowledge and norms about tax competition. We see new parties to those consultations, like the ITIO and new regulatory bodies in the countries targeted, like the Financial Services Commission of the British Virgin Islands. Whether or not it represents a co-optation of the initiative, the imagination and deployment of the 'level playing field' is, after all, a measurable effect of it and, specifically, of its incorporation of 'society' into the deliberative process.

And that incorporation felled a powerful beast – or at least radically transformed it. The OECD, a large, rich organization, found its effort redirected by a collection of small states whose interests were represented by tiny organizations with minuscule budgets. This was not a case of a multilateral organization being bought off by rich lobbyists, as Jason Sharman has demonstrated. While the outcome might ultimately serve business interests, those interests did not bankroll the attack on the OECD's campaign. Instead, true ideologies from the Centre for Freedom and Prosperity – three individuals, one full-time staff member, a budget for this purpose of only $600,000 (Sharman 2006, 67) – lent the power of persuasive ideas and rhetoric to the counter-campaign. And the ITIO, with a budget of around $200,000 and an 'intermittent' (Sharman 2006, 67) existence (it seems to come to life just before every biannual Global Forum conference), could hardly be said to be a 'front organization' (Sharman 2006, 67) for other interests.

It would be a mistake to see the CFP and ITIO as not true social actors because of their smallness, however. It would be the same category error as claiming that an individual English speaker could not provide insight into the grammar of the language, or assuming that individuals are datapoints and societies are aggregates. The whole is not only greater than the sum of the parts; the parts themselves contain wholes. And, within the logic of the OECD, as soon as such a social whole is conjured into existence, it must be invited into the consultative process. The 'currency' of the OECD's influence is precisely its identity as a consultative body; to act otherwise in the face of people with whom to consult would have debased that currency (Sharman 2006, 69).

The discursive convergence around the effort's 'failure', however, turned on a number of other questions. Was the initiative scuttled by the reluctance of the United States government under President George W. Bush, which withdrew its support for the effort? Or was it hijacked, or at least watered down, by new professional bodies, new transnational actor networks of consultants, tax planners, lobbyists, and government officials? Was it a pointless endeavour from the beginning, given the refusal of some OECD members to abide by the same rules as the non-OECD countries it targeted, and given the fact that several US states permit practices deemed harmful, like anonymous corporate ownership? Does it demonstrate the effectiveness of so-called soft law, non-binding directives, principles and commitments? Or does it rather show how easily soft law can be co-opted – and, if so, by whom, and how?

Again, these questions are shared by both analysts of and participants in the tax competition debate. This is a significant part of the social field within which the initiative has taken place. As such, these questions are 'data' rather than second-order commentary on another, prior phenomenon, for these kinds of questions are exactly the stuff of the OECD's consultative process. Furthermore, the individuals and groups involved constitute overlapping constituencies and co-constitutive knowledge practices. Scholars have been enlisted into the policy and regulatory debate and activity (see, for example, Sharman and Rawlings 2005), and terms from the policy debate have wended their way into the scholarly argument, in a continuous loop (see Elyachar 2006, 416). This is a part of the representational or narrative dilemma at issue in Sharman's statement, quoted at the beginning of this chapter, that 'social' approaches to politics and economics may not have the ends anyone intends.

This convergence was possible because there is no place to stand, politically, ethically or epistemologically, in the debate over harmful tax competition *as it was constituted here* without having the rug ripped out from underneath one's starting premises. For example, there are two widely held criticisms of the OECD effort in the literature and among the parties to the debate itself: (1) that international institutions like the OECD, in promulgating best practices, are engaged in a neocolonial project, and (2) that the OECD has double standards and unfairly targets small, powerless states while it allows its big, rich member countries to continue to engage in practices it otherwise condemns (like anonymous corporate ownership, permitted in several US states). However, arguments like these against the OECD fail to address that here, at least, it was trying to curtail unfettered capital mobility, restrain tax evasion by the ultra-rich and prevent corrupt regimes from using tax havens to hide revenues skimmed for the profit of elites or rulers. Alternatively, if analysis or critique begins from a position critical of capital mobility, tax haven abuses or money laundering, then the argument quickly becomes a colonialist one: it denies tax haven countries their sovereignty and supports soft law imperialism; it refuses small countries the options for attracting investment afforded big countries, and it cannot account for the fact that, in this case at least, multilateral, neoliberal organizations that supposedly serve business interests were here acting against them. How much simpler, then, to worry over success or failure.

Conclusion: Reassessing the Social

What interests me about soft law is that its practitioners, proponents and critics alike all presume something called the 'social'. This holds true for proponents and critics of soft law in the world, as well as proponents and critics of the *analytical concept* or the *analytical utility of the concept* of soft law. For proponents of soft law in the world – true believers, or more cautious advocates who see a role for it in certain places or for certain issues – the incorporation of the social into governance has the potential profoundly to democratize and to allow other, diverse voices into the domain of policy-making and implementation. Critics of the analytical concept of soft law, like Finnemore and Toope (2001), seem to agree that law is more 'social' than those who endorse soft law as an analytical concept might allow. It is a truism in law and society scholarship that law is always-already a 'social' phenomenon, full of custom, norms, so the concept of soft law has little analytical utility. But why this rush to the 'social' for analytical purposes or the embrace of the 'social' for policy objectives?

The nature of the 'social' enlisted in soft law social governance projects went relatively unquestioned in the OECD's harmful tax competition initiative. Regardless of whether one deems the OECD effort a success or failure, it proceeded through the type of consultative bringing together of a number of actors for which the OECD is well known. The use of audit, standards and peer review, which are simultaneously 'autonomizing and responsibilizing' (Rose, O'Malley and Valverde 2006, 91), have been understood as hallmarks of neoliberal governmentality. Yet the very idea of curbing harmful tax competition depended on a vision of the maintenance of the fiscal state's integrity, not its evaporation; the initiative was trying to promote a non-market-based system of payments in the form of revenue collection that was detached from the market; indeed, it was trying to preclude or close off the formation of a market in sovereignty (see Palan 2003). It did so in terms of the logical extension of a theory about that market in sovereignty. One analytical lesson, then, is that evidence of the infiltration of market logic does not always guarantee 'marketization' as an outcome. There are other things going on besides markets, calculation, equivalence and so on, even when – indeed, I would argue, especially when – we see markets, calculation, equivalence going on.

In the case of the harmful tax competition initiative, a 'social governance' entity, the OECD, which was originally trying to curb 'neoliberal' competitive deregulation, was opposed by a collection of unlikely partners which joined market freedom with political freedom. These partners used the OECD's own practice of partnership to bring 'society' into the discussion, not to reduce, but to protect tax competition. The effects were complicated: small states 'won', but meanwhile, onshore jurisdictions, not subject to the same level of 'peer review', have become more competitive (such as the US states of Delaware and Wyoming, which permit anonymous corporate ownership). Some small states used their enhanced sovereignty to engage in Double Taxation Treaties with the United States, thereby even further enhancing their sovereignty (Rawlings 2007).

At least three meanings of 'society' cohere in the debate over offshore finance charted here. First is the social as an object of social policy, and particularly as an organism fed by the fiscal state. This is the social of the welfare state, and it was constructed as being under threat by tax competition. Second is the social of 'participatory' forms of governance that involve the bringing together of various stakeholders and interest groups to discuss regulatory matters of mutual concern. Who gets invited to the table and who does not is a highly politically charged affair. The tale narrated here, however, is one of ever-increasing inclusion: as more parties and potential partners were identified, they were invited into the process.

I am hoping to withhold the cynical scholarly rejection of such invitations as a cover for brute interests only so that we may better see the shape of this kind of process. Like Sharman, I note that in the case of offshore finance, brute interests did not so straightforwardly 'win' or carry the day. We can only sustain that cynical critical posture towards offshore finance if we think that ongoing colonial relationships – actual, not metaphorical, colonial relationships – are just fine, and that the livelihoods of people living in tax havens do not matter. This is why some scholars (like Sharman) argue that the best solution to the problem of tax competition is to buy the tax havens off, and others (like myself, Maurer 2007) point out that this could take the form of reparations for slavery and colonialism.

This brings us to the issue of 'soft law' itself, and whether it is worth sustaining as a concept. Soft law relies on social as opposed to formal legal mechanisms. Yet the anthropology of law and socio-legal studies have long acknowledged that the law is far more than formal. It is the particular manner in which soft law 'makes' society that is of interest here. If the statistics of the nineteenth century constituted a particular kind of society that could then be intervened in, contained or channelled, the soft law of the late twentieth and early twenty-first century creates a society not to be tinkered with like the elements in a scientific experiment, but rather to be 'invited to participate' in its own self-construction. As an analytical concept, soft law may not carry much water. But it is an important ethnographic object in many of the worlds anthropologists of law are currently moving in.

In this chapter, I have been more interested in the process than the outcome, however. In *The Law of Primitive Man*, E. Adamson Hoebel wrote: 'International law, so-called, is but primitive law on the world level' (Hoebel 1954, 331). Michael Barkun (1968) extends the argument. Sally Merry writes, in a review essay on the anthropology of international law:

> Some intriguing parallels can be found between the way international law works and the law of villages without centralized rulemaking bodies and formal courts …. Both rely on custom, social pressure, collaboration, and negotiations among parties to develop rules and resolve conflicts. In both, law is plural and intersects with other legal orders …. Each order constitutes a semiautonomous social field within a matrix of legal pluralism. Both depend heavily on reciprocity and the threat of ostracism, as did the Trobrianders in Malinowski's account. Gossip and scandal are important in fostering compliance internationally as they are in small communities. Social pressure to appear civilized encourages countries to ratify international legal treaties much as social pressure fosters conformity in small communities. Countries urge others to follow the multilateral treaties they ratify, but treaty monitoring depends largely on shame and social pressure. Clearly there are many differences between social ordering in villages and in the world, but there are some similarities. (Merry 2006, 101)

While the anthropology of law and socio-legal studies have been saying for some time that law is a profoundly social affair, the rise of governance explicitly articulated in terms of peer pressure and peer review, such as that promoted by the OECD, brings to the fore the conceptualization and the pragmatic unfolding of the 'social' as a social artifact itself. That pragmatic unfolding poses analytical challenges to social scientific accounts of legal process, not least because it is an explicit and self-conscious effort to acknowledge and then harness the 'social' basis of law. While messy for theory, it is exemplary of the kind of 'practically oriented orders' involved in the continual redefinition and rearticulation of 'society' itself (Thrift 1996, 22).

Acknowledgements

I would like to thank the editors of this volume and participants in the 'Law and Governance' conference for their criticisms of earlier versions of this chapter. I would also like to thank Franz and Keebet von Benda-Beckmann for pushing me to think more about the implications of my argument for 'society'. Special thanks are due Tom Boellstorff, Stefan Helmreich and Gregory Rawlings for their detailed commentary. I would also like to thank Jeff Katcherian and Andrea Ballestero for helping me to think about soft law.

The material presented in this chapter is based on research supported by the National Science Foundation, Law and Social Sciences programme under grant no.

0516861. Any opinions, findings and conclusions or recommendations expressed in this material are those of the author, and do not necessarily reflect the views of the National Science Foundation.

References

Abbott, K. and Snidal, D. (2000), 'Hard and Soft Law in International Governance', *International Organization* 54(3): 401–19.

Barkun, M. (1968), *Law without Sanctions: Order in Primitive Societies and the World Community*, New Haven, CT: Yale University Press.

Biswas, R. (ed.) (2002), *International Tax Competition: Globalization and Fiscal Sovereignty*, London: Commonwealth Secretariat.

Búrca, G. de and Scott, J. (2006), 'Introduction: New Governance, Law and Constitutionalism', in G. de Búrca and J. Scott (eds), *Law and the New Governance in the EU and the US*, Oxford: Hart Publishing, pp. 1–12.

Callon, M. (1998), 'The Embeddedness of Economics Markets in Economics', in M. Callon (ed.), *The Laws of the Markets*, Oxford: Blackwell, pp. 1–57.

Cameron, A. (2006), 'Turning Point? The Volatile Geographies of Taxation', *Antipode* 38: 236–58.

Ciocca, P. (2006), 'Committee on Fiscal Affairs Releases Outcome of Review of Preferential Tax Regimes in OECD Countries', press release, Centre for Tax Policy and Administration, Organization for Economic Co-operation and Development, <www.oecd.org/document/31/0,3343,en_2649_34897_37446047_1_1_1_1,00.html>, accessed 30 January 2009.

Collier, S. and Ong, A. (2005), 'Global Assemblages, Anthropological Problems', in A. Ong and S. Collier (eds), *Global Assemblages: Technology, Politics, and Ethics as Anthropological Problems*, Oxford: Blackwell, pp. 3–21.

Eden, L. and Kudrle, R.T. (2005), 'Tax Havens: Renegade States in the International Tax Regime?', *Law and Policy* 27(1): 100–127.

Einhorn, R.L. (2006), *American Taxation, American Slavery*, Chicago, IL: University of Chicago Press.

Elyachar, J. (2006), 'Best Practices: Research, Finance and NGOs in Cairo', *American Ethnologist* 33(3): 413–26.

Evans-Pritchard, E.E. (1937), *Witchcraft, Oracles and Magic among the Azande*, Oxford: Oxford University Press.

Financial Action Task Force (2001), *Financial Action Task Force Annual Report on Money Laundering, 2000–2001*, Paris: FATF Secretariat.

Finnemore, M. and Toope, S.J. (2001), 'Alternatives to 'Legalization': Richer Views of Law and Politics', *International Organization* 55(3): 743–58.

Hay, R.J. (2006), 'OECD Level Playing Field Report Released: Consensus or Conflict?', *Tax Planning International Review* (June): 1–8.

Hoebel, E.A. (1954), *The Law of Primitive Man*, Cambridge, MA: Harvard University Press.

International Trade and Investment Organization (ITIO) (2003), 'It's Official: OECD Tax Project Depends on Level Playing Field', press release, <www.itio.org/NewPressReleases/PR23-10-03.htm>, accessed 30 January 2009.

—— (2007), 'Little Difference between Onshore and Offshore, New Analysis of OECD Data Reveals', press release, <www.itio.org/pdf/ITIO_press_release_1_May2007.pdf>, accessed 30 January 2009.

James, V.E. (2002), 'Twenty-first Century Pirates of the Caribbean: How the Organization for Economic Cooperation and Development Robbed Fourteen CARICOM Countries of their Tax and Economic Policy Sovereignty', *University of Miami Inter-American Law Review* 34(1): 1–62.

Kirton, J.J. and Trebilcock, M.J. (2004), 'Introduction: Hard Choices and Soft Law in Sustainable Global Governance', in J.J. Kirton and M.J. Trebilcock (eds), *Hard Choices, Soft Law: Voluntary Standards in Global Trade, Environment and Social Governance*, Aldershot: Ashgate, pp. 3–28.

Marcussen, M. (2004), 'OECD Governance through Soft Law', in U. Mörth (ed.), *Soft Law in Governance and Regulation: An Interdisciplinary Analysis*, Cheltenham: Edward Elgar, pp. 103–27.

Maurer, B. (2005), 'Due Diligence and "Reasonable Man" Offshore', *Cultural Anthropology* 20(4): 474–505.

—— (2007), 'Incalculable Payments: Money, Scale and the South African Offshore Grey Money Amnesty', *African Studies Review* 50(2): 125–38.

Merry, S. (1992), 'Anthropology, Law and Transnational Processes', *Annual Review of Anthropology* 21: 357–77.

—— (2006), 'Anthropology and International Law', *Annual Review of Anthropology* 35: 99–116.

Mörth, U. (2004), 'Introduction', in U. Mörth (ed.), *Soft Law in Governance and Regulation: An Interdisciplinary Analysis*, Cheltenham: Edward Elgar, pp. 1–9.

—— (2006), 'Soft Regulation and Global Democracy', in M.-L. Djelic and K. Sahlin-Andersson (eds), *Transnational Governance: Institutional Dynamics of Regulation*, Cambridge: Cambridge University Press, pp. 119–35.

OECD (1998), *Harmful Tax Competition: An Emerging Global Issue*, Paris: OECD.

—— (2003), *OECD Global Forum on Taxation, Ottawa, 14–15 October, Closing Statement by the Co-Chairs*, <www.oecd.org/document/0/0,2340,en_2649_201185_16643264_1_1_1_1,00.html>, accessed 30 January 2009.

—— (2006), 'List of Unco-operative Tax Havens', <www.oecd.org/document/57/0,3343,en_2649_33745_30578809_1_1_1_1,00.html>, accessed 30 January 2009

Oxfam (2000), Tax Havens: Releasing the Hidden Billions for Poverty Eradication, London: Oxfam.

Palan, R. (2003), *The Offshore World: Sovereign Markets, Virtual Places, and Nomad Millionaires*, Ithaca, NY: Cornell University Press.

Rawlings, G. (2005), 'Mobile People, Mobile Capital and Tax Neutrality: Sustaining a Market for Offshore Finance Centers', *Accounting Forum* 29: 289–310.

—— (2007), 'Taxes and Transnational Treaties: Responsive Regulation and the Reassertion of Offshore Sovereignty', *Law and Policy* 29(1): 51–66.

Rose, N., O'Malley, P. and Valverde, M. (2006), 'Governmentality', *Annual Review of Law and Social Science* 2: 83–104.

Sharman, J.C. (2006), *Havens in a Storm: The Struggle for Global Tax Regulation*, Ithaca, NY: Cornell University Press.

—— and Rawlings, G. (2005), *Deconstructing National Tax Blacklists: Removing Obstacles to Cross-border Trade in Financial Services. A Report for the Society of Trust and Estate Practitioners*, Sydney and Canberra: University of Sydney and the Australian National University.

Stoll-Davey, C. (2007), *Assessing the Playing Field: International Cooperation in Tax Information Exchange*, London: Commonwealth Secretariat.

Strathern, M. (2004), *Commons and Borderlands: Working Papers on Interdisciplinarity, Accountability, and the Flow of Knowledge*, Wantage: Sean Kingston Publishing.

Thrift, N. (1996), 'Shut up and Dance, or, is the World Economy Knowable?', in P.W. Daniels and W.F. Lever (eds), *The Global Economy in Transition*, Harlow: Longman, pp. 11–23.

Trubek, D. and Trubek, L. (2005), Hard and Soft Law in the Construction of Social Europe: The Role of the Open Method of Co-ordination', *European Law Journal* 11(3): 343–64.

——, Cottrell, P. and Nance, M. (2006), '"Soft Law" "Hard Law," and EU Integration', in G. de Búrca and J. Scott (eds), *Law and the New Governance in the EU and the US*, Oxford: Hart Publishing, pp. 65–94.

Webb, M.C. (2004), 'Defining the Boundaries of Legitimate State Practice: Norms, Transnational Actors and the OECD's Project on Harmful Tax Competition', *Review of International Political Economy* 11(4): 787–827.

Woodward, R. (2005), 'Offshore or "Shorn off"? The OECD's Harmful Tax Competition Initiative and Development in Small Island Economies', in G. Harrison (ed.), *Global Encounters: International Political Economy, Development, and Global Governance*, London: Palgrave Macmillan, pp. 195–212.

Chapter 11
The Law of the Project: Government and 'Good Governance' at the World Bank in Indonesia[1]

Tania Murray Li

Introduction

Transnational institutions such as the World Bank and the IMF are not supposed to meddle in the political affairs of creditor nations. Indeed, the Bank's charter forbids such meddling. The Bank is supposed to focus on economic matters such as growth and poverty reduction. As Bank experts have come to recognize that these economic goals cannot be achieved without 'good governance', the line between the political and economic has become blurred.[2] But there still is a line. The Bank cannot set the law for a sovereign nation. What it can do, however, is use the leverage of project funds to set conditions to encourage one course of action and discourage another. Such conditions operate at various scales. Nationally, IMF 'conditionalities' were imposed on debtor nations under the infamous structural adjustment programmes of the 1980s and 1990s. In principle – though not in practice – debtor nations had a choice: conform to the conditions of the loan, or decline the funds. At sub-national levels, Bank funds are channelled by means of projects directed to particular sectors represented by their line ministries (forestry, health), or to spatial units (provinces, districts, villages). In these arenas, the project 'target group' does have a choice. So too does the donor – it can select between candidates competing for project funds. In this situation, I argue, the donor can use project rules, or what some have called the 'law of the project', not

1 Parts of this chapter are reprinted, with permission, from *The Will to Improve: Governmentality, Development, and the Practice of Politics* (Duke University Press 2007); 'Social reproduction, situated politics, and *The Will to Improve*', *Focaal* 58 (2008), and 'Neo-liberal Strategies of Government through Community: The Social Development Program of the World Bank in Indonesia', *New York University IILJ* Working Paper 2006/2, Global Administrative Law Series. Funds to support research and writing were provided by the John D. and Catherine T. MacArthur Foundation Program on Global Security and Sustainability, and by Canada's Social Science and Humanities Research Council. Special thanks to Scott Guggenheim for being a thoughtful and engaged interlocutor.

2 F. von Benda-Beckmann (2006, 54); Rawski (2006, 921–2).

as a sovereign uses law, to secure conformity, but as a tactic to educate the desires and reform the practices of the target population. The funds serve as leverage to entice participation, but it is the project rules that take centre stage. By adhering to them, project planners expect participants to learn new and better ways of living, and make them their own.

It is the educative use of the 'law of the project' that I explore in this chapter.[3] My analysis draws on the concept Foucault called 'government' – a term he used in a specific sense. 'Government' refers to the attempt to shape human conduct by calculated means. Distinct from discipline, which seeks to reform designated groups through detailed supervision in confined quarters (prisons, asylums, schools), government is concerned with the welfare of the population at large. Its purpose is to secure 'the improvement of its condition, the increase of its wealth, longevity, health and so on' (Foucault 1991, 100). To achieve this purpose requires distinctive means. At the level of population, it is not possible to coerce every individual and regulate their actions in minute detail. Rather, government operates by educating desires and configuring habits, aspirations and beliefs. It acts on actions. It uses law, rules, incentives and other tactics to set conditions, 'artificially so arranging things so that people, following only their own self-interest, *will do as they ought*'.[4] Note that government in this sense is not the preserve of 'the government' or the state apparatus. Programmes of government are devised by transnational donors, NGOs and a host of other authorities. Nor does the term 'government' equate with governance or 'good governance' – the concern to make institutional regimes transparent and accountable. As it happens, 'good governance' is a central objective of the World Bank interventions I examine in this chapter, but not all governmental interventions have this goal. They are equally concerned with matters such as agriculture, public health and conservation.

Governmental interventions come in various forms, and can be more or less heavy-handed. In other work, I have traced continuities and shifts in governmental intervention in Indonesia from the colonial period to the present (Li 2007). In this chapter, I focus on the World Bank because it offers a striking example of government in a neoliberal or advanced-liberal form. Central to government under advanced liberalism, according to the sociologist Nikolas Rose, is an emphasis on choice. The subtext is game theory: assuming that actors are rational, the planner can devise conditions so that the actor will make the optimal choice – optimal, that is, in terms of the beneficial results the planner has prescribed. Setting choice in a framework of competition increases the leverage: not only will the actor who makes the wrong choice miss out on the promised benefits, others will receive them. Thus, competition and choice are keywords of advanced liberal government, to which is added a third, market, because the market is the operational manifestation of choice and competition. To govern in an advanced-liberal manner, Rose argues, is:

3 For background on the phrase 'law of the project', see F. von Benda-Beckmann (2006, 62).

4 Scott (1995, 202), citing the 'pre-eminent governmentalist' Jeremy Bentham.

> not a matter of 'freeing' an existing set of market relations from their social shackles, but of organizing all features of one's national policy to enable a market to exist, and to provide what it needs to function .... All aspects of *social* behavior are now reconceptualized along economic lines – as calculative actions undertaken through the universal faculty of choice. Choice is to be seen as dependent upon a relative assessment of costs and benefits of 'investment' in the light of environmental contingencies .... And the paths chosen by rational and enterprising individuals can be shaped by acting upon the external contingencies that are factored into calculations. (Rose 1999, 141–2)

My analysis explores how the Bank attempted to use the 'law of the project' to transform the conduct of the Indonesian state apparatus, and millions of Indonesian villagers conceived as members of communities. In the first section, I examine how the Bank used the opportunity presented by administrative decentralization to reform the conduct of senior officials. Then, I examine the billion-dollar sub-district development programme designed by the Bank's social development team to institute new practices of participation and accountability in village-level planning. In the following sections, I examine two extensions of the Bank's sub-district development program, one focused on changing the culture of corruption, the other focused on conflict management. In both cases, the social development team used project rules and incentives to guide behaviour in an 'improving' direction. The latter part of the chapter considers how the Bank's ambitious programme of social transformation worked out on the ground in some Sulawesi villages, where I have carried out long term ethnographic research. This section reveals the limits of the law of the project as a means to govern conduct. I end with a brief conclusion.

Reforming Indonesia in the Age of Decentralization

The 2001–2003 World Bank Country Assistance Strategy (CAS) for Indonesia was phrased in a very different language from the CAS of Suharto's New Order (1966–98). It explicitly engaged with the problem of governance, and discussed the many past and present failures of the ruling regime.[5] These were topics generally avoided in previous decades, when donors applauded Indonesia's steadily increasing Gross Domestic Product and improved health and education indicators, and turned a blind eye to regime-sponsored violence, corruption and authoritarian rule (Guggenheim 2004; Woodhouse 2005). The CAS discussed various causes of poverty. No longer was the focus on deficient farming techniques or the lack of infrastructure. Yet the CAS retained the key feature exposed by Ferguson (1994) in his study of development discourse as an 'anti-politics machine': critical scrutiny of relations

5 There was also frank recognition of corruption within Bank projects. See Guggenheim (2004).

of production and appropriation were still excluded from its analysis. The CAS only identified problems and deficiencies that could be rectified by technical interventions of the kind Bank experts might supply.

Governance, stated the CAS, was 'Indonesia's key medium-term development challenge' (World Bank 2001a, 6). Hence, it was governance that had to be rendered technical: parsed into its components (corruption, lack of accountability, transparency, rule of law), each of which could be rectified by expert design. To emphasize that the focus on governance was not an imposed, World Bank agenda, the CAS referred to development partners, including civil society organizations, who requested Bank support in this area (World Bank 2001a, i–ii, 17, 24). It thus constructed a discursive terrain which positioned the Bank not as a coercive force, laying down the law or dictating how people should live, but rather as a reservoir of expertise to assist indigenous reformers who had set their own agenda.

The techniques through which the Bank proposed to achieve good governance conformed rather closely to the governmental approach characteristic of advanced liberalism described above. Specifically, the CAS argued that good governance could best be promoted in a climate of competition that rewards performance. Indonesia's decentralization programme that went into effect in 2001 presented an opportunity for the Bank to insinuate calculation and choice at multiple spatial scales. In place of standardized national programmes evenly spread, a hallmark of the New Order, Indonesia's provinces, districts, sub-districts and villages would have to compete for Bank support. Bank experts designed the competition to direct conduct in quite specific ways. At the provincial level, the Bank would:

> seek to support reform-minded, pro-poor leaders and performing governments, through on-going supervision, project preparation, and sub-national dialogue. Selection criteria and a short-list of areas would be reviewed with the central government, to seek agreements on 2–4 provinces in which the Bank could initiate deeper engagement through consultations with local governments and civil society, and through provincial public expenditure reviews. (World Bank 2001a, 28)

To receive Bank support, in other words, candidate provinces must first demonstrate that they had absorbed appropriate values or, better still, had autonomously arrived at a position that was reform minded, and pro-poor. They must be 'performing', according to Bank standards. Selected provinces would then become eligible for a further intensity of World Bank expert supervision, including scrutiny of their accounts.

Why would a province's senior officials volunteer to submit to World Bank tutelage or, indeed, compete for the role of tutees? Access to Bank money was the 'external contingency' that enterprising leaders would learn to factor into their calculations. The CAS did not stress the persuasive power of cash, however, perhaps because money might complicate the idea that being 'pro-poor' is a characteristic of authentic leaders, a group needing only to be encouraged and supported by the Bank and other pro-poor reformers in collegial partnerships. It hints at bad faith, dancing to the donor's tune. Through the CAS, the experts implied, the Bank sought merely to strengthen the indigenous virtues of responsibility and accountability already present in embryonic form.

The attempt to foster competition between provinces, restated and intensified in the 2004–2007 CAS, was in tension with the Bank's 'overarching goal … to reduce poverty and vulnerability' (World Bank 2001a, ii). It was markedly at odds with the rights-based approach to development strongly advocated by the UNDP in the same period, which argued for higher public spending to meet the health, education and other basic needs of the poor, with a focus on the poorest provinces.[6] Caught in this contradiction, the Bank could not support only a few 'performing' provinces. In the CAS, neoliberalism and poverty reduction were brought into alignment by deflecting responsibility downwards. Through its 'community-driven development' programmes, the World Bank would 'empower communities so that poor everywhere have an opportunity', even if they happened to live in districts or provinces where authorities were 'reluctant to undertake reform'.[7] What was proposed in this neoliberal vision was equal opportunity to compete for funds, not equality of outcomes. Moreover, access to this opportunity required conforming to strict conditions.

Social Development and the By-pass Model

Empowering communities fell within the remit of the Bank's social development team. Before the CAS was written, the team had been carrying out studies of social capital in Indonesian villages, and had devised a programme that would give 'teeth to the reform agenda laid out in the CAS and Indonesia's decentralization program by turning broad principle into a program of action' (World Bank 2001a, 3). This was the Kecamatan ('Sub-district') Development Programme (KDP). It was ambitious on several fronts. First, the team intended from the outset that the KDP would serve as both a programme of action and a policy argument. They would use '"facts on the ground" to show that properly designed community empowerment programs lead to higher returns, greater benefits for the poor, and more sustainable outcomes' (World Bank 2001b, 5). They would demonstrate how

6 BPS, BAPPENAS and UNDP (2004).

7 World Bank (2001a, 28, 26). The role of the social development programme in ensuring access to 'development' in the context of Bank-enforced competition and 'selectivity' was further emphasized in the subsequent CAS (World Bank 2004a, 28). A Bank study of decentralization recommended a role for the central government in defining standards that lower levels of government must meet, pushing responsibility downwards (World Bank 2003a,). The proposition that properly designed decentralization would make political and administrative elites more accountable, rather than intensify the authoritarian tendencies of 'predatory networks of patronage', is critically examined by Hadiz (2004).

to do development better – a demonstration aimed both at the development industry, including the Bank, and at the Indonesian bureaucracy. Second, the scope of their transformatory ambition was extraordinary. They did not set out to transform one or other delinquent sector of society (farmers, the poor and so on), but society itself. As one expert put it, the goal was to 'get the social relations right'.[8] Third, the KDP was unprecedented in its scale: no previous community development programme had become so large so fast. In Phases 1 and 2 (1998–2003), the KDP was implemented in tens of thousands of villages across the archipelago: one in three. With its offshoots, it absorbed US$1 billion of loan funds. It accounted for more than half World Bank lending to Indonesia in 2001–2003.[9] Finally, the KDP was ambitious in the extent to which it took over the entire process of project delivery, completely by-passing the national planning and disbursement systems, substituting its own rules and the labour of up to 4,200 consultants supplied through private-sector contracts. These consultants, almost all of them Indonesian, operated as a loyal, parallel bureaucracy, answerable to the Bank and the KDP's official sponsor, the Central Planning Agency.

The by-pass strategy seems counter-intuitive. In a programme that aimed to have an educative effect, why by-pass the officials whose conduct needed to be reformed? Explaining the reasons for the by-pass strategy, the project designers argued that they needed space to demonstrate the effectiveness of their approach. In the early phases, 'KDP did not allow local governments to meddle much in the project. The risks of misguided government takeovers were too high' (Guggenheim et al. 2004, 2). Further, they argued that contract workers were more flexible, and could be hired without inflating the civil service payroll (Guggenheim et al. 2004, 9). Not until Phase 3 of the KDP (2005–2008), after the virtues of its approach had been confirmed, did the social development team attempt to integrate KDP delivery and normalize its rules as part of the regular legal and administrative system (World Bank 2003b). Although reform of the state apparatus was one of the KDP's long-term goals, its principal point of intervention was tens of thousands of rural 'communities'. These communities had, the team argued, natural capacities for self-management – a social capital that was damaged by the military-dominated regime of the New Order, but was still present and could be restored. KDP would set the conditions for this natural capacity to re-emerge by empowering communities to plan their own projects and manage conflicts. Then, through the force of popular demand, they would reform the state apparatus from below.

The template for the KDP was simple. It provided block grants of US$60,000–110,000 to sub-districts, where an elected committee comprising a man and a woman from each village adjudicated between competing proposals prepared by

8 This expression appeared in Woolcock (1998, 187).

9 Guggenheim (2004, 2, 8). Further phases and offshoots of the programme were scheduled to receive 25 per cent of all World Bank lending to Indonesia in the period 2004–2007, and were a cornerstone of the Country Assistance Strategy (World Bank 2004a, ii).

villagers. The menu was open, but most of the proposals were for infrastructure projects (local roads, water, irrigation) or for small enterprise credit.[10] The KDP team insisted on competition as a means to reward performance: The villages with the best 'pro-poor' proposals would win. Villagers had a choice: they could elect to join the competition, and play by the rules, or they could stay away. As the social development team stressed, the innovations of the KDP lay not in its activities, rural infrastructure and credit, which were conventional, but in the mechanisms of project planning and delivery. Indeed, one observer who studied the project in 2002 concluded that the objective of raising rural incomes had actually been dropped, due to the difficulty of measurement and 'the primacy of the overarching objective – creating participatory institutions and processes'.[11]

Every technical feature of the KDP was designed for a transformative purpose. Project funds were to serve as leverage. In order to access these funds, villagers had to subscribe to a very detailed set of rules that obliged them to form committees, hold consultations, and interact with each other in new forums and new ways (World Bank 2001b, 3). They were required, for example, to post notices of meetings in public places for a set number of days – reversing the usual practice in which plans were made and deals done in private. A meeting could not proceed without a representative from each of the outlying hamlets – a measure to prevent capture of the project by the elite families that typically reside in the village centre, to the exclusion of the poor. The budget for approved projects had to be posted publicly and itemized, so that everyone would know where the money went. The rules were elaborated in manuals, checklists, information sheets and other documents. They were also presented verbally and reiterated constantly by the army of consultants and facilitators hired by the project to work at village or sub-district level, and by selected residents – a man and a woman from each village – who received training and stipends for their work on project implementation.[12]

There was a rather obvious tension between the KDP's claim to be building on the social capital naturally present in Indonesian communities, and the detailed specification of nationally standardized KDP rules. Indeed, requirements for elections by secret ballot, decisions by vote, and gender equity were deliberate reversals of customary practices in many parts of the archipelago. As the project's chief architect, Scott Guggenheim, observed: 'KDP could not function without its operational manual, disbursement system, poverty targeting criteria, and innumerable "coordination teams" …. KDP villages 20 kilometres from Jakarta use the same formats, planning cycle, and facilitator structure that villages in the jungles of Papua do' (Guggenheim 2004, 38). How, then, did the KDP claim to support 'local forms of organizing' and 'local adaptation and ownership?'

10 Block grants had been used before, under the New Order and during the 1997–98 crisis, but without such tight control (Guggenheim 2004).

11 Edstrom (2002, 2). Guggenheim et al. (2004, 6) still listed poverty alleviation as the KDP's prime objective.

12 World Bank (2001b, 13); Guggenheim et al. (2004, 9); Woodhouse (2005).

(Guggenheim 2004, 39, 40). The claim came down to the way the KDP granted villagers responsibility and choice *within* the project framework.

The KDP's rules were designed for their educative effect. They would reform practices and desires. Neither the ends they sought to achieve nor the means were up for debate. The social development team argued that the KDP's detailed rules and constant monitoring were necessary because of the complexity of the social terrain they aimed to transform. Their ethnographic studies showed that villages had the potential 'to become self-managing actors in development programs', but warned against overly romantic assessments: 'Most villages are not egalitarian, harmonious units, but conflictive and highly stratified entities with internal problems of exclusion, corruption, and conflict of their own.' In view of the high risk of elite capture, procedures must be designed to prevent it. The KDP set out to correct the deficiencies of past projects that 'simply "gave" resources to villages with no planning structure for negotiating through these problems' and watched 'their funds slip through village fingers with little return for the investment' (World Bank 2001b, 4–5).

Techniques for Corruption Reduction

The anti-corruption strategy of the KDP was not an add-on; it was integral to the objective of the project (Woodhouse 2005, 1). Every step in the project process was designed to prevent corruption within the project, and to establish new habits that would carry over into other arenas. The anti-corruption strategy occupied a seven-page annex in the KDP Phase 2 project appraisal document (World Bank 2001b). Corruption was also the subject of special ethnographic studies, case reports and experiments. Corruption was rendered technical, parsed into components for remedial intervention as the KDP design team set out to 'chip away at the fortresses of monopoly power and impunity' (World Bank 2002b, 54).

Three approaches to corruption reduction can be discerned in the KDP. The first was to design the project to maximize transparency. The block grant funds were sent directly to a bank account in the sub-district, cutting out the many layers of bureaucracy through which 'leakage' normally occurred (World Bank 2002b, 15). The amount of funding available was publicized. Once a proposal was accepted, villagers had to monitor to ensure that contracts for construction were awarded competitively and materials met quality specifications. Transparency rules required project implementers at the village level to hold open public meetings to account for how the money was spent, and to answer questions (World Bank 2002b, 54). There was a complaints procedure to handle breaches of the project rules. The Bank contracted independent NGOs and journalists to monitor the project, and publicize its successes and failures. Their job was to draw attention to cases of corruption, and to the efforts of villagers to get corrupt individuals convicted (Guggenheim 2004, 7). Sanctions were built into the project cycle, well publicized, and followed through. Corrupt facilitators were fired, some officials went to jail, and 'non-performing' sub-districts were cut from the programme (Woodhouse 2005, 18).

The second approach to corruption treated it as a problem of culture. The Bank's ethnographic studies and case reports showed that corruption was accepted as normal. Funds were routinely siphoned off as a reward for public office (Evers 2001, 15–16; World Bank 2004b). Villagers were driven to complain only when they deemed the balance inappropriate – when too much money was extracted from a project budget, and not enough shared with other claimants. When corrupt parties were confronted, KDP studies showed that villagers were mainly interested in having the money returned so the project could be completed. They were not interested in prosecution or other forms of punishment (Evers 2001, 14). To the KDP design team, the finding that corruption was accepted by villagers flagged a problem in need of correction. They argued that this cultural norm was not authentic – it had emerged historically in the distorted context of the New Order, when development assistance was understood as a gift. Villagers were told they should be grateful for gifts, however small, and not ask too many questions (World Bank 2002b, 52). To restore traditions of accountability that were still present, though weak, the design team proposed that KDP village facilitators should engage in moral argument, explaining to villagers why corruption should not be tolerated. KDP researchers should also identify 'key opinion makers, channels of information, and the forums where communities discuss among themselves local forms of anti-corruption action' (Guggenheim 2002, 4). Once these opinion makers, channels and forums were identified, the team thought they could be optimized to achieve the results – transparency, empowerment – desired not only by outsiders, but also by villagers who were already engaged in 'anti-corruption action' of their own. Further, the team proposed to use ethnographic 'thick description' of corruption cases to reveal how social norms entered into incentive structures (Woodhouse 2005, 6).

The third approach to corruption in the KDP was to work directly and minutely upon the incentive structure. This approach treated corruption as a rational response to a given set of incentives and disincentives. It would occur wherever the benefits of corruption outweighed the costs, or, from the victims' perspective, the costs of protest outweighed the benefits. In this spirit, a Bank researcher analysed the cost benefit equations for each step of the KDP process for the different parties involved. Based on the findings, the researcher proposed adjustments to the reward structure to close loopholes, increase the risks and reduce the benefits from corrupt behaviour to the point where such behaviour would no longer be rational (Woodhouse 2005, 35–9).

The KDP team also worked on changing the cost–benefit equation from the perspective of the victims. Their studies showed that the victims of corruption often had quite complete knowledge about how, when and by whom project resources were stolen, but the costs of protest were too high for them to use the information. Costs included harassment or intimidation by the perpetrators or by police and other officials; being accused of giving the village a bad name, reducing prospects of receiving development funds in future; the cost of transportation to make repeated visits to the city to present information to the police and prosecutors, and time and energy spent in a legal process that few believed would produce any result. To change this equation, the team experimented with the use of informal or customary settlement procedures, which they thought might be more effective and less costly for the complainant, both socially and financially (Evers 2001; Woodhouse 2005). Researchers also documented cases where 'poor people have been able to use the justice system successfully to defend their interests and rights'. From this analysis, they identified the enabling conditions for successful village action, and devised schemes to replicate them (World Bank 2002a, 4; 2004b). The KDP also piloted a programme of legal assistance to support village groups wishing to take a corruption case to court. In its usual comprehensive fashion, the team set rules for legal aid lawyers, who should be volunteers committed to public service, not individuals seeking private gain. They should abide by 'rules of the game', which included breaking from the customary practice of paying off judges (Evers 2001, 5-8).

Conflict Management

Initiatives in conflict management developed as an extension of the KDP. Just as the team had parsed the problems of participation and corruption, the team parsed conflict into its components – its triggers and pathways – in order to identify points of intervention. They identified existing social capital and local mechanisms for dispute resolution that could be supported, enhanced and replicated. They studied innovative approaches that villagers had devised for themselves. As with the KDP more generally, the assumption was that communities already held the secrets to overcoming violence (and poverty, for that matter), but they needed Bank assistance to recover virtuous habits and practices damaged by the New Order.

The team argued that communities were previously less prone to conflict, because customary norms were agreed, rules were enforced, and there were respected leaders capable of mediation.[13] These conditions no longer existed, due to the mixture of populations and attenuation of custom brought about by migration, and by the New Order's deliberate displacement of customary institutions in favour of standardized, national ones. Yet the New Order's standardized national institutions had not taken hold. There was no functioning, impartial justice system (police, courts) to which aggrieved parties could turn. The result, the studies found, was confusion. There were formal and informal rule systems that overlapped and conflicted. Rules were interpreted differently, poorly enforced and easily manipulated.

13 Smith (2005) describes past customary regimes in Kalimantan in these terms. Madden and Barron (2004, 67) describe the attenuated mediation skills of villagers.

For the Bank experts, confusion about rules emerged as a significant cause of conflict. The solution they proposed was to craft coherent rules to restore what was naturally present, and supply something new to meet the needs of the time. Local knowledge and practice should be nurtured, the experts argued, but also adjusted through the 'application of general democratic principles of conduct' (Smith 2005, 45). 'Outside technocrats' should not be the ones to determine new rules or resolve disputes. Instead, 'spaces, incentives, and resources need to be created and sustained by a range of actors that make it possible for disputants to craft resolutions that all sides can own, uphold and enforce' (Barron, Smith and Woolcock 2004, 33). The role of the Bank would be to supply the 'mediating institutions' and the 'meta-rules', or at least the 'minimum standards' for meta-rules that villagers would craft within the space the Bank's programme would provide (Barron, Smith and Woolcock 2004, 34). The initiative to alter patterns of conduct, the experts stressed, must come from below. All parties must uphold agreements and be accountable for their actions (Barron, Smith and Woolcock 2004, 36, 37). In social life, as in the marketplace, the experts insisted, only good performance should reap rewards.

In tension with the stress on initiative from below, the team proposed to use material incentives as leverage to 'encourage different communities to participate in the process and agree to certain baseline rules' – minimally, the outlawing of violence as a way of solving problems (Barron, Smith and Woolcock 2004, 35). The proposed incentive package was the standard KDP fund for small infrastructure projects. Of equal value, according the team, was the KDP process, which provided 'relatively neutral inter-group forums within which villagers are potentially … able to more peacefully mediate conflicts of certain types'.[14] The proposition, in short, was that hostile groups would choose to set aside their differences because they wanted access to resources such as new roads and bridges that they could only obtain if they agreed to abide by Bank rules. Yet Bank-supplied incentives would only add weight to the protagonists' own cost–benefit analysis. Rational actors would desire to stop fighting when the costs of conflict outweighed the benefits (Tajima 2004). At that point, all that was needed was the appropriate mechanism. Once they experienced the benefits of peace, the cost of conflict would no longer seem acceptable.

Grafting conflict resolution onto the KDP had risks, as Bank experts acknowledged. Competition between groups over scarce resources was the source of many conflicts, yet they proposed to use more competition – well-crafted, managed and 'facilitated' competition – as the solution.[15] Nevertheless, the chain of reasoning linking diagnosis to remedy was persuasive enough for the team's proposals to be turned into a project funded with millions of dollars in loans. The

14 Barron, Smith, and Woolcock (2004, 34). See also Smith (2005, 48–50).

15 The risks are described in Smith (2005); Tajima (2004, 29). Bank social experts planned a controlled study of the risks and benefits of using KDP-style mechanisms for conflict management (Barron et al. 2004).

Bank approved the Support for Poor and Disadvantaged Areas Project (SPADA) running from 2005 to 2010 with a loan of US$104 million. SPADA aimed to help break the conflict cycle by improving relations between groups, engaging villagers in KDP-style participatory planning, and providing incentives to co-operate (World Bank 2005c, 3). Although the design team recognized that feelings of social injustice were widespread in the Indonesian countryside, they had no proposal to transform the material roots of those feelings. Rather, participation in SPADA would transform the feelings themselves, replacing them with feelings of trust, co-operation, (healthy) competition, and empowerment. Monitoring in SPADA would include the use of 'tracer methodologies' to track the effects of training interventions on 'changes in knowledge, attitude, and performance at periodic intervals'. Household surveys would evaluate impacts on social capital and attitudes towards conflict and violence, together with economic and other indicators (World Bank 2005c, 31). As with the KDP more generally, the project rules were designed to instil new practices and beliefs – a transformation far more significant than the dispersal of funds.

Project Law and its Limits

The social development team's interventions in Indonesia were unabashedly governmental. They set conditions to reform not just the practices, but the desires and beliefs of their target population. In terms of reformed desires, the KDP claimed some evidence of success, as villagers started to demand efficiency, effectiveness and accountability from the state apparatus, augmenting transformation through what the team called a 'multiplier effect' (World Bank 2002b, 9; Guggenheim 2004, 33).

As a quantitative measure of uptake, KDP planners anticipated that project procedures which had proven effective would be packaged and sold. The goal – becoming a reality by Phase 3 – was for the KDP to become a 'Golden Arches' or 'franchise' model, in which 'participating districts would "buy" the rule book and staff training/management procedures … with the project funding the full cost of the technical assistance, but a decreasing share of the Kecamatan grants'.[16] There was uptake across borders too, as the programme pioneered in Indonesia was declared 'best practice' and replicated. By 2005, there were clones of the KDP in the Philippines, Timor Leste and Afghanistan (Guggenheim et al. 2004, 4).

Reactions to the KDP from the Indonesian state apparatus, and its willingness to take on US$1 billion of debt to finance the project, suggest that the KDP offered them something of value. Although the by-pass model caused some officials to

16 World Bank (2001b, 20). In 2004, 40 per cent of districts opted to provide matching grant funds to the KDP. The team proposed to make matching contributions from districts a requirement for those districts to retain access to KDP funds after an initial three-year period (Guggenheim et al. 2004, 12; 16).

avoid involvement in the KDP because it cut them out from their customary share of project resources, others reportedly welcomed it (Evers 2001, 10). Supporters claimed to recognize the virtues of the participatory, bottom-up process, and wanted to replicate it (World Bank 2002b, 40–42). Perhaps the officials who spoke in these terms knew how to please the donor. Perhaps the KDP provided sufficient benefits for officials to offset the frustration of lost income. Villagers who received high-quality infrastructure projects that met their needs were a satisfied constituency.

In the early years of post-Suharto reform, the repeated failure of state-sponsored development projects was a problem for administrators and politicians alike. Their job security depended upon being able to lay claim to at least some success, especially success of the measurable, visible kind KDP-funded roads and bridges provided. Despite its by-pass procedures, the KDP was still a project of the government of Indonesia, one which strengthened the claim of the regime to govern in the interest of the people and promote their wellbeing. Further, as explained earlier, donors operating in a decentralized environment could choose their 'partners', cutting off troubled or 'non-performing' provinces, districts and sub-districts. Officials who co-operated with the consultants hired to deliver the KDP acted within a field of constraints and opportunities that had been structured to guide their actions in calculated ways. Nevertheless, the social development team was all too aware of the fragility of its interventions. Once the incentives and the massive monitoring apparatus of the KDP is dismantled, 'it remains an open question', KDP architect Scott Guggenheim observed, whether reformed village and sub-district councils 'can avoid slipping back into the authoritarian traditions of rural politics' (Guggenheim 2004, 33).

To monitor the effects of its programme, the KDP team continued to engage in ethnographic research in various sites across the archipelago. The programme is so vast, and conditions so varied, that many studies will be needed to discover the range of outcomes, both in the short run and over time, as processes stimulated by the programme shift and evolve. Here I can offer some observations from one of my field sites in Central Sulawesi, which I revisited for two months in 2006, following up on field research I conducted intermittently throughout the 1990s.

Since my last visit in 1998, not only had the KDP arrived, there had been other transformations, notably the end of the Suharto regime, administrative decentralization giving more authority to the districts, and intensified interest in the rugged, mountainous interior of the peninsula where indigenous farmers, migrants and regional elites scrambled to profit from the arrival of new commercial tree crops, especially cacao. The visit gave me the opportunity to see what difference the KDP had made in village-level planning, something I had observed quite closely throughout the 1990s, and to situate the KDP in relation to broader shifts in social forces, including the emergence of landlessness and a new landlord class in the hills.

My first indication of a shift was a meeting with the district head, at which he talked enthusiastically about the new focus of government on improving the lives of the poor living in the hills, who had been sorely neglected during the previous era. His narrative had a patriotic twist: it was shameful, he said, that six decades after independence the people of the hills were still living in a primitive state, without roads or access to education. The last time I talked to a district head, neglected highlanders were nowhere on his horizon. So this was different. To solve the problem, he was determined to build roads into the hills, combining funds from the KDP with routine budget allocations. I described to him the results of my studies about the link between road-building, the arrival of outsiders and the rapid dispossession of highlanders, who retreated further into the hills – away from the schools and the road intended to help them. He acknowledged the problem: 'I gather them together and I tell them,' he said, 'don't sell your land.' In his vision, wise words from a paternalistic politician would be enough to stop dispossession in its tracks.

The sub-district and village heads I spoke to next echoed the district head's concern for the poor, and his enthusiasm for the road-building programme. The material incentives are easy to spot: access to the hills would give them the opportunity to play broker, allocating land to outsiders as well as expanding their own landholdings. But according to KDP rules, government officials and their allies in the regional economic elite are not the people who decide on the use of project funds. As I explained earlier, plans are the result of a carefully managed consultation process in which every hamlet, even the most distant and marginal, *must* participate. If they are absent, a planning meeting cannot proceed. The KDP facilitator – a paid consultant from outside the local government apparatus – is charged with ensuring that these rules are followed, and applying sanctions if they are not. So I went along with one of the facilitators when she was working in a hill area I know quite well, to see how this worked out in practice.

Faithful to KDP principles, the facilitator insisted that the planning meeting to initiate a new project cycle should be held in the hills, or at least as far into the hills as she and her team could go without walking – at the end of the new road, built in the previous year's KDP project cycle. When our group arrived on the back of a small fleet of motorbike-taxis, a few people had gathered, but not the crowd the facilitator expected or required if she was to proceed. After waiting a couple of hours, she called on a sub-district official who was serving as interpreter to ask if a representative of each of the hamlets was present. There was an awkward pause. The official called off the numbers – hamlets 1–12 – asking if a representative was present. Different voices from the crowd responded with vague shouts that could be taken as affirmative. Since she did not know the village and could not speak the local language, she was not in a position to verify. I later confirmed that no one from the more distant hamlets was present at the meeting. In conversations with me over the following week, they described their exclusion in terms of a barrier that blocks information and resources in the path. They also described the 'crocodiles' who guard the path, to make sure this situation does not change. The KDP has rules to prevent this – an elaborate system to prevent elite capture. Yet the carefully crafted control system was defeated by the pragmatics of a long, hot, tiring day, the likelihood that the crowd would dissipate because they had no lunch, and the facilitator's need to keep to a rigorous schedule for programme delivery, report writing and audit. So she ticked the box, and moved along.

The first activity on the meeting agenda was to elect the villagers who would lead the consultation process. Candidates were proposed, and the illiterate crowd placed paper ballots in containers. It turned out that the person handing out the ballots had signalled to the voters that the correct answer was number 3. Number 3 was duly elected. There were grumbles about that too, as I learned in subsequent conversations, as number 3 was a person the highlanders did not trust. Caught in webs of debt and dependence with the village elite who live on the coast, and ashamed at their inability to speak Indonesian in front of high-status outsiders, they had been intimidated. Later, they regretted that they had not had the courage to speak out. As the meeting rolled along, the official/interpreter talked about the opportunity provided by KDP funds to extend the new road further into the hills, and to build a bridge connecting the hamlets on the other side of the river. The facilitator, through the same interpreter, emphasized that they – the people – would decide about the use of the funds, through a consultation process that would involve many meetings over many months. But the highlanders had already got the message – the correct answer was the road and the bridge. So they did not see much point in meetings.

Even if the highlanders had discussed their preferred uses for KDP funds in their hamlets, the outcome might have been the same. The better-off highland farmers would opt for the road, because roads enable them to get their cacao down to the market by motorbike instead of by paying porters. The poorer highlanders, who work as porters, would be silent or absent from the planning meetings. Portering is the most lucrative income-earning opportunity for the new landless class in the hills, those who have sold their land to neighbours who have been more successful at establishing and extending productive commercial farms. It is back-breaking work. The teenage son of a widow I knew well died of a haemorrhage as he forced himself to carry excessive loads. When I discussed with landowners what would happen to the porters when the road arrived, they had no comment. As I noted earlier, the KDP's designers understood very well that there is little natural solidarity in Indonesia's villages. Yet they still believed they could intervene on the side of the poor simply by insisting on procedures for including their voices, and their choices, in the proceedings. In this case, not only have the benefits of voice failed to materialize or to result in poverty-reducing shifts in power, the processes of poverty-production have actually intensified. Coastal elites have moved in wherever new roads are planned, buying up or simply laying claim to the land, and holding it for speculation. Meanwhile, the poor still walk along the old footpaths that follow the riverbeds, since these are shorter and not as hot as the new roads. They cannot afford to use the motorbike-taxis. Thus, the KDP's micro-managed planning process did not alter the social forces that perpetuate inequality and inadvertently supported them.

In another case I tracked in a different village, highlanders mobilized to protest against corruption, in just the way KDP planners promoting village empowerment intended. Armed with crucial information, namely the amount of money allocated for building a road to their hamlet, they monitored closely. They interviewed the driver of the bulldozer hired to do the work, and found out the cost per day for the machine and his labour. They calculated that the budget was more than sufficient for the road to reach their hamlet. Instead, it stopped about half way. The village headman told the highlanders the money was insufficient, but because of KDP's transparency rules, the highlanders knew precisely how much had been stolen from them, and they were furious. Learning that the district head was to visit the highlands, a group of men, some of them clutching blowpipes, waited where the road ends to present their grievance. Unsurprisingly, although they waited all day, the district head did not arrive. Their protests to the village head and the sub-district head fell on deaf ears, and the highlanders' assumption was that they had all been paid off. So the highlanders had information and they united to take action, but they still had no means of redress. The KDP's attempts to increase villagers' access to the means of holding corrupt officials to account have yet to reach this corner of Sulawesi, where powers are entrenched and project rules easily circumvented. This particular road-building project, although it used the KDP rulebook, was one of the new-generation 'indigenized' versions of KDP that no longer use facilitators hired directly by the Bank, but return control of the project process to bureaucrats who are presumed to have learned – and to desire – new and improved ways.

How reformed is the bureaucracy in this area? Sub-district officials I knew from the 1990s acknowledged that the KDP was much tighter than the old system – there were far fewer opportunities to steal funds. As they pointed out to me, this gave them less incentive to be involved, and it also made them impatient with endless meetings to elicit the planning priorities of backward highlanders in distant hamlets. The aspect of the project they and the villagers appreciated least was the KDP proposal procedure that sets hamlets and villages in competition with each other over project funds. Although the criterion for selection was supposed to favour proposals that were most convincingly 'pro-poor', comparing the list of KDP projects in the sub-district with my knowledge of patterns of poverty did not convince me that this process was working, and no one else with whom I discussed the matter thought it was either. All too obviously, equal opportunity to compete did not produce equitable results. Overall, my conclusion was that neither the KDP nor the 'reform' movement that removed Suharto from power, nor the two together, had been able to engineer a shift in social forces sufficient to reorientate planning towards the poor in this part of Sulawesi. Such a shift may still emerge, and irate highlanders scrutinizing a project budget and uniting to protest are possibly an advance sign of it, but the counter-forces are still formidable.

The limit of the 'law of the project' as a vehicle for social transformation under 'normal' conditions might explain why the Bank's social development experts have been strongly attracted to post-conflict and post-disaster situations. In these situations, experts can imagine building upon a clean slate, not just physically but socially – constructing a new society in which the delinquent structures of the old order would not intrude. Under the label 'Community-Driven Reconstruction', Bank experts devised strategies explicitly designed to take advantage of vacuums in state capacity in order to instil new practices that, in normal times, officials might oppose. They envisaged an 'opportunity to re-define the social and institutional relationships that led to the conflict in the first place' (Cliffe, Guggenheim and Kostner 2003, 1). They planned to use the incentive of access to Bank funds as leverage to reform, or indeed to constitute, 'communities', and to reform a weakened state apparatus that needed rapid and tangible reconstruction to establish its credibility. Under disaster conditions, they reasoned, ruling regimes lose their capacity to dictate the terms of donor assistance, enabling experts to rebuild society according to their own prescriptions.[17] Yet the experts recognized a limit to this approach: when a project is designed as 'an island of integrity outside state structures, there is a risk of low government ownership undermining sustainability in the long term' (Cliffe, Guggenheim and Kostner 2003, 20). In Aceh after the tsunami, where the KDP was one of the primary vehicles for aid delivery, I was struck by a passage in a World Bank bulletin: 'Don't forget the Government.'[18]

Conclusion

The World Bank in Indonesia has devised a massive programme to reform conduct. Its mode of operation is governmental. It sets out to reshape desires and set conditions in which the targets of reform will find it in their interest to configure their practices in an 'improving' direction. It uses the 'law of the project' not in the way a sovereign uses law – as a means to secure the authority of the sovereign – but rather relies on project rules as tactics to transform the behaviour of subjects who retain the freedom to choose. As I have demonstrated, freedom is not the converse of government, it is its instrument. Choice is a keyword of governmentality in its advanced liberal mode. When the Bank social experts designed their interventions, they had very specific objectives in mind: they would make decentralized provincial and district governments accountable and 'pro-poor'; they would alleviate poverty; they would restore the natural capacities and

17 The approach is described in Cliffe, Guggenheim and Kostner (2003). The Bank duly noted that its activities in conflict zones might be opposed on 'nationalist' grounds (World Bank 2005c, 41).

18 World Bank (2005b, 4). Rawski (2006) examines the use of KDP-type mechanisms in Timor Leste, where the Bank team imagined a clean slate, but its interventions were opposed on two fronts: by the resilience of the patriarchal, clan-based loyalties and aristocratic privileges that continued to shape local relations of rule, and by the UN-mandated transitional government authority that was convinced it alone had responsibility for defining the new institutional structure and legal regime, while the Bank was merely supposed to deliver a poverty alleviation project. In Afghanistan, the KDP concept of an elected sub-district body responsible for planning and disbursement not only became law – it was enshrined in the post-invasion constitution.

social capital of Indonesian villagers, and they would use villagers' experience of the benefits of efficient and transparent planning to reform the state apparatus by pressure from below.

The desirability of the ends sought by the Bank's social development programmes was simple common sense: who would not prefer a well-built bridge to one built with inferior materials, washed away at the first flood? Which villagers would prefer to remain ignorant about what happens to budget lines designated for the poor when given the opportunity to hold authorities accountable? Wasn't it reasonable to reward performance? Shouldn't rules be clearly laid out and followed? Even if the social experiment were to fail, the KDP was efficient: Village infrastructure built under KDP rules cost 23 per cent less than equivalent infrastructure built through the routine planning mechanisms (World Bank 2001b, 6; 2002b, 6–8, 20–21).

Putting the questions this way, within the logic of the programme, I would be among those offering applause. Yet the benevolence of a programme does not excise the element of power. Even when they set out to learn from the best practices of Indonesian villagers, members of the World Bank team positioned themselves as experts who knew what was wrong with Indonesian society and how to correct it. They envisaged a two-step process in which project incentives would be used to create the conditions in which actors would adhere to the 'law of the project'. Later, they would adopt project rules as their own, absorbing them into their everyday practices, their common sense. Without engaging in an explicit debate on the matter, they would come to understand justice as a matter of distinguishing the legal from the illegal, the accountable from the corrupt, the plan that was 'pro-poor' from a plan that would benefit the rich, and the deserving poor from those whose failure to perform made them ineligible for assistance. They would govern themselves according to a framework in which competition, choice and the transformation of social relations into a vast cost–benefit equation governed by transparent 'rules of the game' were the optimal arrangements. My approach in this chapter, drawing from Foucault, examines the 'law of the project' in a critical light that does not revolve around good versus bad intentions, or good versus bad outcomes, but focuses, rather, on understanding the kind of power exercised by experts who set out to transform society by design.

References

Barron, P., Diprose, R., Madden, D., Smith, C. and Woolcock, M. (2004), *Do Participatory Development Projects Help Villagers Manage Local Conflicts? A Mixed Methods Approach to Assessing the Kecamatan Development Project, Indonesia*, Washington, DC: World Bank.

——, Smith, C. and Woolcock, M. (2004), *Understanding Local Level Conflict Pathways in Developing Countries: Theory, Evidence and Implications from*

Indonesia, Social Development Papers, Conflict Prevention and Reconstruction 19, Washington, DC: World Bank.

Benda-Beckmann, F. von (2006), 'The Multiple Edges of Law: Dealing with Legal Pluralism in Development Practice', in World Bank (ed.), *The World Bank Legal Review: Law, Equity, and Development*, Washington, DC: World Bank, pp. 51–86.

BPS, BAPPENAS and UNDP (2004), *The Economics of Democracy: Financing Human Development in Indonesia*, Jakarta: BPS, BAPPENAS, UNDP.

Cliffe, S., Guggenheim, S. and Kostner, M. (2003), *Community-driven Reconstruction as an Instrument in War-to-Peace Transitions*, Social Development Papers, Conflict Prevention and Reconstruction 7, Washington, DC: World Bank.

Edstrom, J. (2002), *Indonesia's Kecamatan Development Project. Is it Replicable? Design Considerations in Community Driven Development*, Social Development Paper 39, Washington, DC: World Bank.

Evers, P. (2001), *Legal Assistance Program for KDP Communities: A First Assessment of the Legal Assistance Pilot Project in Central Java and North Sumatra (August–October 2001)*, Jakarta: World Bank.

Ferguson, J. (1994), *The Anti-politics Machine: 'Development', Depoliticization, and Bureaucratic Power in Lesotho*, Minneapolis, MN: University of Minnesota Press.

Foucault, M. (1991), 'Governmentality', in G. Burchell, C. Gordon and P. Miller (eds), *The Foucault Effect: Studies in Governmentality*, Chicago, IL: University of Chicago Press, pp. 87–104.

Guggenheim, S. (2002), *Proposal to the Norwegian Trust Fund for Environmentally and Socially Sustainable Development*, Jakarta: World Bank.

—— (2004), *Crises and Contradictions: Understanding the Origins of a Community Development Project in Indonesia*, Jakarta: World Bank.

——, Wiranto, T., Prasta, Y. and Wong, S. (2004), *Indonesia's Kecamatan Development Program: A Large-Scale Use of Community Driven Development to Reduce Poverty*, Jakarta: World Bank.

Hadiz, V.R. (2004), 'Decentralization and Democracy in Indonesia: A Critique of Neo-institutional Perspectives', *Development and Change* 35(4): 697–718.

Li, T.M. (2007), *The Will to Improve: Governmentality, Development, and the Practice of Politics*, Durham, NC: Duke University Press.

Madden, D. and Barron, P. (2004), *Violence and Conflict Resolution in 'Non-conflict' Regions: The Case of Lampung, Indonesia*, Social Development Paper 2, Jakarta: World Bank.

Rawski, F. (2006), 'World Bank Community-driven Development Programming in Indonesia and East Timor: Implications for the Study of Global Administrative Law', *International Law and Politics* 37(4): 919–51.

Rose, N. (1999), *Powers of Freedom: Reframing Political Thought*, Cambridge: Cambridge University Press.

Scott, D. (1995), 'Colonial Governmentality', *Social Text* 43: 191–220.

Smith, C. (2005), *The Roots of Violence and Prospects for Reconciliation: A Case Study of Ethnic Conflict in Central Kalimantan, Indonesia*, Social Development Papers, Conflict Prevention and Resolution 23, Washington, DC: World Bank.

Tajima, Y. (2004), *Mobilizing for Violence: The Escalation and Limitation of Identity Conflicts: The Case of Lampung, Indonesia*, Jakarta: World Bank.

Woodhouse, A. (2005), *Village Corruption in Indonesia: Fighting Corruption in the World Bank's Kecamatan Development Program*, Jakarta: World Bank.

Woolcock, M. (1998), 'Social Capital and Economic Development: Toward a Theoretical Synthesis and Policy Framework', *Theory and Society* 27: 151–208.

World Bank (2001a), *Indonesia: Country Assistance Strategy*, Jakarta: World Bank.

—— (2001b), *Second Kecamatan Development Project: Appraisal Document*, Jakarta: World Bank.

—— (2002a), *Idea Note, Justice for the Poor: Program for the Reform of Legal Institutions in the Local Environment*, Jakarta: World Bank.

—— (2002b), *Kecamatan Development Program Phase One: Final Report 1998–2002*, Jakarta: Ministry of Home Affairs (Community Development Agency), KDP National Secretariat and National Management Consultants, World Bank.

—— (2003a), *Decentralizing Indonesia: A Regional Public Expenditure Review Overview Report*, Jakarta: World Bank.

—— (2003b), *Third Kecamatan Development Project: Appraisal Document*, Jakarta: World Bank.

—— (2004a), *Indonesia: Country Assistance Strategy*, Jakarta: World Bank.

—— (2004b), *Village Justice in Indonesia: Case Studies on Access to Justice, Village Democracy and Governance*, Jakarta: World Bank.

—— (2005a), *Community Recovery through the Kecamatan Development Project: Appraisal Document*, Jakarta: World Bank.

—— (2005b), *Conflict and Recovery in Aceh: An Assessment of Conflict Dynamics and Options for Supporting the Peace Process*, Jakarta: World Bank.

—— (2005c), *Support for Poor and Disadvantaged Areas: Project Appraisal Document*, Jakarta: World Bank.

Chapter 12

Corruption as Governance? Law, Transparency and Appointment Procedures in Italian Universities

David Nelken

> Another factor that contributes to Italian originality is the non-admirable ease by which the reigning laws are ignored and quite different ones are applied, laws which have never been formally approved but belong instead to a sort of material constitution which is stronger than the legislative apparatus. (Melotti 2005)

Introduction: Corruption and Transparency

The current period is one in which international and non-governmental organizations expend considerable effort trying to negotiate or impose international standards of behaviour on matters that concern, for example, health, food, safety, the environment, the economy and the banking system, immigration, and responses to crime or discrimination. States and other public and private organizations, for their part, need to find ways to signal their willingness to conform to such standards (Nelken 2006; Whitehead 2006) if they are to gain, or continue to benefit from, trading and other benefits of being part of the global or more restricted political or economic groupings. One of the many standards in play here – the one on which we shall be concentrating – concerns what states are doing about corruption. To some extent, being seen to be dealing effectively with this problem may even be considered a *sine qua non* of credibility in tackling others. A major player in trying to establish improve standards in this sphere is the non-governmental organization Transparency International (TI), which produces widely reported yearly check-ups on the levels of corruption in a large number of countries (see Figure 12.1). TI is engaged in valuable work. But there are also important questions that can and should be raised about the methods it uses to make its judgements as well as the remedies it suggests.

Is TI only engaged in discovering different rates of corruption – or is it also trying to bring about common definitions of what counts (or what should count) as such? Where do its standards come from? In one way, the subjective aspect is predominant, given that TI league tables are explicitly a construction of others' constructions.[1] What is being compared is influenced by the ability and willingness of observers to see and describe local behaviour as corruption. But this means that societies where a sharper line is drawn between public and private life are also likely to be places where subjective perceptions of corruption will be higher (see Haller and Shore 2005, 5). But, at the same time, its judgements are also artefacts of objective differences in socio-political models of governance. Given that they define corruption largely in terms of the use of public office for private gain, the changing relationship between the private and public sphere in a given country will often be the key to the opportunities for what can or cannot be called corruption. Thus, it is interesting to note that the countries which do best in its league tables are either neoliberal ones such as New Zealand (in which the role of government is reduced) or social democratic ones like the Scandinavian countries (where the role of government is less challenged).[2] But it would not be safe to assume that the reason for the alleged low level of corruption is the same in each case.

We could say – at a minimum – that corruption, as defined by TI, is that which does not conform to the ways of governance of neoliberal or social democratic societies. But Nuijten and Anders (2007), in their recent critical remarks about TI, go further. They argue that there are '"orientalist" overtones to the fight against corruption' and see TI, 'founded by a former world bank manager', as in some way linked to neoliberal hegemony (Nuijten and Anders 2007, 3). For them, we should reject the dichotomization which sees corruption as having a distinctive presence in the South and East as compared to the Western world – the assumption that 'they' have 'structurally embedded corruption', whereas 'we' have only 'rotten apples'. According to them, by uncritically depicting corruption as an absolute evil, these anti-corruption programs disregard the close relationship that exists between corruption and state power.[3] Corruption cannot be understood as an individual act but only as one embedded in a wider matrix of power relations in society.[4] There are many situations where people justify behaviour on moral grounds, even though it is prohibited by the state, because they rely on alternative sets of social and moral norms.

---

1 The Websites <www.transparency.org> and <www.transparency.it> provide some explanation of the sources (experts, businesspeople and others) on whom they rely in drawing up their assessments.

2 See the map of global corruption at <www.transparency.org>.

3 But, paradoxically, it is the neoliberal (anti-statist) project which tries to build up the power of the local state to deal with corruption in the developing world.

4 For some writers, what Western observers categorize as corruption in economically less developed countries is in fact less exploitative for those involved than everyday labour relationships in their industrialized societies. And its openness is a virtue. Pepinsky argues that 'corruption and other violence are more directly expressed in Tanzania and more indirectly expressed by Americans who as a consequence are more enslaved to corruption and violence than Tanzanians' (Pepinsky 1992, abstract). Bribery is an equitable 'solution', rather than a problem; on the other hand, it is patriarchy and domination that keep American poorly paid workers in their places.

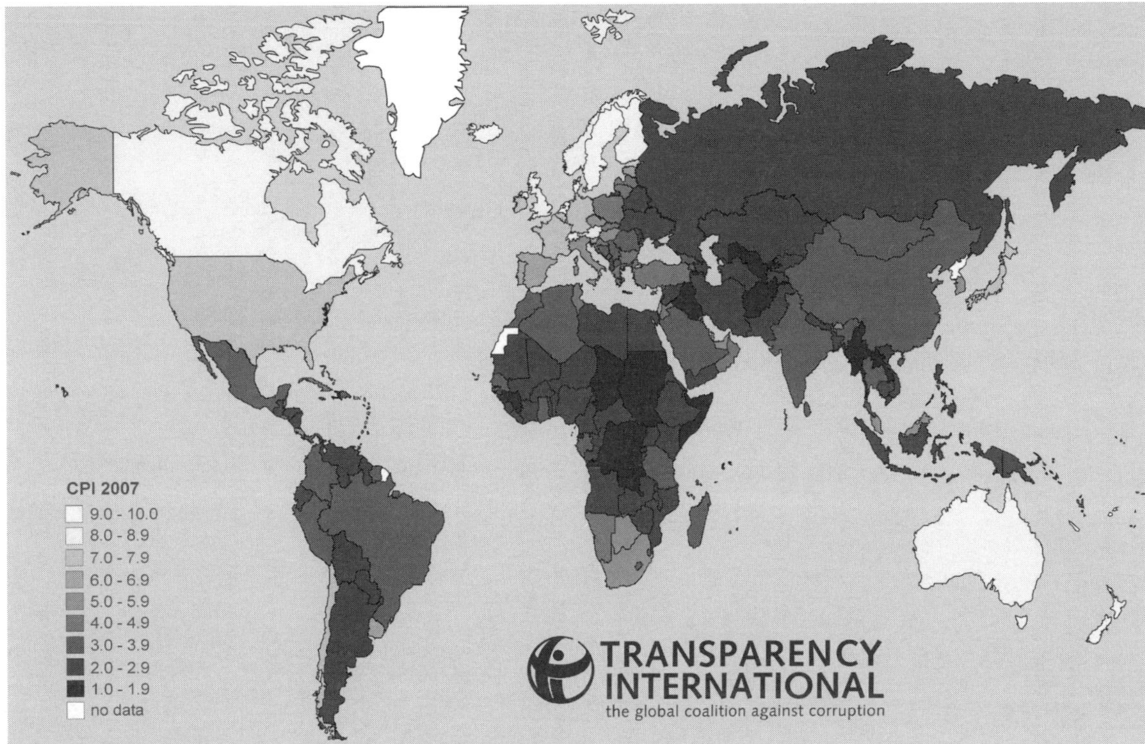

Figure 12.1 **Transparency International's 2007 Corruption Perceptions Index. Reprinted from 2007 CPI. Copyright © 11 September 2008 Transparency International: the global coalition against corruption. Used with permission. For more information, visit <www.transparency.org>**

But, under the influence of organizations such as TI, instead of talking of patronage or brokerage, people are increasingly encouraged to speak the judgmental language of corruption. The authors end by suggesting that corruption and law should not be seen as opposites, but as constitutive of each others' identities. Corruption is not law's negation, a vice afflicting the body politic, but is in continuity with it.

Our concern here is with Italy – a developed country of the West. As Nuijten and Anders comment:

> Italy is something of a special case. Although it has become one of the leading economic powers in the world, in northern Europe it is still regarded as a hotbed of corruption. But because of its economic prowess it is not a prime target of the global anti-corruption coalition. (Nuijten and Anders 2007, 3)

Italy certainly has an ambiguous status in the struggle to impose standards on others. It is a leader, for example, in the call for the worldwide abolition of the death penalty, and – of more relevance for the subject of this chapter – through the Bologna initiative it also has an important role in the effort to produce convergence in higher education. At the same time it is disproportionately likely to be rebuked for malfeasance by the European Union Commission or the European Court of Human Rights. And Italy does get poor marks for corruption. According to TI's 2006 report, Italy came in at 41st place, after Dominica and Botswana. Do Nuijten and Anders' comments about the need to avoid confusing patronage with corruption also apply here?

I shall be taking as my case study what goes on in the Italy's university appointments system. In this system, almost all such jobs are allocated through a public procedure known as *il concorso* – literally, 'the competition'. As we shall see, many people claim that these procedures are more corrupt than those elsewhere. But are we comparing like with like? Academic manoeuvring has much in common everywhere (Bailey 1977); all methods of appointment sometimes involve improper pressures or produce surprising and even inappropriate outcomes. In so far as the judgement is a relative one, much will depend on what system we are comparing it to, and the laws governing each system. It may be particularly instructive, for example, to contrast the constraints on appointment procedures in many of the countries where university posts are considered part of the civil service with the ease by which single universities or departments can fill jobs simply through advertisement and interview, as in much of the English-speaking world.

One English academic working in Italy in fact claims that it would be misleading to describe Italian practices as more corrupt than those in the UK (Eve 1993; 1996).[5] In the UK, he explains, there is much less obsession with the

5 We could also add that Italy suffers less from such problems as the hold that business has over university research in some of the most famous universities in the USA and elsewhere.

intrusion of the personal into public life. Appointment committees are so obviously 'subjective' that any serious candidate is well advised to try to discover the names and interests of those who will be making the decision. But despite (or just because of) an acceptance of the role of personal factors, people do not emphasize the networks that may condition decision-making.[6] Matters are decided in a club-like way, and candidates are not usually scandalized if beaten by an 'insider' unless this is obviously attributable to differences of class or race. Committees can do things openly that would be unthinkable in Italy. In the UK (and the USA), it is acceptable to recruit an international 'star' by also offering a post to a perhaps less stellar husband or wife – whereas Italians would see this as nepotism. Doctoral candidates are taken on (and funding sought) precisely because their projects are of interest to their potential supervisors. But in Italy, this would not be legal; these awards, too, have to be gained through impersonal competitions. In short, many of the same practices which would be condemned in Italy are simply taken for granted in the UK.

There is much in this argument. One reason for the constant succession of 'scandals' in appointments to academic posts in Italy is undoubtedly the difficulty of maintaining the kind of extremely impersonalized distribution of public resources which the law purports to lay down. But the point should not be taken too far. Even if it is true that some of the methods which are used to rig job selection in Italy would not be forbidden in many English-speaking countries, and that academic merit is not the only thing that counts, it is also important to ask why it is that co-option in the UK does not have the same effect of preventing foreigners and other meritorious 'outsiders' from obtaining posts. In my experience, the ideas of academic merit held by Italian academics do *not* differ from those shared in what are considered the world's leading universities. It is just that proven ability in research and teaching are typically made subservient to other requirements – they are neither necessary nor sufficient for obtaining posts. Many Italians themselves insist that their appointment system is corrupt (and not only because they have been told so by others). It would surely be another sort of 'orientalism' just to tell them that they are wrong. In trying to destabilize the obviousness of transnational labels, we should therefore not fall into a relativism where something is 'right' just because it is being done (Nelken 2008). There may be reasons to be cautious about adopting the neoliberal (and more specifically US) reforms that some critics of the *concorso* system in Italy advocate. But the alternative should not be unthinking 'resistance' in defence of current practices (which are not even liberal ones).

My aim in this chapter will not be to 'expose' the Italian system as 'really' more corrupt than other ones, though I will need to offer some account of how the system operates. Nor will I try to find 'solutions' to the problem other than by pointing to the 'social traps' (Rothstein 2005) that underlie its current functioning. On the contrary, I am more concerned with showing the general limits of a strategy

6 But one does hear complaints about the success of what is called – tellingly – 'the Oxbridge Mafia' in placing its graduates in jobs.

that relies on exposure as a way of putting pressure on societies to change their 'corrupt' practices. I shall be giving special attention to the limits of law as a means of producing more transparency. The assumption built into the work of TI is that public decision-making is less transparent in relatively corrupt societies, and hence that more transparency would be a good thing. But can there be too much transparency? Does not authority always require some dissimulation? What if the means of exposure are themselves part of the problem? As we shall see, the living law of the Italian *concorso* has as much to do with hiding what goes on in the university appointment system as it does with making decision-making transparent.

The 'Law' of the *Concorso* (This is Not a Competition)

The Italian university appointments system – on paper – is one of the most meritocratic and transparent that could be imagined. In the university version of the usual means by which jobs are allocated in the public sector,[7] the merits of candidates are assessed by some combination of assigned written work, published writings or sample lectures (depending on the different academic position being competed for). Judging is carried out by commissioners, who attain their positions through processes involving a mixture of election by peers from the same academic discipline and random selection. The judgements they formulate at each of the various formal stages of specifying the criteria for merit and the actual comparative evaluations of the candidates are obligatorily published on the Internet. But is any of this a guide to what actually goes on? For the purpose of answering this question, I shall discuss what is said in the academic literature, newspapers and on the Internet about the problems concerning these competitions, but I shall also draw on my direct experience of being a commissioner in various types of *concorsi*.

The media regularly carry reports of *concorsi* procedures going badly wrong. There are also regular stories about widespread nepotistic preferences being shown in all types of *concorsi*, with those involved also including leading professors whose institutional responsibilities should make them a guarantee against this being done by others. And there are recurrent scandals and discussions centring on the way that more able candidates are rejected in favour of 'protected' insiders. Are these only exceptional cases? Diego Gambetta, a brilliant Italian social scientist working in Oxford, tells us that they are rather the rule.[8]

---

7 There are differences in the extent to which such competitions are thought to be 'fixed'. The *concorso* for magistrates, for example, is considered pretty well uncorrupted (especially in its written part), though later promotion can depend on allegiance to different internal factions. Interestingly, by contrast, the method of selecting judges in UK jurisdictions relies largely on co-option.

8 Gambetta concedes that those fields that are more linked to international scholarship are less likely to be corrupt, and that 'there are exceptions who slip through the net'.

'Most academic positions in Italy', he writes, 'are allocated through national competitions held at irregular intervals, sometimes several years apart.' 'Those giving out jobs', he explains, 'operate on a pact of reciprocity – I promote yours and trust you to promote mine in the next round.' 'The system is corrupt because academic achievement counts little in determining the chances of promotion. … there is near-universal agreement that loyalty and subservience to the "barons", as the powerful professors are dubbed, are the currency that gains promotion to applicants' (Gambetta 2006, 89–90).[9]

Many of those working inside the system agree. As a pressure group association of Italian professors (Coordinamento Intersedi Professori Universitari di Ruolo, CIPUR) explains:

> CIPUR has been running a campaign for years against the malpractices of the university competition system and everyone knows that the scandals that are reported are only the tip of the iceberg. Few of the rejected candidates have courage enough to appeal against the decision knowing that they will come up against retaliation … the system of organizing competitions at a local level has been applied in a distorted and, often, mafia-like way.[10]

In general, academic commentators on the Italian university (for example, Froio 1996; Simone 2000) investigative journalists (Zagari 2007), as well as innumerable contributors to Internet discussions all agree that the actual rules that govern Italian appointments are quite different from those set down by the law. Those who succeed in the *concorsi* are almost always co-opted – on the basis of past services rendered and assumptions of future loyalty[11] – by powerful professors and/or their academic 'schools'. These usually operate through disciplinary sub-groups that are linked to 'factions' that claim to stand (if sometimes only loosely) for values belonging to the different parts of the political spectrum (as with aspects of most public and social life in Italy).

---

9 Gambetta offers further proof of the corruption of the system from the fact that the Italian government has had to establish funds for inviting back accomplished Italian researchers who have gone abroad. As he puts it, 'no matter how internationally distinguished, their chances of obtaining a chair in the regular competitions were zero'. It may be added that there are now frequent reports of how these funds are either unused or misused.

10 From <www.cipur.it/>, accessed 30 January 2009.

11 At this point, the reader may well want to ask how I got *my* job! The answer is that I was recruited using a provision in the 1980 law on universities which allowed for direct appointment of so called distinguished (*chiara fama*) full professors working abroad. It is highly unlikely that I could ever have got any position through a *concorso*. Although no bargain was ever specified, soon after my 'call', my sponsor stood for high office in an election in which I was eligible to participate. To remove any doubts, a professor of theology sat down beside me during the vote and whispered into my ear, 'Loyalty is the highest value.'

In my discipline, for example, there are the ex-socialists, the ex-communists (or lay group) and the Catholic (or central) group. Each has established historical dominance in certain sub-areas, and seeks to recruit new entrants. Because universities and faculties cannot appoint to posts directly, but only via the *concorso*, this means that appointments are in fact the outcome of multiple processes of negotiation: between barons and powerful figures outside the university, among barons who head the disciplinary factions, between barons and more lowly professors within their groupings or 'schools', and between barons, professors and candidates, and so on. These discussions largely pre-determine who will be on the commissions, who they should appoint, when, and why. Those professors unwilling to go along with this system will not receive the help they need – most importantly perhaps, if they cannot manoeuvre their assistants into jobs they are unlikely to attract any; hence, the system eventually reproduces only its own.

Those who are critical of the current system have made a number of attempts to spell out what are the applicable *unofficial* rules. A public prosecutor involved in arresting seven medical professors came up with the following five rules which he said showed how an organized crime model is used to control public competitions in the Italian university system:

1. A job must be advertised by the university only when the local full professor wants it.
2. At the national level, the group of colleagues dealing with the relevant subject matter has to approve this even before the official institutions do.
3. The local professor is allowed to select one candidate who is to be considered qualified for the job; colleagues are allowed to select the other.
4. The candidate who wants to win will have to have been totally faithful to the local full professor and to have satisfied all his [*sic*] expectations.
5. To make further career progress, it will be necessary for the winning candidate to obey whenever required to do so by the group (Zagari 2007, 93).

These allegedly 'criminal' rules are hardly different from those said to characterize the everyday functioning of the appointment system. Raffaele Simone, the leading commentator on the problems of university governance, claims that there are unwritten rules that regulate the corporations, create beliefs and convictions, and orient individuals and groups, and that everyone who enters the university world knows them off by heart (Simone 2000, 68ff.). The first and most important is the law of 'primordial affiliation'. To get a job, you must be the 'son' or 'daughter' of someone already there, whether by real kinship or a 'family-like' or 'client-like# relationship. Following this are rules such as that of 'egoistic reproduction', meaning that the new professor must be as much like his protector as possible and guard his academic territory; that of academic symbolism, the candidate 'representing his academic father till death or an irresolvable public disagreement'; the law of exchanging academic favours, which forms the basis for *pax academica*; the advantages of fitting in with the political complexion of the faculty, and the right to return to a university in one's home town at a later stage of career progression.

Judging a *Concorso*: When in Rome …

But all such attempts to spell out the unofficial rules of the appointments system can give at best only a partial and misleading picture of the *concorsi.* Not only are there other rules than those mentioned,[12] but the meaning of the rules is often unclear[13] and only emerges as they are actually used. If we are to gain a better sense of this process, we need to go beyond de-contextualized descriptions. As Georgio Blundo points out, rather than focusing on sensational cases, 'a good description of the practices of corruption must, on the contrary, restore them to their triteness, their daily character, their ordinary dimension, and their ambivalence' (Blundo 2007, 34). I therefore offer here some insights which may help fill in the picture based on my own experience of the system as an 'observing participant' (Nelken 2000). I shall also try to cast the difference between the 'normal' and the 'exceptional' *concorso* in a new light. It is often arbitrary when a *concorso* becomes newsworthy, since this depends on judicial intervention that casts a past *concorso* in a poor light retrospectively. For those involved in running a *concorso*, however, what counts is what prospectively causes the routine application of the unofficial rules to break down.

One of the first things I learned was that trying to apply practices from elsewhere in a different system could easily cause havoc. Once, in a low-level *concorso*, I confidently chose the academically most meritorious person, only to discover later that this person was about to move to another university, following their 'patron' professor. Before long, I found some of my ideas being used as his by the other professor. On the other hand, trying to run a *concorso* only by following the written rules can equally lead to trouble. As already noted, because they involve the disbursement of public funds, PhD candidates are also supposed to be awarded their posts by open, blindly marked examinations. But if this were adhered to rigorously it could mean that a person ended up joining a department even where their academic interests were quite different and they could not easily be supervised in their work. Moreover, they would almost certainly continue their collaboration with their previous professor in another university and not spend

12 A practice has grown up, for example, by which candidates send in their publications but do not actually turn up at the *concorso,* or do not see it through to the end. This strange behaviour is meant to signal their availability for future employment, but also their willingness to abide by the unofficial rules of the system and their acceptance that they do not expect to be appointed simply on their academic merits.

13 It is the barons who make the rules. But it is far from obvious what entitles someone to be considered a baron. Such recognition of entitlement as often follows the successful assertion of power as vice versa.

much time or contribute anything to the university that gave them the award. As these examples show, in deciding who is the 'best' person for a post, it is essential to give attention to whether the candidate's loyalty is likely to be given to one's institution (even though these considerations are not written into the legal rules).

But it is one thing to recognize the sense of unofficial local practices, and quite another to break faith with universal ethical principles. What were the principles that commissioners respected? My participation in the discussions of commissions, particularly ones for higher-level positions, helped me understand that, for my colleagues, a single *concorso* did not and could not exist as an independent unit. Much like a game of three-dimensional noughts and crosses, what is decided in any given competition depends on what has been decided in previous *concorsi* going back many years, as well as what is already decided for, or likely to be decided in, future *concors*i. In keeping with the principles of distributive justice that regulated the division of posts among factions, candidates were expected to wait their turn irrespective of whether they had more academic merit than the candidate whose turn it was.

Normal Cases

A good illustration of how a smooth *concorso* runs its course is offered by one of the first competitions for full professors in which I was involved. In this competition, our task was to choose three eligible candidates who would later be called to posts by different universities. The majority of the commissioners had allegiance to the central faction of my discipline; therefore, according to the unofficial rules, two of the winning candidates would have to be chosen from this faction. With the packs of candidate's materials still unopened, the decision was soon made to choose two of the central candidates. There remained the question of who would be the winning candidate from the minority faction (to which I was, by default, aligned). I had identified by name one sociologist who had published widely and was therefore on my list of likely favourites. But I was told we could not choose her, as there were already agreements between the heads of the factions that she would be made to win a forthcoming *concors*o elsewhere. Instead, my colleagues proposed promoting a candidate I had not heard of, and whose writings I had not received by post.

The other members of the commission spent the rest of the day at the computer, carefully drafting each of the various reports that were to serve as a legally satisfactory record of our deliberations (*il verbale*). But I decided that I needed to find out more about this candidate before I could give him my vote. I untied the relevant package of publications and read enough to convince myself that I was not agreeing to support a candidate without any merits. Once they were satisfied that the *verbali* had been completed correctly, the other professors returned and sat down in front of the large (or small) packs of candidates' materials in front of them, each of which was still tied together with string. The senior professor of the central faction now made a move to gather up the candidates' materials and take them away. Since mine were the only ones which were in part opened and not so easy to gather up under his arm, I apologized for this fact, trying in this way to make a subtle allusion to the fact that my colleagues had found it unnecessary to read the materials because the winners had been selected beforehand. I thought he might tell me that I had clearly only been doing my duty by reading the materials. But with great charm, he simply replied that I should not worry about it as it was no problem for him to gather up my papers even as they were. Clearly, my attempt at irony was out of place. What was happening was entirely normal. I felt (and I was) stupid for having made such a comment. Yet the inability or unwillingness to see or respond to such irony does also tell us something about the seriousness with which proceedings are taken in their own terms.

Most of the other *concorsi* I was involved in were similarly routine. It was usually clear who was supposed to win, often on the strength of past services rendered to their faction or their university. Although in the higher competitions the publications of some of the candidates were impressive, at lower levels they were few and poor. The agreements between the factions, or the understood wish of the local faculty, made for 'competitions' in which there was in fact nothing to decide. Often, only one candidate turned up – though it was still necessary to go through the rigmarole of procedure. But there are certainly also often cases of *concorsi* where factions fight it out for a while before reaching agreement, and uncertainties can also arise when there is more than one well-backed candidate from the same faction. In one commission of this sort, I helped make a decision to give a post on the merits to a candidate more junior than the one who (I later discovered) had been 'intended' to win, and no doubt had been made to wait for this chance. We later learned that this had created some distress for the losing candidate. It is not clear whether the decision would have been the same had we known of this extrinsic claim (or whether it should have been). But the case illustrates how the opportunity to play off different kinds of 'merit' can add a considerable element of unpredictability to outcomes.

Uncertainty was also increased as a result of the law reform in 1998 (now repealed) which gave local universities more responsibility for the *concorsi.* This created more of an opportunity for competition between the candidate the factions in the relevant discipline wanted to win and the one favoured by the local faculty. In one such *concorso*, I found myself the so-called 'internal' commissioner, whose task it was to defend the local candidate, who already taught there. But another roughly equal candidate belonging to my faction had also decided (been told?) to compete. This led to quite a battle within the commission, with the members of the other two factions not knowing which of the two contenders represented our 'official' unofficial candidate who was meant to get the post. In the end, the problem was solved because the second candidate from our faction, on instructions from above, withdrew at the last minute (to the fury of those who were backing him).

A Really Exceptional Case

These kinds of struggle form part of the story of many a *concorso* (or series of them). But they are usually resolved to maintain a system which it is in the interest of all (insiders) to keep going. For those playing the game, keeping to the unofficial rules means that you are sure to eventually have your turn without unpleasant surprises. The following case, however, stands out as the only *concorso* in which I participated in which the commissioners were unable to bring the proceedings to any sort of closure.[14] It is therefore in some ways the exception that proves the rule – showing what would happen if the unofficial rules broke down completely. It also shows the ways in which official law can also be invoked to obstruct or contest *concorsi* decision-making and, on the other hand, the way unofficial rules may be used to try and make *concorsi* yield pragmatically sensible results.

The *concorso* in question had to be organized for a rather special reason. An earlier commission dealing with same job had made its decisions some twelve years previously. But two of the losing candidates had appealed the decision to the courts. After a lengthy series of claims and counter-claims, it had finally been decided that because of a formal error in procedure (which is almost the only way to get a *concorso* reopened), the original *concorso* had to be nullified. This meant that, legally speaking, since we were being asked to re-do the *original concorso*, we were only allowed to consider publications that had been submitted up to that date of the original competition so long before. Legal time and scientific time did not coincide. Hypothetically speaking, if one of the candidates had been awarded the Nobel Prize in the years following the earlier *concorso*, it could not be taken into account.

In this new–old contest, the leading candidates whose merits we had to (re-) evaluate were Professor A, the winner last time round, and the two who had brought the successful legal action to have the *concorso* reopened, a lady, Professor B, and another man, Professor C. As the only member of the commission who knew anything about the subject matter, the view that I formed after reading their work was that Professor B had had the most relevant publications at the time of the last *concorso*. But it soon became clear that the relevance of publications was not the (only) issue that mattered. We were informed that the post had indeed originally been created so that Professor B could be promoted at her university. But because of better backing from the factions, Professor A had been appointed. He had since moved university, but because of the legal action taken to reopen the *concorso*, his promotion had never been fully recognized. The unsuccessful local candidate had meanwhile spent the last twelve years of her life trying to get 'her' job back. It was as much because of these other factors as questions of academic merit that

14 Because much of this account is necessarily based on hearsay and partial understanding of the higher levels at which bargaining is carried on, this description (like the other accounts of *concorso* proceedings) expresses only my fallible understanding about what I perceived was happening.

three of the other four commissioners agreed that the post should now be awarded to Professor B.

Given the number of commissioners ready to vote in Professor B's favour, it might have been thought her victory this time would have been a foregone conclusion. But this underestimated the determination of Professor A, something which had manifested itself even before the first meeting of our commission. At an early stage, one powerful professor (not on the commission) had rightly foreseen trouble in resolving the competing claims of Professors A and B. He had therefore sought to see if a *new* job could be created for Professor A (the original victor, who had, however, now lost the court case) to win at the university where he now worked. This would have left the way clear for us to award Professor B the post we were supposed to be re-deciding. But Professor A saw this as an effort to take away from him what he considered his rightful post. He used this attempt at a pragmatic 'solution' as an opportunity to attack the commission for committing the crime of 'the use of public functions for private ends', and launched various court cases and sent warning threats to commission members. Various strange messages arrived by email. One sent to me explained that he had interested himself 'in my friends and influence', and had been told that I liked 'to play the Englishman'; it added that he liked English novelists and had enjoyed spending time in England.

Professor A continued to cast a shadow over our proceedings. Of the five commissioners, only one of us had been a member of the earlier commission whose decision had been nullified. As it happened, this professor, the most left-leaning, ex-communist, member of our commission, had voted against the winning candidate last time (perhaps also because he was opposed to the majority faction then), and in favour of the loser, Professor B. But it was exactly this commissioner who was to prove the undoing of this *concorso*. As soon as we sat down to discuss the candidates, he announced that this time he intended to vote for Professor A, who had been the winner last time. 'What?', we asked astounded, 'How come you have changed your mind? We are looking at the same candidates and the same books as when you were involved in the last *concorso* – and that time you were the only one who was in favour of our candidate!' 'It's true,' he replied, 'the candidates are the same and the books likewise. But I am different! I have changed my mind in the mean time.'

Obviously, we then tried to find out why. 'Well,' he said 'because I am left-wing I always vote for the weakest candidate. Last time the woman candidate was the weakest, so I supported her. This time the one who won last time is the weakest, so I am supporting him!' But there was more to the story. It seemed that Professor A, for all his insistence on reminding commissioners of their legal obligations, had 'got at' this commissioner. Professor A had persuaded him that he would kill himself if he did not get his promotion confirmed. As a matter of conscience, he therefore felt bound to support him. I protested that with this type of argument, the woman who had lost last time might also threaten to kill herself. After all, it was probably her last chance at promotion, to the job which had originally been meant for her. We also noted that if our colleague changed his vote between the previous *concorso* and this one, she would certainly appeal his decision on the basis of inconsistency, so the matter would still not be resolved. But he refused to give way, and announced that he would block our proceedings if we sought to decide against his favoured candidate. Frustrated at what seemed an impossible situation, I suggested at this point that we could consider awarding the post to the other professor, Professor C, who had been the joint winner of the appeal against the decision of the previous commission. I had read the publications that we had been sent and found them relevant and of a decent standard.

The only small problem was that he was dead. But – and this was crucial – he had *not* been dead at the time of the original *concorso*. So, I suggested, just as we were only allowed to consider the candidates' publications as they were then, the same applied to the candidates. Appointing Professor C would have a number of advantages. Professor A would be less likely to kill himself (even assuming that he was serious about this threat) if he was beaten for the post by a dead person rather than by his old, living rival. Also, since the ministry would, eventually, discover that Professor C was unable to actually take up his post, there was a good chance they would advertise a new *concorso* for someone able to deliver their lectures. In this competition (open also to Professors A and B), the commissioners would be allowed to read work that had been published since the date of the nullified *concorso*, something which was forbidden to us.

I was gratified – if also a little surprised – that some of my colleagues seemed to take this proposal seriously.[15] After considering the matter, however, they told me that there was a technical problem with it. Even though we had for some reason been sent his books, Professor C himself had not replied to the minister's letter asking previous candidates to indicate whether they wanted to be considered in this re-enactment of the *concorso*. Of course not, I answered – he was dead! (And we should not be discriminating against the dead.) Ah, said my colleagues. After further examination of the issue, however, they found out that at that point, he *had* in fact been alive. He had not asked to be evaluated again because in the mean time he had won a *concorso* for another university position (which he unfortunately did not live to take up). So this solution, too, turned out to be unworkable.

While we tried to get on with the work of the commission, Professor A kept up his guerrilla tactics. At one stage, the president of the commission had been sent a large bunch of flowers which purported to come from the ex-communist commissioner. It was only at one of our meetings that they both realized who must have sent them. At another, we were told that Professor A had stationed himself in front of the president's residence, something that he found threatening. The ex-communist did his best, as promised, to delay our meetings, and then resigned, making it necessary to postpone matters until a replacement could be appointed. Professor A went on making threats of legal action against the commissioners. Worn out by all this, and unable to get any helpful advice from the ministry, the

15 Of course, it is possible that the joke was on me. But it is not unusual in Italy to look for formalistic ways round formalistic obstacles.

president advised us all to submit our resignations, which we did. I lost touch with what happened afterwards. But it seems that Professor A is still at his post, while Professor B (who quickly accused the newly appointed commission which replaced us of being demonstrably biased towards Professor A) has never received promotion. Instead, a new *concorso* was set up and another candidate (linked to one of the previous commissioners) has been appointed at a more junior level.

Corruption as Governance

What conclusions can be drawn from these experiences? I would not want to claim too much for accounts based on only a limited experience of commissions. 'Observant participation' excludes the possibility of systematic study of a random sample of *concorsi*. In the commissions in which I took part, it was never necessary to reject the academically best qualified candidate. And the more dramatic stories of corrupt commissions that appear in the newspapers do tend to come from subject areas where there is more power and money at stake than mine. If we are to believe reported telephone interceptions, there commissioners sometimes take 'macho' pleasure in being able to block the candidates who are clearly the most qualified. But even in my disciplinary area, I heard indirectly of highly qualified candidates trying and failing to get appointed, of candidates obtaining promotion for reasons that were not strictly academic, and of progress being blocked because a patron had died or gone abroad, or more rarely, because candidates had dared to disagree with or defy a baron. Given what goes on, it is not surprising that many describe the Italian appointments system as corrupt, and even Mafia-like in its *modus operandi*. At a minimum, there is no doubt that many appointments involve at least some measure of legally borderline behaviour. Almost all public discussions of the *concorso* system are critical, and it is difficult for those involved to find universalistic language to justify what seems undeniably a particularistic form of decision-making.

None the less, it is important to appreciate that, for the commissioners actually involved, it usually feels more as if they are involved in solving a difficult problem of micro-politics than in engaging in forbidden exchanges. It is clear to all involved in a *concorso* that the larger agreements that frame its deliberations are made by the barons. In most cases, they do not even need to be physically present. But the placemen on the commissions see themselves as part of a scheme of (self-)*governance*, rather than slaves of the personal whims or ambitions of faction leaders. The overriding responsibility of the commission is to ensure that posts are allocated between the known candidates of different schools and factions, according to their relative levels of electoral support among the relevant professoriate as expressed in a given *concorso*. Only in this way can conflict between the different academic 'schools' or the disciplinary factions be avoided. There have been and can be genuine and serious political and cultural divergences at stake. It is for this reason that the merits of candidates can only be relevant after, and subject to, this overriding requirement of political 'mediation'.

The major task of the commissioners during *concorsi* meetings is not to decide the winner, but rather to create a legal record that candidates will not be able to challenge. This involves ensuring that all procedural requirements (ostensibly there to prevent corruption) can be seen to have been satisfied. In the normal *concorso*, the 'extraneous' considerations that dictate which candidate should win are not usually discussed when dealing with the paperwork. Phone instructions from faction leaders are received, if possible, in another room, and cross-dealing with other commissions which happen to be meeting simultaneously takes place between working sessions. Only exceptionally, as in the dead professor case, does the 'outside' erupt dramatically into the *concorso* itself. The crucial deals which create preferential links and encourage (and, above all, discourage) applications are established *before and outside* the most legally regulated moment of the proceedings.

But even if we accept that the appointment system is a form of governance, this does not prevent our asking, as a normative question, whether we should consider it as an example of good or bad governance. In terms of the different possible principles of ordering recognized by political scientists –network, state and market – what we see here are networks profiting from the trust delegated to them by the state in order to limit the turbulence that could be created by market competition in university posts.[16] Rather than offering a robust alternative to official law, the unofficial rules of the *concorso* live in parasitic symbiosis with it. Even though there are no procedures for resolving disputes over single cases, factions do generally respect each other's selections – because, as I was once told, 'otherwise everything would collapse'. Outside the moment of the *concorso*, representatives of the different factions sometimes even make efforts to modify the operating rules, by specifying, for example, the number of publications that would normally be expected for positions at each level. But these decisions are not easily enforced, and the factions have so far been unable even to establish minimal common criteria to exclude unworthy insider candidates. There has certainly not been any concerted effort to ensure that the *concorso* is genuinely open to outsiders: that would go against the interests of those playing by the unofficial rules.

The *concorso* system is connected to other problems found in the world of Italian universities[17] (Zagari 2007) as well as public life in general, and tinkering with the *concorso* system may not be the only or best way of improving matters. In the 1998 reform, for example, it was decided the *concorsi* should no longer be organized at the national level, but instead held at each of the universities that were seeking to appoint people. The idea was that this would make universities more transparently 'responsible' for their choices on the merits. But this turned out to be

---

16 Rather against Giglioli's (1979) predictions, government bureaucracy has not tried to overcome the power of the barons.

17 Simone (2000) focuses mainly on the distracting effects of the heavy involvement of professors in professional or political activities outside the university. Interestingly, the role of the 'public intellectual' is now becoming *more* prized in the English-speaking world.

a complete failure, leading to what was described as 'the rise of the local cretin', with allegedly as many as 90 per cent of candidates simply being promoted within each university itself. As a result, the system has now been returned to operating at a national level. Getting entirely rid of the *concorso* would also offer no guarantee that merit would then become the guiding criterion of decision-making. At the time of the expansion of higher education in the 1970s, there was massive *direct* recruitment of former assistants to professorial roles, without any real *concorsi*, but most of these had not published much – and have not published much since.

Those who advise moving to systems of recruitment more similar to those used in the English-speaking world admit that this would only produce decisions based on merit if other more fundamental changes were made, including abandonment of the current equal legal value of all degrees, introduction of competition between different universities, the reduction of job security, and so on. But each of these issues is highly controversial. External pressures towards harmonization may, eventually, bring about change, and there is likely to be increasing political embarrassment over the haemorrhaging of talent as academically able Italians are forced to go abroad to find work. But reforms which go in the direction of more individualism and neoliberalism would be hard to reconcile with the many other structural features and values of Italian life that stress group loyalty.

Law and the Secret of Corruption

We may now return to our starting question. How does the *concorso* help maintain what many Italians themselves describe as their 'corrupt' system of university appointments, and what implications does this have for the pursuit of transparency as a purported solution to the problem? As we have shown, the *concorso* usually does more to conceal than to expose what is really going on. In routine cases, it does nothing to stop outcomes being pre-determined. In these cases of *de facto* co-option, its main role is therefore to conceal the range of extra-legal criteria (both those ethically defensible and those quite indefensible) that have in fact been taken into account. In the exceptional cases, such as the one described above, resort to law can upset the well-laid plans of the commissioners. But it is an open question whether it helps produce the best outcomes. And it typically does more to impede or annul deliberations than improve them.

Looked at in terms of their role in fighting corruption, the role of the courts is also complex, and often contradictory. Resort to the courts can serve as a weapon for the relatively powerless, for example in annulling a *concorso*. But this depends on the willingness of victims to come forward. The courts are slow and costly, and the results are uncertain as compared to the high risk of permanent exclusion from the unofficial system. As in many other areas of social life, when state-guaranteed rights do not work as they are purported to do, the courts tend to arrive too late on the scene. Judges are usually only willing to consider formal errors, and are unable or unwilling to go into substantive questions about the quality of scientific work.

What is more, courts can also be used for their own reasons by those who run the system. For example, a *querela* (a private legal action) for defamation may be threatened against those who try to expose 'fixed' competitions.

Nuijten and Anders (2007) claim provocatively that 'corruption is the secret of law' – because real power lies in the ability to *apply* the rules. But this tension between the rule of law and the role of law – between law as a constraint on power and law as an instrumentality of power – can and does vary in time and place. What is special about this relationship in Italy? Most of the individual elements that play a part in this story have parallels elsewhere. Other systems have laws that are made in the interest of powerful groups (even more so, in some ways). There is nothing specific to Italy about the ubiquity of informal norms, organizational working rules or plural legal orders, laws that are 'dead letters', or gaps between 'law in books' and 'law in action'. But the skill at playing off official and unofficial rules does seem remarkable. Commissioners not only exploit to the maximum the margins offered by the *concorsi*, they use them for purposes which often contradict the explicit statements they make about choosing the academically most qualified candidates.

There is evidence from levels of tax evasion and other forms of illegal behaviour in many other areas of social life that suggests that ordinary Italians often find ways to get round what they treat as over-formalistic legal regulations, and no doubt this, too, plays its part in the way the official rules governing the *concorsi* are (not) observed. But 'the problem' starts at the top. In Italy, it is difficult to control the controllers, and it is sometimes even hard to tell controllers and controlled apart.[18] Ministers know what actually goes on in the *concorsi*, but do not (or cannot?) find effective ways to regulate them. As scholars keep rediscovering, Italian governments employ the art of 'not governing' (Di Palma 1977; Ricolfi 2007), and 'ruling through leniency' (Melossi 1994), especially – though not only – where the powerful are concerned. Expressions commonly heard in Italy, such as 'the law is *applied* to enemies, but is *interpreted* for friends' or 'as soon as a law is passed, a way of outwitting it is found', are used to describe the behaviour of those *making* the laws as much, if not more than, that of those *subjected* to them (as suggested by the quotation that serves as an epigraph to this chapter).

The ability to manipulate the law in the way we have illustrated does not show it to be irrelevant. Far from it – no one in Italy can feel securely beyond the reach of the courts. (Most recently, the barons have decided that deals will no longer be conducted by telephone, but only in person). The need to provide a patina of legality itself produces a 'dirty togetherness' by which participants know that they are all at risk unless they keep to their pacts. Thus – perversely – the threat of legal sanctions for any abuse of procedures helps to induce reliability rather then

18 The Italian branch of Transparency International broadcasts its public service appeals for less corruption on the Berlusconi-owned Mediaset television channels. And, on the other hand, as I write this, the centre-left Minister of Justice and his wife (also a politician) are both being investigated on corruption charges.

defection. Thus, it may not be going too far to say that not only may corruption be called the secret of law, but law itself may be the secret of corruption. The 'law' of the *concorso* serves, above all, the purpose of making it more difficult for excluded candidates to complain – and forces them to do so in terms of procedure rather than substance. By arranging for decisions to be taken collectively on allegedly technical criteria, the *concorso* diffuses responsibility for outcomes. Above all, it offers legitimization for a process that would otherwise be seen more clearly for what it is: an exercise of power by insiders, for insiders.

Italian political clientilism used to be defended as a form of democracy which has the advantage of openness (as compared to the hidden power of 'Anglo-American lobbies'). Because power is palpable, one knows where it lies (La Palombara 1987). It is true that candidates understand that they have little if any hope of getting a job unless they can identify the barons in their fields and create a long-term relationship with a protector. But as the *concorso* system shows, this is only half the story. Those involved in university appointments send out two types of signals, at the same time, to two different audiences. One is meant for those in the university world, the other for those outside it. Even an open secret is still a secret. While purporting to control corruption, the *concorso* also hints at the power of those it pretends to control. In this way, the legal facade raises hopes, but the system, in practice, sends the message that personal links of dependency are the only way to secure a job and make progress in one's career.

Is the answer even more 'transparency', and what would that mean? Why has the frequent exposure of *concorsi* through the courts and the media not already torn away the facade? If the *concorso* maintains its place despite the frequent scandals, this is because it allows the issue to be posed as one of wrong procedures being followed – implying that right procedures would solve the problem. But also, and this is just as important, a society which has too many scandals become de-sensitized to them. The tendency is for each political or other grouping to focus on the faults of the others. Different media sources, few if any of which are perceived as independent, tell incompatible stories with different heroes and different villains. People become suspicious of the motives of those who launch corruption accusations, and 'facts' are easily reduced to opinions (Travaglio 2006). In the many cases that go through a process of trial by newspaper, the sentence, if any, issued much later after going through various court stages, reports circumstances which seem quite different from the facts as they had first been reported.

In a society where appearances mean everything, appearance is always suspect. As a condition of social survival, people learn to use *dietrologia* (or 'looking for what lies behind'). This suggests the need for rethinking the work of Transparency International and similar bodies. The TI experts who give Italy a low ranking are not offering an assessment that is different from that shared by many Italians themselves. But – just because of this – the risk of spreading these rankings (whatever other good this may do) is that of inducing a self-fulfilling prophecy. Those who see corruption as the result of a 'social trap' (Rothstein 2005) explain that the trap is set by the belief that, if others are corrupt, you would be a fool not to behave the same way. So it would be naive to assume that simply generating more transparency about what goes on in the university appointment system would inevitably lead to improvements in the behaviour of those involved in the system.[19] Under conditions of 'pervasive corruption' (Varese 2000), more information about what is really happening may only reinforce candidates' apprehensions that without protectors, they have no future. This said, the 'law' of the *concorso* offers little more than a simulacrum of legality. Both falsely transparent and transparently false, it can do little to create a virtuous circularity of trust through which academic merit could come to have greater weight in relation to the criterion of loyalty to a patron.

References

Bailey, F.G. (1977), *Morality and Expediency: The Folklore of Academic Politics*, Oxford: Basil Blackwell.

Blundo, G. (2007), 'Hidden Acts, Open Tales: How Anthropology Can "Observe" and Describe Corruption', in M. Nuijten and G. Anders (eds), *Corruption and the Secret of Law*, Aldershot: Ashgate, pp. 27–52.

Eve, M. (1993), 'Paradigmi Nazionali: Percezioni del "Particularismo" in Italia e in Inghilterra', *Rassegna Italiana di Sociologia* 34: 3.

—— (1996), 'Comparing Italy: The Case of Corruption', in D. Forgacs and R. Lumley (eds), *Italian Cultural Studies*, Oxford: Oxford University Press, pp. 34–51.

Froio, F. (1996), *Le Mani sul'Universita*, Rome: Riuniti.

Gambetta, D. (2006), 'Trust's Odd Ways', in J. Elster, O. Gjelsvik, A. Hylland and K. Moene (eds), *Understanding Choice, Explaining Behaviour: Essays in Honour of Ole-Jørgen Skog*, Oslo: Unipub Forlag/Oslo Academic Press, pp. 81–100.

Giglioli, P. (1979), *Baroni e Burocrati*, Bologna: Il Mulino.

Haller, D. and Shore, C. (2005), *Corruption*, London: Pluto Press.

Melossi, D. (1994), 'The Economy of Illegalities: Normal Crimes, Elites and Social Control in Comparative Analysis', in D. Nelken (ed.), *The Futures of Criminology*, London: Sage, pp. 202–19.

Melotti, U. (2005), 'Globalizzazione, Migrazioni Internazionali e Culture Politiche', in D. Nelken (ed.), *L'integrazione Subita. Immigrazioni, Trasformazioni, Mutamenti Sociali*, Rome: Franco Angeli, p. 92.

Nelken, D. (2000), 'Virtually There, Researching There, Living There', in D. Nelken (ed.), *Contrasts in Criminal Justice*, Aldershot: Ashgate/Dartmouth, pp. 23–48.

19 Della Porta and Vannucci (2007) emphasize the failure of the many years of media discussions of the Tangentopoli corruption scandals to produce movement towards genuine reform of its underlying causes.

—— (2006), 'Signaling Conformity: Changing Norms in Japan and China', *Michigan Journal of International Law* 27: 933–72.

—— (2008), 'Comparing Criminal Justice: Beyond Ethnocentrism and Relativism', in A. Groenemeyer and X. Rousseaux (eds), *Assessing Deviance, Crime and Prevention in Europe*, report of the First CRIMPREV Network of Excellence, <www.gern-cnrs.com/gern/fileadmin/documents/CRIMPREV/WP1/Report_WP1/rapportWP1_final_28jan08.pdf>, accessed 30 January 2009.

Nuijten, M. and Anders, G. (2007), 'Corruption and the Secret of Law: An Introduction', in M. Nuitjen and G. Anders (eds), *Corruption and the Secret of Law: A Legal Anthropological Perspective*, Aldershot: Ashgate, pp. 1–24.

Palma, G. Di (1977), *Surviving without Governing*, Berkeley, CA: Berkeley University Press.

Palombara, J. La (1987), *Democracy: Italian Style*, New Haven, CT: Yale University Press.

Pepinsky, H. (1992), 'Corruption, Bribery and Patriarchy in Tanzania', *Crime, Law and Social Change* 17: 25–51.

Porta, D. Della and Vannucci, A. (2007), *Mani Impunite*, Rome: Laterza.

Ricolfi, L. (2007), *L'Arte del non Gioverno*, Milan: Longanesi.

Rothstein, B. (2005), *Social Traps and the Problem of Trust*, Cambridge: Cambridge University Press.

Simone, R. (2000), *L'Universita dei Tre Tradimenti*, 3rd edn, Rome: Laterza.

Travaglio, M. (2006), *La Scomparsa dei Fatti*, Milan: Il Saggiatore.

Varese, F. (2000), 'Pervasive Corruption', in A.V. Ledeneva and M. Kurkchiyan (eds), *Economic Crime in Russia*, The Hague: Kluwer, pp. 99–111.

Whitehead, C.K. (2006), 'What's Your Sign? International Norms, Signals, and Compliance', *Michigan Journal of. International Law* 27: 695–742.

Zagari, C. (2007), *Processo all'Universita*, Bari: Dedalo.

Index